Spirituality and Psych

Edited by
Richard H. Cox
Betty Ervin-Cox
&
Louis Hoffman

Colorado School of Professional Psychology Press
Colorado Springs, CO

Published by
Colorado School of Professional Psychology Press
555 E. Pike's Peak Avenue, #108
Colorado Springs, CO 80903-3612

Spirituality and Psychological Health
Edited by Richard H. Cox, Betty Ervin-Cox, & Louis Hoffman
Table of Contents

Part I   Foundational Issues

Part II   Developmental Perspectives

Dedication

To the Rev. Dr. Jack Hart whose inspiration led to the establishment of the Hart Pastoral Care program at the Forest Institute of Professional Psychology.

To the Rev. Dr. Garrett tenZytoff whose initial lecture, encouragement, and support were instrumental in the Hart Program coming into existence.

ACKNOWLEDGEMENTS

This book would have not come about had it not been for the late Rev. Jack Hart, pastor of the First and Calvary Presbyterian Church, Springfield, Missouri, and of course, without the help and encouragement of a host of other persons. Dr. Hart was relentless in his search for ways to integrate faith and life and his vision led to a program that is carrying on his dream long after his physical departure from us. The late DeArmand Moore, M.D. and his surviving widow, Leona Moore, R.N., who initially funded the Hart Pastoral Care program, are to be graciously remembered. It, as always, is not possible to list all who helped in this project and we hereby plead for the forgiveness of ones that we will surely forget to mention. The spouses, friends, and families of all who have contributed to this volume are obviously to be thanked for their inspiration and willingness for academic minds to devote the time to this task. The office staff at the Forest Institute of Professional Psychology, particularly Marcie Johnson, is thanked.

Dr. Christopher Grimes reviewed much of the book and offered some extremely helpful editing assistance. Dr. Stephen Diamond of the Center for Existential Depth Psychology offered some very helpful feedback and assisted in securing some of the contributors to the book. Their assistance, along with their contributions to the book, is greatly appreciated. Dr. Glen Moriarty of Regents University and Dr. Rodney Hesson offered helpful feedback and critiques, particularly on the God Image chapter. Several other individuals should also be thanked: Dr. Robert Murney for expert psychological insight and editing; Michael Mitchell for corrections and theological assistance; Brittany Garrett-Bowser for support and editing assistance; Tifany T. Jones for her editorial assistance and expertise, and there must be special thanks given to the students in the Psychology of Religion and Spirituality classes at Forest Institute of Professional Psychology. An additional thanks and credit should be given to the Forest Institute of Professional Psychology, as much of time Dr. Hoffman spent editing was while he was serving as a faculty member at Forest. The students of Vanguard University's graduate psychology students who offered feedback on several chapters are also thanked. Additionally, we would like to thank the *American Journal of Psychotherapy* for permission to reprint the article which is Chapter 7 in the current volume and to *Tikkun* magazine for allowing Kirk Schneider's contribution, which originally appeared in their magazine, to be included as the Epilogue.

Finally, we'd like to thank all those at the Colorado School of Professional Psychology for their support and contribution to getting *Spirituality and Psychological Health* in print.

Richard H. Cox,
Betty Ervin-Cox,
Louis Hoffman, Editors

Forward

Frances M. Parks, Ph.D., ABPP
Forest Institute of Professional Psychology
Springfield, MO

Over the course of its one hundred twenty-five years or so history, psychology has had, at best, an ambivalent relationship with the fields of religion and spirituality. Some aspects of this relationship can be understood by looking at the bifold roots of modern psychology. The typical history of psychology text sees the advent of the discipline in Wilhelm Wundt's laboratory at the University of Leipzig in 1875. Wundt was committed to the scientific measurement and description of the sensory experiences of the human being with the idea that human experience could be described scientifically. It is from this tradition that psychologists have insisted that the field is a science following the philosophy and theory of scientific method. At about the same time at Harvard University in Cambridge, William James, who had studied in Europe and was well aware of Wundt's work, was offering the first college courses in "psychology." While honoring the scientific orientation of the new field and supporting work in applied experimentation, James was also writing *The Varieties of Religious Experience* (1902). Were both the scientific approach and the study of religious experience "psychology?" Both give important insights into the aspects of humanness; are the approaches diametrically different or are they different approaches to the same questions? We struggle still with the same questions one hundred plus years after Wundt and James.

This collection of papers does not attempt to give definitive answers to the relationship between these fields but helps to define and clarify the questions with insight and contemporary thinking on the issues. Four of the papers review with new perspectives the concept that spiritual development may be studied and viewed as a progressive developmental process in the same vein as psychology has studied the development of cognition, social behavior, and moral values. This perspective represents the more scientific (and more linear) attitude of studying persons from childhood through old age and measuring religious and spiritual attitudes and experiences. One chapter examines spirituality across cultures and presents cultural variations and models of healing/healers basically from the point of view of the scientist observer. Three papers speak to issues of religion and spirituality as they relate to the process of psychotherapy. With these latter papers there is a shift from the "scientific" laboratory perspective of Wundt to the more philosophical interest of James. There are fewer objective studies here, more descriptions of experience and philosophical questions. Existential, transpersonal theories, and values discussed in other chapters give a language and orientation for the more subjective realm of spirituality. This difference in perspective, this tension, is reflected in the modern field of psychology as a debate between the ultimate value of the scientific vs. the applied (therapeutic, healing) approach. This debate must seem rather silly to the outside observer. Both perspectives add to human knowledge and hopefully to human development and to the alleviation of suffering. Both are about *psychology*, the scientific study of behavior and the mind.

I appreciate that the editors of this book, Drs. Cox and Hoffman, did not choose to be hindered by this split/debate/ambivalence in the profession. Rather they have chosen to present relevant material and perspectives and allow the reader to partake of separate aspects or integrate them.

One way of viewing the two approaches is to see one as rational (the approach of science) and the other as irrational (religion and spirituality). Theology at times bridges the two. The problem arises mainly from our learned, cultural valuing of the rational and from that perspective our devaluing and dismissal of the irrational. Since most human behavior is irrational, this seems a rather dangerous point of view but it is the one we are taught throughout our formal schooling.

C.G. Jung placed equal value on the rational and irrational aspects of the psyche. The central theme of his psychological theory is spiritual development. He viewed himself as a scientist who studied and reported on phenomena of the human psyche. In 1932 he delivered a lecture entitled "Psychotherapists or the Clergy – A Dilemma" which is contained in his *Modern Man in Search of a Soul* (Jung, 1933). In the Translator's Preface to this book, Cary F. Baynes sums up the dilemma to which Jung refers and which is present for us today:

> Between these two extremes of traditional faith and militant rationalism, every conceivable shade of opinion about this great problem of humanity's next step in psychic evolution is to be found. It may be said that the middle position is held by those people who know that they have outgrown the Church as exemplified in Christianity, but who have not therefore been brought to deny the fact that a religious attitude to life is as essential to them as a belief in the authenticity of science. These people have experienced the soul as vividly as the body, the body as vividly as the soul. And the soul has manifested itself to them in ways not to be explained in terms either of traditional theology or of materialism. They do not wish to severe the real piety they feel within themselves from the body of scientific fact to which reason gives its sanction. They are convinced that if they can attain to more knowledge of the inner workings of their own minds, more information about the subtle but none the less perfectly definite laws that govern the psyche, they can achieve the new attitude that is demanded without having on the one hand to regress to what is but a

thinly veiled mediaeval theology, or on the other, to fall victims to the illusions of nineteenth-century ideology (Jung, 1933, Translator's Preface, no page numbers).

As a psychologist who teaches and a psychoanalyst who has the privilege of companioning patients in their uncovering of their psychic pain, trauma, evil, wisdom, compassion, and creativity, I know the joy and suffering of the soul and the inspiration of the spirit bring healing. In order to be a competent psychologist and psychoanalyst, I need to understand to the best of my ability the science and the spirituality of humanness. Science and spirituality are two different ways of knowing but if we can *be* in this paradox, a new dimension of knowing may develop. This tension is within each of us as persons and is reflected in the cultural/political dichotomies between the East and the West. Our world situation makes our efforts to work toward such a way of knowing of vital importance.

Forest Institute of Professional Psychology is one of the few non-denominationally affiliated schools in the United States that has maintained within its graduate training in clinical psychology a cluster of courses on psychology, religion, and spirituality. Several of the following papers were written by persons who have contributed to and been influenced by this program. Perhaps the effect of such training programs and the papers here presented will help the profession of psychology and our culture to grow from the psychology/spirituality tension.

Frances M. Parks, Ph.D., ABPP, Diploma C.G. Jung Institute, Zurich
Dean/Chief Academic Officer, Forest Institute of Professional Psychology
Springfield, MO
28 November 2003

REFERENCES

James, W. (1997). *Varieties of religious experience*. New York: Simon & Schuster. (Original work published in 1902)
Jung, C.G. (1933). *Modern man in search of a soul*. New York: Harcourt Brace.

Introduction

H. Newton Malony, Ph.D.
Professor Emeritus
Graduate School of Psychology
Fuller Theological Seminary
Pasadena, CA

Spirituality is in; *Religion* is out! So goes popular culture. Nevertheless, there is significant truth to such a statement – at least in the field of mental health. It is no accident that the volumes published by the American Psychological Association in this field have progressed from one titled *Religion* in the clinical practice of psychology (Shafranske, 1996) to the more recent title A *Spiritual* strategy for counseling and psychotherapy (Richards & Bergin, 1997). This volume on *Spirituality* and Psychological Health is right in vogue with this new trend.

However, Cox, Cox, and Hoffman along with the authors in this volume take this development one step further – they focus less on treatment and more on practice. They are concerned with the kind of spiritual behavior that results in being healthy in mind and spirit. Only in passing do they deal with how to use spirituality in helping persons return to health who have become sick.

Much study has been made of the "health" that results from being *religious*. What is needed now is reflection on the "health" that results from being *spiritual.* Of course, such an assertion is grounded in the conviction that being religious and being spiritual are two different things – a conviction which to which I personally subscribe. I contend that *spirituality* is the *human capacity to experience transcendent reality* while *religiosity* is the *labeling of such transcendent experience in a manner that is shared by two or more persons.* Such definitions may not have absolute validity, but they do afford us some basis for clarification.

Spirituality is not an *instinct* – otherwise everybody would express it in the same manner. Nor is spirituality a *drive* – or we would find everybody doing it. Spirituality is a *capacity* – a potentiality, an ability, even a skill. Spirituality is a universal possibility, but it is not a universal practice. Recently, I participated in a discussion of whole-person health care at the retirement community where I live. This discussion illustrates my contention that spirituality is a potential for inducing health that is not affirmed by all care givers – contrary to what this volume clearly asserts. The discussants at the meeting I attended seemed so intent on not offending anybody's "religiousness" that they were willing to ignore the current mandate to provide aging persons with *spiritual* alongside *physical, social, and emotional* care.

Humans do seem to have the *capacity* to experience transcendent reality and those who plan for the care of persons during life transitions and crises have come to believe strongly in the value of *spirituality* for psychological health. This is not a novel idea but it is being reemphasized anew here in the 21st century. As early as 1986, psychologist Benjamin Beit-Hallahmi contended that the process of "imagination" was the same in religious and aesthetic experience. Using a definition of religion similar to my understanding of spirituality, Beit-Hallahmi suggested that the catharsis persons received by leaving pragmatic reality and entering into a world of transcendence had immense health-giving power. He pictured such experience as reinvigorating and re-creative in those who returned to empirical problem solving after time spent in the trans-empirical reality of art and/or religion. The present volume is grounded in this conviction. The value of spirituality is in no way compromised by relating it to the same cognitive process as artistic imagination and aesthetic appreciation. In fact, spirituality may be greatly enhanced by the recognition that experiencing transcendent reality is an embedded human capacity – not some esoteric option given to a precious few.

Of course, several aspects of this volume's theme beg for further elaboration. The first pertains to the *nature* of transcendent reality itself. Beit-Hallahmi noted that religionists, after returning to daily experience, contended that they had been in touch with absolute reality. After returning from aesthetic experiences at concerts or galleries, however, persons would never ascribe such objectivity to such events. It is no coincidence that much theorizing about spirituality has chosen to ignore this issue. They have preferred to emphasize the process rather than the substance of spirituality – perhaps because of the immense diversity among those who talk about what they experience. Several chapters in the current volume reflect this trend. Tillich's dynamics of faith as well as the chapter on *existential* spirituality deal with pre-cursors to spiritual encounters. Life's "boundary" experiences, such as distress and tragedy, are often thought to prompt the search for meaning that leads to spirituality. Of course, many modern yearnings for personal development trigger this same search prior to the experience of any such crises.

However, the fact still remains, the substance of transcendent reality is left undefined. The chapter on spirituality across cultures and religions addresses the almost inevitable compulsion to put words to spiritual experience. Once words are applied and shared, spirituality becomes "religion." By religion, I simply mean the labels put to spiritual experience – labels can be shared and that make repetition of the experience highly likely. Spirituality could be understood to be the inevitable precursor to religion, if by religion we mean a set of behaviors and constructs that give overarching meaning to life. I think we need to broaden religion to mean any set of such constructs, be they simple or extensive. I recognize that many who emphasize spirituality in contrast to religion will take issue to my model, but I remain convinced that the dynamic of spiritual experience mandates that a set of words be applied to it and that it is these words that both motivate one toward the repetition of the experience as well as the sharing of the experience with others. I believe that in the final analysis language is the quintessential trait of humanness and that psychological health includes an essential verbal core.

This leads me to a final sense of where this volume will make an important contribution – in an enlightened definition of psychological health. As Margaret Mead suggested so many years ago, "Mental health is a moving target." We have tended to speak of psychological health in purely mid-adult terms. Where else but here can one read about the development of spirituality over the life span? Where else but here can one reflect on the difference between spirituality and psychological health for children, adolescents, and aging persons as well as those who face the crises of the adult productive years? As addressed by Cox, Erik Erikson remains the seminal theorist about what adjustment means for humans at different periods of their lives. One would hope that such a collection of chapters as appear here would leave us with a post-Eriksonian sense of what optimal adaptation might mean when it is grounded in spirituality. Health is never self-defining. It always demands a stage of life and a culture context to give itself a specific definition. When health is infused with spirituality, we can hope for an understanding that reflects values and ideals significantly beyond simple adjustment to the environment.

In conclusion, let me note the psychological truth that offends theologians so much, namely that "knowledge begins with experience." Many religious scholars would prefer that we start with proclamations, dogma, and creeds. The writers of these essays know better; you can only talk about what you have seen, heard, tasted, felt, and smelled. Spirituality will have its effect on psychological health as experiences that cannot be forgotten and that continue to impact the present and the future. To use a biblical event, Philip, in trying to counter the misgivings of his brother Nathanel's about the identity of Jesus says, "Come and SEE" (John 1:46). C.S. Lewis suggested in a Pentecost sermon that having a charismatic (spiritual?) *experience* was a prerequisite to understanding Pentecostalism. Prior to such a personal experience, one would be like trying to explain sounds on a piano as representative of instruments in a symphony orchestra to those who had never heard a performance. Or, he continued, it would be like attempting to understand what a house was like simply by looking at a blueprint if one had never seen a house. Spiritual "experience" is an absolute necessity if spirituality is to be related in any way to psychological health. Trying to convince others of its power and impact will fall on deaf ears until they, too, experience it.

Of course, being a set of behaviors, spirituality will need some help and direction – as many writers have noted and as the chapter on "practical matters" addresses directly. Since, as I suggested, spirituality is a "capacity," not a drive or instinct, it is a skill that must be developed and practiced if its impact on psychological health is to be of any significance. Walter Houston Clark, the author of *Chemical Ecstasy: Psychedelic Drugs and Religion* (1969) commented on a truth about the 20th as well as the 21st century. He opined that having a religious (spiritual?) experience was difficult in the pragmatic and problem focused world of everyday life. His solution was to recommend the ingesting of psychedelic drugs, such as peyote, as a means of triggering the experience of transcendent reality. That suggestion never caught on in the late 1900s nor I do not think it would be received with much applause today. The issue is still with us today, however, and the question of how to induce spirituality in a post-modern environment remains a viable question. Perhaps this volume will carry up one step close to solving that riddle.

REFERENCES

Beit-Hallahmi, B. (1986) Religion as art and identity. *Religion, 1,* 1-17.

Clark, W. H. (1969) *Chemical ecstasy: Psychedelic drugs and religion.* New York: Sheed & Ward.

Richards, P.S. & Bergin, A.E. (1997). *A spiritual strategy for counseling and psychotherapy.* Washington, D.C.: American Psychological Association.

Shafranske, E. P. (Ed.). (1996). *Religion and the clinical practice of psychology.* Washington, D.C.: American Psychological Association.

Part I

Foundational Issues

1

Training Issues in Spirituality and Psychotherapy: A Foundational Approach

Louis Hoffman, MAT, Ph.D.
Vanguard University of Southern California
Costa Mesa, CA

Richard H. Cox, Ph.D., M.D., D.Min.
Provost
Colorado School of Professional Psychology
Colorado Springs, CO

Betty Ervin-Cox, Ph.D.
Dean of Students
Colorado School of Professional Psychology
Colorado Springs, CO

Michael Mitchell, M.A.
Southwest Missouri State University
Forest Institute of Professional Psychology
Springfield, MO

Spirituality in psychotherapy has rapidly moved from a marginalized issue toward the forefront of psychological training. For many years it was difficult to find quality training, education, and supervision for religious and spiritual issues in psychotherapy unless attending one of several specialized training programs which focus on integration issues. Times have changed. There is an increasing abundance of schools which focus on the 'integration' of spirituality and psychology, many other schools are offering more courses on these content areas, continuing education is readily available, and an increasing number of quality books addressing these issues are available (Miller, 1999; Moriarty, in press; Olthius, 2001; Pargament, 1997; Richards & Bergin, 1997; Shafranske, 1996; Sorenson, 2004).

Therapists and counselors are also much more aware of the importance of spirituality and religion in relation to mental health. Still, most therapists do not feel they have been adequately trained to deal therapeutically with these issues. Perhaps what is more disconcerting is the number of therapists who do feel adequately prepared solely because they themselves are religious and/or spiritual. Any therapist who believes that their own spiritual commitments are adequate preparation for dealing with their client's spirituality clearly lacks an understanding of the diverse and complex issues surrounding spirituality and mental health. Two important factors should be considered in this discussion.

First, early research suggested that psychologists tended to be less religious than the general population. However, upon further analysis, it was found that they were not necessarily less religious; they were religious in different ways (Shafranske, 1996). Psychologists tend to be more open to different perspectives and to think more critically about religious matters. Another way this information could be interpreted is that psychologists tend to be just as spiritual, but less religious. This interpretation, however, makes many assumptions about how religion and spirituality are defined and what the relationship is between them. This topic will be pursued by many of the different authors throughout the rest of the book.

Second, religion and spirituality are becoming much more complex and diverse. The early days of the interface between religion and psychology referred almost exclusively to Western approaches to religion, primarily Christianity. Furthermore, Christianity was assumed to be in agreement on most of the essential issues. However, as pointed out by Kathryn Tanner (1997), Christianity can no longer be assumed to have such monolithic beliefs. There are very few, if any, issues with which all people calling themselves Christians can agree. Even if they agree upon the truth of a particular statement, they cannot agree on what that statement means or how it should be interpreted.

Pluralism is an important factor contributing to the increasing complexity of religion and spirituality. Fifty years ago the interaction between different world religions was limited with the exception of missionaries who were sent to convert people of different faith backgrounds. Today, many, maybe even most, Americans have friends of a different religious background than their own. This increasing dialogue between religious groups has formed the impetus for many hybrid churches and religions.

As stated by Hoge (1996), "Religion is as alive as ever, but it is diversifying" (p. 38). As such, it is necessary for adjustments to be made in how therapists are trained to deal with religious and spiritual issues. Attempts such as these are often referred to in the professional literature as "integration." Integration, when applied in this context, means a way of bringing psychology and religion and/or spirituality together. Historically this has often been associated with Christian approaches; however, in the course of this book there is no assumption that any one religious group needs to be identified with the term integration. Still this term is preferred over "the psychology of religion" or "the psychology of spirituality," as these terms often suggest an approach which places psychology in a superior position over religion or spirituality. This assumption is not made in integration movements.

This chapter introduces a new training model for preparing therapists interested in working with religious and spiritual issues in psychotherapy. However, despite calling it a new model, we must acknowledge Elizabeth Bowman (1998), whose chapter "Integrating Religion into the Education of Mental Health Professionals," provided an important stimulus to the current endeavor. Bowman made the distinction between *essential*, *important*, and *helpful* material in training mental health professionals about religious issues. While agreeing with this basic structure in the current model, we differ as to what should be placed on each level.

A FOUNDATIONAL APPROACH

The model is called a foundational approach because of the authors' conviction that therapists must first establish a strong, foundational knowledge and understanding before moving to application. As with any new area of clinical practice, it is very dangerous to read a book or attend a workshop on integrating spiritual techniques or approaches and then begin to apply these new ideas, approaches, or techniques without obtaining a foundational knowledge of spirituality. With an increasing number of books on "technique" available to therapists, this point cannot be stressed enough.

One of the better books which introduces new spiritual techniques is Glen Moriarty's (in press) *Why is God Always Mad at Me?* In this book, Moriarty spends a good deal of time building the theoretical framework which supports the technique he develops. While still unable to control that some irresponsible readers will jump right to the techniques and begin applying them, this is a more responsible approach to teaching technique.

The foundational approach being proposed is a three-tiered approach to training. Each progressive level is intended to build from the previous one. Ideally, each of these levels would comprise the equivalent of one 3-credit graduate level course or approximately 100-hours of training (in class and outside of class preparation). While this may not be possible in many training programs, it is still recommended that the same progressive approach be applied when less time is available.

The most critical placement in this approach is locating the application portion of the training in the final tier. It is the belief of the authors that this is both a matter of clinical integrity and ethics. Until this foundation is firmly established, therapists should not make attempts to work too directly with spiritual issues without the close supervision of a professional with expertise in this area.

LEVEL 1: DEFINITIONS, INTERRELATIONSHIPS, DEVELOPMENTAL ISSUES, AND ETHICS

The first level is the broadest of the three levels of training. This is partially due to the need for establishing foundational concepts which will be built upon in the later training tiers. Additionally, it is essential to have an understanding of the basic dynamics of faith before being able to understand how this faith relates to other important topics.

Definitions

Developing an adequate professional language is part of becoming a psychotherapist or a professional in any field. This can be an intimidating and frustrating aspect of training. The thought of concurrently learning the language of spirituality, in addition to the language of psychotherapy, may not be the most endearing part of becoming a therapist. However, it is necessary. While therapists don't need to become religious scholars or theologians, they should be familiar with some of the important terms used by individuals from different traditions.

Some terms have more than one definition. For example, religion and spirituality are defined in many different ways. To work with a client who is spiritual, it is important to be able to understand what that means to them. This means, in part, that therapists should have some familiarity with different ways this term is used. The same is true of religion.

Some of the other terms necessary to be familiar with include transcendence, faith, salvation, karma, God, ritual, tradition, creed, theism/theistic, agnostic, and theodicy. Additionally, therapists should become at least somewhat familiar with the different traditions associated with religious and spiritual approaches to mental health. These include spiritual direction, pastoral counseling, shamanism, and religious counseling (i.e., Christian counseling, Jewish counseling, Buddhist counseling).

The Relationship Between Religion, Spirituality, and Psychology

Since Freud provided his first critique of religion and before, there has always been tension regarding how psychology and science are related to religion and spirituality. This topic is important partially because of its historic origins. Additionally, this is a major concern for many clients, especially those coming from religious or spiritual backgrounds which are suspicious or critical of therapy. There are a couple of important issues for therapists to be aware of in this regard.

First, therapists should be familiar with the spiritual and religious critiques of psychology. This includes some preparation as to how to answer questions critical of psychology in a non-defensive manner when voiced by a client. Second, though clients often are not able to articulate how they conceptualize the relationship between spirituality and psychology, they still have some beliefs about the matter. In particular, they may have some important beliefs about epistemological issues. In other words, which is the more authoritative source of knowledge and/or truth: psychology or spirituality? Are the sacred texts more authoritative than science? How is spirituality knowledge attained versus psychological knowledge? Which is better? Which is more important?

Barbour (1997; 2000) provides an excellent overview of various approaches to the relationship between science and religion, though his focus is more on the hard sciences than the social sciences. Several authors in the current book have devoted some time to this issue.

The Relationship Between Religion, Spirituality, and Mental Health

There are two basic questions which are addressed here. First, how do spirituality and religion impact mental health? The answer to this question forms an important basis for applications issues, too. Are there spiritual practices which improve mental health? Are there spiritual practices which interfere with mental health? Cox, Hoffman, and Grimes, in the final chapter of this book, provide an overview of many ways in which religion and spirituality are beneficial for health. However, what is often not addressed is ways in which spirituality and religion interfere with mental health. For example, it is common for spirituality to be used in the service of suppression, repression, and denial. Through various means, spiritual people often send the message that it is not okay to feel bad or angry or that people should just be able to magically let go of their hurt or angry feelings if they are *really* religious. However, as depth psychotherapy has pointed out for years, this form of repression or suppression can be very destructive to both mental and physical health.

Second, how do life events and mental health affect spirituality? This is a question that has been drastically underrepresented in the literature and deserves more attention. The current volume attempts to address one aspect of this issue which has not been given sufficient attention: development. Various aspects of normal development, not to mention complicated development, influence a person's spirituality. Additionally, the awareness of evil, suffering, mental illness, and many other psychological issues impact a person's spirituality. Therapists must be aware of these issues to not misunderstand a person's faith.

Developmental Issues

Religious, spiritual, and faith development is one of the most neglected aspects of religious psychotherapy. Religious and spiritual health has received much attention, and the relationship of faith to mental health has been a focus of a great deal of research, but relatively little writing and research has emerged around the application of development perspectives to psychotherapy. It is not that the developmental theories don't exist; they just haven't been applied to psychotherapy.

James Fowler (1981), in his classic book *Stages of Faith: The Psychology of Human Development and the Quest for Meaning*, articulated the most popular of the various developmental approaches. Relying heavily on Kohlberg and Piaget, Fowler developed an approach to interviewing people of faith to assist in developing and substantiating his theory. In the over 20-years since it was first published, *The Stages of Faith* continues to be the influential.

Developmental theories, such as Fowler, have been used more in the assistance of promoting spiritual growth than as a way of determining appropriate therapeutic intervention. Yet, a therapist who is sensitive to the worldview and beliefs of their clients will readily understand that different therapeutic interventions may be more appropriate, respectful, and effective with clients at different levels of faith development.

One controversial topic within the developmental perspectives relates to how well the developmental models apply across belief systems and religions. While there are similarities in patterns, certainly there will be some variations which are dependent upon the religious or spiritual group. As a training issue, it becomes important to have exposure to several different developmental models in order to increase the therapist's ability to establish a flexible approach to conceptualizing developmental processes.

Ethics

While this is possibly the most important issue of the first tier, it is probably best dealt with toward the end of this phase of the training.[1] Most clinicians will not be able to fully grasp some of the important ethical issues until they have established a basic understanding of the dynamic process of spirituality and faith. It is also important to note that ethics should not just be addressed in one phase of training. Rather, this issue should be continually dealt with throughout the training process. While it is impossible to note all the important ethical issues, a few desire some specific mention here.

It is important for therapists to learn how to not impose their values or beliefs upon their clients. While this seems like common sense, it often is not. Through experience in teaching and providing supervision to many therapists in training, the authors' have noted that many neophyte therapists make this mistake without even being aware of it. If a therapist is unaware of the complex issues of spirituality, they will often be unaware of when they may be imposing their values on clients.

A second important issue is dealing with limitations. For many therapists there may be spiritual issues and/or beliefs that they feel uncomfortable working with because of their personal values. Because of this, part of the training process should be a thorough examination of their belief system. If a client does not have a good awareness of their own spiritual process, they may have a more difficult time avoiding imposing their beliefs on clients and working effectively with a broad range of spiritual people.

There are many religious and spiritual issues which can also be impacted by the setting (i.e., government settings require certain restrictions) and carry with them additional ethical concerns. This issue is still just beginning to be fleshed out, but is receiving additional attention in more books on this topic (see Richards & Bergin, 1997). Therapists need to be aware of the applicable ethics codes and related issues.

---

[1] Bowman (1998) even suggests this may be best placed in the second tier (important, rather than essential material).

Summary

A major emphasis on this level of training is developing an understanding of the dynamics of spirituality. This topic is addressed more thoroughly as the dynamics of faith in the next chapter. Essentially, therapists must learn the language, process, and ethics of spirituality as pertaining to mental health and psychotherapy.

LEVEL 2: DIVERSITY ISSUES

Diversity is an increasingly important issue in psychotherapy. As psychologists have become more aware of the essentialness of dealing with diversity, they have also discovered it to be increasingly complex. At one time, diversity primarily was used to refer to cultural and ethnic diversity. However, today there are many different ways to talk about diversity. The authors maintain that at least four different categories of diversity are important to address.

Diversity in Psychological Approaches to Spirituality and Religion

Different theoretical orientations and approaches to psychology bring different conceptualizations of religion. For example, cognitive approaches to religion are drastically different from existential or transpersonal approaches. It is important for therapists not only to understand the approaches to spirituality and religion from within their own therapy orientation, but it is also good for them to have some understanding of alternative approaches. This may be covered, in part, during the first level of training.

Spiritual and Religious Diversity

Spiritual and religious plurality is an extremely important issue far beyond the walls of the therapy room. Since 9/11, in particular, the tension between religious groups has received more attention. For therapists, this is important in being able to work with clients in a sensitive manner and in assisting clients become able to use their spiritual beliefs in ways conducive to mental health.

Two recent edited books gave attention to religious diversity (Koenig, 1998; Richards & Bergin, 2000). While these books were extremely important contributions to the field, they only addressed the major world religions. Koenig's (1998) *Handbook of Religion and Mental Health* did acknowledge some of the variations within Christianity, but not the other world religions. Several chapters within Richards and Bergin's (2000) *Handbook of Psychotherapy and Religious Diversity* also provided some, albeit limited, information on religious diversity within the major world religions. However, neither of these books examined any of the indigenous religions or emergent trends in spirituality.

David Tacey's (2004) *The Spiritual Revolution: The Emergence of Contemporary Spirituality* provides one example of an examination of contemporary trends in spirituality. New spirituality trends are occurring within the major world religions, but also external from them. Oftentimes, they occur by blending themes from various world religions or reinterpreting traditional religious believes from new cultural contexts. As these trends continue to develop they are likely to become increasingly influential upon clients entering the consulting room.

The chapter by Krippner in the current volume provides one example of attempts to go beyond the major world religions through an examination of the more indigenous approaches to spirituality. Transpersonal psychology has also made many attempts to give indigenous traditions their appropriate attention (Cortright, 1997; Walsh, 1996), yet precious little is included in the mainstream psychotherapy literature.

The coverage of religious and spiritual diversity must include these various approaches if it is to comprehensively train therapists to work with clients from the various backgrounds. For some therapists, they may only be interested in working with clients from a particular world religion. For these therapists, it may be more important for them to receive training on variations within that particular tradition.

Cultural and Ethnic Diversity

One of the important factors accounting for intra-religious variation is cultural differences. Theologians have been giving increasing attention to this topic (see Brown, Devaney, & Tanner, 2001; Hopkins & Davaney, 1996; Tanner, 1997). Most people will recognize that there are some common differences between many African American churches and Caucasian churches in American. Similarly, there are some common, significant differences between Muslim clients who grew up in the Middle East versus Muslim clients who grew up in America. Variants of Buddhism which emerged in Western society have often strayed far from they way Buddhism is practices in China, India, and Japan.

While it is not possible for therapists to know all these differences, they should be aware of some of the major patterns and themes. This will help them be able to adjust their framework and better recognize differences when they occur. When the therapists then encounter a new approach to spirituality, they will better be able to learn about this from the client in a manner which is respectful of their beliefs. The untrained therapist may not even recognize the divergences and continue to follow their assumptions based on general features of the spiritual group. This is one example of how a therapist can unknowingly impose their values on a client.

Other Diversity Issues

Several other important, and often controversial, topics should be addressed in training. This includes social economic status, disability, gender, and sexual orientation. Several of these issues are intertwined with a long history of debate and feuding within religious circles. For example, the role of women is an often controversial issue within the church. For some, a patriarchal system is part of their religious beliefs and value system. While this may be offensive to some therapists, it may be the individual or family's religious beliefs and should be respected. Another very controversial example is the issue of homosexuality. This has been controversial both in the history of psychology and the history of religion. However, the psychological community has become more accepting of this issue and there are an increasing number of religious groups which are now changing their position on homosexuality. For some therapists with strong religious convictions, it may be difficult to accept that not all Christians (or Muslims, Jews, etc.) believe homosexuality is a sin. Yet, again, it is important to be able to respect these different belief systems when working with clients who espouse them.

Therapists will have difficulty handling these situations ethically if they have not adequately established their own personal beliefs about the matter. At times, when the therapist's beliefs and sensitivities become clarified, they may come to the realization that they cannot work with clients from particular belief systems. These diversity issues, closely tied to the intra-religious group diversity, are extremely important in maintaining an appropriate ethical stance.

Summary

Diversity, when applied to spiritual issues, must take on a broad connotation. Students and therapists should be exposed to the various ways of conceptualizing differences in religion and spirituality. It is likely that the number of diversity issues will continue to expand, requiring therapist to maintain ongoing training to prepare themselves to work with emergent spiritual trends.

LEVEL 3: APPLICATION

The application level of training is more straight-forward, however; a couple of important distinctions are still necessary. This section will briefly highlight three issues to consider in regards to application. The authors maintain that all three of these issues should be contained within the final level of training. None of these, with the possible exception of the exploration of beliefs, should be applied without the establishment of a foundation. Ideally, the first two levels of training will be obtained prior to being exposed to application. However, if they are taught out of sequence for any reason, students or therapists should be informed of the dangerous ethical and clinical issues of using applications without an established foundation as discussed in the previous two levels.

Exploration versus Active Integration

An important distinction can be made between exploring spiritual beliefs and using spiritual applications (i.e., approaches and techniques). Most therapists, even those who are not specifically trained in these issues, utilize some exploration of spiritual issues. This can be a part of gathering a client's history, encouraging a client to talk about what their spiritual beliefs mean to them, or having a client explain aspects of what they believe to the therapist. While, in general, this is much more benign than the active approaches, it is still best to have

11

some training background in religious and spiritual issues prior to utilizing in-depth spiritual exploration.

Approaches

Many approaches to therapy, such as humanistic and existential psychotherapy, focus more on *approaches* to therapy rather than *technique*. For example, Carl Rogers (1980) focused on the idea of therapy as *a way of being* that is healing. In spiritual application of relational psychotherapy, James Olthuis (2001), in *The Beautiful Risk*, lays the framework for an approach to therapy than is non-technique driven. Similarly, Viktor Frankl (1984, 2000), the founder of logotherapy, delineates an active approach to spiritual issues without applying techniques. Randall Sorenson (2004), in his book *Minding Spirituality*, integrates a relational approach to analytic therapy with spirituality.

Approach based therapies tend to be rather abstract and difficult for neophyte therapists to grasp. For example, empathy is rather straight forward when thought of as a technique, but much more complex when thought of as an approach. As a technique, a person acts in such a way to reflect concern for what the client is feeling. While the therapist may be emotionally moved in the process, there is still a distance which is implicit when the technique of empathy is applied. Conversely, when a person is truly empathetic, this becomes a natural process which flows from them. They are moved more genuinely by the client's experience as it is shared in the therapy relationship.

Therapy approaches are still intentional and grounded in a solid theoretical base, but they must be learned at a more abstract or experiential level. Many young therapists shy away from these approaches because they are much more challenging and time consuming to learn.

Techniques

Techniques are more focused and specific than approaches or exploration methods. Technique is generally emphasized more within the solution-focused approaches to treatment, though not exclusively so. Robert McGee (1990) is an example of an application of cognitive behavioral therapy with Christian clients. While this book is well written and quite popular, there can be unique dangers to using techniques with religious clients. For example, some clients who have had a negative church experience may react negatively to a therapy that utilizes quoting scripture or an active approach to challenging problems spirituality.

Moriarty (in press) utilizes both cognitive behavioral and psychodynamic techniques in working with clients who have a negative experience of God. This book begins by providing an in-depth discussion of the problem and surrounding theory. Mark Epstein (1995), in an integration of Buddhist mediation with clinical practice, provides a blending of a religious practice with a depth psychology approach to therapy. This book, which also provides an excellent brief overview of Buddhism, is one example of using a spiritual practice in conjunction with psychotherapy. The strength of both of these books is their grounding in solid theoretical and theological implication.

Techniques can be either a therapy technique modified to address spiritual issues or a spiritual 'technique' or practice applied in the context of therapy (i.e., confession, prayer, readings from sacred texts, engaging in religious rituals). When applying a spiritual technique, therapists should be sensitive to beliefs about who is able to engage in these practices. For example, there are some practices which are reserved for clergy or religious leaders. Therapists should also have an understanding of the symbolic meaning associated with the practice.

Summary

Three different ways of addressing spiritual issues were discussed in the section: spiritual exploration, a spiritual approach, and spiritual techniques. All therapists can benefit from learning about how to utilize spiritual exploration, particularly in the context of gathering history information. It is good for therapists to have some exposure to both approaches and techniques, but many therapists may want to focus on practices that are more consistent with they way they approach therapy.

CONCLUSION

This chapter provides a very brief overview of a long, complex process. The organization of this book follows nicely with the Foundational Model presented in this chapter. While variations will be needed to accommodate unique programs, training situations, and the availability of continuing education opportunities, the authors believe the basic progressional structure of this model is important in providing optimal training which is sensitive both to the issues of integrity and ethics.

REFERENCES

Barbour, I. (1997). *Religion and science: Historical and contemporary issues.* San Francisco, CA: Harper.

Barbour, I. (2000). *When science meets religion: Enemies, strangers, or partners?* San Francisco, CA: Harper.

Bowman, E. S. (1998). Integrating religion into the education of mental health professionals. In H. G. Koenig (Ed.), *Handbook of religion and mental health* (367-378). San Diego, CA: Academic Press.

Brown, D., Davaney, S. G., & Tanner, K. (Eds.). (2001). *Converging on culture: Theologians in dialogue with cultural analysis and criticism.* New York: Oxford University Press.

Cortright, B. (1997). *Psychotherapy and spirit.* Albany, NY: State University of New York Press.

Epstein, M. (1995). *Thoughts without a thinker: Psychotherapy from a Buddhist perspective.* New York: Basic Books.

Frankl, V. E. (1984). *Man's search for meaning*. New York: Simon & Schuster.

Frankl, V. E. (2000). *Man's search for ultimate meaning*. Cambridge, MA: Perseus.

Hoge, D. R. (1996). Religion in America. The demographics of belief and affiliation. In E. P. Shafranske (Ed.), *Religion and the clinical practice of psychology* (pp. 21-41). Washington, DC: American Psychological Association.

Hopkins, D. N. & Davaney, S. G. (Eds.). (1996). *Changing conversations: Religious reflection and cultural analysis*. New York: Routledge.

Koenig, H. G. (Ed.). (1998). *Handbook of religion and mental health*. San Diego, CA: Academic Press.

McGee, R. S. (1990). *The search for significance* (book & workbook, 2nd ed.). Houston, TX: Rapha.

Miller, W. R. (1999). *Integrating spirituality into treatment: Resources for practitioners*. Washington, DC: American Psychological Association.

Moriarty, G. (in press). *Why is God always mad at me?: Understanding and changing how people who are depressed experience God* (working title). Haworth.

Olthuis, J. H. (2001). *The beautiful risk*. Grand Rapids, MI: Zondervan.

Pargament, K. I. (1997). *The psychology of religion and coping: Theory, research practice*. New York: Guilford Press.

Richards, P. S. & Bergin, A. E. (1997). *A spiritual strategy for counseling and Psychotherapy* (2nd ed.). Washington, DC: American Psychological Association.

Richards, P. S. & Bergin, A. E. (Eds.). (2000). *Handbook of psychotherapy and religious diversity*. Washington, DC: American Psychological Association.

Rogers, C. R. (1980). *A way of being*. Boston, MA: Houghton Miffin.

Shafranske, E. P. (1996). Beliefs, affiliations, and practices of psychologists. In E. P. Shafranske (Ed.), *Religion and the clinical practice of psychology* (pp. 149-162). Washington, DC: American Psychological Association.

Sorenson, R. L. (2004). *Minding spirituality*. Hillsdale, NJ: The Analytic Press.

Tacey, D. (2004). *The spiritual revolution: The emergence of contemporary spirituality*. New York: Routledge.

Tanner, K. (1997). *Theories of culture: A new agenda for theology*. Minneapolis, MN: Fortress Press.

Walsh, R. (1996). Shamanism and healing. In B. W. Scotton, A. B. Chinen, & J. R. Battista (Eds.), *Textbook of transpersonal psychiatry and psychology* (pp. 96-103). New York: Basic Books.

2

THE DYNAMICS OF FAITH: HOW CAN THE PSYCHOLOGIST UNDERSTAND RELIGION AND SPIRITUALITY?

Joey Pulleyking, MTS, Psy.D.
St. John's Clinic
St. John's Regional Health Care Center
Springfield, Missouri

Religion without science becomes superstition;
science without religion becomes a monster.
-- The Rev. Dr. Gerrit tenZythoff[1]

The task of integrating spirituality and psychology is a popular pursuit in current academic and clinical psychology. The level of interest in this task appears to be steadily growing as is evident by an increasing number of research studies, journal articles, and books on the topic. Professional schools of psychology and university psychology departments are offering courses and seminars on the psychology of religion and on spirituality. The interest of psychology students and psychological trainees is part of the force that has created these new areas of learning and training. The research finding that 72% of the general population describe religious faith as the most important influence in their lives while only 33% of clinical psychologists place this sort of value on their faith (Jones, 1994), has also served as something of a wake-up call to the field of psychology to a pragmatic need to better

---

[1] This quote, made by Rev. Dr. tenZythoff at his retirement party, paraphrases a quote from Albert Einstein (1941), "Science without religion is lame. Religion without science is blind."

understand spirituality. Even in the public domain there is a level of interest in things spiritual that has not been seen in several decades.

The integration of spirituality and psychology is a complex task whose features are just being discovered as the attempts at integration are made. A current review of the literature on the psychology of religion displays a wide range of perspectives as to how the psychologists define and integrate spirituality into his or her clinical or academic work. This lack of common ground in definition and in integration methodology creates a confusing array of options and an inability to develop clear criteria and appropriate goals for integration.

A basic sense of balance and an awareness of the dangers of extreme thinking and believing are the starting criteria suggested by the quotation that begins this chapter. It would be wise for the field of psychology to consider how other disciplines have approached the integration of scientific knowledge with religious knowledge. The author of this quotation, Dr. Gerrit tenZythoff, was the founding chair of a department of religious studies established in a state university in the Midwest. This department of religion had to integrate the scientific methodology of biblical and theological studies with the religious beliefs of many traditions to exist, function and thrive as it has for over twenty years in a publicly-funded, state university. The primary assumption that has guided this kind of integration is that both the intellect and the spirit are necessary for a successful merger of these two ways of knowing. A secondary assumption is that the scientific way of knowing and the spiritual way of knowing have different connotations but share equal value in human endeavors to understand and live well.

Superstitions develop and play themselves out when the religious way of knowing is utilized without an accompanying sense of rationality and reason. Superstition occurs on the individual level or in the context of a larger group or community. Some examples of superstitious extremes are the destructive cults formed around people like David Koresh and Jim Jones. Superstition functions on the individual level with magical beliefs in events and rituals which do not carry ultimate meaning or significance. One of the common manifestations of individual superstition is an overwhelming sense of anxiety resulting from beliefs and actions that do not have a connection to reality.

Monsters are created when the ideals and methods of scientific knowledge are applied without a corresponding sense of ultimate value and reality. The classic tale of *Frankenstein* by Mary Shelly first presented this question of purpose, meaning, and value in regard to the advances in scientific knowledge and the new creations of scientific methodology. Scientific monsters frequently carry out their destruction on the individual level in the form of arrogance, narcissism, and intolerance of differing theories or methodologies. Notable scientific monsters created on the corporate level in the past century include atomic weapons and other technologies of mass destruction, ideologies of eugenics and political fascism, and certain medical and psychological treatments such as frontal lobotomies and the early, extreme uses of electroconvulsive therapy (ECT).

Another way the extreme of superstition has been described in academic literature is as an irrationalism, which is sometimes understood as the core feature of being religious. The notion that religious faith is a "blind faith" which accepts and follows certain dogma, beliefs or rituals despite any rational knowledge to the contrary is a commonly held definition of spirituality. "Blind faith" readily becomes superstition and is promptly rejected or refuted by the methods of scientific knowledge. It does appear to be the case that a part of the historical schism between religion and psychology is based on the assumption that all religious faith is "blind faith." However, all religious faith is not of a "blind" sort and many theologians from many eras have also rejected and refuted religious faith that is irrational and uncritical.

Scientific monsters have also been academically described and critiqued with the terms of reductionism and naïve realism. While the knowledge gained from breaking a complex phenomenon like depressive thinking down into it's neurological parts is beneficial knowledge, is this information sufficient for a comprehensive understanding of the existential experience of depression and for a meaningful treatment method? One of the main ways in which the monsters of science are set free to roam is in the assumption that empirically gained knowledge is without bias and interpretation and that this sort of knowing is comprehensive of all aspects of reality. As Jones (1994) points out in his *American Psychologist* article, contemporary philosophers of science are aware of the flaws in positivistic empiricism and now are beginning to "not support a radical or categorical separation of science from other forms of human knowing, including religious knowing or belief" (p. 188).

The errors of the extremes of scientific thinking or of religious believing are sometimes costly and very destructive to human life. Psychologists striving to integrate spirituality into their research, theory, and and/or clinical work would do well to place their work on a knowledge continuum between the superstitions and the monsters.

The main purpose of this chapter is to present a definition of religion and spirituality that does not fall into the errors of the extremes as described above. A secondary purpose is to demonstrate how a balanced definition of religion and spirituality is essential to the integration of psychology and spirituality. The potential for the integration of religious knowledge and scientific knowledge is still an impossibility according to Krauss (1999) who writes that "Science deals with ideas that are falsifiable. Religion deals with matters of faith. It is of vital importance for both fields that they stick to their separate turfs" (p. A88). However, for Krauss and those who fall into this separatist camp, there appears to be a lack of depth to their definitions of both science and religion. An integration of psychology and religion requires definitions capable of seeing the ways religious and scientific knowledge can interact and inform each other. A first step toward such a definition is to propose some criteria for the task of integrating the scientific way of knowing and the religious way of knowing.

As already implied earlier in the chapter, a primary criteria is the assumption that the intellect and the spirit are both needed for a successful relationship between these two ways of knowing. A second criteria is assuming these ways of knowing have different connotations but share equal value in human endeavors to understand and live well. Jones (1994) asserts that psychology has typically interacted with religion in three ways that are all "unidirectional, with psychology being unaffected in any substantive way by the interaction" (p. 184). The first mode of interaction has been the scientific study of religion from a psychological viewpoint such as the works of Paloutzian (1983) and Wulff (1991). The second mode of interaction has been the psychologizing of pastoral care and counseling in the past eighty years. Jones observes that before 1920, pastoral care texts primarily referred to their theological roots and history and after 1920, these texts referred primarily to psychotherapy theorists. Even today, clergy readily look to psychological concepts to guide their work in pastoral counseling.

A third mode of interaction cited by Jones is "the use of psychological findings or theories to revise, reinterpret, redefine, supplant or dismiss established religious traditions" (1994, p. 185). This mode of interaction is one of the oldest trends in the history of psychology and religion and is perhaps the main cause of the animosity and suspicion that still exists in certain religious traditions toward psychology and mental health professionals. It is a frequent occurrence in some clinics that patients seeking therapy will present with the request for a therapist who will not attack their religious beliefs as wrong and as something that must be given up.

"In each of the three modes discussed above, religion is treated as an object, either of study, for education and provision of services, or for reform. In none of the three is religion a peer or a partner" (Jones, 1994, p. 185). Jones goes on to call for a relationship of mutuality and respect to be formed between psychology and religion. Perhaps the term acquisition is more appropriate for the kinds of interactions that have taken place between psychology and religion. When seen in this light, it is not surprising that frequent conflicts or power struggles have erupted between religion and psychology.

Integration implies the utilization of comparable methods or epistemologies considered to carry similar levels of validity. If psychologists cannot step away from viewing religion as an object and move to viewing religious knowledge as a partner to psychological knowledge, then efforts at integration will fail and perhaps transform into other monsters of extremism. One of the primary reasons that the field of psychology finds itself unable to make this move is the genuine study of theology and references to theologians and their work is quite rare in most psychological literature and research. Many psychologists and scientists have an impoverished and narrow understanding of religion, and they are unaware of how limited and unsophisticated their working definitions of religion are.

A third criteria for the integration of psychology and religion is that critical thinking and objective and rational methodology be utilized along with serious consideration of ultimate values and historical traditions of religious knowledge. A successful integration between religion and psychology cannot form and survive without a tie or connection to an established religious tradition and it's accumulated store of values, rituals, and systematic beliefs. Researchers and clinicians can fall prey to utilizing spiritual methodologies and interventions that are taken piecemeal from a variety of religious traditions and only end up creating a harmful mix of superstitious treatments that do not fit together spiritually or psychologically and may in fact do harm to those who seek treatment. In some situations these clinicians may even create a cult-like atmosphere to their work and begin to wander into methods of practice that go beyond professional standards of ethics and care.

An additional criteria for integration is the necessity to bring together similar levels of psychological knowledge and religious knowledge. As one who first completed graduate study in theology in a divinity school and then completed graduate study in a professional school of psychology, this author is keenly aware of the tendency of some psychologists to attempt to integrate advanced levels of psychological knowledge with simplistic levels of theological and biblical knowledge. This mismatch of levels of understanding can result in a variety of integration problems ranging from the reductionistic error of positivistic science to misusing the influence of psychological knowledge for purposes of proselytizing.

When similar levels of religion and psychology are brought together, then one comes closer to creating the kind of a dialectical relationship that Jones (1994) has called for in his article: "a willingness to establish such a dialogical relationship with religion will necessarily presume the willingness of scientists and professionals to become theologically literate and for theologians and philosophers to become scientifically and professionally literate" (p. 195).

With these criteria in mind, this author hopes to avoid some of the pitfalls that have previously occurred in the complex task of integrating religion and psychology. These parameters are not assumed to be comprehensive nor are they without problems of their own. However, it is from these guidelines that it now is appropriate to look more directly at the thinking and understandings of theological writers.

The endeavor to define religion and spirituality is an age-old quest. Taken in its broadest sense, this seeking to define things spiritual is a life-long process of experience, study, and discernment. In the context of this chapter, the need is to provide a definition that can fit the requirements and situation of the academic or clinical psychologist. Many different types of definitions utilized in theological studies can be found in Wilson and Clark (1989).

First, religion can be defined in a descriptive way. A descriptive definition is simply whatever someone calls his or her religion, such as "I'm a Baptist," or "I'm a Buddhist." In a descriptive definition there is no assessment or evaluation of religion, it simply is the label used to identify a tradition. Descriptive definitions of religion are routinely integrated into the demographic information gathered in psychological research or psychosocial histories. Since this definition type is only a label, drawing psychological or theological implications from this kind of information is not recommended or appropriate for the kind of integration work we are discussing here.

A normative definition implies what religion should be or what it ought to do. This type of definition is a kind of judgment or evaluation of rightness or wrongness. Religion ought to provide a person with high morals. Religion should help a society improve itself and the quality of life of its peoples. Religion ought to improve one's psychological health. The weakness of normative definitions is that they are highly subjective and do not lend themselves well to the tasks of integration and critical evaluation. The normative type of definition is sometimes seen in statements or professions of personal faith.

A functional definition describes religion according to what it does or what its consequences are. Religion as the "opiate of the masses" was Marx's functional definition of religion. Freud's conclusion that religion is an immature wish-fulfillment approach to reality is also a functional type of definition. The functional definition is the type most commonly utilized by scientific methods and theories seeking to understand religion. It is the kind of interaction that Jones refers to as making religion an "object" of study. The thinker or scientist makes an assumption of objectivity in attempting to understand and describe just how religion works. Any sort of participation or involvement with the "object" of study is not desired. If the purpose of understanding the mechanisms of religion is the stated goal of research or study, then functional definitions can generate very helpful kinds of information and knowledge. However, the error of scientific reductionism is a prevalent danger of functional definitions of religion.

Additional types of definitions of religion are summarized in Rahner's (1975) *Encyclopedia of Theology*. A single and comprehensive type of definition of religion does not exist. Even the words we use to describe religion are bound to particular languages and the cultures that are associated with those languages. While an etymological study of the word religion will lead us to the notions of re-connecting and "binding oneself back to one's origin and goal" (Rahner, 1975, p. 1359), these notions are somewhat artificial and stilted when applied to religious traditions that do not have ties to Latin or its family of languages. The purpose of considering these different types of definitions of religion is to create an awareness of the type that a psychologist may be using and to allow for an evaluation of the appropriateness of that type to the task at hand.

The type of definition of religion striving to be comprehensive and to consider all forms of religious expression is a type called essential by Wilson and Clark (1989). This type is also known by the philosophical term--phenomenology of religion. A phenomenological definition of religion strives to take an overview of all religious traditions and to bring together the common features of the human experience of religion and spirituality. According to Rahner,

> the aim is to understand, not to evaluate these phenomenon. It is therefore an empirical procedure, methodologically close to the history of religions, inasmuch as its *epoche* – 'bracketing out' – precludes the application of preconceived judgments. The researcher becomes a 'hearer of the word', i.e. the facts of the religions which from his own standpoint appear as alien. (p. 1392)

However, the phenomenological understanding of religion does not separate out the "researcher" to the extent that she or he is above being a participant in the described religious experience.

Phenomenological definitions of religion are by nature quite broad and look beyond particular religious histories, writings, or terms. A definition of religion not bound to a particular tradition or description of the ultimate is difficult to develop. Yet, as we consider potential errors of superstitions and/or monsters and look at the criteria presented here for the undertaking of integrating psychology and religion, the phenomenological definition of religion appears to be the most appropriate type.

The main weakness of a phenomenological approach is its non-contextual and non-historical stance. The potential problem here is the ideas generated by this approach could miss the actual meaning of religion in its historical context. And this type of definition could also lend itself to the kind of spiritual syncretism or hodgepodge approach to spirituality warned against earlier in this chapter. Still, on the methodological basis, the phenomenological type of definition of religion is a most suitable place to start the process of integrating of psychology and religion. The understandings gained from the phenomenological perspective then have to be taken back into the appropriate religious context in a meaningful way that does not violate the theological system of a particular tradition.

A brief survey of current psychological literature regarding the integration of religion and psychology shows that many of the definitions of religion and spirituality currently used fall into the functional type of definition. Religion is frequently described according to how it may operate or how people behaviorally express their religion. In the research literature, operational definitions such as church attendance and frequency of meditation or prayer are a common form of functional definition. Yet, with functional definitions and measures, the question remains as to whether one is actually measuring what one is attempting to test or falsify. For example, in a study that found people who attend church frequently live longer than people who attend less frequently (Koenig, 1999), what can really be inferred about the nature of religion and it's relationship to longevity? Without some definition of religion addressing the possible theological and psychological meanings of church attendance, how can anything be implied beyond going to a certain building at a certain time? Functional definitions of religion lack the depth of meaning necessary to make substantial theological and psychological implications.

A recent book by Richards and Bergin (1997) on spiritual strategies for psychotherapy simply offers a descriptive and somewhat confessional definition of religion: "God exists; is humankind's Creator; embodies love, goodness, and truth; and acts on people's behalf and for their sakes." (p. 76). A functional type of definition is also given for spirituality "as attunement with God, the Spirit of Truth, or the Divine Intelligence that governs or harmonizes the universe" (p. 77). While every person is entitled to their own theological beliefs and to the expression of those beliefs, it does not appear to this author that these definitions possess enough intensity and intricacy to be integrated in a balanced and comprehensive way with the complex issues and dynamics that occur in psychotherapy. The spiritual or theistic strategies proposed by Richards and Bergin will only appeal to a select group of therapists and patients who share a similar theology. A broader definition of spirituality such as can be found in the phenomenology of religion would help some of the their integration strategies go much further and apply to a wider audience of professionals.

21

One of the major definitional events in psychology of religion is the distinction drawn between religion and spirituality. In this two-dimensional definition, religion is understood as pertaining to the corporate dimension of cumulative tradition, history, and rituals. Spirituality, on the other hand, has to do with the individual experience and the inner beliefs and experiences that pertain to one's notion of God or the ultimate. This functional distinction between spirituality and religion made a forceful effect in the literature and continues to be used regularly. The distinction is helpful in better understanding some of the ways in which the religious experience of the individual is independent of the community and it has been a beneficial concept for the study of internal and external religious dynamics.

Yet, from a phenomenological perspective, this division between religion and spirituality is reductionistic and is more problematic than helpful in the task of the integration of scientific knowledge and religious knowledge. How can one of these dimensions really exist and function without the other? An individual does not live, think, feel, believe and act in isolation. A religious institution with its history, traditions and rituals will not form, reform or survive without the individuals who make it up and whose spirituality drives the tradition. Even in most all psychological theories both the intrapersonal and the interpersonal dimensions are considered together. A definition of religion that does not examine both of these dimensions cannot function as a peer or partner to psychological concepts. A definition of religion that is too narrow in either of these ways will only be another limited description of behavior interjected into a psychological construct or theory.

In order to emphasize the need to move away from the descriptive and functional definitions of religion that have been utilized thus far in attempts at integration, a change in the vocabulary of definition is required. Rather than attempt to define "religion" or "spirituality" and risk confusion with the prior meanings of these terms, the definition developed here is the essence, the meaning of "faith" as seen in the religions of the world. This definition is taken closely from the work of the theologian Paul Tillich, as found in his book, *Dynamics of Faith* (1957). To focus on a definition of faith that is applicable to all forms of religious and spiritual expression is the kind of starting place comparable to the assumption that psychology has as its focus - the study of all human personality and behavior. To employ a definition of faith which was developed with an empirical approach comparable to the empiricism of psychology is also a good methodological match. To look at the experience of faith in a dynamic way, as Tillich does, is also a strong similarity to the dynamic quality of many psychological theories. With a closer kind of match of definition and methodology between psychology and faith, psychologists and theologians can hope for an interaction of epistemological partners or peers as Jones (1994) calls for in his article.

Tillich (1957) begins his definition with the phrase, "faith is the state of being ultimately concerned" (p. 1.), and from this point he goes on to expand in detail the meanings of these terms. An ultimate concern is one that requires a complete surrender of the one who accepts it. The exact content of the ultimate concern is of little attention to the phenomenological definition as the dynamics described are primary over the content. The ultimate concern which expects a complete surrender also provides an ultimate promise of complete fulfillment to the one who chooses to surrender. The content of the fulfillment is also relative to the believer and to the religious tradition. Both the ultimate concern and the ultimate fulfillment defy simple description and are expressed in symbols and in rituals. The ultimate fulfillment is not attained by those who do not completely surrender to the ultimate concern.

In Christian theology, the believer is committed to a belief in one God and in God's incarnation into the human realm in the person of Jesus Christ. Complete surrender to the truths, values, rituals, and behaviors taught by Christ is the ultimate demand required of the Christian. The ultimate fulfillment resulting from the Christian's ultimate concern is the experience of God's kingdom of peace and justice both in the present life and more completely in the eternal life after death with God in heaven.

In Hindu theology, the believer is committed to a belief that the divine Brahman is one reality that takes on an infinite number of expressions or manifestations in the human realm. The Hindu totally surrenders to following the rituals, actions and stages of life that aid one in moving beyond the cosmic chain of cause and effect to harmonizing with the total pattern and motions of the cosmos. The ultimate fulfillment for the Hindu is called *moksha*, which is to find liberation in the awareness of complete identification with the absolute divine consciousness.

In illustrating his ideas, Tillich readily suggests there are concerns to which people as individuals or groups may be ultimately committed that are not really at the level of ultimacy. Nationalism, or the concern that one "people" or "race" is the ultimate race to which one must be completely devoted no matter what, is one of the non-ultimate concerns people will easily surrender to and kill for. The 20th century has illustrated terribly the potential of nationalism, e.g. Nazism and genocide, to be believed in and acted on as an ultimate concern.

A combination of success, social standing and economic status can also be the highest concern that organizes all of the aspects of a person's life.

> It is the god of many people in the highly competitive Western culture and it does what every ultimate concern must do: it demands unconditional surrender to its laws even if the price is the sacrifice of genuine human relationships, personal conviction, and creative eros. Its threat is social and economic defeat, and its promise—indefinite as all such promises—the fulfillment of one's being. (Tillich, 1957, p. 3)

However, the fulfillment of a non-ultimate concern such as materialism is impotent and the one who has completely surrendered to it is damaged and may even pay the consequence of losing their very existence.

Tillich is well aware the term faith carries with it some history that is very destructive and has a variety of negative connotations. His objective is to rescue "faith" from the inadequate and confusing meanings that have come to be linked with the word and to put forth a balanced and beneficial understanding of the authentic experience of faith. Thus, according to Tillich's definition, the first point of evaluation of how healthy or pathological a

23

person's faith is whether the concern to which they surrender is an ultimate concern. Those concerns that are not ultimate have been described in more traditional theological terms as demons or idols.

Some psychodynamic constructs are also woven into Tillich's thinking as he defines faith as ultimate concern.

> Faith is an act of the total personality. It happens in the center of the personal life and includes all its elements…faith is not a movement of a special section or a special function of man's total being. They all are united in the act of faith. But faith is not the sum total of their impacts. It transcends every special impact as well as the totality of them and it has itself a decisive impact on each of them. (p. 4.)

The polarity of the conscious and the unconscious are each integral components of the dynamics of faith. Faith being in part a conscious act reveals the freedom of the individual to participate and to surrender to the content of their ultimate concern. Yet, faith also contains unconscious elements that shape its beginnings in the life of a believer as well as its expressions and manifestations in the believer's daily living. If faith is dominated by unconscious forces, then it ceases to be a centered act of the personality and it becomes a matter of compulsion or neurosis. Tillich's definition suggests a balance of conscious motives and unconscious forces as the hallmark of faith. Attaining such a balance in the personality structure has long been one of the main features of psychodynamic theory and therapy.

In discussing the id, ego, and superego, Tillich asserts Freud's notion of the superego is unclear and too negative in regard to the norms and principles, which make it up. Faith may well have its beginnings in the father image, yet as faith matures, it transforms this image into the principles of truth and justice that are able to be critical even of the father image. Tillich appears to place the role of genuine faith in something more akin to the place and role of the ego.

The cognitive and emotional aspects of the personality also participate in the state of being ultimately concerned.

> In the ecstasy of faith the will to accept and to surrender is an element, but not the cause. And this is also true of feeling. Faith is not an emotional outburst: this is not the meaning of ecstasy. Certainly emotion is in it, as in every act of man's spiritual life. But, emotion does not produce faith. Faith has a cognitive content and is an act of the will. (Tillich, 1957 p. 7)

Here Tillich clearly confronts the notion that faith is "blind" to the rational side of human existence, and that anyone who is religious has surrendered their cognitive abilities to the passion of belief. As a centered act of the total personality, faith takes place in the tension between the affective and the intellectual dynamics of the personality. When faith lies too much in the emotional realm, then there is the danger of magical belief and superstitions.

When faith falls too much in the cognitive domain, one runs the risk of creating a monster spawned of a non-ultimate concern.

Considering this broad type of phenomenological definition, other theologians since Tillich have argued that every person has an ultimate concern and is in some sense a person of faith. The content of someone's concern may lie in a traditional religious tradition or it may be found in more finite aspects of human life. Just as in a mental status evaluation the question of congruence between mood and affect is assessed, in the dynamics of faith the question of congruence between the faith a person professes and the faith by which they actually live is assessed. Genuine faith that is a centered act of the total personality would exhibit a high degree of congruence between that which is avowed and that which is lived out in one's behavior and beliefs.

Yet, incongruence can readily be observed in the faith of some people. Wilson and Clark (1989) offer two ways to label this sort of inconsistency. Cryptoreligion, meaning "hidden religion", describes an ultimate concern by which one lives but, does not openly acknowledge. A cryptoreligion, such as materialism or nationalism, may even be below a person's level of conscious awareness. Pseudoreligion, or "false religion", is when someone may outwardly claim to surrender to a specific ultimate concern and its content, but they do not actually believe and behave according to this ultimate concern. Pseudoreligion is evident when someone faithfully attends a worship service where certain truths or values, such as honesty or respect for all persons regardless of race, are taught as the content of ultimate surrender—yet, this person regularly is dishonest or behaves in a racist manner. Incongruence of this sort between the faith professed and the faith actually lived out, would be a symptom of inauthentic or uncentered faith according to Tillich's definition.

In the field of pastoral psychotherapy, Jordan (1987), addresses this matter of incongruence as he discusses the clinical necessity for understanding the operational theology versus the professed theology of the patient. "Operational theology refers to the implicit religious story by which one is living, including unconscious material" (p. 29). In the listening perspective that is a key part of the therapeutic endeavor, the therapist identifies the operational theology by attending to "what or who is perceived as the ultimate authority in the psyche of the [patient] and of how he or she experiences being defined or valued by that ultimate authority" (p. 22). Jordan argues that self-concept and one's concept of the ultimate go hand in hand. The definition of pathology emerging from Jordan's psychospiritual object-relations theory is that the root of neurotic pathology is idolatry or finite understandings of the ultimate.

Tillich speaks at length of the dangers and implications of idolatry or false ultimacy as the content of the act of faith. Faith as the state of being in a non-ultimate concern is a distortion of faith. Many of the misconceptions of faith are key forces behind the breach between the scientific way of knowing and the religious way of knowing. Distortions of faith occur in two related dimensions, one is in the personality of the believer and the other is in the content of the ultimate concern.

The expression and representation of the ultimate can only occur in symbol. If the ultimate were to be completely described or contained in symbol or language it would automatically cease to be ultimate. According to Tillich, symbols point to something beyond themselves; they participate in that to which they point; they open up levels of reality that are otherwise closed; they cannot be produced intentionally, and they cannot be invented and constantly maintained. "Like living things, they grow and they die. They grow when the situation is ripe for them, and they die when the situation changes" (p. 43). Symbols are the dynamic means of understanding one's ultimate concern, but always they are incomplete modes and as such are understood as inadequate. Idolatry takes place when any of the symbols of faith, including physical and mental symbols, are believed or felt to be complete, perfect, or comprehensive of the ultimate. Religious fundamentalism, scriptural literalism and creedal exclusivism all then fall into the category of idolatry and not genuine faith.

Faith which avoids becoming idolatry must then contain the sort of skepticism, doubt, or falsifiability which is usually associated with scientific epistemology. From time to time the symbols of faith may well undergo revision, conversion or destruction. Tillich speaks quite clearly of the risk of faith and the existential courage required to participate in faith.

> Courage does not deny that there is doubt, but it takes the doubt into itself as an expression of its own finitude and affirms the content of the ultimate concern. Courage does not need the safety of an unquestionable conviction. It includes the risk without which no creative life is possible. (p. 101)

Here is the symmetry of faith and reason that was referred to in the quotation at the start of this chapter.

Faith as a centered act of the total personality into the state of being ultimately concerned is the positive definition proposed by Tillich. When the action of faith is not balanced along the various components of the personality structure, i.e. conscious and unconscious, cognitive and emotional, then various distortions of faith emerge and those distortions are discussed by Tillich in greater detail than is suitable for the scope of this chapter. Here is where psychologists who aim to integrate faith and psychology are called upon to further delve into the scholarship of phenomenological theology

Tillich's definition of faith also engages the interpersonal domain or the necessity of a community in which one participates and makes the act of faith. Individual spirituality is not possible without the greater context of a religious community and tradition. The reason for this individual impossibility is that the expression of faith occurs in symbols of which language is a main type. Language as a system of symbols presupposes a community in which the language is meaningful. "The life of faith is life in the community of faith, not only in its communal activities and institutions but also in the inner life of its members" (p. 118). Withdrawal from the community may be a customary habit of some individuals, but for the life of faith to be sustained this practice of withdrawal is a temporary one. For the genuine community of faith to guard against corporate idolatry, there is the need for a similar dialectic of ultimate surrender and skepticism regarding the content of the ultimate concern as within the faith of the individual.

The dynamic definition of faith proposed by Tillich strives to be a positive understanding of the experience of religion. Others such as Clinebell (1986) have constructed clinical criteria for describing spiritual health and wholeness that can apply to all religious traditions. Clinebell's criteria exhibits the kind of integration of psychological knowledge and faith experience which the methodology of this chapter advocates.

While the phenomenological definition of faith seeks to present an overview of all religions, it may not naturally follow that a theologian or a psychologist can then observe or intervene in an authentic way in all and every religious tradition. Tillich argues that this sort of objectivity is really not possible.

> There is no faith without a content toward which it is directed. And there is no way of having the content of faith except in the act of faith. All speaking about divine matters which is not done in the state of ultimate concern is meaningless. Because that which is meant in the act of faith cannot be approached in any other way than through an act of faith. (pp. 10-11)

This requirement of participation in the particular content of an ultimate concern runs counter to the idea that the objective psychologist can effectively work in and out of various religious traditions.

Perhaps Tillich's notion here can be related to the role of the psychologist as a participant-observer. Each researcher or therapist does have a particular ultimate concern with its particular content and historical context that may be the tradition she or he can best utilize this phenomenological model in the task of the integration of faith and psychology. As was mentioned earlier in this chapter, for integration to work remain theologically balanced and to avoid syncretism there is a need for the psychologist to be linked to a particular tradition and it's theological values and structures. Jones (1994) also proposes that a psychologist form a formal type of relationship to a particular religious tradition for the purposes of greater accountability and theological responsibility (p. 197).

The integration of religion and spirituality with clinical and academic psychology is a work in progress. It is easy to overlook the kind of methodology that is necessary for an adequate combination of these different ways of knowing. In clinical terms, when the therapist acts without some awareness or in response to countertransference, there is the requirement to step back and identify its content and work through the personal issue at hand. It would be fair to say all us have our own spiritual countertransferences and good methodology aids us in not bringing those underlying issues into our psychological work. The definition and criteria advocated here are intended to build on the ideas which others have presented and to advance this undertaking of integration.

In summary, these criteria are: 1) that the rational dimension and the ability to look to the ultimate are both needed for a balanced and successful relationship between faith and psychology; 2) that these two ways of knowing and have different connotations but share equal value in human endeavors to understand and live well; 3) that psychological theory and objective methodology be utilized alongside meaningful consideration of the ultimate values, historical context, and religious knowledge of a particular tradition; and 4) to bring together similar levels of psychological knowledge and religious knowledge.

The phenomenological definition of religion appears to best meet these criteria for bringing the religious way of knowing together with the knowledge of psychology. In particular, Tillich's understanding of the dynamics of faith furnishes a reliable understanding from which to build. Defining faith as the state of being grasped with an ultimate concern and that this state is a centered act of the total personality, offers the psychologist a valid and broad theological epistemology from which psychospiritual integration theories, techniques and interventions, measurements, additional definitions, and greater understandings can emerge and find meaningful application.

REFERENCES

Clinebell, H. (1984). *Basic types of pastoral care and counseling*. Nashville: Abingdon Press.

Coon, D. J. (1992). Testing the limits of sense and science: American experimental psychologists combat spiritualism 1880-1920. *American Psychologist, 47(2),* 143-151.

Ellwood, R. S. (1982). *Many peoples, many faiths* (2nd ed.). Englewood Cliffs, N.J.: Prentice Hall.

Haug, I. E. (1998). Spirituality as a dimension of family therapists' clinical training. *Contemporary Family Therapy, 20(4),* 471-483.

Jones, D. R., Ripley, J.S., Kurusu, T. A., & Worthington, E. L. (1998). Influential sources in the integration of psychology and theology: A decade summary. *Journal of Psychology and Christianity, 17(1),* 43-54.

Jones, S. L. (1994). A constructive relationship for religion with the science and profession of psychology: Perhaps the boldest model yet. *American Psychologist, 49(3),* 184-199.

Jordan, M. (1986). *Taking on the gods: The task of the pastoral counselor*. Nashville, Abingdon.

Koenig, H. et. al. (1999). Does religious attendance prolong survival? A six-year follow-up study of 3,968 older adults. *Journal of Gerontology: Medical Science, 54A(7),* M370-M376.

Krauss, L. (1999). An article of faith: Science and religion don't mix. *The Chronicle of Higher Education*, November 26, 1999.

McCullough, M. E. (1999). Research on religion-accommodative counseling: Review and meta-analysis. *Journal of Counseling Psychology, 46(1),* 92-98.

Miller, W. R. (Ed.). (1999). *Integrating spirituality into treatment*. Washington, D.C.: American Psychological Association

Paloutzian, R. (1996). *Invitation to the psychology of religion* (2nd ed.). Boston: Allyn & Bacon.

Parker, S. (1999). Hearing god's spirit: Impacts of developmental history on adult religious experience. *Journal of Psychology and Christianity, 18(2),* 153-163.

Richards, P. S. & Bergin, A. E. (1997). *A spiritual strategy for counseling and psychotherapy*. Washington, D.C.: American Psychological Association

Rahner, K. (Ed.). (1975). *Encyclopedia of theology: The concise sacramentum mundi*. New York: Crossroad.

Shelley, M. (1816). *Frankenstein, or the modern prometheus*. New York: Penguin Books.

Tillich, P. (1957). *Dynamics of faith*. New York: Harper Collins.

Wilson, J. F. & Clark, W. R. (1989). *Religion: A preface.*(2nd ed.). Englewood Cliffs, N.J.: Prentice Hall.

Wulff, D. (1991). *Psychology of religion: Classic and contemporary views*. New York: Wiley.

Part II

Developmental Perspectives

3

A PROPOSED PARADIGM FOR THE DEVELOPMENTAL STAGES OF SPIRITUALITY

Richard H. Cox, Ph.D., M.D., D.Min.
Provost
Colorado School of Professional Psychology
Colorado Springs, CO

Nearly every philosopher, psychologist, and theologian, to name only a few professions, has spoken regarding spirituality. Some have lumped spirituality into the broader concept of religion. Many have separated religion from spirituality. Fewer have attempted to develop a theory regarding the development of spirituality. Some have recognized that it is possible to be religious without being spiritual, and that it is possible to be spiritual without being religious. Some have tended to equate morality with spirituality and vice versa. Kohlberg, one of the foremost thinkers in the field of moral development does not equate moral development with spiritual development. Indeed, he does not so much as mention the latter term. "Kohlberg's approach to the study of moral reasoning is based upon a complex set of philosophical and psychological assumptions" (Kuhmerker, 1991, p.21).

The problem is that spiritual development is almost universally seen by behavioral scientists as being synonymous with psychological development. Kohlberg based his concept of moral development on philosophical theories that were subsequently elucidated in psychological terms by psychologist James Baldwin, then later by sociologist George Mead, and finally by Jean Piaget the child epistomologist. Kohlberg anchored his theory in *cognitive* development, meaning *thought production*. This anchoring is fine for *moral* development because morals are a result of reasoning, which of course is cognitive. Spiritual development precedes cognition, and therefore is a foundation for moral thinking but not at all synonymous with morals.

James Fowler's developmental model of the stages of faith is relied upon heavily by many persons who write regarding the development of spirituality. His model provides a bridge from psychological development to spiritual development, although he does not conceptualize his stages in that fashion. His stages utilize psychological language and are as follows:

Stage One: Intuitive-projective faith
Stage Two: Mythical-literal faith
Stage Three: Synthetic-Conventional faith
Stage Four: Individual-reflexive faith
Stage Five: Conjunctive faith
Stage Six: Universalizing faith

A more thorough discussion of these stages may be found in two chapters in this book, "Spirituality and Old Age" and "Spirituality and Children". Unlike most other theorists, who discuss spirituality, Fowler relates his thinking to emotional development and I find his work very helpful in attempting to define the stages of spiritual development. Psychiatrist M. Scott Peck (1997) condenses Fowler's six stages into four which are as follows:

Stage One: Chaotic
Stage Two: Formal, Institutional
Stage Three: Skeptic
Stage Four: Mystical, Communal

Peck states, "Jim speaks of six stages, which I condense into four in the interest of simplicity, but basically we are saying the same thing" (Peck, 1997, p. 124). I do not see Fowler and Peck in accord with each other. Fowler's description seems to be more consistent with traditional religious and psychological language, while Peck's first two stages appear social and the latter two appear philosophical. However, both he and Peck in the basic content of their paradigms clearly have a spiritual base of operation, and have helped us to understand the need for a developmental spirituality. Neither of them base their developmental stages on a specific theology. I am not proposing that to be "spiritual" in and of itself requires that one be theological in orientation in the usual sense of the word. However, by necessity spiritual thought requires that we believe in a force greater than ourselves, a *theos* of some sort. My addition to their conceptualization and discussion is regarding the time in our lives when spirituality begins. It is my firm belief that spiritual development begins long before organized thinking enters the picture, therefore if one is stuck at any given level, the predilection for such begins long before we are consciously aware of it.

My first post-doctoral residency assignment was observing neonates and their mothers in the same room and through a one-way mirror, studying their behavior intently and writing about it. Those two years left no doubt in my mind as to when spirituality begins. I am convinced that what Tillich (1951) calls "Spirit" (capital S) and what he calls "spirit" (small s) is increasingly demonstrable throughout life from the very moment of birth. Tillich helps us to understand the basic nature of Spirit and that of spiritual development. He differentiates the two aspects of spirituality as follows: "The term 'spiritual' (with lower case s) must be sharply distinguished from 'Spiritual' (with a capital S). The latter refers to activities of the divine Spirit in man; the former, to the dynamic-creative-nature of man's personal and communal life", (Tillich, 1951, p.15). I saw both Spirit and spiritual development in action in the newborn and watched both aspects of the human grow in the very early weeks of life.

Further, both Spirit and spirit continue to develop, sometimes in harmony with psychological and physical development, and sometimes quite apart from it until we die. The synchronicity of spiritual with chronological development is not as easily observed as is physical and psychological development. However; as the physical and even the psychological dimensions of human existence fade and sometimes fail altogether in later life and old age, there is no evidence that spiritual development declines. As a matter of fact, some would argue that we have seen spirituality grow by leaps and bounds even as the body and mind fails.

The question arises as to whether as we move through the developmental stages we may become "stuck". Some theorists maintain that if we become arrested at a given stage we cannot move on to the next stage. Some conceptualize that we can skip stages and thus be deficient in one or more of the benefits of that stage in later life. Some would say that we can be deficient in part of a stage, yet move through to the next. I believe that all combinations are possible in spiritual development, i.e., we can be deficient in part or in whole at any stage of spiritual development. The question arises as to the effect of partially or wholly becoming arrested at a given stage or what happens if one skips a whole stage of spiritual development.

There is also the question as to whether the directionality of spiritual development can change, and if so, how does that happen. Most persons see "spirituality" as a positive, i.e. benevolent result of the inner person. By the same logic, we must accept the opposite as malevolent. Both are spiritual forces and both have directionality but are opposites in our value system. As a matter of fact, we must conclude such if we are to establish a basis for what might be called "evil spirituality". Evil spirituality is no less "spiritual", it is only a matter of directionality of the spiritual energy. Malevolent spirituality is systematized into religious systems the same as is benevolent spirituality. Since the beginning of time there have been benevolent and malevolent spiritual leaders. Temple priests and pagan sorcerers have similarly vied for allegiance from their followers. Both were practicing "spirituality". While Christians celebrate Christmas and the birth of the Christ Child, Wicca celebrate the sun, moon, stars, and seasons of the year. Other religious systems celebrate other aspects of belief. All utilize formalized symbols and rituals. All are highly "spiritual". In order to practice as a priest or as a sorcerer it was necessary to believe the opposite side was evil, or to word it in common parlance, each thought the other was "wrong". It is no different today. Both priests and sorcerers/Wicca rely upon symbols and rituals to reify their beliefs in concrete practices. Among the symbols and rituals, the priest has at command the wine and bread of the Eucharist, oil for anointing, water for baptism, and many creeds and liturgies. The sorcerer has available, potions, charms, hexes, chanting, hypnotic practices and other formalized and informal symbols and rituals. Modern Wicca claim to be benevolent. I was recently informed of a modern witch who nailed the tail of a cat to a friend's garage door to drive off the evil spirits. Although this practice may sound incredulous to Christians, to covens anointing with oil for healing would sound equally bizarre. Both are results of belief systems believed to be benevolent by the practitioner. The major difference between "good" spirituality and "evil" spirituality is that benevolent spiritual practices do not attempt to work evil upon others whereas malevolent practices cast hexes, spells, and ill will upon one's enemies. Extreme examples have led to animal and even human sacrifice.

Neither benevolent nor malevolent spirituality is devoid of human bodies. They are both embodied and are seen in action in varying degrees in living human beings. Christian theology asserts that "God (the Word) was made flesh and dwelt among us" (John 1:14, RSV); illustrating the anthropomorphism of benevolent spirituality. Many would assert that the Devil is the same anthropomorphism of evil. Just as God becomes flesh in each believer, according to Christian theology, would it not also be possible for evil (the Devil) to become flesh as well? Christian theology recognizes the existence of both benevolent and malevolent spirits and exhorts the Christian to "test the spirits to see whether they are of God…" (I John 4:1, RSV). That same New Testament text continues to exhort Christians to know the difference between spirits that are of the antichrist rather than of God, thus establishing a distinct differentiation between benevolent and malevolent spirits. The New Testament speaks of the Evil One as the embodiment of malevolence, (I John 2:13, RSV). The book of I Samuel in the Old Testament particularly emphasized anthropomorphic evil. Evil is spoken of as entering Saul, (I Samuel 19:9) and on another occasion leaving him, (I Samuel 16:23 RSV). The Old Testament has many such narratives regarding both good and evil "coming upon", "entering", "residing", and "taking on flesh". Just as benevolence can indwell persons and evidence goodness through that person's actions, malevolence can indwell persons and evidence evil through that person's actions.

Hitler, Dahmer, and other infamous persons were not devoid of spirituality, but evidence of the embodiment of evil spirituality. For reasons that we do not know or understand, their spiritual development progressed in a manner which assumed an evil, malevolent, rather than a righteous, benevolent direction. As a matter of discussion, we could look at these kinds of persons in the light of Tillich's Spirit (capital S) and spirit (small s), i.e., the internal person being the true S and the actions of the person being the s. Erich Fromm, in *The Anatomy of Human Destructiveness*, quotes Speer, "Hitler lacked all the more gentle virtues of man: tenderness, love, …were alien to his nature. On the surface he showed courtesy, charm, tranquility,…The outer skin obviously had the function to cover up the really dominant traits, with a complete, although thin layer" (Fromm, 1973, p.409) . In reality his Spirit which was devoid of tenderness, etc., evidenced itself in this destructive behavior or spirit. For the most part, and to most persons, he apparently was able to disguise his true

Spirit (destruction) with external charm that duped at least some of his followers. One might say that even though the chameleon can change its color it cannot keep from being a chameleon, or the clown can change his costume but he cannot change who he is as a person by changing clothes. Hitler then would be an example of a person who did not change his true Spirit by the cover-up behavior.

Peck (1985), in his book, *People of the Lie*, more than any other behavioral scientist has forced us to recognize evil as the basic Spirit (capital S) in some persons. In my opinion, evil is highly spiritual. Simply stated, it is the reversal of what we usually think of as spiritual. We normally consider "spiritual" as being benevolent and for the betterment of self and others. In the case of evil, we are speaking of Tillich's capital (S) as being an evil Spirit that produces evil "spiritual" results. Results that to most of us seem destructive and negative. Such conceptualization, i.e., spiritual either as benevolent or malevolent, is not inconsistent with either the Old Testament or the New Testament. Both of these literatures recognize evil as an active force in the universe and more explicitly in human beings. Even in the understanding of physics, every force has an equal and opposite force, as per Sir Isaac Newton's third law of physics. Therefore, it is entirely conceivable that if there is a "spiritually" driven "good", there is also a "spiritually" driven "evil."

Consider the story of Saint Paul who prior to his conversion is reported to have persecuted Christians, then after his conversion turned his wrath on the heathen and unconverted Jews. The New Testament narrative indicates it is possible to become stuck, and as a result, develop a totally different direction of behavior. To those who are on Paul's side, when he became "unstuck" and changed his spiritual direction, it was good. To others it was doubtless seen as a betrayal and anything but good. I do not use this illustration to give or take away from the Christian belief regarding Saint Paul's conversion, but to show that a change of direction in one's spiritual energy is possible. If we look at the possibility of a turn of direction toward evil, this may help us to account for persons such as Hitler. If he was basically an evil person, are we to assume that he was conceived that way, or did his directionality change at some point in his life? I believe that the direction of the Spirit may change due to human and divine external and internal forces, thus reversing previous stages of spiritual development. This one account of Saint Paul helps us to see that there can be a change of Spirit and a dramatic change in the directionality of one's Spirit and the resultant spirituality.

One could reasonably argue that Saint Paul maintained the same Spirit and energy drive but upon his conversion totally re-directed that Spirit. New Testament theology would maintain that with conversion comes a new Spirit. The spiritual and psychological aspects of religious conversion are beyond the scope of this writing, however, they no doubt occur, and present us with a myriad of questions regarding the immutability of the Spirit and our spiritual directionality.

Peck (1997) seems to agree that one can get stuck at a given stage and illustrates his thinking by stating that fundamentalists are arrested at his level II, "Formal, Institutional" (p. 124). He gives great hope for persons to move from one stage to the next, and posits that without a theology, movement in a positive direction is impossible. He states that even "humanism which believes that humans are precious…is often like a house built on the sand. Having no roots in theology, …people may be blown away quite easily in times of stress and temptation." (p.125). His emphasis upon a theological base is consistent with the necessity of *theos* which I discuss in this writing.

Although persons may be partially "stuck" at a given stage, every stage is highly individualistic, personal, intrinsic, and often quite unknown and unrecognized by the individual. This is, in my opinion, due to the fact that so much of spiritual development is unrecognizable by any of us in ourselves. Most of us recognize that we are stuck at a given stage only in retrospect as we attempt to move into a higher stage and find that we are unable to free ourselves from the baggage of the former stage. The development of a spiritual dimension far precedes the human's knowledge of the value of spirituality for dealing with the *angst* of life, or for that matter the knowledge of *angst* itself. We must conclude that there is an *in utero* presence of a Spiritual beginning and incarnation of Spirit that at least partially determines one's life long spiritual direction. However, as we have already discussed, the *in utero* presence does not eliminate the possibility for a change of spiritual direction as we develop. Anything that helps build the foundation for any structure, whether it be spiritual or physical, must be taken seriously and seen as a basic building block upon which everything else that is built is based. Therefore, influences, especially spiritual influences upon the fetus must be taken very seriously.

In order to understand the essential nature of spiritual development it is necessary to conceptualize spirituality within the confines of ontology (being) rather than epistemology (knowing), teleology (purpose and order), or philosophy (theorizing). Although a sense of being, a foundation of knowledge, and some idea of purpose and order are all contributory, we must be willing to admit the existence of a real entity called "spirituality". We must be willing to recognize that some part of the human being is distinct from (although related and relating to) both psyche and soma. Spirituality must be seen as the all embracing, all encompassing, totally inclusive part of the human, out of which all else physical, mental, and emotional flows. Most concepts measure spiritual development against psychological constructs (emotional maturity), moral dictums (right and wrong), and religious affirmations (ecclesiastical acts and confessions). Spiritual development may involve one or all of these dimensions, but cannot be measured by any one of them alone. It is in this context that we begin to understand many of the great theologians and many of the great philosophers who spoke of the human being as a unified whole, in contrast to the Cartesian concept of dualism, i.e., mind and body, rather than mind/body.

Paul Tillich, probably more than most theologians, understood and dealt with the psychological aspects of human existence. He postulated that "God" is the word we use to describe the ground of being (our ontology). It is in this concept that we find human wholeness rather than biological or philosophical fragmentation. The word "Spirit" is used to unify the mystical with the existential. Spirituality (with a capital S) in the Tillichian sense deals with the existential and the eternal. When we speak of spirituality (with a small s) we are dealing with most of the stages discussed by Fowler and Peck. Valid as they are, they are primarily related to terrestrial imminence (Cox, 1996). It should be noted that both Fowler and Peck in their overall philosophies give unspoken credence to Tillich and include a definite base of *theos* in their overall considerations.

We must move beyond the concepts of even our finest human attributes such as love, grace, kindness, caring, etc., and find the source of that energy. The basic source and resource of the human being is in a unification of the human Spirit with the universal Spirit. To the theistic person, this is God. To others it is a more amorphous universal energy. Most people relate well to an abstract, yet concrete concept that allows an intellectual and emotional cathexis, such as God. The abstract part allows for the indefinable emotionality, and the concrete part allows for the creeds and confessions of most religions. We reify both our emotionality and concreteness with the many symbols and rituals of daily life, both "religious" and "secular". Since spirituality is all encompassing, there of course can in reality be no difference between sacred and secular. The "secular person" sees all things as *secular*, whereas the "spiritual person", sees all things as *sacred*. Since I believe that life is sacred, the Spirit and all spirituality which develops from the Spirit is sacred. As difficult as it is to understand, the person with a malevolent Spirit would also consider everything as sacred even though it would be destructive in our opinion.

Symbols and rituals allow us a bridge from the internal to the external. That which we feel inside, know "in ourselves", and consciously and unconsciously believe, is amplified into practice and into demonstrable daily living by the rites and rituals each of us develops. The question of how our internal beliefs become external thoughts and deeds is answered by understanding the role and meaning of symbols and rituals. The methods by which we deal with birth (baptism), death (funerals) and marriage (weddings) are only a few of the illustrations as to how we externalize our (s)piritual expressions of our internalized (S)pirit. The Judeo-Christian doctrine of God manifesting Himself in the prophets of the Old Testament, and later in the New Testament concept of God being in Christ, then as Saint Paul preaches, God (Christ) in the believer, are all illustrations of our belief that what we have internalized, i.e., the (S)pirit becomes manifest in our daily (s)piritual living. Our symbols and rituals validate by externalization that which has been anthropomorphized in our Spirit. The Book of Proverbs (23:7) states this concept much more simply, "as a man thinketh in his heart, so is he". This verse is not speaking to the process of *thought* but the fact of *being*.

We don't develop spirituality for specific aspects of future need, but rather, it is much like a savings account maintained against an unknown but certain future need. Furthermore, true spirituality (small s) is developed naturally out of Spirituality (capital S) and is developed not for need but for the intrinsic value of being Spiritual.

The question addressed here is the process by which the larger spiritual aspects of the universe become part of the developing human being. I propose that spiritual growth occurs through a developmental process that begins in the embryo, long both before there is conscious thought or deed and continues throughout the entire life cycle. This process encompasses the total person, therefore the concepts of mind and body, thought and action,

39

means and end. Both the intention and the result are holistic and cannot be separated. There are no dichotomies and therefore there can be no division between sacred and secular. In truth, every single thought and every single deed is sacred beyond definition. Everything we think and do is sacred because it emanates from our deepest Spiritual being and is intended to achieve our own spiritual ends.

It is extremely difficult to get beyond the imminent (that which is happening or could happen at any moment) and pay attention to the immanent (that which is within, indwelling). However; Spirituality (capital S) does just that. Spirituality (with small s) serves to deal with events, happenings, results, and externalities. Spirituality (with a capital S) turns itself toward causes, beginnings, creations, and internalities. It might well be said that (S)pirituality receives from the Spirit that dwells within us and within the universe, and that (s)pirituality produces and becomes the true "fruit of the Spirit" as spoken of in New Testament theology; "the fruit of the Spirit is love, joy, peace, patience, kindness, goodness, faithfulness, gentleness, self control…" (Galatians 5:22-23 RSV).

Although I may be taking unwarranted license with the teachings of Paul Tillich, I believe that we can accept the internal, therefore intangible as Spiritual (capital S) and the tangible, external, results as spirituality (with a small s) in our daily lives, i.e. to quote Tillich, "…the activities of the divine Spirit in man" (Tillich, 1951, p.15).

Although the Old Testament mostly uses less specific vocabulary, as does the Koran and the literature of other world religions, the concept of Spirit and the results of that Spirit are the same to all theistic religions, i.e., spiritual (Tillich's small s) manifestations of Spirit. We may conceive of "growth of the Spirit" by virtue of living the honorable life, but actually it is the other way around, since Spirit precedes all thought and action. Yet, lest we fall into the thinking that since Spirit precedes all thought and action the way we live life does not matter, here is where the scientists of human behavior are helpful. They help us to see that the way we live matters socially and psychologically. Theologians tell us that the way we live matters not only for immediate results but also for "eternal reasons".

We readily see that Spirit can be enhanced and Spirit can be damaged, maybe even destroyed. If such were not the case, it would be totally in vain to educate, attempt to redeem and otherwise "help." Ernest Becker (1973) in his brilliant critique of psychoanalysis sees Otto Rank and Kierkegaard as coming to the same conclusion regarding the human conflict, and thus helps us to understand the battle between the flesh (thought and deed) and the Spirit, "…the only way out is full renunciation, to give one's life as a gift to the highest powers. Absolution has to come from the absolute beyond…To renounce the world and oneself, to lay the meaning of it to the powers of creation, is the hardest thing for man to achieve –and so it is fitting that this task should fall to the strongest personality type, the one with the largest ego" (Becker, 1973, p.173).

Saint Paul apprised us of his own dilemma in a very human fashion and similarly came to the same conclusion as did Rank and Kierkegaard in his confession to the Romans, "We know that the law is spiritual; but I am carnal, sold under sin. I do not understand my own actions. For I do not do what I want, but I do the very thing I hate…I can will what is

40

right, but I cannot do it. For I do not do the good I want, but the evil I do not want, it is no longer I that do it, but sin which dwells within me", Romans 7:14-20 RSV). We could get into Pauline theology, but that is not my point at this time. Saint Paul was struggling with the very problem with which we are faced in this discussion, namely, thoughts and deeds, regardless of how religious we may be do not always match our spiritual development. It could be fairly argued that the very fact that Saint Paul had this soliloquy and went public with it was in and of itself more than admirable evidence of his own spirituality. He often spoke of the contradiction between the "spirit" and the "flesh", which I would interpret as his struggle between the Spirit (capital S – the internalality) and the spirit (small s – externality).

The differentiation between Tillich's "Spiritual" (capital S) and "spiritual" (small s), is only possible in the light of a belief system. All theistic belief systems allow for this differentiation, possibly because theism unifies thinking and gives credence to that which we do as being a result of that which we are.

Spirituality as a subject matter or primary content for a course of study in most colleges, universities, medical schools, schools of psychology, and for that matter theological seminaries, is doubtless a rarity, if existent at all. I agree with Miller's statement in his book, *Integrating Spirituality into Treatment* " The training of psychologists and other mental health professionals is expected to include education about cultural and individual diversity – preparation to work competently with a broad spectrum of people – and such diversity surely includes varieties of spirituality" (Miller, 1999, p.*xvii*). Perhaps it is my differing definition, however, it is my opinion that whereas varieties of religious experience, ala William James, may be studied, little if any attention is paid to spirituality, per se. Spirituality and religion tend to be treated synonymously – and they are not the same.

While reviewing the literature on this topic I remembered a very large book entitled, *Measures of Religiosity* edited by Peter Hill and Ralph Wood (1999). It is an entire volume containing literally dozens of tests, questionnaires, and measurements of religious belief and practice. Although several of the measurements are called "spiritual" measurements, they are in reality all measures of religious practice and intellectual belief, not spirituality in the Tillichian sense of Spirituality (capital S). The authors are certainly not to be criticized for such; they do not claim otherwise in the book's title. It is quite certain that one cannot measure spirituality by parametric or non-parametric means. Likewise, it is my belief that the tools of psychology and the social sciences do not have the ability to measure Spirituality (capital S). They may be able to observe and even measure by assumed and presumed "norms" very small ingredients of spirituality (small s).

As far as we know only human beings experience what we call spirituality. We have no evidence that the lower animal kingdom experiences this dimension of existence. Of course, we do not know that beings in the lower animal kingdom do not experience some state of existence that could be called "spiritual". We do not know at what stage of life spirituality starts to manifest itself in human beings. It is my contention, as stated previously, that it starts in the womb, thereby laying down a foundation for all spiritual experiences that will follow. If what we mean by spirituality is "oneness with the universe", we can observe it

41

in very tiny children. Some newborns seem to embrace and enjoy their new world, whereas others seem to fear and shun it. Some tiny infants are curious, excited, and seem to absorb every detail of everything they see, feel, hear, taste and smell literally drinking in everything around them. Others seem to reject everything around them, even their own mothers. It is fascinating to watch very young children. While one infant embraces new faces, new places, new smells and sights, others shy away and show facial fright at almost anything new.

Why are such simple observations that important? Spirituality assumes a trust factor. Trust in one's environment, trust in relationships, trust that the world is a friendly place, and trust that conquers fear of all sorts. Spirituality necessarily assumes that our weakness will not devour us. The confident and self-assured infant is the embodiment of trust. Surely the energy for this behavior began in the womb. Can a fetus be terrified in the womb? Can it be tranquil and satisfied in the womb? No doubt.

Dr. Ursula Anderson (2000) sheds considerable light on this subject in her lectures on *The Immunology of the Soul*. The earliest immunology begins as cell division starts *in utero*. It is as if the very earliest cell division becomes the mitosis of harmony or of conflict. Mothers who are in tune with their bodies can tell us of the subtle, and not so subtle, movements, feelings and changes, both physical and emotional, that occur within them during gestation. They know more about the embryo and the gestating infant knows more about the mother than either will ever be able to tell us. These feelings of oneness or separation are surely the embryonic beginnings of spirituality, either positive or negative.

Spirituality, like all other human growth, occurs in stages. The stages are not uniform and they are not all experienced at the same rate of speed. There are times of slow growth and there are spurts. Spiritual growth may accompany chronological maturation, but most often it does not. Spiritual growth is dependent upon variables that are not well understood. The starving child with Marasmus (a disease due to malnutrition) may be developing spiritually at a rapid pace, while the well-fed healthy looking infant may be starving from spiritual deficiency. It seems that at times even adults must regress to earlier years of development and literally "go back" and pick up what they did not develop.

Religious persons are not necessarily spiritual. Attendance to religious rites is not necessarily related to true spirituality. A person may be simultaneously spiritual and attend to such, however, in others, the obsessive attendance to religious practices may signal an actual deficit of spirituality, hence the attempt to compensate. It might even be said that the more one is insistent upon the rightness of his/her religion, to that extent he/she does so out a deficit for true spirituality and is substituting form for faith. In that case, external acts of spirituality are in psychological language compensations.

Rules, regulations, dictums, canons, creeds, and statements of faith are for those (all of us) who need guideposts, fences, and controls. We all, however free our spirit may be, are at times confused if not lost, and doubtless benefit from these signposts on the road of spirituality. Some of these road signs help us to read the map for our own spirituality, but they may also inhibit our progress toward a maturity of individuated spiritual knowledge. Like the Pharisees we get caught up in the action rather than the purpose behind it, confusing religious observance with spirituality. If we can't read, signs are of little value, and if our inner Spirit is not willing to follow, no amount of external assistance will help. Following external signposts is not a mark of deficiency of the Spirit but displays a universal inability to live as spiritually as our Spirit would dictate. Of course we cannot assume that because one has no formalized or organized religious observance that he/she is not spiritual in the deepest and most profound sense. Religious observance and spirituality are not mutually exclusive, nor are they mutually inclusive.

Some theologians have attempted to equate religion, spirituality, and piety. These are three very distinct concepts, inter-related to be sure, and not mutually exclusive, but certainly not necessarily mutually inclusive. Piety is more closely related to spirituality than is religion. The practice of one's religion hopefully contains considerable spirituality, however, there is no assurance that the formalisms, even the symbols and rituals of organized religion contain true spirituality, because spirituality emanates from within the person not from within the formalism.

Pietists often assumed that piety was a display of spirituality. The term "Pietism" was born out of a movement within the Lutheran Church in Germany in the 17th Century that stressed personal piety over the formalized aspects of orthodoxy. The act of being "pious", i.e., "devout or showing religious devotion" (Cayne, 1989, p. 764), is assumed to be the manifestation of God within us, i.e., the projection of our internal Spiritual person in our external spiritual living. The New Lexicon Webster's Dictionary (Cayne, 1989) defines spiritual, "of, relating to, or concerned with the soul or spirit, relating to religious or sacred matters" (p. 958) helping us to further define the internal Spirit and the external spiritual manifestations.

We must also consider the concept of "morals" since they may also be confused with spirituality. Our previous discussion of Kohlberg helps us to understand that moral thinking is not necessarily spiritual thinking. Morals have to do with conducting oneself in accordance with "right" and "wrong." However, it cannot be successfully argued that one always acts in accord with one's own morals. The question can be asked, "Can one be spiritual without being moral?" Or, can one be moral without being spiritual?" This becomes a moot point in the latter question, in that everyone is spiritual and evidences his/her true morals in behavior. When we consistently act in opposition to our stated morals, we must assume that our internal Spirit and our external spirituality are in conflict and question which statement (the word or the deed) is the real person. The question is not whether one is spiritual or moral, but whether one's morals are consistent with one's Spirit. It could be argued that one is always consistent with one's Spirit in truth, and that it only *appears* inconsistent because our stated beliefs do not match our Spirit. Moral thinking is always evidence of one's Spirit, meaning the intellectual conceptualization of what we really believe, but one may display a given moral kind of behavior for other than spiritual reasons. One may betray his/her own Spirit in conscious and unconscious thought and deed. Our daily spiritual living may at times be at odds with what the Spirit within us would demand. Therein may lie the true *angst* of life and the challenge of our theology.

We might then ask the question as to how we become spiritual. What is the process? Are there distinct developmental stages as we have outlined for psychological and physical development? How one becomes spiritual is a non-question since it is impossible not to become spiritual. The problem is that our spiritual manifestations in daily living are not always (and in some not at all) in accordance with our stated beliefs. Even the most evil person who ever lived is spiritual. The Spirit within, however, may be in severe contrast to our idea of goodness and right. Since this is the case, it behooves us to take seriously the spiritual development of the human being from conception to the grave. Insufficient attention has been given to the spiritual development of the embryo and infant. Since theistic religions believe that "God is Spirit," and that mankind is made in the image of God (*Imago Dei)*, and therefore by necessity God lives within us, it is not even a short step to understand that the moment the sperm and egg join, Spiritual life begins.

Authorities on human behavior have arranged many elements of maturation into various stages that more or less accompany chronological age. Others have ordered life's energy in terms of health and illness. Neither should be ignored. Spiritual development, by its very definition, must accompany every developmental stage physically, psychologically, and emotionally, and be present in every degree of health and illness.

Psychological systems for the most part approach the study of the person from an illness or negative model. Erikson created a paradigm that contrasted positive development with the negative, such as "trust vs. distrust". Abraham Maslow developed one of the more positive models and spoke in terms of self-actualization. This more positive approach came from his belief that the study of psychopathology tended to limit the true understanding of human behavior and encased it in negativity. In social work vocabulary these models would be referred to as "strength" or "deficit" perspectives. Han Selye perceived the struggle of the human spirit in terms of stress. His work regarding stress is relevant since stress results from blocked positive growth. An impressive and very inclusive approach for studying spiritual development, is that of Ursula Anderson who deals with *soul* development and utilizes the paradigms of both Selye and Erikson.

Spirituality and spiritual growth depend upon a confident, contented, firm belief that guilt, anxiety, and fear can be managed. Without the ability to manage guilt, anxiety and fear, the end result becomes a disablement against spiritual growth. The well recognized developmental stages of Erik Erikson provide a paradigm for emotional development. However, none of these paradigms in and of themselves provide an adequate understanding of spiritual development, including the one I propose here.

Spiritual development is not the same as emotional development, and it is not the same as the absence of stress. There is no such thing as a "stress-less" life, however if such were possible, that state would not necessarily be spiritual. Stress pulls, pushes and acts upon developing spirituality much the same as physical exercise encourages and forces our muscles and bones to grow. Spiritual development is a process different from both emotional development and coping skills for stress, but it can be dwarfed or grow as a result of both.

Because spiritual development is a distinct process does not mean that all other factors of human existence are not germane.

Psychological thinking too often assumes the psyche to be the primary element that makes us human. Not so. It is the *neumos*, the Spirit. All else is subrogated to the Spirit and all thoughts and deeds emanate from that basic Spiritual being. As this discussion unfolds, it will be seen that the Spirit, regardless of how strong it may be at times does not seem to direct one's actions in predictable ways.

A holistic philosophy requires that the human being be understood as a unity and does not allow for the separation of the mind, body and soul. Yet, in an attempt to understand the whole person, it is helpful to look at each part in the best singular light possible. Although we can talk in terms of holism, most of us have a difficult time translating that concept into any understanding of the person. To the person who assumes that physical prowess is supreme, such as some of the Greek writers, all else, i.e., mind and spirit are secondary. To the one who places the psyche in the supreme position as do some psychologists, the body and the spirit become secondary. I am making the same mistake, of sorts, in placing the spirit as supreme, since it is in truth integrated into the mind and body as well, however, I would argue for the supremacy of the spirit in that without it there is no purpose.

One way to discuss the elements of human existence independently without fragmenting the person is to view the person as a three-tier pyramid with the spirit on the foundation level, the psyche on the next, and the body on the third. This would indicate that all that is included in human existence must be derived from our spiritual base. It would also presume that a weak Spirit would produce a weak psyche and a weak body. One could be very intelligent and extremely physically strong, yet have a weak psyche and misused physical strength. The Spirit helps to direct thought and deed and establishes purpose.

God, as the "ground of being" establishes spirituality as the absolute foundation level of the pyramid. Spiritual development, psychological development and emotional development may in many aspects be similar. They may be like looking at a prism from different angles. They may be different ways at looking at the same thing, however, in order to accept this position one must maintain that emotional being, psychological being, and spiritual being are the same. Given that position one must be willing to say that when the emotional person is healthy, the psychological person is healthy and the spiritual person is healthy. Does this mean that one cannot be psychologically ill without being spiritually ill as well? As we learn more and more about the biological and chemical bases of psychological illness, we discover that much psychological illness is chemical illness. Are we than to say that one cannot be physically ill without also being spiritually ill? This argument could take on a life of its own and we could "split hairs" over various meanings. I would argue that spirituality has similarities to psychological health but is the foundation of psychological health, not one and the same thing. Similarly, emotional health has similarities to spiritual health but is the result of spiritual health rather than synonymous with it or a substitute for it. Spirituality must be seen as a the beginning of all else and has an existence and essence of its own, not dependent upon anything else, but benefiting or being hampered by all else. To understand Tillich is to recognize that the Spirit (capital S) precedes all else and until Spirit (S) and (s)pirit are in accord with each other there is discord. The discord may reveal itself in ill-ease and dis-ease. Much psychopathology and many physical ailments may well be the end result of this conflict.

Spiritual development becomes the basis for purposeful behavior. All behavior is of course purposeful. That is inherent within all of life, human and sub-human so far as we know. However, the idea of purpose takes on a meaning that is beyond the immediate result of an action in human behavior. In other words, we are able to anticipate future needs and take primary action to meet those immediate needs and prepare us for meeting future needs at the same time. Spiritual development must be seen in the same light. The Spiritual development of the fetus allows its survival in the womb and begins to build the blocks for the first level of the holistic pyramid of spirit, psyche and body. The Westminster Confession attempted to encapsulate thinking of this nature by stating that the purpose of man is to "love God and enjoy Him forever". If we view that statement fully and apart from a strictly theological position, it essentially says that spiritual life is purposeful and that the purpose of life is spiritual.

Although some of Selye's thinking may be seen as far from spirituality, it soon becomes apparent that although he does not speak of spirituality, the foe of spirituality is dissonance; dissonance of any sort. Certainly stress is the dissonance of life itself, and can be a hindrance to all human growth, physical, emotional, or spiritual. There can be little doubt that stress, i.e., dissonance, can be the enemy of spirituality, however it may also be the grist for positive spiritual growth. It is difficult to keep focused on the larger picture when immediate details of our life are in turmoil. By the same token, we must not think that stress, turmoil and disturbance are not an integral part of spirituality, for they are, and when dealt with healthfully, help us grow as spiritual persons.

Dr. Ursula Anderson (2000) rightly considers stress to be likened to soul trauma. At any stage, the soul can be traumatized by emotional, physical or spiritual assaults. She relates Selye's first stage "alarm reaction" to soul confusion. Selye's second stage, "stress becomes distress" with enduring effects of trauma upon the soul, and his third stage "overwhelmed and death" she likens to trauma which takes up permanent residence in the soul. Her concept of soul development is the fullest discussion of what I consider "spiritual development" in the literature. Additionally, it may be clearly seen that her understanding of an "immunized" soul allows for a "non-immunized" or "insufficiently immunized" soul which furthers our understanding of the development of the dimension of evil spirituality. By relating the immunology of the soul, i.e., spiritual development, to Selye's stress model, she may be giving us some of the answers for how and why the directionality of spirituality changes.

If we substitute the word "Spirit" for "soul" (and they may well be synonymous) Anderson's model contributes to our understanding of spiritual development in that she combines Selye's treatment of stress with the developmental model of artist/philosopher/psychoanalyst Erik Erikson. The combined thinking of these three theorists provides a framework for understanding that spiritual development is a natural process that is always accompanied by conflict/resolution, starts/stops, ease/disease and encouragement/discouragement.

Without doubt the most theistically harmonious approach is that of Anderson's paradigm of soul immunology. The soul which is immunologically prepared for the "bacteria", "viruses", stresses and assaults of life is surely a soul that has the spiritual development for a full holistic and holy maturation.

Erikson, by virtue of his initial training as an artist seemed to conceptualize the human in a different light than those trained in the sciences. Although he does not state his spiritual position in theological terms, it is apparent that Erikson had strong spiritual underpinnings for his developmental stages, and did not rely primarily upon scientific and psychological models. While his developmental stages are highly individualistic, they are also deeply interpersonal and in that sense seem to be grounded more closely to what I am calling spiritual development.

This chapter proposes that we view Erikson's paradigm as related to spiritual development in a parallel manner as illustrated in Table 1. Like Erikson, I see human development as a continuum. Although persons may become arrested at any stage of development, more often, the stages are partially fulfilled, and continue to be completed as we move through subsequent stages. When development is arrested at a given stage, spiritual pathology results. The manifestations of spiritual pathology are probably similar to what psychologists call psychopathology. It is important, however, to see that the origin of such arrest is due to spiritual rather than purely psychological factors. It is also important to recognize that the remedy for these two pathologies is quite different. For instance, "guilt *feelings*" arising from psychopathology are irrational feelings of guilt arising from a dysfunctional psyche, whereas "guilt" from a spiritual pathology result from one's thoughts and actions that are dissonant with one's Spirit. The spiritual is in opposition to the Spirit.

Table 1

Comparison of Erickson's Developmental Paradigm and Cox's Spiritual Development Paradigm	
Erikson's Stage	Cox's Stage
Trust vs. mistrust	Belief
Autonomy vs. shame and doubt	Spiritual self-hold apart from universe
Initiative vs. guilt	Self-affirming faith
Industry vs. inferiority	Positive productive faith
Identity vs. inferiority	Established Personal Belief
Intimacy vs. isolation	Interpersonally shared belief system
Generativity vs. stagnation	Contributory belief system
Ego integrity vs. despair	Confident internalized hope

Psychological and spiritual underdevelopment and dysfunction are similar in that both effect one's personal growth as well as expressed thoughts and actions. One difference is that spiritual deficiency (or presence) cannot be measured by any known scientific instrument or psychological test. The evidence is nonetheless seen in societal actions, interpersonal relationships, and the relationship one has to him/her self.

Spiritual development is far less predictable than physiological, psychological, social, or intellectual development. However, "approximate age" references are being proposed here for discussion and general observational purposes in that they may be helpful in contrasting what we think might occur spiritually with the proposed developmental stages of Erikson.

Stage One: Infancy (Approximate age: birth to 18-months)

Spirituality and Tillich's concept of Spirit develop within the womb and are very present from the moment of conception. Although we may not be able to observe the attributes of Spirit and spiritual activity, we surely do not believe a child is truly *tabla erasa* at birth as proposed by Locke (Jones, 1969). We do not think all experience is only the result of experience and nothing precedes it. As with all learning, experience requires that learning precede it. Even Locke believed "we start life with a certain number of 'native ideas and original characters'…being in our minds from their first beginning, are antecedent to all experience and must have been implanted in them by God himself" (Jones, 1969, p. 242).

There is probably little if any difference between what Erikson (1979) called trust and what is referred to here as belief. The infant through human bonding comes to believe (trust) in its all encompassing love and support systems. Belief starts with that which is presented to the infant in a consistent and reliable manner. Belief is a brain function and in Anderson's model it is the "soul" function. The brain does not start to work the moment it is expelled from the womb, it has been working all along since it was formed. The brain, hence the process of thought is in operation very early in the womb, hence, belief – the basis of spirituality. We do not know the precise gestational moment when the brain as an anatomical unit starts to function. We do know that in the genetic sense, thinking begins as soon as the sperm and ovum meet and DNA starts to do its work of remembering how to produce daughter cells. Either the cell is non-spiritual and functions entirely as a chemical bond or it is spiritual and functions as it will throughout its entire life as an holistic entity of body, mind, and soul. To assume that the fetus subsequent to conception begins to function as a spiritual entity is to accept an arbitrary time, usually for personal, medical, or legal convenience.

Accepting the conception basis for the beginning of spiritual development is important since trust/belief starts with a pre-partum relationship between the fetus and the mother. To assume anything else is to believe that the infant begins to bond after delivery and all the learning necessary for that bonding takes place post-partum. We can see evidence of a trusting relationship within only hours after birth and certainly without enough chronological time to have amassed that learning after delivery.

The child must trust that to which it bonds, even if the end result is disastrous. One is reminded of the famous study of Lidell (Kaplan, Sadock, & Grebb, 1994) who found that infant sheep would starve to death rather than to leave the substitute maternal object (a large rock) for food placed only a few feet away. Spiritual development does not necessarily start

48

or progress positively. It may be very negative, nonetheless firm. "Some weep their way out of the womb and go on weeping through life and into old age" (Eckstein, 1970, p.562). Utilizing Erikson (1979), distrust can be just as strong and enduring as trust. Thus, disbelief can be equally as strong as belief. It must be recognized that disbelief is not the absence of belief, but the opposite of belief. Actually, disbelief is very strong belief in an opposite force, making it far more destructive than simply a neutral position. Unlike Erikson's stated position, it is my contention that the development of belief begins at the moment of conception and continues throughout one's entire life. We know that every cell has memory and this includes the sperm and the egg.

Stage Two: Older Infant (Approximate age: 18-months to 3-years)

Erikson's (1979) stage of autonomy vs. shame and doubt is helpful in understanding spiritual development. The child that develops shame and guilt instead of autonomy cannot develop a positive spiritual self. Rather he or she is tied to the non-nurturing environment and like Lidell's (Kaplan, Sadock, & Grebb, 1994) sheep cannot venture away from the only attachment they know. Spiritual selfhood is a building block placed atop the infant's already bonded trust/belief. The internal Spirit has begun to learn what I would call "spiritual congruence," i.e., those external actions that are in accord with the internal Spirit. It could further be proposed that the more important aspect of behavior at this stage of life is not the presence of shame and guilt. Rather, it is the internal sense of spiritual well-being (or spiritual illness) that comes from the congruence (or lack of congruence) with what psychologist Maslow called self-actualization. The concept of "self-actualization" is usually thought of as a development at a more mature stage of life. In fact, there can be no self-actualization without the basis of it starting very early in life, possibly even within the womb. Erickson and Maslow both include a definite spiritual dimension to their developmental models, but do not identify it as such. I think it is important to specifically state that there is a developing Spiritual self-hood in each of these stages.

The spiritual basis of the human is the "real" part at all stages of development. Belief, which began before birth is certainly a major theme not only in the birth to three year period of life, but belief is the continuing spiritual life force throughout all subsequent stages. The child between 18 months and three years is building a structure for all personal thinking, therefore the Spiritual structure as well. For Erickson, this is a period of developing autonomy. Part of that autonomy is the Spiritual. Since the brain tells the body what to think and what to do, the directionality of spiritual energy for the rest of his/her life is also developing.

Stage Three: Young Child (Approximate age: 3-years to 6-years)

The child of this age undertakes self-initiative, confident steps, and reaching out and testing the limits, and is clearly developing self-affirming faith; faith in oneself, others and the universe. Such a faith reminds one of the teaching of Jesus who queried his disciples as to how they could believe in God whom they had not seen if they could not believe in that which they had seen. Erikson (1979), juxtaposes initiative against guilt. One does not develop initiative out of the presence or absence of guilt, but out of the basic Spiritual development present in the first place. Although the three to six years old is certainly continuing to learn "right" from "wrong," the driving force for the child is not the externally derived guilt that produces growth but the child's awakening internal congruence between his/her Spirit (real self) and the externally manifested spiritual actions. This is self-affirming faith. It may well be that at this critical stage of development the child self-affirms a faith in benevolence or malevolence and sets the tone for future behavior. Once we see the developing Spirit as the most important aspect of human development, how we handle human behavior is no longer a matter of "behavior modification" but of spiritual re-direction.

Stage Four: Older Child (Approximate age: 6-years to 12-years)

The early productivity of the developing child is a marvel to watch and can be identified with Erikson's (1979) industry vs. inferiority. It is the period in which a positive, productive faith manifests itself. The young child enters society, goes to school, starts various kinds of musical and artistic endeavors, and in a very real sense starts to "grow up". Their faith becomes creative and beneficial. By six years of age the foundation for all abilities needed for life has been laid down. So it is with spiritual development. What Erikson speaks of as inferiority, is identified here as Spiritual Doubt. Inferiority is overcome from the spiritual point of view only when a personal belief system becomes internalized. This internalization is well on its way by one's sixth birthday.

Erikson (1979 uses the term "inferiority" in contrast to "industry". Inferiority tends to be comparative. Although I would not deny that children compare themselves to others (and that we do at any age), stressing inferiority takes our thinking away from the inner Spirit and contrasts it into the external world. The basis for what Erikson calls "industry", and what I call "positive productive faith" are probably very similar concepts and are found within the person, deeply inside the Spirit, not in comparison to anyone or anything else. The child by six years of age has learned that trust/belief has provided the basis for spiritual self-confidence, and positive, gratifying results. Further, the child's trust is reaffirmed because of the observed and experienced beneficial ends. Certainly this experience is internal yet based on both internal and external reward. The concept of an "ego ideal" is established internally and mythically exists even if not in an identifiable, known individual. Religious organizations have long recognized age 6 through 12 to be important for developing a personal productive faith, hence programs such as catechism, confirmation, and other educational pursuits in an effort to establish a congruity between thought and deed, i.e., internalized belief and externalized daily living.

Stage 5: Adolescence (Approximate age: 12-years to 18-years)

Somewhere between older childhood and adolescence, the human must come to grips with personal beliefs. Erikson (1979) would consider persons of this age to be experiencing "identity vs. role confusion." The dictums of parents, organized religion, educational systems and political systems all come under rapid-fire doubt. A driver's license, to be tried as an adult for criminal activity, draft age, right to vote, and many other societal markers establish the necessity of personal views and responsibility for one's actions. Erikson's "identity vs. role confusion" becomes very real, however, role confusion is only augmented by external forces. Identity is a deeply spiritual concept and role confusion cannot develop in the presence of a positive productive faith established in the previous stage. Role consciousness is a deeply spiritual force, namely, a force that tears at the adolescent's already acquired Spiritual self and the desire to behave in manners not consistent with it, hence role confusion. It is not a confusion that comes only from societal and demands of the psyche but attempts to force a disparity between societal/psychological demands and the internalized role consciousness (Spirit) of the individual.

This is the stage of "established personal belief" and the term spiritual does not make it any less tangible. In contradiction to his disdain for anything called spiritual, Freud describes this conflict as the struggle of the Id against the Super Ego. Had Freud not been so theologically hostile, his term "Super Ego" might very well have been called the Spiritual person.

Most, probably all, adolescents suffer from an overdose of inferiority at some time. Even into young adulthood one may still be searching for the perfect ego ideal, but hopefully through experience has learned that such does not exist. "Role confusion" does not occur because of one's confusion over one's place in this world. The confusion is a spiritual battle and utilizes all the spiritual development that has developed since conception. It develops primarily because of a Spiritual confusion, hence a confusion of one's practices of thought and behavior. Dependency upon an ego ideal wanes during this adolescent stage of life and other external systems are accepted in favor of his/her own developing self-spirituality. The Spirit of the adolescent finds compatible friends, organizations and functions. They may be benevolent or malevolent and are built on the goodness or evilness of the Spirit to this point in life.

Personal belief sets the tone for what we describe in later life as flexible or non-flexible thinking. Although not always seen as a positive attribute, rigidity of thought, when it comes to morals, values, and other spiritual matters, is doubtless due to a firm personal belief system. The belief system is not always benevolent. During this stage of life there is frequently a violent intellectual, spiritual, social, and psychological warfare waging. Childhood beliefs are challenged, the adult world is still not a comfortable place to be, and the adolescent's personal belief is not entirely established. More consideration is given to developing one's own ego as *the* ideal within the greater Spiritual world with some "higher power" or *theos* as the scale of weights and measures. Changes in one's spiritual beliefs after this stage of life are the exception rather than the rule.

Stage 6: Early Adulthood (approximate age: 18-years to 29-years)
In later adolescence and into adulthood we experiment with intimacy. The question to Erikson (1979) is whether we develop intimacy or isolation. From the point of view of

spiritual development, this stage has to do with isolated, private beliefs or shared beliefs. Erikson's isolation would be seen in spiritual development as private beliefs that are not shared. Most psychological histories of mass murderers, reveal secretive, private, persons who do not share their beliefs. They are usually non-communicating, internally scheming, individuals. When some of the belief systems become known in examination after criminal conviction, it becomes evident that they had few, if any, shared belief systems. They had few friends with whom they shared any of their thinking. They are not usually members of organized groups that would challenge their beliefs. The current spiritual model has no conflict with Erikson regarding this stage, per se. However, we must deal with the isolated beliefs for what they are – the Spiritual foundation of the person, not just *beliefs*. The usual laboratories for experimenting with intimacy at this stage of life are frequently sensually and sexually devious and often resulting in death and destruction.

Intimacy must not be seen as being limited to the physical. The mind becomes intimate with knowledge and power and the use of knowledge and power. Knowledge is power and power is spiritual energy. Every building block to that point in life is used to balance the rewards and disappointments of ever intimacy that has been established or broken. The young adult over and over again tests their unique spiritual verities that are only found in themselves rather than in external ego ideals. They have by this time arrived at a definition of their own *theos*, whether they can put it into words or not. They look for mutual beliefs, agreed upon prejudices, and group agreements regarding what is "true". This is why peer pressure is no less powerful in the young adult than it is in the adolescent. They measure their own thinking and actions by their peers. Joining, affiliation needs, and belonging becomes important to this age group in order to find and further prove their individual belief systems. Individual spirituality at this point in life becomes arrested unless supported by peers, a strong and ego strength, which would better be called Spiritual strength.

Many of he attributes of this stage of development are usually discussed in psychological terms and as having to do with adolescent years, however, those who have personally experienced their own, and observed other's development, know that these young adult years are filled with tremendous internal struggles regarding spiritual development. Although the utilization of non-psychological language is preferable in this discussion, the term "ego ideal" is the most universally understood term for our internal, real self. What is called the stage of "interpersonally shared belief systems" becomes the spiritual bridge into adulthood. It establishes the verity of the person, allows for the more serious journey of transcendence that is to follow, and allows others' Spirit into one's Spirit as equals. Without these building blocks, adulthood is doomed for broken relationships, vocational disappointments, and spiritual defeat. Unfortunately, it is in this young adult time frame that many learn that they have not established a deep faith in themselves or in others and as a result they are in emotional turmoil and cannot share their Spirit in meaningful interpersonal relationships.

Stage 7: Early through Late Adulthood (Approximate age: 30-years to 55-years)

The adult soon learns that there is no standing still in any kind of growth, spiritual or otherwise. That which is not generating is stagnating, hence, the correctness of Erikson's (1979) generativity vs. stagnation stage of development. However, since life is always moving, stagnation is a difficult concept to accept. This stage is a period of time in which we contribute our belief systems to various actions and purposes. The person who has an "evil bent" will continue to join groups that allow participation in purposes of evil intent. This is hardly stagnation. It is simply not "generativity" as a positive force as idealized by Erikson. Further, even the person who is seen as a loner and stagnating is brewing, stewing, or otherwise spoiling in some fashion. A stagnant pond with green, putrid looking scum on the top is far from inert. It is generating more putrefaction.

Everyone shares his/her belief systems in some way –either constructively or destructively. In that sense, all persons are "generative"; i.e., they generate something, if not good – then evil. At this stage of spiritual development, we share our beliefs, involve ourselves with groups that believe similarly, and join groups that "do things", such churches, civic clubs, etc. We want to see our faith produce results. It is therefore of serious consequence what our Spirit (faith) is in, since our spiritual "joining" will evidence our true inner Spirit. In our industrial world, these are seen as the pre-retirement years when we amass sufficient monetary means to live without active employment until we die. It is important to recognize that what we have "saved" is not only money but also values, beliefs, practices, friendships, and spiritual connections with our own internal Spirit and with those who mutually share our acquired "spiritualness."

Stage 8: Late Adulthood and Aging (Approximate age: 55-years to death)

The last of the Erikson stages is "ego integrity vs. despair." The highest stage of spiritual development, perhaps, is that of an internalized, highly self-confident belief system that has withstood the test of growing up and is now ready for the highest form of all spiritual beliefs which is hope. Erikson may well have seen Ego integrity similarly as a deep "confident hope" of the Spirit. Psychological systems have failed largely because they have promised happiness rather than hope. Many religious systems have done the same thing. Throughout the most of life, a majority of persons seek happiness. Sooner or later, (although we all continue to search for and attempt to find happiness), most persons come to realize that there must be something greater than our three-score and ten years on this earth. Our hope is in leaving a legacy that is greater than ourselves and going on to something greater after we shuffle off this terrestrial globe.

This is where true spirituality enters the picture and one must deal with his/her *theos*. In the later years of life there is frequently spiritual despondency as a result of taking inventory of what has been accumulated and appropriately or inappropriately believing that we have not stored up enough of what we should have. This may be financial, communal, material or all of these and more. However, the most important is the spiritual and recognition that it is too late to start all over. While for most persons it is too late to acquire wealth and material goods, frequently the latter years of life are the most productive in developing friendships and the more meaningful spiritual relationships with self, others and God.

Many philosophers and psychologists have grappled with the problem of despair vs. hope. However, because of their humanistic thinking, they have been trapped into pseudo-scientific language. Although psychology is seen as a behavioral *science*, in truth it is a language of behavior, not a true science at all. Once behavioral "scientists" are able to get outside the language and entertain a spiritual dimension, psychological, emotional, moral, and religious development takes on a new meaning and becomes much more useful both in understanding and changing human behavior.

Maslow (1972) helped us to understand spiritual growth when he spoke of "transcendence". In order to benefit from his thinking we must understand what he meant by the term transcendence. Maslow defines 'transcendence" as follows:

> Transcendence refers to the very highest and most inclusive or holistic levels of human consciousness, behaving and relating, as ends rather than means, to oneself, to significant others, to human beings in general, to other species, to nature, and to the cosmos. (p. 279)

Having written and spoken extensively regarding transcendence, Cox adds "Transcendence is a spiritual quality. It probably cannot be learned but may be acquired by the disciplines of introspection and unconscious recognition."

Spiritual development takes into account that the part of our person that defies definition but is most certainly our transcendence; i.e., that which is the soul; the part of us that I believe was with us before we were physically born and will survive our physical demise. Maslow (1972), although coming from a strongly Watsoninan background, began to believe many of the "orthodox" and "scientific" approaches were insufficient to understand human behavior. Thus, he postulated that health and self-growth are rooted in "self-actualizing creativeness". He called "ego-transcending" experiences "peak experiences". His description of these experiences sound very spiritual.

> A peak experience…is an episodic, brief occurrence in which a person suddenly experiences a powerful transcendental state of consciousness. During that state a person experiences…intense euphoria, an integrated nature, unity with the universe, and an altered perception of time and space. (Kaplan, Saddock, & Grebb, 1980, pp.257-258)

The stages of spiritual development as postulated here are not seen as stepping stones that one can skip over rather than step upon. Rather, they are building blocks without which each one in order cannot produce a solid structure. Furthermore, although this chapter has taken considerable liberty with Tillich and stand upon much of his thinking, it is not believe that he wanted us to separate the *theos* within us from what psychologists would call the "self." Stages of development are theories; just that, guesses and hopefully starting points for productive thought and discussion. Nonetheless, whether stages are seen from any point of view, psychological, physical, emotional, or spiritual, they are not experiences occurring in a straight line. The detours, the stops and starts, the influences, the balances and counterbalances are forever unknown to all including the person experiencing them. The developing human from embryo through adulthood can become arrested partially or even totally at any point. Adults are observed being stuck at various points in the building order, even at the first stage of distrust/disbelief. By the same token, there is evidence that the direction of one's Spirit may be reversed, and therein lies the hope for the helping professions. This is not the place to discuss the relevance of arresting at an earlier stage of spiritual development to psychopathology, although, there is no doubt a close relationship.

There are no instances of success/failure. All striving proceeds inevitably and uncontrollably toward spiritual resolution. The resolution may be seen as acceptable, socially congruent, or socially deviant, but there is always a resolution. It is also difficult, perhaps even impossible to conceive of spiritual resolutions as positive or negative. Whereas one culture may deem a given resolution as acceptable, even divine, another may see it as sinister and of the Devil.

Immediate resolutions may in the long-term become positive and vice versa. Certainly resolutions that do not necessarily "feel good" are sometimes in the larger picture very beneficial. The conflict can be a spiritual process just as can the resolution. Similarly are stops as well as starts, dis-ease as well as ease, and discouragement as well as encouragement. We cannot think in terms of spiritual failure in temporal terms. Further, spiritual development is difficult to verbalize since human language does not lend itself to life's experiences that are intensely personal and most often non-visible. Even that which appears to be failure is in the long scheme of life actually success. Just as the infant does not fail when it falls while learning to crawl, so it is with us; even falling down is a small success in the long road that does not end in this lifetime.

REFERENCES

Anderson, U. (2000). *Immunology of the soul*. Winter Park, FL: InSync Press.

Becker, E. (1973). *The denial of death*. New York: Free Press.

Cayne, B. S. (Ed.). (1989). *The new lexicon Webster's dictionary of the English language* (Encyclopedia Ed.). New York: Lexicon Publication.

Cox, R. H. (1996). *Transcendence and imminence in the art of healing*. Keynote address at The Charter Declaration, Brazil, World Congress on Comprehensive Medicine, World Health Organization, Rio de Janero, October 30, 1996.

Eckstein, G. (1970). *The body has a head*. New York: Harper & Row.

Erickson, E. H. (1979). *Childhood and society*. New York: Harper & Row.

Fowler, J. W. (1981). *The stages of faith*. San Francisco: Harper & Row.

Fromm, E. (1973). *The Anatomy of Destruction*. New York: Holt, Rinehart, & Winston.

Hill, P. & Hood, R. (1999). *Measures of religiosity*. Bermingham, AL: Religious Education Press.

Jones, W. T. (1969). *Hobbes to Hume* (2nd ed.). New York: Hartcout Brace.

Kaplin, H. I., Sadock, B. J. & Grebb, J. A. (1994). *Kaplan and Sadock's synopsis of psychiatry* (7th ed.). Baltimore, MD: Williams & Wilkins.

Kuhmerker, L. (1991). *The Kohlberg legacy for the helping professions*. Birmingham, AL: Doxa Books.

Maslow, A. H. (1972). *The farthest reaches of human nature*. New York: Penguin.

Miller, W. R. (1999). *Integrating spirituality into treatment*. Washington, D.C.: American Psychological Association.

Peck, M. S. (1985). *People of the lie*. New York: Simon & Schuster.

Peck, M. S. (1997). *Denial of the Soul*. New York: Harmony Books.

The Presbyterian Church (USA). (1983). *The book of confessions* (Pt. 1). New York: Office of the General Assembly.

Random House Value Publishing. (1996). *Webster's encyclopedic unabridged dictionary of the English language*. New York: Gramercy Press.

Seyle, H. (1975). *Stress without distress*. New York: Signet.

Tillich, P. (1951). *Systematic Theology* (Vol. 1.). Chicago, IL: University of Chicago Press.

4

SPIRITUALITY AND CHILDREN

Barry Nierenberg, Ph.D.
University of Miami School of Medicine
Miami, FL

Alissa Sheldon, Ph.D.
Private Practice
Weston, FL

Americans are a religious people. In fact, in a recent Gallup poll of the American public, some interesting facts were highlighted. For example, 94 percent believe in God, 85 percent believe that religion is a "fairly" or "very" important part of their lives, 76 percent report that prayer is an important part of my daily life, and 61 percent believe that religion can answer all or most of today's problems. In our role as psychologists working with medically ill children, we stand with parents at their bedsides and have often seen them take comfort, as well as blame, and guilt in their religious and spiritual beliefs. We have also seen children use prayer. For example, recently, a 16-year old boy came to the Pediatric Rehabilitation Unit at our hospital after surviving a Traumatic Brain Injury following a gang related shooting. Prior to his injury, he was heavily involved in a gang which had frequent brushes with the police and had not attended school in some time. After the shooting, recovery was slow. After regaining the ability to communicate, he told almost everyone who would listen that while he was in a coma, he saw Jesus come to him with his dead brother. They told him he would not die and would get better in order to "have a second chance at life, to not mess up this time." The patient swore he would not go back to what he called, "my old ways," and at his insistence, went to church during his weekend passes home and avoided contact with his old friends. After discharge, the boy continued on this path and directly attributed "turning my life around" to his religious experience. During his stay in the

Rehabilitation hospital, the staff used his religious approach to help encourage participation in required therapies.

The religious experience of this 16 year-old-boy led the authors to the question of how children use spirituality as a way of coping with chronic illness. In recent years this topic has just begun to be studied with adults (especially senior citizens) and families, but not to a great extent with children. One place to begin understanding is to take a look at theories of how children and adolescents develop a sense of spirituality in the first place.

THEORIES OF SPIRITUAL DEVELOPMENT

Two theories that attempt to explain the presence and development of spiritual beliefs in children. They utilize two different approaches that deserve detailed discussion, and both are related to principles of general child development. Fowler's (1995) theory is extrapolated from the works of Erik Erikson, while Oser's (1991) theory is derived from that of Jean Piaget (See Tables 1 & 2).

Table 1
Fowler's Stages of Faith and Erikson's Developmental Stages

	Age 0-6	Age 6-12	Age 12-18
Fowler	Primal Faith	Intuitive-Projctive	Mythic/Literal
Erickson	Trust v. Mistrust	Autonomy vs. Shame/Self doubt	Industry vs. Inferiority

Table 2
Comparison of Oser and Fowler's Stages

	Age 0-6	Age 6-12	Age 12-15	Age 15-18
Oser	Unknown	Stage 1	Stage 2	Stage 3
Piaget	Sensorimotor	Concrete Operational	Formal Operational	Formal Operational

Fowler's Theory of Faith Development

James Fowler (1995) derived a theory of faith development that was similar in construct to Erikson's theories of general human development. Like Erikson, Fowler suggested a set of discrete, hierarchical stages that a person may pass through as he or she develops a greater sense of "faith." "Faith" is defined as "the personal appropriation of a relationship to God through and by means of religious tradition" (p. 42). Also in keeping with Eriksonian thought, Fowler assumed that movement from one stage to the next required a successful resolution of each stage's inherent task. As a result, faith development can arrest at any level, regardless of chronological age.

The first stage of faith development is referred to as *Primal Faith*, and begins in infancy (Fowler, 1995). This stage lays the foundation upon which later faith is built. It stems from the successful completion of Erikson's Trust vs. Mistrust task, and forms the basic rituals of care, interchange, and mutuality.

The second stage, according to Fowler (1995), is *Intuitive-Projective Faith*, and it corresponds with the awakening of moral emotions and standards in the young child (approximately at age 6). Increased faith at this stage results from the resolution of Autonomy vs. Shame and Self-Doubt. Here, representations of God are drawn from early childhood experiences with parents or caregivers, and generate "faith images." These images are believed to express the emotional orientation of the children toward their world, and their experience of the support they have received.

Fowler's (1995) next stage begins in middle childhood, and is called *Mythic-Literal Faith*. Children begin to think concretely and organize the world in distinct categories. As a result, children perceive events in literal terms and their beliefs are often derived from authority figures, such as parents and teachers. This stage usually occurs between ages of seven and twelve and parallels the Industry vs. Inferiority task of Erikson. It is often the first time that the child is faced with the contradictions between scientific and religious explanations of events.

Fowler's (1995) following stage begins in early adolescence, and is termed *Synthetic-Conventional Faith*. Given children's developing cognitive capacities, they can only now begin to think hypothetically. This may be the first time they can reflect on past experiences and examine them for patterns and meaning. According to Fowler, this stage of faith development stems from the completion of Identity vs. Role Confusion. This process occurs in conjunction with the establishment of the young teenager's identity, and becomes a unique set of beliefs, values, and commitments.

The last stage involving children is referred to as *Individuative-Reflective Faith*, and often occurs in late adolescence (Fowler, 1995). In this stage, reflecting the increasing sophistication of the teen's thinking, previously formed values and beliefs are now questioned. The result of this process is that these beliefs become consciously chosen, and critically supported commitments. A process of discovery thus begins, in which a meaning greater than the individual events of one's life is perceived and a sense of significance is found in one's roles and activities. This faith stage corresponds with the Intimacy vs. Isolation psychosocial task.

Fowler (1995) goes on to describe the continuing development of faith into adulthood. Individuals at the *Conjunctive Faith* stage embrace and integrate opposites and polarities into their lives. They develop a new appreciation or their own traditions, as well as the traditions of others. The last stage of faith development Fowler referred to as *Universalizing Faith*. He believes people at this stage have a foundation consisting of feeling a unity with the power of God. He also describes a process of decentralization of self as the basis for being able to identify with the concerns of others. There is a commitment to overcoming division and oppression. Fowler contends that not all reach this stage and those who do may be significant spiritual leaders, such as Martin Luther King, Jr. and Mahatma Gandhi.

Oser's Theory of Religious Development

Another way to think about children and spirituality is given by Oser (1991). Like Fowler, he takes a developmental approach, but bases his ideas on the pioneering work of Jean Piaget. Oser takes a more cognitively based approach and has created five hierarchical, non-age dependent stages of religious development, like Piaget's theory. Fowler similarly believes that an individual can be in any stage at any age. Also, there is no judgment implying that one stage is inherently better than any other. Each stage is merely a different way to understand one's relationship to God.

Stage 1: The Ultimate Being Does It... Oser's first stage is characterized by an anthropomorphic representation of God. God is understood as being active and moving unpredictably in the world, while people are seen as being reactive. The Ultimate Being is seen as having absolute power, causing all events, and intervening directly in the world and in individual's fates. God's will must always and unreservedly be fulfilled. If not, the relationship breaks and God will inflict sanctions on the disobedient. This stage often occurs in early childhood and individuals at this stage view their influence on the Ultimate Being's actions as minimal.

Stage 2: The Ultimate Being Does It, If... In this stage, God is still viewed as an external, all-powerful entity that either punishes or rewards. However, God's actions are now characterized by the principle *do et des* (give so you may receive). People at this stage believe that prayers, good deeds, and adherence to religious rules and customs can influence the Ultimate Being's will and mood.

Stage 3: The Ultimate Being and Humankind Do... Oser's third stage states that the Ultimate Being is viewed as apart from and outside of the world. It is assumed that God has a specific realm of action. The idea of a God in charge of all details of human existence and nature is abandoned. When it comes to individual and social matters, it is the individual's will that is crucial.

Stages 4 & 5: Humankind Does Through an Ultimate Being's Doing... Oser combines the fourth and fifth stages of religious development, suggesting that one builds on the other. These stages do not usually occur until adulthood. God is now considered to be not only the base of the world, but of each individual's existence. People in this stage believe that their freedom and lives cannot originate and give meaning only within themselves. Instead, they take a broader perspective, and see their freedom and lives as having been made more meaningful through an Ultimate Being. Individuals see themselves as having an indirect, mediated relationship with God. The fifth and final stage is seen as an extension of the fourth, and is only rarely found. Here, the Ultimate Being informs and inhabits each moment and commitment, however profane and insignificant. The Ultimate Being is realized through human action, wherever there is care and love. Again, people such as Martin Luther King, Jr. and Gandhi typify this stage.

Examples of the first two of Oser's stages can be found in Hemple and Marshall's (1991) book, *Children's Letters to God*, where the authors published the writings of grade school children, ages six through twelve, who were simply asked to write God a letter.

Oser's first stage, characterized by an anthropomorphic representation of God, is typified by the letter from Donny who wrote, "Is Reverend Coe a friend of yours, or do you just know him through business?" As we can see, Donny is addressing God here as if God is a kindly grandfather.

In a similar way, Jane addresses God in her letter as if God is a friendly adult she's met and was curious about his work: "In Sunday school they told us what you do. Who does it when you are on vacation?"

Eugene paid God a compliment when he wrote, "I didn't think orange went with purple until I saw the sunset you made on Tuesday. That was cool." And finally, Seymour wonders in his letter, "How come you did all those miracles in the old days and don't do any now?"

Stage 2 is typified by the addition of the idea that prayers can influence God's actions, can be found in Janet's letter. She asks God, "I wish you would not make it so easy for people to come apart. I had three stitches and a shot." Here, Janet is attempting to influence God by wishing or praying for improved manufacture of our all too human bodies.

Joyce expressed her disappointment in God's answer to her prayers when she wrote, "Thank you for the baby brother but what I prayed for was a puppy." In her letter, Jane asks God to implement an idea she's had, "Instead of letting people die and having (sic) to make new ones, why don't you just keep the ones you got now?" Finally, Mark states his wish in his letter where he wrote, "I keep waiting for spring but it never come yet. Don't forget."

As we would predict, since Stage three occurs after age twelve, there were no examples represented in this book. However, an example can be found in other literature. In *Death Be Not Proud* (Gunther, 1949), the adolescent boy writes just before his impending death:

> Almighty God
> Forgive me for my agnosticism;
> For I shall try to keep it gentle, not cynical,
> Nor a bad influence.
>
> And O!
> If thou art truly in the heavens,
> Accept my gratitude
> For all thy gifts
> And I shall try
> To fight the good fight. Amen.

Here the adolescent author clearly views God as apart from the physical world and sees his own individual will and attitude as crucial. As Oser predicts, no examples of Stages four or five were found in any of the child or adolescent literature.

Research utilizing Oser's Theory

In a manner similar to Kohlberg's building a theory of Moral Development on Piaget's work, Oser was able to derive a semi-clinical structured interview whereby he could attempt to measure religious judgments to hypothetical situations. He gave participants three dilemmas, and asked each to describe, "What you would do, and why, if you were the actor in this story?"

Dilemma One. A young medical doctor sits in a plane that is about to crash. Out of desperation, he promises to devote his life to helping the sick and the poor in underdeveloped nations, should he survive. He does survive the crash, but struggles with whether to keep the promise he has made.

Dilemma Two: A judge has led a good and responsible life. As he gets older, he finds he is in misery and pain, and questions why such a just man has to suffer so much.

Dilemma Three. Do certain events, such as winning the lottery, occur solely by chance or are they part of a divine plan?

By using this interview technique, Oser attempted to determine if there were any trends in responses based on age, as would be expected according to Piaget's theory of increasing cognitive ability. Oser and colleagues (1992) then went on to prove that these trends were robust enough to be seen across religions and cultures. They studied the Bantu Cult and Christianity in Rwanda and found similar results. This is an excellent example of the adaptability of Oser's work to clinically based research. The addition of the semi-structured interview made it is possible to place children in their appropriate stage of religious development across cultures, which is also what Piaget would predict.

The authors have done just this in two pilot studies (Nierenberg et al, 1997; Nierenberg et al, 1998). These are included here for two reasons, the first being some of the more intriguing directions the findings suggest for future research and the second reason being that they are examples of how to apply Oser's work in clinically based research. Oser's theory is particularly adaptable to research due to its Kohlbergian approach allowing for easy identification of the stage that each child is operating from. The authors used this approach to begin to investigate the possible relationship between spirituality and health in children.

Extending the paradigm of psychospirituality offered by Oser, the authors tried to better understand and intervene with children, focusing on dealing with young children's illnesses and their use of spirituality and values as a way of coping. As demonstrated by Piaget, in the school age population, children's ideas about death and loss begin to incorporate the concept of irreversibility and one can start to appreciate the psychospiritual effects on them directly. As they approach adolescence, hypothetical thinking allows for a more complex and abstract understanding. At times, beginning at this stage, one can see the

62

psycho-spiritual struggles affecting the individual's balance of hope and reality in adopting an optimistic vs. pessimistic view of the long term effects of the trauma affecting them.

The authors began by looking at children who were Human Immunodeficiency Virus (HIV) positive since birth. The idea was to investigate whether there was a measurable connection between their degree of spirituality and their physical health. In one of our Pediatric HIV clinics, we had 33 children age 7 to 17 with an average age of 10.8. There were 20 males and 13 females. These children were interviewed over a two-day period and data were collected on their health. The interviews utilized Oser's dilemmas to find a stage of religious development and gave the patients a chance to state whether or not they attended church and prayed on their own. Researchers who did not know the interview results or the premise of the study collected the health measures blindly. The health measures included the Center for Disease Control (CDC) classification of their symptoms, T cell count, and number of hospitalizations over the past year. Simple correlations were then run on the spirituality and health measures (see Table 3).

Table 3
Relationship Between Religion and Health Factors

	Correlation	Significance Level
Religion and Health	.466	.006
Religion and CDC Symptoms	.438	.05
Religion and T Cell Count	.413	.05
Religion and Number of Hospitalizations	.366	ns

To summarize the results, the religion and health measures correlated significantly at the $p = .006$ level. Of the religious measures, the one that added the most degree of significance was self disclosed church attendance. Since the correlations were positive, the more religious the children said they were the healthier they were. The T cell counts were significantly higher, and CDC symptoms lower. Number of hospitalizations over the past year was not significantly correlated with church attendance, meaning that being hospitalized did not affect the religion measure. By knowing church attendance, one could predict how sick the child was. Oser's stages did not correlate significantly with the health factors, but did correlate significantly with age.

As pointed out by a colleague, there is a problem with Church attendance being the highest factor. Namely, that as the disease progresses, there can be significant wasting of the body's tissues, which can significantly alter the person's appearance. Our colleague pointed out that the sickest children may not be attending church secondary to these appearance issues, perhaps skewing our results. Taking this seriously, the team decided to choose another disease entity to determine if a similar relationship could be found between spirituality and health.

A second group was found in Pediatric dialysis patients with End Stage Renal Disease. These children and adolescents were on Hemodialysis three times per week for 3-4 hours at a time and blood work, reflecting their current health status, was drawn once per week. This allowed for both the time necessary to interview them and access to objective health related measures.

Sixteen children were recruited for the study, ranging from ages 6-20, with 14.7 being the mean age. The children were from a variety of cultures, representing Anglo, Hispanic, African American and Haitian backgrounds. Interestingly, age and Oser level correlated highly ($p = .009$).

To add another measure of spirituality, along with a colleague Steve Katsikas, the authors developed a pencil and paper measure of children's' Spiritual Attitudes and Beliefs (SAB). This consisted of 20 items constructed so that half covered attitudes and half covered behaviors. Items are arranged in a four point Likert type format and the reliability analysis yielded a .78 alpha coefficient. Interestingly, data analysis revealed a strong relationship between Oser level and SAB (see Table 4). As one would expect, high correlations were also found between Oser level and age.

Table 4

Correlations Between SAB and Oser Level

	Correlation	Significance Level
SAB Total/Oser Level	-.677	.004
SAB Behavior/Oser Level	-.486	.05
SAB Attitude/Oser Level	-.703	.002

Physical measures included the standard ones measured in the dialysis literature: number of access problems, amount of interim weight gains, number of hospitalizations in past year, and various blood levels of minerals and metabolites. Of these measures, one of the more important ones is the Blood, Urea, and Nitrogen (BUN). Usually a measure of overall health and compliance to the rigid and demanding dietary restrictions, the BUN has lower readings indicating more health. The SAB correlated to a significant degree with the BUN as can be seen in Table 5. It is interesting to note that the highest correlation is with the total SAB score, i.e. the more spiritual the outlook, the healthier the child was. A multiple regression analysis showed that the SAB score accounted for over 40 percent of the variance in the BUN, which was significant at the .035 level.

Table 5

Correlations Between SAB and BUN

	Correlation	Significance Level
SAB Total/BUN	-.632	.009
SAB Behavior/BUN	-.561	.024
SAB Attitude/BUN	-.449	.081

There are several possible explanations for these results and at the time of this writing, we are actively investigating some of them. One is the possible intervening variable of family so, one possible outcome of the follow up study is that the, "family who prays together," has healthier children on Dialysis. Currently other possibilities are also being explored.

FACTORS TTHAT AFFECT SPIRITUAL AND RELIGIOUS DEVELOPMENT

Although much is believed, little is actually known about the role that spiritual beliefs play in the lives of children. Several factors have been explored in the published literature in an attempt to account for the origin of these beliefs including the family environment, cultural and ethnic variables, and children's cognitive abilities. The impact of a variety of negative life events has also been reported. Since spirituality is a complex construct, it is likely that many factors are responsible for the formation of the child's spiritual and religious beliefs. The literature that does exist seems to indicate that spiritual development is a multiply determined phenomenon: a result of the complex interactions between cultural, familial, personality, developmental stage, life events, neighborhood, and friends' influences. In our opinion, the most important factors for development of spirituality in children are the interaction of individual factors (personality, intelligence, developmental stage), family (family structure, what parents teach) and how life events are interpreted by the child/family unit. Elaboration of some of these factors, supported by research and clinical findings, follow.

Family Environment
As is the case with many aspects of child development, the family environment plays a large role in both spiritual and religious development. Families that engage in religious activities are more likely to have children and teens that are religious. The religious beliefs are also more similar to their parent's beliefs, especially if there is a warm, nurturing relationship between parent and child. Some feel that this similarity in beliefs is due to secure attachments formed during childhood (Granqvist & Hagekull, 1999; Granqvist, 1998), while others state that it may be a result of common personality traits (Brubaker, 1998). Regardless of the etiology, children often view God in much the same way their parents do. These similarities are true across race, socioeconomic status, and religious affiliation (Dickie et al., 1997).

Culture and Ethnicity
While children may view God the same way their parents do, that does not mean all children see God the same way. There are some differences in the role that religion plays in various cultures. For example, African-American teens are more likely to report higher levels of spiritual support than their Caucasian counterparts (Maton, Teti, Corns, Vieira-Baker, & Lavine, 1996). Also, when faced with a stressful situation, such as teen pregnancy or

65

childhood illness, African-Americans are more likely to utilize religion and spiritual support, and this often results in higher levels of self-esteem and better adjustment (Rogers-Dulan, 1998). Regional differences are also found with children from rural/farm areas displaying greater religious behaviors than their urban or rural/non-farm cohort (King, Elder, & Whitbeck, 1997).

Clinically, this variance in religious belief is seen in many other cultures. For example, in the traditional Haitian culture, health and disease are not generally viewed in the same way we do in the West. For the traditional Haitian, disease is not seen as a function of germ theory, but as a direct measure of an individual's relationship to God. If one is not healthy, the culturally syntonic explanations are either the individual did something to directly impair their own relationship to God or a second individual, using various religious rites, has impaired the relationship, leading to disease. Either way, traditional Haitians are not likely to immediately view administration of medical technique (e.g. drugs, surgery, etc) as a primary cure. For them, the proper intervention that follows is to perform a healing religious ritual. Several medical teams in our hospital have permitted the use of healing religious rituals with a sick child with the understanding that nothing would be done that the team believed to be harmful to the patient. For ill Haitian children whose family's still use traditional cultural beliefs, it is not unusual to find a faith healer by the child's bed performing various rituals.

Cognitive Level

In keeping with Oser's theory of religious development and Piaget's cognitive development theory, spiritual development is influenced by an increased cognitive level. As a children grow their capacity for abstract reasoning increases. The preoperational child may perceive God or religion in very simple or even magical terms, whereas the concrete-operational child may have a more logical view of the role of religion. Children show an increase in religious knowledge as their age increases and they may even report increases in levels of faith (Bourdeau & George, 1997). It is interesting to note, however, that spiritual development is not necessarily tied to chronological age as there are reports of gifted children displaying heightened levels of spiritual sensitivity. Despite being younger, these children show an increased knowledge of spiritual concepts and an ability to examine belief systems in advance of their cohort (Lovecky, 1998).

Negative Life Events

Abuse. There are two different views as to the effect that childhood abuse has on spiritual development. One view states that incidents of abuse create such a high level of stress and discomfort that the child must begin to search for a higher meaning in life and is therefore, compelled to grow spiritually (Garbarino & Bedard, 1996). The other commonly held view is that spiritual development ceases at the time the abuse occurs, leaving that child forever stuck at an immature level of spirituality (Ganje-Fling & McCarthy, 1996). A more temperate alternative was proposed by Ryan (1998). After reviewing the literature in this area, it is suggested that there is no one response pattern to abuse. This is only to say that views of religion are strongly influenced by the experience of childhood violence. A study designed to distinguish which theory, if any, holds the most validity, has yet to be published.

Bereavement. The concepts of death and dying are challenging for anyone, but especially for young children. The relationship between views of death and spiritual beliefs are even more difficult to ascertain. There has been little research on the role of religion and spirituality in children's concepts of death, but what has been done has shown that increased spirituality correlates with better adjustment (Batten & Oltjenbruns, 1999; Sormanti & August, 1997). Some feel that children's understanding of death is less influenced by spiritual factors, and more so by age and cognitive level (Cuddy-Casey & Orvaschel, 1997). The impact of death on spiritual development is seen by some as being a catalyst for growth, in much the same way abuse is viewed.

Illness / Disability. For children, teens, and families that are coping with a chronic illness or disability, spiritual and religious beliefs play a special role. Families coping with these stressors report increased levels of spiritual support, and state that they engage more regularly in religious activities. Also, families who are more religious, report greater levels of adjustment (Mawn, 1999; Yachtmenoff, Koren, Friesen, et al. 1998). Attributions of blame for childhood illness or injury can even be related to spiritual factors and adjustment. Those families who blame fate or God's will for their children's distress were more likely to be better adjusted than those families who blamed themselves or the environment (Mickelson, Wroble, & Helgeson, 1999).

FUTURE ROLE OF SPIRITUALITY IN CHILD/ADOLESCENT PSYCHOTHERAPY

The majority of mental health professionals polled responded that an increased awareness and inclusion of spiritual factors in psychotherapy is warranted (Burke et al.,1999). In addition, both psychotherapists and clergy acknowledge a need for collaboration, as there is considerable overlap in the issues they address (Weaver, Koenig, & Larson, 1997). Despite these acknowledgments, spiritual and religious concerns are often ignored or not appropriately addressed by care providers (Henley, 1999). There are many areas that could potentially benefit by including assessment of spiritual factors. For instance, home hospice for the dying child is one place that spiritual issues need to be addressed as it has been shown that spiritual and religious factors can increase family adjustment (Goldman, 1996). Likewise, some cultural groups characterize childhood mental illness in spiritual ways and being able to diagnose and treat in a culturally sensitive fashion may be more accepted (Barlow & Walkup, 1998). While there are certain caveats that must be considered when exploring the relationship between spiritual and psychological variables, such as maintaining rigorous testing practices and employing methods of experimental design (Thorsen, 1999), it would be short-sighted not to acknowledge their importance.

The area of spirituality and adult psychotherapy is currently under much investigation. At present, the child/adolescent analogue is not represented well in the literature. Many questions need to be addressed. Under what conditions does spirituality play a positive role in negative life events for children? Under what conditions does it play a negative one?

For example, we have dealt with a number of children who are non-adherent to their medical regimens, some to the extent where it is life threatening. When asked, some of these children have stated a belief that their illness is "a punishment from God" and it is not up to them to prematurely "end the punishment with medicine." Unfortunately, the child persisted in this belief in spite of continued therapy and intervention from his church clergy.

If as psychologists we are supposed to effect change in the attitudes, attributions, and behavior of those people seeking our help, how can we not understand more about their spiritual lives and how it develops?

CLINICAL EXAMPLES

All the theories presented in this chapter are helpful, but skirt the issue of how they can be used in a clinical setting. Given the relative recent development of the concept of psychospirituality and the absence of an extensive literature base, the following clinical examples are offered.

Spirituality Cases
Case 1: Using the Oser levels clinically. C.M. is a 19-year old girl with ESRD, Lupus, and HIV. She had been on Hemodialysis since age 10 when complications from Lupus almost completely eliminated her renal functioning. C.M. was well known to our service, having been followed on an as needed basis since age 12 due to previous referrals re: problems with diet adherence. C.M. was once again referred at age 19 following her diagnosis of HIV. Due to staff concerns that she had increases anxiety and a re-occurrence of non-adherence to her prescribed medical regimen which now required her to take over 20 different medications per day. Dialysis staff was frustrated, complaining that educational techniques were ineffective and requested a psychological consult for assistance.

During the interview, C.M. did express some anxiety and insight into her problem. She understood the importance of taking the medication and understood the negative consequences of taking her medication on an irregular basis. C.M. explained that the problem, as she saw it, was the size of some of the pills, stating that they were simply too large for her to swallow. She described her experience as her throat, "getting tight and small," whenever she attempted to take them. C.M. also shared that this was the first time the staff had no other alternative methods of taking the medication (e.g. liquid, smaller pills, etc). When offered the choice of a relaxation therapy or hypnosis, she surprisingly refused. We had worked well together in the past and successfully utilized other similar behavioral interventions. When asked what the problem was, she explained that she had become more religious since our last meeting and would not do anything that could, "invite the devil into me." She had exclaimed that hypnosis and relaxation could, "open me up to possession."

After further discussion, it was clear that she wouldn't change her mind. The situation was serious since the staff explained that if her adherence did not improve quickly, C.M. could invite further physical complications. After assessing her Oser Level as two, it was asked if she believed the Lord wanted her to stay alive for a while longer. C.M. said she believed he did. Then C.M. was asked if she believed in prayer, she replied that she did and added that she prayed daily and believed God answered her prayers. It was then suggested that C.M. use her favorite prayer to ask Jesus to help her body accept the medicine by relaxing and opening her throat, allowing her to swallow her pills and stay healthy. It was explained that in this manner she might be able to "be well and do God's work." It was hoped that by allowing her to choose her own prayer, it would increase her sense of control and make the intervention more syntonic with her present worldview. Additionally, asking C.M. to directly petition her Lord was a way of respecting her personal view of God. In this example, the fact that C.M. was already using prayer was utilized for the therapeutic end of increasing her adherence and decreasing her anxiety. She was clearly in Oser's stage two of development and by understanding this; it became possible to use her spiritual understanding to help her achieve her therapeutic goals.

After this intervention along with continued follow up psychotherapy where C.M. was encouraged to continue to pray, compliance went up dramatically and she reported being significantly less anxious. C.M. understood the improvement to be the direct result of, "Jesus answering [her] prayers." Since this explanation gave her a profound sense of peace and probably would have been resistant to change under any conditions, C.M.'s attribution was left intact.

Case 2: Premorbid ability to use prayer as a support. T.S. is a 16-year old girl who was referred to Psychological Service from the trauma unit, having survived three gunshot wounds which left her paralyzed with incomplete quadriplegia. T.S. was originally from the Caribbean. She and her Mother had moved to the United States approximately three years earlier. After experiencing a series of unfortunate family financial reversals, T.S. and her mother reluctantly came to the decision for T.S. to move several states away to live with extended family. The family consisted of her maternal aunt and uncle, their 18-year old son and the maternal grandmother.

Shortly after T.S.'s arrival, her aunt and uncle were divorced and a restraining order was placed on the uncle. The uncle returned to the house one day, sat his ex-wife down, then forced her to watch as he first shot and killed the grandmother. He put three bullets into T.S., shot and killed their son, and then committed suicide. Two of the bullets caused only muscular damage to T.S., but one bullet lodged in her spinal cord at T-3 leaving her with incomplete quadriplegia.

T.S. was very religious prior to the shooting. Early in her hospitalization she asked various staff members such as nurses and physical therapists to pray with her when she was afraid or in pain. Several of the therapists expressed some serious reservations in supporting her praying by arguing that this would, "interfere with her coming to terms with her disability." During several team meetings we were able to reframe the group's understanding of T.S.'s praying in terms of a coping style. Once this was done, team members had an easier time supporting the patient's wishes. Following the prayer, T.S. would be visibly calmer and more able to participate in therapies. She also used prayer to begin to come to terms with forgiving her uncle, who had known her all her life.

The staff complied with her requests and meetings were continued with the team to support their strong reactions to T.S.'s experiences. Closer to discharge, many team members stated they were impressed with T.S.'s ability to use prayer as support and to resume her life.

Case 3. Team Consultation on Oser Level with Parents. Another clinical example is the case of B.A., a 7-year old girl who sustained a significant spinal cord injury following a motor vehicle accident, leaving her with quadriplegia. B.A. and her family were quite religious and her parents were open in sharing their belief that God would help heal their daughter. The family went on to share their belief that God works through people on earth and frequently thanked the team members for their help. They carefully explained to the medical team members that it was their practice to pray several times each day and asked that they not be interrupted during these sessions. The team agreed and the parents became active partners in their child's care, often assisting in her therapies. Her parents were quite religious prior to the accident and were convinced that the Lord would heal their daughter. In keeping with this belief, they asked staff to not say anything in front of B.A. that could negate this belief and they went on to pick a date by which the healing would take place and she would again walk. In the meantime, the team spoke with the parents and they decided that, at times, the Lord may work through people on earth and, regarding their daughter, those people might be members of our Rehabilitation Team.

As is the practice of this rehabilitation unit, shortly after admission, a family-team meeting was scheduled. The parents requested that the team members perform a prayer circle just before the start of the meeting so that, "God could bless their work." The day before the meeting was scheduled, a brief discussion was held regarding each team member's opinions and feelings. Following this, the team agreed to the family's request and a prayer circle was performed. This allowed for some measure of increased comfort on the part of the parents who were given a rather pessimistic prognosis for recovery. The medical director was able to frame the difficult news within a spiritual paradigm by adding the explanation that it appears that, "God has not yet decided it is time to fully heal your daughter." It should be noted here that neither the team nor the physician normally uses a spiritual paradigm in explanations to patients or their families. Because the team was able to adapt to the stated spiritual needs of this family, it helped to facilitate the entire family's recovery.

Case 4: Maladaptive Spiritual Coping in a 9 year old. B.C. is a 9-year old boy with HIV who was perinetally infected and experiencing multiple medical complications. Both his parents had already died when we met him in the medical clinic and he was living with an overburdened grandmother. B.C. presented with numerous behavioral problems and had poor peer relations. During the course of intake, when asked about spiritual practices that could affect his care, B.C. was also asked if he ever prayed. He sadly shook his head no and said, "I used to pray everyday to be healthy, but I stopped." He went on to explain that, "even God gave up on me – that's why I'm still sick and the doctors can't do anything." He wondered aloud what he could have done to make "God so mad at me." When questioned further, B.C. explained that he stopped because "everyday I asked God to heal me and all that happened was I got sicker."

When an alternative explanation was offered he again sadly shook his head and told the interviewer, "You don't understand. I done something bad that God is punishing me for. I don't know what it is, but that's why he took my parents away and that's why I'm sick. I ain't gonna get better until God is done punishing me." B.C. persisted in this belief in spite of continued therapy and repeated attempts to reframe his understanding. This was part of an apparent general belief that he deserved "nothing good in life." In fact, B.C. was eventually placed into a therapeutic foster home with a couple that initially wanted to adopt him. However, he subsequently went on to continue to behaviorally act out and had to be placed into a group home.

Case 5: Maladaptive Spiritual Coping in an Adolescent. T.C. is a 15-year old with Lupus who had been followed by our service for over 3 years. Persistent problems existed with compliance and she was frequently hospitalized. During one of her more painful hospitalizations, we were discussing coping strategies and she tearfully admitted that she deserved "to be sick and in pain." When questioned further, she stated she had murdered her sister. Thinking it she was confused by her pain medication, she was reminded she didn't have a sister. She went on to explain she did when she was younger.

Apparently at age 6 her Mother asked her to watch her sister, aged 2, while she quickly went to the local market. While alone with her sister, the toddler got hold of some matches, burned herself and died from her resulting injuries. T.C. was diagnosed with Lupus approximately 6-months later and always saw her illness as a punishment from God. She tearfully explained that she had no right to stop God's punishment by taking her medications and that she could be well only when God forgave her or was simply done "punishing me."

Unfortunately, shortly after this hospitalization, she and her family were lost to follow up and never returned to our clinic.

Case 6: Working with Parents. Our service was recently consulted regarding a 15-year old boy. His parents initially brought him in to be evaluated for a heart transplant, but after seeing him, the team told his family that his condition had seriously deteriorated to the point where he would also need a lung transplant. This was a surprise to the family who, up investigation, learned that a significant number of adolescent heart-lung transplant candidates died while waiting for the operation. Afraid their son might die before receiving the transplant, the father tearfully asked me, "How do you tell a kid he's going to die and how do you keep his faith in God?"

After interviewing both parents and their son, it turned out this spiritual aspect was not a primary issue for son (who was more focused on short term implications). But this was for his mom and dad. With further work, parents revealed that the initial spiritual focus was reflective of their deeper problem with suddenly learning that their son was much sicker than they initially thought. Then it was possible to work with them around gaining an idiosyncratic balance of hope and the reality that they did not know if their son would die prior to a transplant simply because of group statistics. Their question about keeping their son's faith in God was more related to their own faith being shaken. This was explored with them within a therapeutic relationship. Their child got well enough to go home and, at time of this writing, he's still healthy enough to be out of the hospital, waiting for the transplant at home.

Case 7: Parental Coping. A final example is a family of Orthodox Jews. The father was walking his 6-year old daughter home from school when they were both struck by an out of control car. Both of them sustained multiple and serious orthopedic injuries. At the child's bedside, her mother constantly found herself stuck on the question of "How could God allow this to happen?" She believed that since her family was religious and "good," they would be protected from random injury. She saw the accident and resulting injuries as proof that God broke an implied covenant to keep them safe from harm. As Harold Kushner (1981) suggests in his book *"When Bad Things Happen to Good People,"* this may be the wrong question. The answer, which would include something about the physics of an out of control motor vehicle hitting an all too human body, is deeply unsatisfying. He argues that a more viable approach to the problem is to say to yourself that since this happened without your permission and, given the choice, you wouldn't choose it. What can you do anyway? When this was given to the Mother as a possible method for dealing with her anger at God, she was able to initially take it in. After thinking about it, she offered it did give her both some relief and a path. She decided that her husband and daughter now need her "more than ever" and she would "do what it takes to make them better." Again we find that by directly addressing someone's spiritual concerns they found a measure of relief and a way to continue to live their lives.

CONCLUSION

Certainly more research and work needs to be done on incorporating psychospirituality into child and adolescent psychology in order to better help those children who come into our care. What the above examples have in common is a lack of judgment on the part of the therapist and seeing the patient's religious views as similar to a "world view." It is possible to sometimes use this view to effect psychotherapeutic change. We do have a long way to go, but at least the journey has begun.

REFERENCES

Batten, M., & Oltjenbruns, K. (1999). Adolescent sibling bereavement as a catalyst for spiritual development: A model for understanding. *Death Studies, 23(6)*, 529-546.

Barlow, A., & Walkup, J. (1998). Developing mental health services for native American children. *Child and Adolescent Psychiatry Clinics of North America, 7(3)*, 555-577.

Bourdeau, M., & George, D. (1997). Changes across age groups on measures of knowledge, faith, and belief of god's personal concern. *Psychological Reports, 80(3, Pt 2)*, 1359-1362.

Brubaker, L. (1998). Parental bonding and religiosity in young adulthood: Comment. *Psychological Reports, 83(3, Pt 1)*, 1089-1090.

Burke, M., Hackney, H., Hudson, P., Miranti, J., Watts, G., & Epp, L. (1999). Spirituality, religion, and CACREP curriculum standard. *Journal of Counseling and Development, 77(3)*, 251-257.

Chamberlain, T. & Hall, C. (2000). *Realized religion*. Philadelphia, PA: Templeton Foundation Press.

Cuddy-Casey, M., & Orvaschel, H. (1997). Children's understanding of death in relation to child suicidality and homicidality. *Clinical Psychology Review, 17(1)*, 33-45.

Dickie, J., Eshleman, A., Merasco, D., & Shepard, A. (1997). Parent-child relationships and children's images of god. *Journal for the Scientific Study of Religion, 36(1)*, 25-43.

Erikson, E. (1963). *Childhood and Society* (2nd ed.). New York: W. W. Norton & Company.

Fowler, J. W. (1995). *Stages of faith*. San Francisco, CA: Harper.

Ganje-Fling, M., & McCarthy, P. (1996). Impact of childhood sexual abuse on client spiritual development: Counseling implications. *Journal of Counseling and Development, 74(3)*, 253-258.

Garbarino, J., & Bedard, C. (1996). Spiritual challenges to children facing violent trauma. Childhood. *A Global Journal of Child Research, 3(4)*, 467-478.

Goldman, A. (1996). Home care of the dying child. *Journal of Palliative Care, 12(3)*, 16-19.

Granqvist, P. (1998). Religiousness and perceived childhood attachment: On the question of compensation or correspondence. *Journal for the Scientific Study of Religion, 37(2)*, 350-367.

Granqvist, P., & Hagekull, B. (1999). Religiousness and perceived childhood attachment: Profiling socialized correspondence and emotional compensation. *Journal for the Scientific Study of Religion, 38*, 254-273.

Gunther, J. (1949). *Death be not proud*. New York: Harper & Row.

Hemple, S, & Marshall, E. (1991). *Children's Letters to God*. Workman Publishing Co.

Henley, L. (1999). A home visit programme to teach medical students about children with special needs. *Medical Education, 33(10)*, 749-752.

King, V., Elder, G., & Whitbeck, L. (1997). Religious involvement among rural youth: An ecological and life-course perspective. *Journal of Research on Adolescence, 7(4)*, 431-456.

Kushner, H. S. (1981). *When bad things happen to good people*. New York: Avon Books.

Lovecky, D. (1998). Spiritual sensitivity in gifted children. *Roeper Review, 20(3)*, 178-183.

Maton, K., Teti, D., Corns, K., Vieira-Baker, C., & Lavine, J. (1996). Cultural specificity of support sources, correlates and contexts: Three studies of African American and Caucasian youth. *American Journal of Community Psychology, 24(4)*, 551-587.

Mawn, B. (1999). Raising a child with HIV: An emerging phenomenon. *Families, Systems, and Health, 17(2)*, 197-215.

Mickelson, K., Wroble, M., & Helgeson, V. (1999). "Why my child?": Parents attributions for children's special needs. *Journal of Applied Social Psychology, 29(6)*, 1263-1292.

Nierenberg, B. & Katsikas, S. (1998, August). *Psychospirituality's role in Pediatric End Stage Renal Disease.* Paper presented at the 106th Annual APA Convention, San Francisco, CA.

Oser, F. (1991). The development of religious judgment. In F. Oser & G. Scarlett (Eds.), *Religious Development in Childhood and Adolescence* (New Directions for Child Development, (No. 52; pp. 9-68). New York: Jossey Bass.

Piaget, J. (1967). *Six psychological studies.* New York: Random House.

Rogers-Dulan, J. (1998). Religious connectedness among urban african american families who have a child with disabilities. *Mental Retardation, 36(2)*, 91-103.

Ryan, P. (1998). Spirituality among adult survivors of childhood violence: A literature review. *Journal of Transpersonal Psychology, 30(1)*, 39-51.

Sormanti, M., & August, J. (1997). Parental bereavement: Spiritual connections with deceased children. *American Journal of Orthopsychiatry, 67(3)*, 460-469.

Thorsen, C. (1999). Spirituality and health: Is there a relationship? *Journal of Health Psychology, 4(3)*, 291-300.

Weaver, A., Koenig, H., & Larson, D. (1997). Marriage and family therapists and the clergy: A need for clinical collaboration, training, and research. *Journal of Marital and Family Therapy, 23(1)*, 13-25.

Yachtmenoff, D., Koren, P., Friesen, B., Gordon, L., & Kinney, R. (1998). Enrichment and stress in families caring for a child with a serious emotional disorder. *Journal of Child and Family Studies, 7(2)*, 129-145.

5

SPIRITUALITY IN THE DEVELOPMENTAL STAGE OF ADOLESCENT

Betty A. Schlesing, Psy.D.
Besuda Psychological Center
Ozark, MO

To be spiritually minded is life. - Romans 8:6

Adolescence is a time when the adolescent experiences rapid growth physiologically, psychologically, and spiritually. This stage of accelerated growth is surpassed only by an individual's growth during the first five years of life. Spirituality in the adolescent manifests in a myriad of ways. There is a press for a different type of connection, not only with peers and adults, but also with a Greater Power than the self or others. The adolescent is searching for his or her identity within their totality of life. This includes the social, occupational, psychological, educational, physiological, developmental, and spiritual spheres of life. This search for meaning in the adolescent's life together with the physiological and psychological changes the adolescent is experiencing evokes an existential crisis resulting in anxiety that incorporates all facets of the adolescent's life, and results in a connection between and among all spheres of the adolescent's life, including the connection with a Higher Power. The connection between physical growth, psychological maturation, and spirituality brings the adolescent to a search for meaning for their life that is manifest in an intensive focus on various ways in which the adolescent might fulfill that need for spiritual meaning. This intensive focus is unique to each adolescent in his or her particular rite of passage to adulthood.

In the physical sphere, the adolescent is experiencing a time when the body in which he or she has lived for many years is no longer familiar. During adolescence, each part of the body seems to grow at a different rate of acceleration. One day the arms may actually be several centimeters longer than they were on the previous day, and this phenomenon precipitously results in clumsy behaviors. The adolescent may reach for a glass of milk at meals and tip the glass spilling the milk. He or she may experience rapid growth of the length of his or her legs and have "accidents" when attempting to perform the same athletic feats as had previously been performed successfully. As a result of this adolescent growth spurt, the individual feels awkward and clumsy, as if the body that was previously home no longer belongs to the adolescent, but is that of a stranger with whom he or she is unfamiliar. This results in anxiety and a physical existential crisis whereby the adolescent is concerned about what is happening to his or her body.

The adolescent also experiences hormonal changes that result in the body that was formerly familiar becoming a stranger. Both male and female adolescents begin to manifest secondary sexual characteristics causing fluctuating moods, oily skin, skin moisture change, acne, and hair growing on the body in places where none had previously appeared. The female adolescent begins to menstruate, and this natural process starts without warning, resulting in blood appearing. This may evoke ridicule and embarrassment for the adolescent who is unprepared as stains may appear on the clothing. Blood also may initiate feelings of fear and evoke images of death for many adolescents. Blood may be equated with death due to fatal shootings observed on television news programs and shows, as well as in the movies, death due to injuries or automobile fatalities where blood is predominantly evident, or death due to school shootings that now appear to be prevalent in our society. This may be especially frightening if the adolescent female were to begin menstruating while at school and then sees the blood coupled with death of a classmate or peer. Blood also may evoke concerns about external forces over which the adolescent has no control and which may determine his or her destiny, such as happened when the planes crashed into the Twin Towers and the Pentagon, and suddenly our country was at war. This can be particularly anxiety provoking if the adolescent has been planning to serve his or her country in a military capacity.

The male adolescent may have the experience of the once familiar becoming unpredictable. He begins to experience nocturnal emissions and may also experience unexpected penile erections. When walking down the hall at school, the male adolescent may see an attractive female and suddenly begin to feel that his trousers no longer fit, but rather have suddenly become very tight. Embarrassment and fear may result for the unprepared adolescent, even for the adolescent who has been forewarned of what bodily changes to expect. The unpredictability of the body that was once familiar, but now "out of control," evokes feelings of disintegration, an existential crisis, and death imagery. The body, or house that had been, is no more; resulting in a major turning point for the life of the individual.

While the internal world is changing, the adolescent also perceives external world as changing. Society, via usual and customary expectations for social roles that are consistent with those expected of adults, demands that adolescents begin making plans for the future.

Role expectations include, but are not necessarily limited to, obtaining a job, deciding on an occupation or career, formulating an individual identity apart from that of the parental figures, becoming independent, and moving toward intimacy, marriage, and progeny. The increased responsibility is a role expectation the adolescent must address. The past life of childhood with few responsibilities is "dead" forever.

Simultaneous with the loss of the past is a press for developing an individual identity separate from the parental identity that was manifest in the past; that of mother's and/or father's daughter or son. Now there is the present press for connection with another within the cohort group. This present press for connection is for one of a different form of intimacy which involves erotic components not experienced previously in the adolescent's past. This loss of typical past patterns or styles of relating to significant others in the adolescent's life evokes images of death. The past attachment to parental figures and/or peers is appreciably different and the difference appears to have its origins in the hormonal changes in connection with the cognitive, emotional, behavioral, and spiritual aspects of the being. Concurrently, chronological age peers who were previously regarded as good friends now seem to have changed as well. They now appear to be highly competitive, critical, and even derisive at times. This results in loneliness for the adolescent and feelings of being apart from others within the adolescent's cohort group.

For the first time in the life of the adolescent, he or she becomes painfully aware of the void and has experiential corroboration that nothing is constant, or that constancy does not exist. The adolescent becomes aware that the past life is over, that it is dead, and that bodily demise can happen to him or her personally. Awareness of personal mortality evokes concerns about the future, which is inconceivable to the adolescent, and results in an existential crisis.

Previously the adolescent has perceived his or her parents as omnipotent and omniscient. These perceptions of parental figures are now shaken. Shattered suppositions leading to an existential crisis include (a) belonging to and viewing his or her parents as "higher beings," (b) the current press to individuate from parents, (c) the simultaneous need to be linked to someone and to a greater power, and (d) the previous experience of death of life as if it did not apply to him or her.

An existential crisis has been defined as a time when several salient factors are the focus of the existence of the individual (Frankl, 1963, Steele & Colrain, 1990, Yalom, 1980). These include (a) perceived prospective threatened death, (b) perceived actual or prospective meaninglessness, (c) an experience of isolation or lack of linking with another human being, and (d) intent, responsibility, culpability, independence, and freedom. For the adolescent, accompanying his or her rapid, immutable bodily changes that he or she is unable to prevent or obstruct, is the feeling of annihilation; that is, the death of the past existence, never to be relived in reality. The bodily changes also result in a crisis of meaninglessness, as the adolescent is little able to categorize the bodily changes as he or she has done in the past, but rather, must now find a new way of coping with this metamorphosis.

The adolescent has previously gained meaning from his or her relationships with parents and peers. The changes in relationships with parents and with the peer group result in a loss of previous identity, and the press for individual identity for which no meaning has as yet been established. The result is a sense of isolation from and a perceived lack of linking with those individuals instrumental in supplying meaning previously, but who are now perceived as "different" in a substantive way.

The issues of intent, responsibility, culpability, independence, and freedom appear insurmountable to the adolescent, who now recognizes that he or she must forge an individual identity in some responsible fashion. He or she feels helpless to do so without links to others who have given life meaning and identity in the past years and from whom the adolescent is now pressed to individuate. Life decisions loom before the adolescent in an ominous fashion with the perception that one must formulate his or her entire life span in a very short duration of time. This time pressure results in exacerbating the stress, which in turn affects physiology and behavior, causing the existential crisis to be perceived as more severe and thus creating a vicious cycle. This existential crisis faced by the adolescent results in the intense search for new ways to affirm life: (a) to search for meaning, (b) to search for linkage with others, (c) to search for linkage with someone greater than one's self such as a Supreme Being or God, (d) to develop a sense of relationship with meaningful philosophies, and (e) to find a way to bring about purpose for being. Some adolescents may search for new ways to affirm life in a trial and error fashion, resulting in a cycle of disappointment and frustration.

According to Morin and Welsh (1996), spirituality is the most important factor to consider when faced with the finality of life. As a consequence of the existential crisis, the adolescent struggles to seek life and avoid deadness; to experience integrity rather than disintegration; to have substance and meaning in life rather than superficiality, shallowness, or absurdity; to be responsible instead of unreliable, independent rather than dependent; to experience freedom rather than bondage, and linkage rather than separateness. As this struggle transpires, the adolescent begins to process his or her spirituality in various ways with many choices, some of which he or she is aware, and others that are outside of the awareness.

The word "spirit" has it's origins in the Latin word "spiritus," which is defined as "the breath of life; the animating of vital principle giving life to physical organisms" (Grove et al., 1981, p. 2198). It is the ethereal, rather than the material, aspect of the person that lives on after death, and affects the sense of connection with self, others, God, and/or the greater forces of the universe. The spirit is the process that effects integration of all human aspects, including cognition, emotion, behavior, integrity, creativity, motivation, desire, personality, mind, body, and ego functions. It is the aspect that instills hope for current life and the life hereafter. The spirit is the aspect of the human being that gives meaning to life in all of life's various spheres and provides a sense of totality, serenity, and acceptance of self and others. It is the power that enables one to open one's self to love, caring, and emotional maturity that enriches life. The spirit is the life force that enables one to become vulnerable to disillusionment and loss, enables energetic creativity, and the development of goals that are meaningful. It is the ethereal energy that promotes the psyche toward goals that result in linkage to rather than separation from others; goals that result in a sense of integrity for the individual rather than a sense of disintegration.

Spirituality is that aspect of the adolescent that moves the adolescent toward integrating various aspects of his or her self and life in the struggle to work through his or her existential crisis. Spirituality provides the impetus to work through the adolescent's sudden awareness that the past life is gone forever and can only live on in the adolescent's memory. As the struggle to move on to a new form of life transpires, the adolescent begins to process his or her spirituality in various ways, with many choices, some of which he or she is aware, and others that are outside of the awareness. A choice of some adolescents that is outside of the awareness is to disavow the need for attachments. Disavowal can prevent exposure to the possibility of losing someone about whom one cares deeply, and who gives meaning to life through caring, commitment, and companionship. If the adolescent employs disavowal, the grief process is thwarted and mourning cannot occur. Without the normal mourning process transpiring, the adolescent is at risk for clinically significant bouts of future depression, anxiety, and, in severe cases, psychotic features and suicidal behaviors.

Many adolescents manage the existential anxiety that this life stage evokes through conformity with the group and adopting the group spirit. This protects the adolescent from the need to address internal fears, doubts, and anxieties regarding meaninglessness and provides the feeling of being linked to a group Gestalt, with the whole greater than the sum of its parts; thereby filling the need to experience linkage with a Supreme Being or God. When conforming to the values of a cohort group of adolescents, one has many choices of various groups who embrace various ideals, philosophies, social milieus, and causes. Popular groups during adolescence include the Crypts, Bloods, Jocks, Nerds, Preps, Stoners, Dragons, and Wasps as well as many others that are named descriptively according to the purpose or meaning that they perceive themselves as embracing. Linkage with specific group members is indicated with tangible symbols of belonging with body markings. These are indelible marks or figures in the form of a brand or tattoo that is fixed on the body. It is a symbol of the group and is recognized only by the group members. As members of these groups, the group determines spirituality and values for the individual member and each member gains a feeling of linkage and safety with their friends within the specific peer sub-group.

Group cohesiveness (Yalom, 1985) results in an "in group" and "out group" phenomenon, with an appearance of global non-conformity, while conforming to the particular sub-groups' norms and values. This phenomenon alleviates the need for and peril of individuality while simultaneously appearing to be unique individuals to those who are not group members. The conformity is kept out of the awareness of the adolescent while the non-conforming aspect is emphasized to enhance the illusion of individuality and unique identity formation.

Another illusive method of appearing to have linkage to a greater power than the self, as well as commitment, responsibility, integrity, and purposeful meaning is through burying oneself in academic pursuits and thereby achieving greatness. Through this method, and utilization of this rationale, actual changes and commitments to others can be avoided while the adolescent can simultaneously seem to have meaningful fulfillment and connection with a supreme power source in a form of "secularized spirituality."

The fear of death that is evoked through the adolescent's realization that his or her former life is dead and their future life must necessarily be of a different form is also managed by some adolescents via death defying feats. Recreational pursuits may take the form of high-risk activities such as playing "chicken," drag racing, bungy jumping, parachuting, and other such activities that are designed to prove that the adolescent can conquer death. The employment of these types of activities exhilarate the spirit, provide the adolescent with a temporary increment in self-esteem, and offer a sense of linkage with a power greater than the self by "beating" the greater power through defying death thereby providing the adolescent with a sense of pseudo spirituality.

Other adolescents choose to refine the expression of the existential anxiety evoked by the struggle to accept the death of the former life as it was known and the formation of a new life through refining past urges that are still prominent, but are outside of the awareness. Thus, some adolescents become embroiled in the "spirit" of the hunt and are driven to "get that deer" during hunting season every year. Others feel the "spirit" of the chase and choose law enforcement. There are adolescents who utilize the "spirit" of the game or sports and become athletes, performing phenomenal athletic feats to sublimate the existential anxiety. Yet other adolescents will externalize their anxiety by refining the competitive drive and/or the urge to hurt others by turning to the medical helping professions. In this way, the adolescent is able to help others heal by hurting them and sublimate the underlying urge to hurt that is outside of the adolescent's awareness.

Living an austere life is the choice of many youths, as an expression of their spiritual quest. This choice was especially popular in the 1960s when thousands of youth migrated to Walden for spiritual fulfillment and joined communes and cults. The austere life required control and discipline whereby strong urges and desires for the materialistic were negated. By living in poverty, the adolescent gained a sense of meaning, a sense that life had purpose beyond that manifest via the parents' lifestyle, and simultaneously the adolescent could appear to be individuating from parental figures while linked to peers and to a higher ideal or Supreme Power. The austere life was also effective in minimizing risks for the adolescent, while providing an idealistic identity.

The search for spiritual identity is manifest in many ways throughout adolescence. Erik Erikson (1959) describes adolescence as a quest for identity versus role confusion. Erikson focuses on the adolescent's need to integrate all earlier identifications, the need to recapitulate the childhood crises, and integrate the end product of the recapitulation into the formation of a new identity. This new identity, according to Erikson, incorporates ethnic, cultural, sexual, and occupational or career identity formation (Erikson, 1968). However, Erikson does not discuss spiritual identity development.

Organized religion has incorporated the identity development stage of life into its programs and rituals for centuries using ceremonies such as baptism and confirmation during the early years of adolescence to assist youth in the development of a spiritual identity. For example, Baptist religions baptize youth during the commencement of the adolescent stage of development into the fellowship of believers. The liturgical religions employ confirmation rites and rituals to indicate the youth has now identified with the spiritual values and beliefs of the particular religious denomination and is considered an adult member of the fellowship. These rites and rituals are preceded by study that requires commitment of intent, time, energy, assumption of responsibility, and the promise of fulfillment of the void resulting from loss of previous identity. Identity as the child of earthly parents transfers to internalization of the concept that the individual is a child of God. In this way the adolescent experiences a new way to affirm life, to find meaning, to experience linkage with a Supreme Being or God, develops a sense of relationship with meaningful existential philosophies, and finds purpose for living.

This purpose for living is established by way of a spiritual identification that transcends those developed through forms of secular spirituality, cultural spirituality, or ethnic or racial spirituality. Although all types of spirituality development require intent on the part of the adolescent and have similarities in the rites and rituals, the purpose for continuing existence and meaning for life appear to be quite different. While all may be subsumed under "rites of passage" from adolescence to adulthood, some may lack continuity for the spiritual sphere that provides the individual with a sense of enduring linkage to significant others throughout the life span. Some forms of spirituality may lack the ability to convey a sense of security with regard to the meaning of death and the opportunity for rebirth that exists throughout the life span for those who embrace any particular organized religious belief system.

Consider the secular rites of passage that every American youth is culturally expected to achieve, such as graduation from high school or a driver's license. While many may not regard these as "rites of passage" into adulthood, each contains the elements required for a "rite of passage." The requirements for a driver's license include a period of initiation, learning, and then taking driver's proficiency examinations. These examinations include an objective, theoretical, and skills components that must be passed prior to attaining the license. Many adolescents "hate" driver's education classes and maintain the belief that they are able to drive without going through the ritual of learning and examination of achieved expertise. After attaining the license the adolescent practices "cruising" and struggles with other peers and adults for the "best" parking place.

The entrance into secondary education has the initiation requirement that lower classmates, who are essentially strangers to each other, go through some form of hazing from "upper classmates." The upper classmates "play tricks" on freshmen, tell horror stories of teachers and the tests they employ, break into cafeteria lines in front of lower classmates, release shaving cream into their lockers, tie almost invisible lines across their paths, and may even physically and/or sexually harass the lower classmates. A lower classmate who endures severe hazing is likely to find membership in the high school group even more appealing because he or she may perceive it as an indicator of his or her readiness to participate in the

81

peer group regardless of the cost to the individual. The adolescent may regard this "test" as a challenge that must be completed in order to participate in the group. Thus, group cohesion and school spirit start to develop in the individual. In the process, the individual's former identity is stripped away and he or she becomes part of a greater whole through the process of suppressing individuality and promoting group identity. This group identity is further reinforced as the adolescent engages in or attends school sports events, pep rallies, proms, and various other school activities. The individual invests four or more years of his or her life to subsume the education that was designed by society to meet the need for preparation for employment, for adulthood, and in the process, develops a secular spiritual identity.

However, while education does begin the occupational and/or career developmental process, for today's society post-secondary education is necessary for most careers or occupations. In addition, the "school spirit" developed through the four years of high school no longer results in the adolescent internalizing enduring meaning for his or her life, nor does it provide enduring spiritual meaning, linkage with others, or moral values for the individual. In our mobile society, enduring contacts with former friends or classmates is decreasing with resultant planned socialization taking place only during class reunions for many. This factor also results in the progressive depletion of school spirit and the linking of emotional and spiritual ties with former classmates. With the advent of ever increasing mobility, alumni no longer attend their former high school's sports activities, and as time passes, school spirit further weakens.

In the development of career identities, a viable option for some adolescents is post-secondary education, whereby college spirit replaces high school spirit. During college, again, initiates experience hazing from upper classmates and hear "war stories" of various professors' requirements for classes or their examinations. College spirit is again developed through participation in or attendance at sports events such as football games, basketball games, or other college activities. Clothing with the name of the team is the means of imparting visible identity with the group and school "fight" songs insure that school spirit is heightened when at sporting events.

Fraternities and sororities are popular college organizations that also employ rites of passage in the form of hazing or initiation rites that result in identifying the inductee into the organization. The spirit of the group along with its values and morals are subsumed by the inductee following an extended period of mentoring by individuals who have been members of the group for a longer duration of time. With these groups as well, the criteria for becoming a member of the group together with the initiation rites and the extended period of demonstrating the group's expected behaviors, makes the group more attractive to the member. It also insures that the values of the group are subsumed by the inductee and imparts meaning and sorority or fraternity spirit for the participating member.

These memberships and rituals form a bridge to the adult world and the expectations thereof. The fraternity or sorority spirit as well as the college spirit extend into the adult world with occupational opportunity preference extended to those who have attained a

82

diploma from a particular college or those who have specific fraternal alliances or former or current memberships.

Other adolescents who may not choose post-secondary education may utilize other means of symbolic separation from their parents, such as tattoos and/or body piercing. For these adolescents, mutilation of the body in the form of body piercing may be construed as a rite of passage into adulthood. Currently, there appears to be a strong trend toward various types of body piercing, such as navel, eyebrow, nose, nipple, tongue, and even foreskin or clitoris piercing in males and females respectively. This is overtly a symbolic separation from and resistance to parental authority. However, the adolescent who employs body piercing also achieves a secular, short-lived, pseudo-spirit of adulthood and peer group identity by employing this practice. Body piercing then affords the adolescent with a sense of connection to the peer group through the suffering of the pain involved in a self-effected initiation rite. It is popular for the adolescent who employs this means of identification with his or her peer group to have this done while other peers are an observing audience. This enables the adolescent to feel the "spirit" of the group while enduring the pain, much like those individuals undergoing other types of rites of passage and thereby experiencing cohesiveness through conflicting emotions of simultaneous pleasure and pain. Also, these tattoos and body piercing that are not immediately evident are frequently "shown off" to other group members at parties and get together. It is interesting that tattooing during the adolescent years is popularly referred to by the group as "sweet pain."

Group identity and assumption of the spiritual and moral values of a group is also accomplished by those adolescents who choose to abuse alcohol, street drugs, and who sniff hair spray, nail glue, or other mind altering substances. Many of these substances have properties similar to peyote, which was employed for sacramental use by the Native American Church members to absorb the power of the Great Spirit in whom their belief system was centered (Neuhaus, 1990). The ritual use of peyote produced a trance-like state and, in this state, special powers were transmitted from the Great Spirit to the individual who ingested the plant in which the Great Spirit had placed its divine power (Blum, 1984, Goode, 1972, James, 1990). Thus, some mind altering substances offer the promise of a spiritual nurture.

According to Hackerman and King (1998), "When drugs and using friends become the spiritual nutrient (for adolescents), family and religion are rejected; chemical use and being with the new friends involved in the drug culture become the new religion" (p. 92). Drugs that are self-administered via needle and syringe also include the pain aspect endemic to rites of passage. Adolescents using or ingesting mind-altering substances assume the spiritual and moral values of the drug culture and are separate from those individuals who were previously important influences in their lives. This involves assuming a life style of secretiveness and compromising previously held moral values to insure continued access to and obtaining of drugs to support the addiction. Even adolescents who previously were linked with mainstream religious spiritual beliefs and values demonstrate a decline in those values and alienation from the former spiritual refueling group in favor of the spiritual values of the drug culture group. In addition to decreasing loneliness via taking on the cultural aspects of the group using drugs, the drugs numb and/or deaden the pain of isolation, responsibility, and commitment required in adulthood.

Some religious orders also practiced rituals, but those rituals, while promoting spiritual maturity, did not involve the use of drugs as mind altering substances. Instead, fasting and an austere life was a popular way to make contact with the Supreme Being. Monastic orders employed dietary rules and abstinence from food, as well as maintaining a daily regimen of waking, dressing in robes, worshipping, working, eating, and sleeping at specified times (Ward, 1999). Some adolescents, too, choose fasting as a way of linking with a spirit of slenderness. In this way the spirit of the fashionable figure is achieved to comply with the adolescent's perception of society's stereotypic fashion model body image and thereby attribute a literal translation to asceticism's power to free and to effect a beautiful person.

In essence, during adolescence, the individual is searching for identity, belonging, self-validation, and meaning for his or her life. The religious individual may look for that personal revelation through a transcendent or peak religious experience (Maslow, 1976). The mystical experience is characterized by the individual's description of ineffability and the sudden, unforgettable knowledge that the mystery of the universe has been revealed. The person who experiences this peak mystical state is convinced that a mystical power has imparted knowledge of that mystery to the core of one's being or the soul of the person via a soundless means that, in and of itself, is a mystery to the receiver and that is indescribable. A light that is not a light is described; a light that is different from any light produced by humans, accompanied by a sense of timelessness. Kaplin and Sadock (1981) cite distinguishing features of the mystical experience as nonverbal thought content that "are probably manifestation of right brain functioning" (p. 234). However, the individuals who experience this phenomenon also manifest a change in their lives and find direction and meaning, both self and other validating insight, and a reason for living. They experience linkage to others, become aware that the world is a mountain of care, and that his or her life belongs to all suffering humans everywhere. The individual experiencing a mystical experience not only assumes a "spiritual identity," but also an occupational and societal identity and the courage to be who they are in whatever occupational and social role they encompass. They have internalized the nature and meaning of life and their role and identity in relationships.

In summary, the adolescent is in a stage of life that manifests rapid growth physiologically, psychologically, and spiritually. Spirituality in the adolescent may be manifest in myriad ways. With the continuing press for connection, the shattered suppositions of the adolescent's previous life as belonging to parents who have up to this time been viewed as perfect and as higher beings, the adolescent experiences an existential crisis. Simultaneously, the adolescent is searching for his or her identity. This search for identity includes all spheres of the adolescent's life; occupational, social, psychological, educational, developmental, and spiritual.

Within the spiritual sphere, adolescents may employ various ways to manage the existential anxiety that this life stage evokes. Some of these methods include conformity with the peer group, an intensive focus on academic pursuits, athletic feats, hunting, living an austere life, joining a commune, or through other secular spiritual means. The quest for spiritual identity may be temporarily fulfilled through secular rites of passage, such as high school, attaining a driver's license, or through body piercing. Other adolescents may fill their spiritual needs through organized religions, and partake in ceremonies of baptism and confirmation. Finally, some adolescents experience spiritual fulfillment via mystical peak experiences that impart meaning for life, provide connection to other persons, and linkage to a Greater Power than the self.

REFERENCES

Blum, K. (1984). *Handbook of abusable drugs.* New York: Gardner Press, Inc.
Erikson, E. H. (1959). Identity and the life cycle. *Psychological Issues,* Monograph 1. New York: International Universities Press.
Erikson, E. H. (1968). *Identity: Youth and crisis.* New York: Norton.
Frankl, V. E. (1963). *Man's search for meaning.* New York: Pocket Books.
Goode, E. (1972). *Drugs in American society.* New York: Alfred A. Knopf, Inc.
Gove, P. B., et al. (Eds.). (1981). *Webster's third new international dictionary of the English language unabridged.* Springfield, MA: Merriam-Webster, Inc.
Hackerman, A. E., & King, P. (1998). Adolescent spirituality: A foundation for recovery from drug dependency. *Alcoholism Treatment Quarterly, 16,* 89-99.
James, J. (1997). Peyote and mescaline: History and use of the "sacred cactus" (Online).Internet:http:/ehostvgw2.epnet.com/ehost1.asp?key=204.179.122. 141_8000_7061986&return=y&site=ehost
Kaplan, H. I., & Sadock, B. J. (1981). *Modern synopsis of comprehensive textbook of psychiatry.* (3rd. ed.). Baltimore: Williams & Wilkins Company.
Maslow, A. H. (1976) *Religions, values, and peak-experiences.* New York: Penguin Books.
Morin, S. M., & Welsh, L. A. (1996). Adolescents' perceptions and experiences of death and grieving. *Adolescence, 31,* 585-595.
Neuhaus, R. J. (1990). Church, state, and peyote. *National Review 42,* 40-44.
Steele, K., & Colrain, J. (1990). Abreactive work with sexual abuse survivors: Concepts and techniques. In M. Hunter (Ed.) *The sexually abused male: Application of treatment strategies* (pp. 1-51). Lexington, MA: Lexington Books.
Ward, B. (1999). Diet for a large soul. *Christian History, 18,* 24-26.
Yalom, I. D. (1980). *Existential Psychotherapy.* New York: Basic Books.
Yalom, I D. (1985). *The theory and practice of group psychotherapy.* New York: Basic Books.

6

SPIRITUALITY AND AGING

George D. Boone, Ph.D., M.S., M.R.E.
Private Practice
Kaufman, TX

INTRODUCTION

Spirituality is an important aspect of human experience that frequently goes unrecognized in today's society. It is, in my opinion, a vitally important aspect of existence that directly influences our mental health, as well as our relationships with others, and we ignore it at our own risk.

The traditional position has been that spirituality is a condition that stems from religious denominational practices. Clergy have considered this to be their domain, and have treated incursions by psychology as intrusive. An ongoing consensus by many clergymen is that psychology is no friend of the Church, that it is a rationalistic form of humanism bent on destroying one's faith in God and replacing it with faith in man. Interestingly, there are strong reasons for such negativism. A certain level of animosity has existed between psychology and the religious world for many years, the roots of which can be found largely within the history of psychology. Possibly the most influential figure in psychology to provide an opinion on religion was Sigmund Freud. Generally speaking Freud did not consider God to be real; on the contrary, he believed God was only a projection of childish beliefs regarding our parents. As children, we develop an understanding of our earthly father as one who protects us from harm and rewards us when we are good. When we become adults our insecurities and anxieties cause us to project the same childish characteristics on some non-existent entity we call "God," which we then use as a crutch in an attempt to navigate life. In his book *Civilization and Its Discontents* (1930), Freud mocks the commandment given by Jesus Christ to "...love thy neighbor as thyself." (Matthew 19:19), presenting it as an entirely unreasonable concept that not only does not deserve to be obeyed, it doesn't even deserve to be considered. He felt we should throw off such ideas (including the concept of God) as superstition and learn to depend upon ourselves. However, Freud also believed we are controlled by our base instincts and unconscious drives, and he never provided an adequate explanation of how we were supposed to reassert control over our own lives to become completely self-sufficient.

After Freud, many took the position that religious thoughts and beliefs were irrelevant at best and pathological at worst. Many prestigious psychologists from other schools of psychology (and contributors to psychological thought) agreed with Freud's attitude toward religion, if not his approach to psychology. Examples would include Edward O. Wilson and B.F. Skinner. The anti-religious attitude of central figures in psychology led to a trickle down effect, in which spiritual values and beliefs were not even considered worthy of investigation. Psychologists as a whole held a very negative view of religion, which inevitably led to ministers and churches reacting with negativism of their own, often denouncing psychology from the pulpit as being insensitive to the beliefs of parishioners and damaging to the mission of their respective churches.

However, it is important to realize that not all psychologists have held to this negative view of religion. For example Edward Tolman, a psychologist who made substantial contributions to learning psychology, was a Quaker whose stance for his religious beliefs probably cost him his first teaching position (Lefrancois, 1995). Rollo May, renown as an existential therapist, began his career by serving two years as a minister. His first two books, *The Art of Counseling* (1939) and *The Springs of Creative Living: A Study of Human Nature and God* (1940), were both religiously oriented. Swiss psychotherapist C.G. Jung, known and respected in both Europe and the United States as arguably the most brilliant scholar psychology ever produced, always emphasized the importance of spirituality in human life and experience. As a result of efforts by people like these, within the past 15 years or so there has been a resurgence of interest in the psychology of religion; research in this area has suggested that both psychology and religion have a great deal to learn from one another.

Some of the effects generated by spiritual practices have surprised psychologists, such as the findings of Myers and Diener (1995), whose review of literature on happiness found happy people tend to have a meaningful religious faith; or the longitudinal study of John Claussen (1993) which found that men and women in middle age who exhibit higher levels of competence are more likely to have a religious affiliation and involvement than those who were less competent; or yet again the discovery of Paloutzian (1996) that some styles of religious coping are associated with high levels of personal initiative and competence. This finding was significant because psychology's traditional position was that religious coping strategies were relatively ineffective.

Additional studies that have raised eyebrows in the world of psychology include the fact that religion has been found to be related to a sense of well-being, especially in women and people over the age of 75 (Koenig, Smiley, & Gonzales, 1988), that older adults' self-esteem was highest when they had strong religious commitment and lowest when they had little religious commitment (Krause, 1995), and that commitment to religion was linked with health and well-being in young, middle-aged and older African-American adults (Levin, Taylor, & Chatters, 1995). Many other examples could be given, but these should be sufficient to point out that psychologists are learning now what clergymen have contended all along, i.e. that religious experience has a healing aspect which promotes adjustment to difficult life events and improves one's satisfaction with life in general. While current work in the area does not argue that certain individuals with mental problems may exhibit symptoms of delusion, obsession or hallucination that may have a religious theme, it has certainly served to point out that religious beliefs and practices in and of themselves are not innately pathological.

THE MEANING OF SPIRITUALITY

The benefits of spirituality are frequently associated with middle-aged (or older) adults. Some of the potential reasons for these age effects will be addressed shortly. But first it is important to clarify what is meant when referring to spirituality in this chapter, because different people define the term in different ways. The concept of spirituality is often taken for granted and can be difficult to define. Some would opt for a simple definition, describing spirituality as being religious or as being a church member or believing in God. Although these may represent honest attempts at defining spirituality, they can be viewed as rather shallow. This chapter will be addressing spirituality with older adults, and it is important that each reader understands precisely what is being referred to in the usage of "spirituality." This chapter maintains that spirituality is a form of ego transcendence. In order to understand ego transcendence, one must understand the ego.

The ego is a part of personality responsible for seeing that the functions of everyday life are carried out, and provides us with the necessities of survival. It is the aspect of personality that provides for our physical needs by seeking out sources of income to pay for necessary food and shelter. It also provides for emotional and social needs by looking for a suitable mate, and when such a mate is found and a family ensues, it provides for the needs of the family. The ego is our sense of identity, the aspect of personality that tells us who we are. It generates a sense of self that has continuity across time. It is the "I" or "me" of personality. Given the complexity of personality as a whole, the ego represents only a small part, but ego itself rarely recognizes this fact. As the individual moves through life other aspects of personality are frequently ignored, while the ego gathers emphasis and importance. The ego has a tendency to get caught up in the mechanics of everyday life, and as a result the ego-centered individual loses sight of the things that are truly important, such as love, beauty, values, relationships, and understanding our place in the world. The ego is very materialistic, concerned with getting *things* and competing with others to obtain status symbols that reflect "my superiority", status symbols such as a better job, more money, a bigger house.

As we move from childhood into adolescence, and from adolescence into adulthood, we become increasingly focused on the ego, until eventually little else seems important. We "love" our children, but often only as ego-extensions. We invest so much of our own lives in raising them that we see them as extensions of ourselves. What is best for us is best for them (we think). In egoistic functioning, we don't love our children for who they are; rather we love them because they are an extension of that which we value most, namely ourselves. As we become increasingly focused on the ego, we move farther and farther away from the values and meanings that connect us with God. The materialism of the ego says *things* are important. Spirituality says *connectedness* is important, i.e. connectedness with God, with His world, and with other people. The two concepts are mutually exclusive. As long as we maintain egoistic functioning, we cannot experience true spirituality. It is only by transcending the ego that we begin to experience life as it was meant to be experienced. When we become less focused on the ego, it becomes easier for us to integrate the other disparate parts of our personality. We begin to develop as a whole individual, we are no longer bound by the materialism of the ego, we begin to *experience* the non-physical values and concepts that provide meaning and happiness, and as a natural consequence we move closer to God or our God-concept. Spirituality is not a dogmatic denominational code that we adopt, it is a state of being.

A JUNGIAN APPROACH TO SPIRITUALITY

Now that we have an idea of what is meant by spirituality, let us return to the question of why so many studies seem to associate significant effects of spirituality with those that are middle-aged or older. There are several possible answers to this question. A good beginning would start with the teachings of Carl Jung. Jung was raised in a family of nine ministers, one of which included his father, a pastor in the Swiss Reformed Church. As a child Jung frequently asked his father deep spiritual questions that he never received an answer to. Jung eventually realized his father had accepted the teachings of the church entirely on faith and was never truly touched by religious experience, therefore he had no foundation to work from. He could not answer his son's questions because he had no spiritual depth of his own. Unfortunately this distanced Jung from his father, but matters of spirituality remained important to him throughout his life, a fact that can be readily seen in his later work in analytic psychology.

Jung believed human development occurred in three stages, childhood (from birth to adolescence), young adulthood (from adolescence to about age 40) and middle age (from about age 40 to the later years of life). During early childhood, creative life force (which he called "libido") is spent in learning to walk, talk, and develop the necessary skills of survival. After the fifth year of life, the libido begins to gradually turn toward sexual activities and it eventually reaches its peak during adolescence. During young adulthood libidinal energy is directed toward learning a vocation, getting married, raising children and relating to community life. However, Jung believed the most important time of life for the individual was during middle age.

During this period the individual is transformed from an energetic, biologically oriented individual to one that is more philosophical and spiritual. At middle age the individual becomes concerned with the meaning of life. Prior to middle age the individual is concerned with the more mundane functions of life, such as establishing oneself in a profession, or making a marriage work, but during middle age the emphasis changes considerably.

> We are no longer concerned with how to remove the obstacles to a man's profession, or to his marriage, or to do anything that means a widening of his life, but are confronted with the task of finding a meaning that will enable him to continue living at all. (Jung, 1956, p. 74)

Because of the need to understand the meaning of life in middle age, religion becomes truly important to the individual for the first time. Jung believed that in middle age a person develops a spiritual need (which demands satisfaction) that is just as real and pressing as any physical need, like hunger or thirst.

How is this spiritual need to be fulfilled? Jung believed it would be accomplished through steady movement towards understanding, harmony and wisdom (i.e. psychological and spiritual growth) which he referred to as *progression*. Jung felt the pressing need to understand meaning in life provided the motive for such forward movement and libidinal energy provided the force to drive it. From time to time, life throws up barriers to our continued progression. When this happens we can regress from our environment back into our psyche (a Jungian term for *mind*) where we can draw on unconscious aspects of personality to help resolve difficulties and allow us to move forward again.

Jung believed the primary goal of life was to achieve self-actualization, which can be thought of as the harmonious integration of the many elements and forces of the psyche. On the surface this sounds simple, but it isn't. The mind is incredibly complex and a large portion of it is made up of unconscious processes that can only be accessed indirectly through great effort as the result of a personal quest for understanding. Jung emphasized that it is impossible to achieve perfect self-actualization. This would imply that the psyche is in perfect balance, in equilibrium where there is no longer any dynamic movement occurring in the mind; such a condition is only possible in death. However, it is possible to *approach* self-actualization, but only through a very long, complex journey of self-discovery.

An important part of self-actualization is tied to Jung's conceptualization of the unconscious. Unlike Freud, Jung believed all people possess two levels of unconscious processing, which he referred to as the *personal unconscious* and the *collective unconscious*.

The personal unconscious is unique to each individual consisting of material that was once forgotten or repressed, or it simply wasn't vivid enough to make a conscious impression at the time it was originally experienced. The personal unconscious contains clusters of emotionally loaded thoughts Jung called *complexes*. These complexes provide a theme that heavily influences behavior. The theme of each complex can be seen reoccurring over and over in the behaviors a person exhibits throughout life. Thus, a person with a mother complex spends large amounts of time involved in activities that will be directly or symbolically related to the idea of mother (Hergenhahn, 1994). Maintaining the complexes requires a huge expenditure of psychic energy, so much so that balanced psychological growth will probably be impossible, or at the very least inhibited. Jung felt it was necessary to discover the complexes in one's personal unconscious and deal with these so that progression toward self-actualization could take place.

The collective unconscious (i.e. the second aspect of the unconscious) was at once Jung's most brilliant and controversial contribution to psychology. The collective unconscious contains the total experiences all humans have had throughout their long history. It contains memory traces extending back untold millions of years to our earliest ancestors. The collective unconscious comes from common experiences all people share and as a result, unlike the *personal* unconscious (which is *different* for each person), the collective unconscious is the *same* for *all* people. Jung believed something is carried from generation to generation and this "something" is an emotional reaction to common human experiences. This emotional reaction can be thought of as a predisposition to respond to certain categories of human experience, categories that have been encountered by humans over and over across countless ages. These are not predispositions to specific response patterns, but a tendency to deal with universal experience in some way. Ancient humans responded to emotional experience in mythical terms, and this is the unit of expression contained within the collective unconscious. The predisposition to respond to certain types of experience becomes embodied in mythical figures or representations that Jung calls *archetypes*. Examples of archetypes would include the hero, the sun, the wise old man, the persona (the "mask" of self, the part of ourselves that we want others to see and respond to), and the shadow (a demonic figure of evil). Archetypes reveal themselves in dreams, fantasies, and symbols. Like the personal unconscious, the collective unconscious influences our behavior. However, influences from the collective unconscious are far more important than those from the personal unconscious because in a sense, the collective unconscious knows vastly more than any single human generation and under the right circumstances it has the capacity to apply that knowledge to the self-actualization process. Jung stated:

> The more we become conscious of ourselves, through self-knowledge, and act accordingly, the more the layer of personal unconscious that is superimposed on the collective unconscious will be diminished. In this way there arises a consciousness which is no longer imprisoned in the petty, oversensitive, personal world of ego, but participates freely in the wider world of objective interests. The complications...are no longer egoistic wish-conflicts, but difficulties that concern others as much as oneself...We can now see that the unconscious produces contents which are valid not only for the person concerned, but for others as well. In fact, for a great many people, and possibly for all. (Jung, 1966, p. 178)

Jung later continued:

> This process is, in fact, the spontaneous realization of the whole man...The more he is merely "I", the more he splits himself off from the collective man, of whom he is also a part, and may even find himself in opposition to him. But since everything living strives for wholeness, the   inevitable one-sidedness of our conscious life is continually being corrected and compensated by the universal human being in us, whose goal is the ultimate integration of consciousness and unconsciousness, or better, the assimilation of the ego to a wider personality. (p. 292)

To summarize the Jungian perspective, fulfilling spiritual needs are necessary for one to approximate self-actualization. However, because of the way human development takes place, a serious striving to achieve spiritual understanding does not begin until middle age. Once it begins, it generally continues as a life-long pursuit, an exciting journey of self-discovery and relationship that produces observable benefits in terms of improved mental health, increased happiness and satisfaction with life.

LIFE CRISES IN SPIRITUAL DEVELOPMENT

One weakness in Jung's system involves why one would embark on the journey toward self-actualization in the first place. Jung suggests this is a natural part of reaching middle age, that we are motivated at this particular time by a need to understand the meaning of life. But this is not a very satisfying answer. It is almost as though we ask "Why?" and Jung answers "Because!" It is commonly recognized that everyone who enters middle age will not necessarily follow this path. In fact, some devalue spiritual development throughout life and become increasingly hostile toward it as they age. This fact alone suggests that whatever motivates a person to begin their journey may not be experienced by everyone. Which brings us right back to the question "What in middle-age impels us toward self-actualization?"

One possible answer may be that a life crisis is necessary to jumpstart the process. This has been the assumption of many transpersonal psychologists for a number of years. In fact, a debate has existed for some time as to whether the event needs to be a single massive crisis or a series of smaller mini-crises. This debate is, as far as I know, an ongoing process. There is little doubt that religions worldwide recognize both. For example, the Rinzai school of Zen Buddhism claims that the path to satori (enlightenment, a state that can be roughly described as an elevation to a high level of spirituality) is achieved through a single intuitive crisis. Once satori is achieved, it is a permanent state that stays with a person throughout their life. The Soto school of Zen states that we go through life achieving glimpses of satori through numerous smaller intuitive crises. After we experience one of these mini-satoris, we tend to forget it over time, but if we continue to practice Zen meditation, we will re-experience a small version of satori at a later date. So for the Soto practitioner, satori becomes a process rather than a state, a process that is propelled from one small intuitive crisis point to the next throughout life.

Christianity recognizes these two modes as well. Fundamentalists emphasize the conversion experience, in which a person arrives at a major crisis point in their lives, they resolve the crisis by accepting Jesus Christ as savior, and they are immediately transformed by the experience into a member of God's family, ready to embark on a lifelong spiritual journey. Denominations that have a long history of tradition and ritual practice (such as the Roman Catholic Church) contend that people can be led to realize that they are spiritually deficient. They can be taught that there are spiritual aspects of human experience they are missing out on and this deficiency can be rectified through accepting the teachings of the church. Each step in the process constitutes a small crisis, because the person must engage in self-examination and reflection, deciding whether they will be able to internalize these teachings by faith. If they decide they *can*, they will embark on a spiritual journey of their own which will be maintained within the church through the use of ritual (confession, partaking of the Eucharist, etc.).

Neither situation results in the new convert emerging from their respective experiences at a level of spiritual development equivalent to a Mother Theresa or a Ghandi, but both provide the incentive to begin the long arduous journey toward spiritual fulfillment. In truth, there may be a number of situations that propel us toward self-actualization, but it certainly seems likely that for many people some form of crisis (or crises) will start the process.

A PERSONAL EXAMPLE OF JUNGIAN DEVELOPMENT

I am drawn to Jung's explanation of spiritual development because it parallels my own experience so closely. I was raised in a fundamentalist Christian family; the only son of a Southern Baptist minister. My father was a deeply religious man with extensive spiritual experience. As a child I was expected to become intimately involved in church affairs, but I was introverted and had little interest in such things. In fact, the church represented an intrusion into my life that I deeply resented. I was required to study the Bible extensively and this led to numerous questions that my father was able to answer to his own satisfaction, but not to mine. As I got older, I recognized many personal deficiencies in my own life that I tried unsuccessfully to correct. When all else failed I resorted to prayer, but it seemed that God was not interested in imposing these corrections on me either. God had made me the way I was, a faulty, flawed human being. I needed to change, but *I couldn't* do it. What's worse, God had the power to make these changes in me from without, but *He wouldn't* do it. Yet He expected me to be perfect. This led to a very deep resentment and anger toward God, and an abiding dissatisfaction and hatred toward myself. Over time, I recognized that my own deficits were bad enough, but the deficits of other people generally seemed to be many times worse than my own. This realization deepened my introversion to the point that my main goal

93

in life became getting away from people. When I was 20-years old I married and had a family. Some of life's frustrations were sublimated into providing for the welfare of my family, but over time the anger and resentment built until at about 40 years of age it became essentially intolerable. A crisis point had been reached.

Around this same time I began practicing Chinese Taoist meditation as an adjunct to martial arts training. I was using martial arts as a pressure valve to release pent up frustration and stress (probably not a very good idea, considering all of the hostility and anger I was feeling). As I got into the meditation practices, I began to have unusual emotional reactions and I began to experience archetypal images in dreams and waking "visions" (although at the time I had no idea what an archetype was). Visions are a normal side effect of certain eastern meditation practices. The Taoist masters recommended ignoring the visions as being irrelevant to the goal of attaining mastery of certain martial arts skills, but I was always a very curious person, and I was unable to follow their teaching in this regard. In all likelihood it is probably fortunate for me that I didn't follow their advice. I began to explore the meaning of these emotions and images I was experiencing and the implications they held for me personally. Through such exploration I came to a number of realizations that had totally escaped me in the past.

To begin with, I came to realize that my personal deficiencies were not the result of God making me this way. In most cases they were the result of my own efforts. I had essentially created the very chains of personal deficiency that I hated so profusely and then I proceeded to use them to bind myself. On top of everything else, I had harbored tremendous anger at God for not liberating me from these bonds when in fact the only one that could liberate me was the one that created the bonds in the first place, namely *me*.

As a result of my meditation practice, I began to balance the forces in my life that were previously out of balance. My personal problems began to change for the better. I began to live in the truest sense of the word and become the kind of person I had always wanted to be. The anger I had earlier held for God seemed childish and absurd, and this began to fade away. As self-imposed barriers dropped, a new relationship with God emerged with a renewed interest in spiritual development.

My attitude towards people changed as well. I began to wonder how many others were experiencing problems similar to my own, and came to the conclusion that probably a good many were. I couldn't change who I was (and honestly had little desire to) but my personal problems no longer threatened me and I discovered a great deal of compassion for the suffering of others. I resolved to help whenever I could, and the extreme schizoid symptomology began to dwindle away as well. I am currently nowhere near being self-actualized in the Jungian sense, but I am also nowhere near the same person I was when I began this journey.

One of the changes that resulted from my experience was a change in occupation from medical technologist to psychologist. You can imagine my surprise many years later when I discovered that Jung had described my journey toward self-discovery in near unbelievable detail.

FOWLER'S STAGE THEORY OF RELIGIOUS DEVELOPMENT

Another approach to understanding spirituality can be seen in a theory developed by James Fowler. Like Jung, Fowler believes spiritual development is motivated by the need to discover meaning in life. Also like Jung, Fowler believes the ultimate expression of such development can take place either within or outside of organized religion. Fowler has proposed six stages of development, related to the theories of Erikson, Piaget, and Kohlberg. John Santrock (1997) has described Fowler's stages as follows:

Stage 1. Intuitive-projective faith (early childhood). Once children learn to trust parents as caregivers, they create their own intuitive images of good and evil. At this age their cognitive worlds become very active. Boundaries between fantasy and reality are very tenuous; the child generally cannot discriminate between the two. Right and wrong are perceived in terms of consequences to the self. Anything that results in negative consequences to the self must be "wrong", and those that result in positive consequence must be "good".

Stage 2. Mythical-literal faith (middle and late childhood). Children at this stage begin to think more rationally and more concretely. They perceive the world as being more orderly than those at stage 1 and they tend to take religious stories at face value, interpreting them in very literal ways. God is conceptualized as a kind of parent figure who rewards us when we are good and punishes us when we are bad. Right is usually seen in this stage as fair exchange.

Stage 3. Synthetic-conventional faith (transition between late childhood and adolescence to early adolescence). At this stage, the emerging adolescent is developing formal operational thought, Piaget's highest stage of cognitive development. Fowler believes that this is the point at which the adolescent integrates everything they have learned about religion into a coherent belief system. Although stage 3 involves ideas that are much more abstract than found in the previous two stages, for the most part adolescents still conform to the religious beliefs of others and have not yet examined alternate religious ideologies. Behavior that involves a question of right and wrong is interpreted in terms of either the harm it may do to a relationship or what others might say. Fowler believes that most *adults* become locked into this early stage of religious development and never move on to higher stages.

Stage 4. Individuating-reflexive faith (transition between adolescence and adulthood to early adulthood). Assuming the young adult does not become locked into stage 3, stage 4 becomes the first point at which the individual becomes fully capable of taking responsibility for their own religious beliefs. As young adults move away from home, they recognize they are in control of their lives and they must select a life course that is right for them. As they exercise the responsibilities that go along with taking control of their own life, they begin to question the religious beliefs they were taught while growing up. They begin to explore alternate religious systems and beliefs, often as a result of exposure to new ideas in College. Fowler feels that formal operational thought (the ability to reason logically and think in abstractions) and intellectual challenges to one's ideologies while pursuing College or

University training are both responsible to some extent for this questioning stage they go through. This questioning process is seen as essential to the development of individuating-reflexive faith.

Stage 5. Conjunctive faith (middle adulthood). According to Fowler, very few adults ever achieve this stage of development. As the adult ages, he/she becomes increasingly aware of his/her own finiteness and limitations. This awareness makes them more cognizant of similar limitations in others. As a result of this awareness, the adult becomes more open to paradox and is more willing to consider opposing viewpoints and integrate these into their own religious experience.

Stage 6. Universalizing faith (middle to late adulthood). This is the highest stage of religious development involving transcending specific belief systems to achieve a sense of oneness with all beings and a commitment to breaking through barriers that are seen as divisive to others in the world. Events that are normally seen as being conflicted may no longer be perceived as paradoxes. Adults that achieve this stage of development are exceptionally rare. Examples of people that have achieved this stage of development would include Martin Luther King and Mother Theresa.

Developmental theories generally hold that normal human development occurs in readily recognizable phases throughout life. How rigidly the theorist holds to these phases (or stages) varies from writer to writer. The less rigid consider human development to be a continuum and the various stages described as a rough approximation of what an outside observer could expect when examining people at various points throughout life. The stages may or may not be experienced in order. Any given individual may experience some stages in reverse, may skip some stages, or may combine stages.

Others in the field believe human development is a discontinuous process. These are more rigid in their approach to understanding development contending that a person must work through each stage in order and that they cannot advance to the next stage without first maturing at the previous stage. Although Fowler's theory presents religious development as a series of discontinuous stages, it does not rule out a continuum interpretation. His theory is consistent with either approach.

At this point it is probably appropriate to point out that Fowler's theory is one of *religious* development rather than *spiritual* development. Religion and spirituality are *not* the same thing. They often go hand in hand, but this is not a preordained 'given' that is set in stone. Ultimately, religion is whatever one gives oneself to without reservation. The enthusiasm accompanying this giving is punctuated by zeal and devotion. This means that religion can include the belief and acceptance of an organized system describing the relationship between God and man, or it can be money and possessions (if this is what is ultimately most important in a person's life), or even atheism. Religion is vastly different than spirituality. It is possible for one to be religious without being spiritual; it is also possible for one to be spiritual without being religious. The Scribes and Pharisees of the New Testament are excellent examples of people who possessed religion without spirituality; they held to the *form* of religion without possessing any of the *substance*. At the opposite extreme, it is a common occurrence for people who have gone through near death experiences to leave organized religion behind while developing a very strong sense of spirituality. Although it is possible for one to possess either religion or spirituality without the other, in everyday life the two often go together. Presumably when the two coexist, each contributes to some extent to the development of the other. Assuming this to be the case, we can see how Fowler's theory impacts spirituality. Using his hierarchy, the higher levels of religious development (stages 5 and 6) are expected to occur in middle adulthood and beyond. Presumably, if true spirituality develops as a result of religious influence, then one would expect spirituality to occur in middle adulthood or later. However, it is possible that adults may become fixated at the third stage (corresponding to adolescence), and not experience any further development, religious or spiritual.

LeSHAN'S ONTOLOGICAL MODES OF REALITY

The last idea this chapter will focus on before putting all of the disparate pieces together is an ontological theory developed by Lawrence LeShan, a psychologist known for his interest and work in the fields of experimental psychology and parapsychology. LeShan wrote a little book titled *Alternate Realities* (1976) in which he produces a layman's synthesis of the research he has been involved with over many years. LeShan believes the world we live in is not made up of reality (singular) but of realities (plural) which we ourselves create as much as we discover. He states that we can conceivably shift from one mode of reality to another without even realizing it and that doing so creates no problems for us unless we inadvertently try to mix modes of reality or try to explain occurrences in one mode using the terminology of another. Reality is composed of certain aspects that we can change and certain other aspects that we cannot change.

LeShan believes there are several world models of reality available to us. These models are not maps of reality, but maps of one way of *organizing* reality. Each model requires that certain of its aspects be taken as axioms and certain other aspects (termed "unreal") be excluded. Because of this, all models are incomplete in the sense that none are all-inclusive of all phenomena and all human needs. The human way to deal with these concepts is to increase the number of world models we can perceive and react to allowing us to choose the concept of reality that fits our dominant needs at any given time, as long as we understand that *none* of these modes of reality are any closer to the *truth* than any other, but that each is merely a different way of perceiving and reacting to what *is*.[1]

LeShan has catalogued four modes of reality, but he admits that there may be more. The total number of "modes" that may exist is unclear. All modes are "lawful," that is, they

---

[1] Please note that LeShan is not suggesting here that truth does not exist. Rather, he is stating that with regard to the nature of reality, truth is much larger than our ability to perceive and comprehend it. The typical approach would be to assume that one of the described modes is truth, and those that remain are not. LeShan is suggesting that the truth may need all four modes for adequate understanding, and even then it is probably incomplete.

are governed by a set of limiting principles within which all occurrences must happen when reality is structured to conform to each separate mode. These laws are *not* the same across modes, but are unique and valid for each individual mode expressed.

Sensory mode. This is the mode of reality adapted to biological survival, with attention given to defining differences, boundaries, and relationships between things. It is the Sensory mode's description of reality that is generally described as "normal" and this is the mode that the population functions in 99% of the time. Its basic laws are as follows:

1. All valid information directly or indirectly comes from the senses.
2. All events happen in space and time.
3. All events have a cause.
4. Causes occur before events.
5. Events in the past can be remembered or (at least theoretically) their effects observed, but past events cannot be changed.
6. Events in the future can be (at least theoretically) changed.
7. Objects separate in space are separate objects; events separate in time are separate events.
8. All activity (movement) takes place through space and takes measurable time units to occur.
9. Action (movement or change of movement) takes place only when one entity is in direct contact with another.
10. All objects and events are composed of parts that can be (at least theoretically) dealt with separately.
11. When objects or events have similar parts, they can be placed in classes for a specific purpose, and the entire class can be thought of and dealt with as if it were one object or event.
12. This is the only valid way to regard reality. All other ways are illusion. (pp. 88-89)

It is apparent that the "Sensory" mode of reality takes in 17th century rationalism, upon which much of modern science is based.

Clairvoyant mode. This mode is adapted to direct experiencing of the oneness of all being and process, or the unity of the cosmos. This is the "oceanic experience" that psychological literature often alludes to when describing transpersonal phenomena. Here the universe is a vast flow-process in a unitary space-time continuum, and *is* that continuum. Its laws are as follows:

1. All objects and events are part of the fabric of the totality of being, and cannot be meaningful separated from it. The most important aspect of any object or event is that it is part of the total *one* and it is to be primarily considered under this aspect. Considering it under any other aspect is an error.

2. Boundaries, borders and edges do not exist. All things primarily are each other, since they are primarily one.
3. This lack of boundaries applies to time also. Division of time, including divisions into the past, present and future are illusory. Events do not "happen" or "occur", they "are".
4. Since no object can be considered itself without considering all of space-time, the concept of good and evil do not have meaning. Any application of them would automatically mean that the application applies to the total context of being, to everything. The universe cannot be categorized in this way (i.e. in terms of good and evil).
5. All forces or situations in space-time, or fields where the forces of activity are weak or strong, move with a dynamic harmony with each other. The very fact of the universe as a flow process means it moves with harmony.
6. One can only be fully in this mode when one has, if only for a moment, given up all wishes and desires for oneself (since a separate self does not exist) and for others (since they do not exist as separate either) and just allows oneself to *be*, and therefore to *be with* and to *be one with* the all of existence. To attain this mode, one must (at least momentarily) give up doing and accept being. Any awareness of doing or the wish to do disrupts this mode.
7. Valid information is not gained through the senses, but through a knowing of the oneness of the observer and the observed, spectator and spectacle. Once this complete oneness is fully accepted, there is nothing that can prevent the flow of information between a thing and itself.
8. The senses give a false picture of reality. They show separation of objects and events in space and time. The more completely we understand reality, the less it resembles the picture given by our senses.I. This is the only valid way to regard reality. All other ways are illusion. (pp. 92-93)

This model is consistent with many eastern religions and philosophical systems, including yoga (Hindu) and Zen Buddhism. LeShan contends that his research into areas of parapsychology suggest that certain phenomena, e.g. clairvoyant episodes, coincide with the person going into this reality mode. The information then comes to the subject, because being one with all, all knowledge is available to the subject.

Transpsychic mode. This mode is not well understood partly because it is often confused with the Clairvoyant mode, although the two are clearly different. In this mode, objects and events are seen as being separate, but flowing into a larger *one* with no clear boundary from it. LeShan uses an ocean wave as an allusion to this mode. The wave is clearly separate from the ocean as a whole, but it has no demarcation line. Each person is separate enough to be aware if his/her wishes (not true in the clairvoyant mode) and connected enough to be able to transmit these wishes to the universal totality (not true in the sensory mode). Its laws are as follows:

1. Each object, entity or event is a separate unity, but has no clear demarcation line with the organic integral unity that makes up reality.
2. There are tremendous forces in the cosmos that can sometimes be brought to bear on a local part or situation.
3. These can be brought to bear by an absolute single-mindedness of purpose on the part of one person (or part of the whole) toward the condition of another person.
4. Space is real and exists, but is totally unimportant. Parts of the whole are separated by space, but since they are also connected through being parts of the same *one*, space essentially does not matter.
5. Knowledge of other parts can come from two sources:
    a. From observation, as in the sensory mode.
    b. From being a part of the whole and so perceiving other parts through the whole.
6. From the viewpoint of the individual part, sentient individuals possess free will. From the viewpoint of the whole, all actions that the part will take are already decided and their events recorded.
7. Since whatever is done to one part affects the whole, an ethical principle is built into the universe. If one part moves another toward greater harmony with the whole, all of the whole benefits. Action between parts which disrupts harmony between one part and the whole affects all being; whatever action you take affects you personally, as well as affecting the whole.
8. Good and evil exist. Anything that moves a part toward its fullest integration with the whole is good. Anything which disrupts this integration is evil. In the long run, the terms *fullest development of a part* and *fulles integration with the whole* mean the same thing. In the short run, they may not.
9. This is the only valid way to regard reality. All other ways are illusion. (pp. 100-101)

This mode is the one primarily utilized by Christianity and Judaism, although some elements relate directly to Hinduism/Buddhism. The concept that whatever actions one takes with regard to another moves one along in some given direction became doctrines of karma and reincarnation within these latter systems. Intercessory prayer has meaning in this mode in both positive and negative senses (as blessing and cursing), but it requires a completely focused will on one thing to produce results. This requires extensive training and exceptionally strong motivation, but given these two, near miraculous events can occur.

Mythic mode. This particular mode is used in play, art and dreaming, and are particularly useful in creativity. Its laws are as follows:

1. There is no difference between perception and symbol, object and image, thing and name. Each "is" and can be used as if it is the other. "Objective" and "subjective" cannot be differentiated.
2. Anything can become identical with anything else or stand for anything else once the two have been connected. Once this connection has been made, time and space cannot break it, but an appropriate act of will, correctly expressed, can.
3. Each part of a thing is the equivalent of the whole. If you break up an object or an event, each of the parts equals the whole.
4. To control a part is to control the whole. To know the real name of something is to have real power over it. To manipulate the symbols of something is to manipulate the thing that the symbols stand for.
5. Space is determined by the connections between things and events. If they are connected (and therefore identical) space between them does not exist. If they are unconnected, space cannot connect them. This is irrelevant to sensory or geometric space.
6. Time is determined by the connection between events. If two events are the same event, time cannot separate them. If they are unconnected, time cannot connect them. This is irrelevant to clock or calendar time.
7. All events begin with a specific act of will. To explain an event is to show the connection to this act of will, which in itself needs no explanation and is inexplicable.
8. There is a substance that all people and things have to some varying degrees that determines their effectiveness, their ability to influence events. It can be gathered and redistributed by appropriate behavior. Its names include "mana", "wakenda", "manitou", "baraka" and "power". It is a sort of material energy that affects things and determines the course of events. It can be used for good or evil, but in itself is neither black nor white, but gray.
9. There is no such thing as accidental. Everything has meaning and is charged with meaning. Since part and whole are one, to understand the smallest part is to understand the whole, and vice versa.
10. Birth and death are a change from one form of existence to another. They are, as are sleep and wakefulness, two similar phases of the same being.
11. This is the only valid way to interpret reality. (pp. 104-105)

This mode has clear application to various states of consciousness found in shamanism and such religious systems as Santeria. LeShan points out that the ordering of reality using this mode predates Plato. He contends the Clairvoyant mode gives us the reason for living, Transpsychic mode provides the guidelines (in terms of ethical and moral structure), Sensory mode gives us the techniques, and the Mythic mode generates creativity for development as needed.

It is important to note that within each of these modes, things are possible that are not possible in the other three; this is true from both philosophical and physical standpoints. For example, free will is possible in Sensory and Mythic modes and possibly in the Transpsychic mode if one is operating from the "individual" point of view. However, it is totally irrational from the Clairvoyant standpoint and also from the Transpsychic if one is working from the position of "wholeness." Intercessory prayer is possible in the Transpsychic mode and maybe the Mythic mode, but it fails entirely in both Sensory and Clairvoyant modes. Certain elements of extra sensory perception should be physically possible while functioning from the Clairvoyant mode, from the Transpsychic mode (when working from the "wholistic" perspective), and perhaps to a limited extent from the Mythic mode, but ESP is both logically and physically impossible in the Transpsychic mode (when working from the "individual" perspective) and when functioning within the Sensory mode.

LeShan claims that each person's being is "nourished" by these various modes of reality. The sensory mode is perfectly adapted to biological survival, but it can never produce happiness. Happiness is the result of the Clairvoyant mode.[2] Each mode adds its own unique characteristics to human experience. Unless we are able to experience these all of these modes from time to time, either deliberately or inadvertently, we remain an incomplete person. He points out that humans often use many undesirable manipulations to gain access to other modes of being including the use of alcohol, drugs, aggression, etc., apparently in a desperate attempt to provide the mode-driven balance we need but are unable to provide if we cannot access the various modes at will.

The condensation of LeShan's book described above is woefully inadequate, but the scope of this paper is unfortunately such that additional time cannot be devoted to it. Too much space has probably already been used, but the information presented above represents a minimum for adequate understanding of reality from LeShan's point of view. The reader would do well to obtain a copy of his book and read it in its entirety.

The relationship between LeShan's thesis and spirituality should be fairly obvious. As a form of ego transcendence, spirituality would only be possible in two particular modes of reality, the Clairvoyant and Transpsychic. Both religion and spirituality would be completely irrational in the Sensory mode (something that rationalistic skeptics, who only seem to be able to function in the Sensory mode, have been hammering into our consciousness for years). Furthermore, the methods of entering into these various modes (which can also be thought of as altered states of consciousness), are generally the result of many years of practice, whether we are talking about practice of western religion, eastern religion, meditation systems, or whatever. Because the Sensory mode is absolutely vital for survival, we have become conditioned to using it in every day life. To break out of this mode and be able to shift to one of the others *at will* requires many years of training. It is extremely

---

[2] Presumably LeShan makes this claim because it is only within the Clairvoyant mode that one yields up all aspects of self. In the other three modes some element of self exists, making dissatisfaction at some level likely. In spite of this position, I would argue that happiness is also possible in the Transpsychic mode, but certainly not in the Sensory and probably not in the Mythic modes.

rare to find someone good at accomplishing this who is not also middle aged or older. These techniques require effort, devotion, and an expenditure of time that is not normally available to the younger generations.

Comparative religion and meditation also offer insights. Being raised Southern Baptist (although I am closer to Quaker now than Southern Baptist), but have studied numerous other Judiastic based religions, as well as many eastern religions, I have studied a number of meditation systems, including Christian, secular, Taoist, and Buddhist. From a purely experiential point of view, LeShan's ontological system rings true. Earlier it was mentioned that spirituality can be defined as a form of ego transcendence which implies *connection*, particularly connection with God or one's God concept. Long-term continuing religious practice may allow one to transcend their own ego and become acquainted with the Transpsychic mode, through which they may eventually achieve connection with the *whole* (an esoteric description of God). Or one might never become involved in religious practice at all, but still accomplish connection with the *whole* through the clairvoyant mode. There are probably a number of ways this can be accomplished, but the best known methods are found in numerous meditation systems. In either case, a connection is made with what can only be described as God (Interestingly, when in the Transpsychic mode you recognize that you are in touch with God. In the Clairvoyant mode you don't recognize this at the time you are experiencing it; it becomes apparent only after you emerge from the state.)

SUMMARY AND CONCLUDING THOUGHTS

As we work toward summarizing the material we have covered so far, we find that studies have shown older adults are more likely to have a strong religious faith and a higher level of spirituality than younger people. We have also seen that those who are more religious and/or spiritually minded seem to be better adjusted, happier and healthier than others who are not. This suggests the Church's mission to all people is a valid one that is likely to enrich the lives of their converts and the community at large as well. The ultimate expression of spirituality can be seen in the spiritual person's overt behavior, characterized by a sense of peace, satisfaction with the path in life one is forging for oneself, generalized happiness, an abiding sense of justice, love and compassion for others. It also includes a learned ability to trust God, oneself, and other people. When characteristics like these are generalized back to the personality, they benefit both the individual and nearly everyone the individual's life touches.

We have looked at a number of theories that shed some light on where spirituality comes from and why it is that the people most commonly associated with spirituality are middle aged or older. Jung's theory stated in essence that spirituality is the result of a quest for self-discovery and understanding that begins in middle age and continues throughout life as one moves toward self-actualization. Spirituality will not develop properly if the psyche harbors pathology, making self-understanding (and sometimes psychotherapy) vitally important. Fowler felt that religious practice (which he defines in a way that includes some

103

elements of spirituality) develops naturally with age and proper exposure to challenging environments. Although Fowler believed many adults would not advance beyond the stage normally encountered in adolescence, he felt the *potential* to advance occurred with increased age and experience. His advanced stages don't begin until middle age. The ontological approach of LeShan's is not a theory of religious development or spirituality per se. It is actually a way of understanding the nature of reality in the universe, but it quite obviously applies to both religion and spirituality. Using his explanation, spirituality is the result of reordering reality in a particular way, which changes not only the way we understand things, but also the way the universe functions. The physical universe is different in each of the various modes of reality. The possibility of our establishing a true connection with God is only possible when we are in either Transpsychic or Clairvoyant modes. Free accessibility to these modes is difficult at best, requiring extensive amounts of practice to overcome Sensory mode beliefs that have been enculturated and conditioned into us. It is unlikely that high levels of spirituality will be found in young people from this perspective either. The three perspectives suggest that spirituality develops as a result of the natural growth of personality free of significant pathology (Jung's), as the result of natural aging associated with judicious use of educational experience (Fowler's), or as a result of a re-ordered understanding of what the physical universe is and how it works (LeShan's).

None of the theories we have looked at have been shown to be "correct" to the exclusion of the others (that's why they are called *theories*). Although Fowler's theory does have merit, Jung's and LeShan's systems have some important advantages. Jung's system is attractive because his description of personality development so closely coincides with my own experience, because there is no doubt that mental development and pathology both affect one's personal growth as well as their spiritual development, and because Jung is the only major personality theorist that even allows for the existence of spirituality as a significant part of personality development. LeShan's explanation is also very attractive because it provides a very reasonable explanation for spiritual being in the physical world. It shows, for example, how claims made by rationalists, mystics, and religions can all be correct. It is inconceivable that God, spiritual experience, and all interactions between the two (including connections to the physical universe) could be nothing more than an epiphenomenon of neurological brain function. Traditionally, Church wisdom has stated God exists only as spirit, and has no direct connection to the physical world. We must accept him by faith. Rationalistic philosophy has stated that God simply doesn't exist, that the Church's call for acceptance by faith is simply a lame attempt to establish belief in a non-existent entity for control purposes. But God *is* real, and He *does* exist in the physical universe. LeShan's explanation of physical reality is the first *reasonable* explanation describing how God can exist and how people can interact with Him in the physical world (although this was undoubtedly not LeShan's original purpose). In addition, it fits personal experiences with both western and eastern meditation methods. Personal experience of thousands of people along with myself confirms both Clairvoyant and Transpsychic modes *do* exist. Interestingly, LeShan's ontological explanation in its entirety does not conflict with the assumptions of Jungian psychology. Although this chapter has not said much about the mythic mode, it meshes well with Jung's concept of the collective unconscious and archetypes.

The reader will notice this chapter has not separated spirituality into two camps (a la Paul Tillich) with one form relating to God or the aspect of God that resides in us and the other relating to the self (i.e. the dynamic nature of one's personal and communal life). In LeShan's clairvoyant mode, the two cannot be separated. They are one and the same. In the Transpsychic mode, they can be separated only when one is functioning as an individual (as opposed to merging with the *whole*). Since spirituality is by definition (given earlier in the chapter) an ego transcendent state, one is moving away from individualism, which means in the Transpsychic mode they are moving toward merging with the *whole* (or uniting with God) and once again specifying two separate forms of spirituality becomes impossible. One can make a separate distinction between the two as an intellectual exercise to facilitate understanding, but it is not possible to separate them experientially.

Although the greatest potential for advanced spiritual development exists at middle age and older, this is not always what happens. Some young people have exhibited a level of spiritual development "beyond their years." While this is relatively uncommon, it does happen. Also, not everyone in middle age and older will develop spiritually. As Fowler pointed out, many will accept the teachings of others as the final authority and their own personal development will go no further. Some may not accept *any* spiritual training or teaching at all. Although Jung did not believe anyone ever completely achieved self-actualization, psychologist Abraham Maslow disagreed, but in his work Maslow estimated that no more than 1% of the adult population was self-actualized (Hergenhahn, 1994). Although spirituality is not completely synonymous with self-actualization, the two do share many characteristics in common and Maslow's data should serve to indicate the rarity of strong spiritual development.

The greatest danger on the part of churchmen/women is the likelihood that another person's spiritual experience will be discounted or assumed to be false if it is not consistent with a particular denominational teaching. This assumption is particularly strong in young people that have never experienced anything other than the Sensory mode of reality. These only know the dogma they have been taught, and sometimes the very people they are trying to proselytize are the ones they should be learning from. All spiritual experiences are not equal, nor are those that may be different or unexpected necessarily invalid.

REFERENCES

Claussen, J. (1993). *American lives.* New York: Free Press.

Freud, S. (1961). Civilization and its discontents. In J. Strachey (Ed. & Trans.), *The standard edition of the complete psychological works of Sigmund Freud* (Vol. 21). London: Hogarth Press. (Original work published 1930).

Hergenhahn, B. (1994). *An introduction to theories of personality*. Englewood Cliffs, NJ: Prentice Hall.

Jung, C.G. (1956). *Two essays on analytical psychology*. New York: Meridan

Jung, C.G. (1966). Two essays on analytical psychology. In *The collected works of C.G. Jung* (Vol. 4). Princeton, NJ: Princeton University Press. (Original work published in 1913)

Koenig, H., Smiley, M., & Gonzales, J. (1988). *Religion, health and aging*. New York: Greenwood Press.

Krause, N. (1995). Religiosity and self-esteem among older adults. *Journal of Gerontology: Psychological Sciences, 50B*, P236-P246.

Lefrancois, G. (1995). *Theories of human learning: Kro's report* (third ed.). Pacific Grove, CA: Brooks/Cole.

LeShan, L. (1976). Alternate realities: *The search for the full human being*. New York: Ballentine.

Levin, J., Taylor, R., & Chatters, L. (1994). Religious effects on health status and life satisfaction among Black Americans. *Journal of Gerontology, 49*, S137-S145.

May, R. (1939). *The art of counseling: How to give and gain mental health*. Nashville: Abingdon-Cokesbury.

May, R. (1940). *The springs of creative living: A study of human nature and God*. New York: Abingdon-Cokesbury.

Myers, D., & Diener, E. (1995) Who is happy? *Psychological Science, 6,* 10-19.

Paloutzian, R. (1996). *Invitation to the psychology of religion* (second ed.). Needham Heights, MA: Allyn & Bacon.

Santrock, J. (1997). *Life-span development* (6th ed.). Chicago: Brown & Benchmark.

7

SPIRITUAL PERSPECTIVES ON SUICIDAL IMPULSES IN YOUNG ADULTS

David Tacey
La Trobe University,
Melbourne, Australia

We are led to a mystery that is embedded in all initiations and in every rite of passage: the end of a previous form of existence is felt as a real death.
– Thomas Moore (1992, p. 63)

INTRODUCTION

This chapter discusses the problem of suicidal impulses in young people within the context of spiritual life. I have been working on the topic of spirituality for a number of years (Tacey, 1995; 2000; 2004), and recently a community of psychiatrists asked me to address this topic in relation to the urgent and pressing issue of suicide prevention.

I have been developing a narrative in which suicide can be read in terms of a rite of passage which has taken a tragic turn. To understand my approach, we need to imagine a 'rite of passage' in psychological terms, as an aspect of ordinary human experience. The term is borrowed from anthropology and religious ritual, but it is used here in a psychodynamic sense, to refer to mental transitions during crucial periods of our lives.

I speak as an intellectual and a writer, but also as someone who has been affected by suicide in my family, friendship circle, and student population. Because of this personal connection with suicide, I feel compelled to find out more about it, even though I am not a medical specialist or a suicidologist. Tragedy motivates my quest, and I like to believe that understanding can make our experience more bearable. More than that, it is hoped that understanding may even have a role to play in suicide prevention.

The suicidal impulse is deep and non-rational. We find it hard to fathom, until we have been there ourselves and experienced the power of this particular impulse. Normal, everyday logic cannot get us far in solving the problem of suicide. I have a hunch or intuition that there is something in suicide that we are still not seeing. The spiritual dimension is largely hidden from our awareness, and is hard to access. However, contact with Aboriginal elders and healers in Australia convinced me that there is a spiritual element in this tragic problem.

CARE OF THE SOUL: RECOGNITION OF THE SECOND SELF

In our responses to suicidal youth, the community seems to recognize that the endangered young adult needs encouragement and support. There is something at work in the psyche that is self-destructive, and we try to counter that impulse by making the at-risk person feel better about him- or herself. We sense the problem of low self-esteem, and we try to help the person feel connected, loved, supported.

Often, no matter how hard we try, our efforts are in vain. Something deep and resistant to outside support is in control. The young person still feels alienated, despite our attempts at love, still feels disconnected, despite our attempts at support, and feels ghostly, despite our attempts to make things real. Something in the unconscious may be urging the person to relinquish or destroy his or her former existence.

How can we know this, and how can we gain access to it? If we reach into this inner life, and listen to its message, we might be able to liberate the sufferer of suicidal urges from the compulsion to suicide.

I want to suggest that we have two selves, and that having two selves is entirely normal; I am not talking about schizophrenia (Jung, 1961). One self governs our conscious realm, and the other our unconscious. The first could be called the ego, or the 'first self,' while the second is the soul, the 'second self.' The ego is not first in priority, only first in terms of our self-knowledge and experience. We come to know it first and refer to it as "I." The second self is unconscious in the beginning, and its appearance comes as a surprise, a shock, or even a traumatic disruption. It is clear that this thing we call the 'self' is complex, multi-dimensional, and contains hidden depths we can hardly imagine.

Our two selves have different points of view about who we are and where we are headed. The ego defines itself in terms of personal likes and dislikes, social adjustment and connectedness with the outside world. The ego feels fulfilled and satisfied when personal needs are being met, and when its standing in the world is being acknowledged.

The second self, however, operates on a different wavelength, and is based on different needs. This is the self that says, "man and woman does not live by bread alone." The

108

soul is concerned with a connectedness of a different kind. It wants to feel connected with Spirit, with the cosmos and the world. It is not nourished by social status or financial success, but only by meaning, value, and purpose. The soul requires meaning that comes from connection to transcendent values. The soul's origin, according to Greek philosophy and most world religions, is transcendent, and it only feels 'at home' in this world to the extent that it is connected with a transcendent source. Some people feel this longing more acutely than others, especially people of highly sensitive or artistic natures.

Needless to say, our society knows very little about the second self and generally does not acknowledge it. Society attempts to be rational about everything, and the second self is not rational; it derives from a different part of human nature (Jacobs, 2003). When a crisis occurs, the needs of the second self become exposed, and its neglect becomes a serious and urgent reality. It therefore becomes quite irrational for our so-called 'rational' society to ignore the reality of the soul.

It is especially important for health and psychological discourses to take the reality of the soul into account, otherwise the task of understanding human nature becomes impossible (Thoresen, 1998; Swinton, 2001; Orchard, 2001). In recent years, the recognition of the spiritual element in human character and development has been strongly emphasized, giving rise to a series of works which point to a fundamental shift in our self-perception (Crick, 1994; Roach, 1997; Rumbold, 2002; Hay & Nye, 1998).

LOSS OF SOUL IN THE MODERN WORLD

The unattended soul is recognizable in terms of its terrible symptoms: there may be a deep, crippling inner emptiness that prevents life from going on in the normal way. This hollowness, which indicates that something crucial is missing, may express itself as despair, chronic anxiety, deep uncertainty, various kinds of addictions, or suicidal feelings. When we look within and see our spiritual poverty, we can be shaken to the core and made to feel worthless. This poverty can assail us, no matter how well adjusted we seem on the surface, and despite the existence of a caring, concerned family, school community, or friendship network.

What we urgently need in society is more emotional literacy; more concern about nurturing the second self. We educate the mind and the intellect, and we do this relatively well, but we leave a lot out. We generally do not educate the heart or the emotions. Where in our society can the soul go to school? The soul or second self has been traditionally the province of the religions. In our increasingly secular society, the authority of religion has been reduced. This means that the second self is no longer bolstered or supported by tradition in the way that it used to be. Without a religious language to access the soul, we are unable to get a handle on this problem most of the time. For the soul is invisible, and is only made visible in symbol, ritual, myth, and religion. It requires courage to treat something invisible as real, and our society does not yet possess this courage.

The job of religion, in a therapeutic sense, is to keep the second self alive, to 'save' our souls from atrophy, repression, or loss. One problem with Western religion is that it has not been alert to the complexity of the inner life. Interiority has been abandoned, and religion has emphasized 'belief' as the path to salvation. But interiority has to be recovered in the West; this is an urgent problem that we face. Young people often turn to indigenous religions, or to Buddhism, to find out more about the soul than is available in our Western traditions. Parents and teachers should be supporting them in this quest, since knowledge of the soul is now a life or death issue.

'Loss of soul' can undermine our life in an instant. It can cause us to be disturbed, depressed, and confused. When soul is lost, the sense of meaning and purpose goes out of life, as if the life-blood had drained from its face. If the soul is unattended, and yet everything else is going fine, our lives can shrivel up and disappear like withered fruit on the vine. One of the core symptoms of this withering is depression, which afflicts us today like an epidemic. Numerous other symptoms, such as anxiety, low self-esteem, fatigue, and suicidal ideation can be read as expressions of the diminished vitality of the soul, although mostly they are read through theories of social behaviour and the bio-medical model. We are 'dis-eased' at the level of meaning, and most of our theories are unable to access this level, because they do not take the spiritual dimension into account. Spirit is seen as too abstract for science to be bothered with, and yet this is an illusion: nothing is more concrete than a reality that bestows purpose and value to life.

Society believes it can get along without spirit, but it cannot. Very soon there will have to be new reckoning, a new kind of enlightenment. We can't keep denying these facts. We will be driven to a new recognition by widespread mental illness and psychological imbalance. This is the dreadful paradox that besets our society: just when things seem to be getting better, easier and more controlled, we are beset by mental health problems. As life becomes simpler, more efficient, it also becomes unjust and more traumatic.

This is the cost of our loss of soul: in normal conditions the soul lifts us beyond the human into elevated heights, but in abnormal conditions, when soul is absent, our experience is debased, so that the quality of life become subhuman, dangerous, and raw. Civilization could be driven to the wall by this problem: the soul needs to be recognized, else we fall into despair. Going back to the Old Testament, we do well to recall the warning of the prophet: "Where there is no vision, the people perish" (Proverbs 29: 18).

It is clear that people are perishing for no apparent reason. The modern sickness of alienation and despair is invisible, and almost impossible to reach with the logic of the left-brain.

SELF-ESTEEM: WHO OR WHAT GIVES VALUE TO THE PERSON?

Today we are bedeviled by the problem of low self-esteem. This is because it is the soul, or the second self, that supplies our sense of deep worth. A great many people are talking about the problem of self-esteem, and there are many secular attempts to resolve it.

But it is hard for secular approaches to deal with this issue, because there is a mysterious dimension to self-esteem. Something other than the ego or society gives us our sense of being worthy.

I have been helped in my thinking about this by Aboriginal culture. I once asked an Aboriginal leader why so many youth – Aboriginal and non-Aboriginal – are harming themselves, sniffing glue or petrol, or attempting suicide. His response was simple and direct, "They don't know who they are" (personal communication, June 2003). He seemed reluctant to say much more, as he was thinking about sacred matters, and the sacred is protected by secrecy. When I enquired further, he did say that the 'natural' self is unable to understand its true identity. The task of culture, he said, is to tell the person who he or she really is. When they know who they are, they no longer want to harm themselves, for they have received, as a gift from life, their true dignity and worth.

We can learn an enormous amount from indigenous cultures, even though we cannot imitate these cultures or appropriate their rituals as sometimes happens in the New Age activities (Tacey 2001).

SPIRIT IN ANCIENT INITIATIONS AND RITES OF PASSAGE

I grew up in the deserts of central Australia and was able to experience, albeit at a distance due to racial barriers, the powerful spiritual world of indigenous people. This is a primal world in which spirit is felt to be close at hand and powerfully real. But it was also a world in which spiritual transformation was never sentimentalized. The *otherness* of the divine remains, for these people, a primal otherness which is never finally humanized or made familiar. The spirit is a taskmaster, not a masseur of our ego or a force that makes us feel comfortable.

In archaic societies, before the experience of spirit had been humanized and rendered relatively 'safe' or harmless by the rituals of the world religions, there was a sense that contact with the spirit was arduous and difficult, involving a complete upheaval of normal life. I think we are gradually moving back to this ancient milieu today, now that many of us are forfeiting the safety and containment of the world religions. Contact with the spirit is problematic at all times, and most difficult of all when it is not controlled by religious tradition.

The movement into the life of the spirit is ritualized in the form of the tribal initiations. There were many kinds of initiations, but they conceived of life as a series of rites of passage from a natural to a higher or spiritual state. The encounter with spirit was often precipitated by personal difficulty, disorientation, trauma, or rupture. The tribal societies held no illusion that the spirit was a friend or helper, but understood that spirit belonged to a different world, even as it attempted to reach into and transform this one.

In his classic work, *The Sacred and the Profane,* Mircea Eliade (1957) shows that in ancient societies the movement from the natural to the spiritual was conceived as a 'violation' of the natural man or woman: "In archaic societies, one does not become a complete man until one has passed beyond, and in some sense abolished, 'natural' humanity." (p. 187). The archaic initiations are always ordeals and trials, involving scarring, mutilations, and great physical and mental difficulty. In symbolic as well as physical terms, the natural state is cut across or impeded, to make way for a different kind of reality, which cuts across the given condition.

I speak of 'cutting across' quite deliberately, to highlight the image of *cutting* in philosophical and literal (scarification) contexts. The movement into maturity is to some extent an *opus contra naturam*, a work against the natural state, and even a violation of it. It is regarded as 'natural' to want to 'stay the same' and resist transformation. In tribal societies, youth often reluctantly set foot upon the initiation fields, as they do not welcome the ordeals that are to follow (Van Gennep, 1908). They have heard how difficult the ordeals are, and rumors abound, often intensified by the secrecy that surrounds the sacred rites. Despite human squeamishness, however, tradition dictates that such ordeals are to be endured.

Central to this ancient thinking is the idea that we are not complete beings at the time of birth. We need to be 'born again,' to grow into a different sense of ourselves and to gain intimacy with our creator:

> Initiation rites express a particular conception of human existence: when brought to birth, man is not yet completed; he must be born a second time, spiritually; he becomes complete man by passing from an imperfect, embryonic state to a perfect, adult state. In a word, it may be said that human existence attains completion through a series of 'passage rites', in short, by successive initiations. (Eliade, 1957, p. 181)

> The man of the archaic societies does not consider himself 'finished' as he finds himself 'given' on the natural level of existence. To become a man in the proper sense he must die to this first natural life and be reborn to a higher life, which is at once religious and cultural. (Eliade, 1957, p. 187)

In the primal experience of early man, the word 'natural' seems to have two meanings. It is 'natural' to be egocentric and contracted, blind or asleep to the life of the spirit. And yet it is 'natural' to be woken up from this sleep, and stirred to new life in a way that demands reorientation. Spirit is seen as a part of nature, but it is a part that is deep, profound, and often hidden. It is natural to hide from spirit and it is natural that spirit should seek us out.

In his writings on these matters, however, Eliade uses a dualistic language. For him, the state of unconsciousness is natural, and the act of waking up from slumber is by implication 'unnatural' or *contra naturam*. I understand what he is saying in terms of my induction into the Christian West, but in terms of my exposure to indigenous Australians, I am not sure he is right. It is not apparent that early man made the same distinctions. While early man understood the conflict between spirit and matter, this was felt to exist in the *one* world. The danger of any Western attempt to describe indigenous religions is that we tend to see spirit as a force outside the natural order, rather than as a transforming energy within it.

112

Spirit is the aspect of nature that seeks transformation. There is no dualism if we understand nature as a self-overcoming unitary system.

THE METAPHOR OF DEATH

Nature desires life but it also asks life to become more conscious, more connected to the whole. Nature is prepared to put a stop to forms of life if they do not cooperate with this evolutionary process. Its credo appears to be: 'sacrifice for the larger design, or be sacrificed to growth denied.' In archaic systems of knowledge, the pattern of spiritual transformation always operates under the insignia of death: "In initiatory contexts *death* signifies passing beyond the profane, unsanctified condition, the condition of the 'natural man', who is without religious experience, who is blind to spirit" (Eliade, 1957, p. 191). Eliade says that "rituals illuminate the symbolism of initiatory death" (p. 189), and "death is the preliminary condition for any mystical regeneration" (p. 190). Initiation is a descent into the condition of death, followed by the hoped-for rebirth and regeneration:

> The novice dies to his infantile, profane, nonregenerate life to be reborn to a new, sanctified existence, he is also reborn to a mode of being that makes learning, *knowledge* possible. The newborn is not only one newborn or resuscitated; he is a man who *knows*, who has learned the mysteries, who has had revelations that are metaphysical in nature.
> During his training in the bush he learns the sacred secrets: the myths that tell of the gods and the origin of the world, the true names of the gods. (p. 188)

This is tough, difficult language, about difficult experiences. We might be tempted to enquire: surely we no longer need to go through these ordeals in today's civilized world? Surely we no longer have to pretend we are 'dead' in order to enjoy a fuller life? Surely we have outgrown the need for such painful initiations?

LIFE CRISES AND TRAUMAS REPLACE THE INITIATIONS

This is where our modern attitudes need some correction. There is more meaning and contemporary relevance in these initiations than we are able to grasp. We are no longer tribalized and no longer suffer the ordeals of the initiations. We read these events and stories as if we are delving into the ancient past, long dead and almost forgotten. But not quite. Eliade (1957) gives us the clue to our present situation, when he writes "In modern nonreligious societies initiation no longer exists as a religious act. But the *patterns* of initiation still survive, although markedly desacralized, in the modern world" (p. 188). The patterns of initiation survive in our lived experience. Society no longer conducts rites of passage for us, but we are forced to go through the sufferings of the soul that bear a remarkable resemblance to the rites of passage from earlier times. We no longer have painful initiations, but instead we have personal traumas, crises, and life-transitions. We no longer have initiatory deaths, but instead phases of depression, burnout, and self-doubt, when our lives appear completely unreal and empty. There are times when we are 'beside ourselves', desperate, suffering, ghostly, and alone. Society no longer initiates us into the mysteries, but the human soul goes through its age-old patterns of change and growth, and reaches for new stages of development.

Today we are burdened with a troublesome inner life, and what society fails to accept as its responsibility falls to the lot of the individual, who has to make of the situation whatever he or she can. Without supervised initiations, we still need to make the perilous transition from one state to another, from innocence to experience, from egocentricity to spiritual responsibility. The spirit still pushes us from one state to another, from inertia to expansion, from self-enclosure to openness. This is an innate, evolutionary process, and nothing can stand in its way, not even a secular, materialist society that has no conscious belief in the power of the sacred. These transitions cannot be reduced to a biological process, because we are being urged to transcend ourselves and embrace something more. It is biological and spiritual at the same time.

Our consciousness may be emptied of all content regarding the initiations, but there is an older, unconscious part of the mind that still thinks in these terms, that continues to imagine life in terms of death and rebirth. Something in us knows that we have to die, be displaced or interrupted, so that a greater life can emerge. The language of our dreams still speak the language of death and rebirth, and our emotions and desires continue to be influenced by this archaic or mythological thinking. We may no longer 'believe' in spirit, but we experience its demands and claims in similar ways to primal man.

Today, instead of being called to the initiation fields, we will suffer a crisis or a breakdown where we realize we can no longer continue in the old way. A previous form of existence has to be sacrificed, and we have to take stock, reassess, and move on. This may occur during adolescence, when we have to put the child in us away and take on a new life as an adult. Or it may be at midlife, when we realize that the old way of being in the world is no longer satisfying to the soul. At such times of transition, something in us has to die, so that something new can live.

We may dream about symbols of death and rebirth at these points, or we may have desires to die and be reborn. But without public symbols or ceremonies, we might not know how to go about this process. We might experience the *impulse* to terminate our previous existence, but not know how to carry it out. Without a symbolic language for the soul and its processes, we stand helpless before these impulses. In this situation, with desperate inner emotions, we might harm ourselves in some way, or entertain the idea of suicide as a way out of the impasse.

Without symbol or ceremony, we are helpless and vulnerable. The psyche impresses the idea of death-and-rebirth upon us, and we are at loss to know how to react. Our doctor might say we are suffering from suicidal ideation, and we should put such morbid thoughts out of our head and embrace the world. But a persistent desire will keep nagging away, demanding attention. 'You can't go on like this', it might say; 'you can't go on as before.'

Indigenous people listened to these impulses carefully, and responded appropriately. But we do not know how to negotiate the psycho-spiritual transitions of our lives. We are blind to the spirit, and mostly we have no markers, rites, or symbols. We have no language except, 'I am not feeling so good today,' or 'I am depressed and fatigued,' or 'I think I want to kill myself.' Needless to say, it was more noble and dignified to speak the language of ritual death and rebirth. It was healthier to mark our transitions by linking our inner lives to ceremony. It was healthier to mark our transitions communally, in society, and to share our suffering with elders, rather than suffer in isolation and in the quiet desperation of our private corner. Where is the advancement in how we live today?

SUICIDAL IDEATION AND INITIATORY PROCESS

The first of the initiatory ceremonies occurs during the teenage years. In Aboriginal cultures, these are referred to as 'men's business' and 'women's business.' There is a complete separation of the genders at initiation, a belief that older members of the same sex are best equipped to induct young people into the spirit (Stanner, 1989). Typically, the candidate is taken to the initiation fields, where a three- or five-day ordeal is constructed to carry the candidate to the condition of adulthood.

The timing of this initiation is significant for us, since it is the teenager or young adult in modern society who is often afflicted by self-harming behaviors or beset by suicidal urges. We say we have no way of understanding these tragic impulses that afflict large numbers of our youth, but indigenous cultures provide a window into a new way of looking at this problem. Certainly, the problem today is huge. According to epidemiologist Richard Eckersley (2004):

> A study of Australian university undergraduates…found that almost two-thirds of the students, with an average age of 22, admitted to some degree of suicidal ideation or behaviour – broadly defined – in the previous twelve months. 21 per cent revealed minimum ideation, saying they had felt that 'life just isn't worth living', or that 'life is so bad I feel like giving up'; another 19 per cent revealed high suicidal ideation, agreeing they had wished 'my life would end', or that they had been 'thinking of ways to kill myself'; a further 15 per cent showed suicide-related behaviour, saying they had 'told someone I want to kill myself', or had 'come close to taking my own life'; and 7 per cent said they had 'made attempts to kill myself'. Another study found 27 per cent of a sample of university students indicated suicidal ideation in the 'past few weeks'. (pp. 176-77)

Psychiatry generally interprets this problem in terms of students' self-punishing responses to the pressures of higher education. The menacing force driving them to suicide is said to be their perfectionism and performance anxiety (Hamilton & Schweitzer, 2000). But in my opinion, this response is too limited. The deeper force driving them is not environmental but internal, not rational but archetypal. That force is the desire to live authentic lives, not to be fake, phony, or feel worthless. Young adults cannot stand an inauthentic life. It is hoped that psychiatry will look beyond its current horizon and begin to address the larger existential issues.

In tribal societies, the young adult is encouraged to embark on an ordeal, or a trial of initiation. In this ordeal, which is supervised by the elders, the candidate is made to experience the 'death' of his or her former self through ritual process. From the symbolic enactment of death, he or she is expected to arise in a new form, as a fully initiated member of the adult community. The young person is no longer oriented around personal goals or needs, but rather around collective, tribal, transpersonal, and cosmic needs. This process is felt to be vital to the health and wellbeing of the soul. The tribal member breaks free of the ego-bound state and enters into relationship with a greater world of sacred values and visions (Thompson, 1982).

He is 'born again' to a larger world, and here the assumption is that the ordinary ego is not an end in itself, but a kind of transitional object. It is a vehicle to carry us to a larger life and worldview. We are not meant to remain as shrunken egos. The ordinary ego is not, in itself, large enough to carry or contain the soul, the whole of life. It must be shed like an animal skin, so we can put on the new body, which is why some indigenous cultures adorn themselves in the skins of sacred totemic animals at the time of the initiations. This is the sign that the profane life has ended, and that the sacred life has begun.

The contemporary education theorist Joseph Chilton Pearce (2002) understands the importance of the role of 'spirit' in the developmental life of the young adult. He argues that young people know, instinctively, that there is more to life than what society presents them:

> A poignant and passionate idealism arises in early puberty, followed by an equally passionate expectation in the mid-teens that 'something tremendous is supposed to happen' and finally by the teenager's boundless, exuberant belief in 'the hidden greatness within me'. A teenager often gestures toward his or her heart when speaking of these sensibilities, for the heart is involved in what should take place. (p. 53)

A transformation *should* take place, but often it does not. The young person can be overwhelmed by negativity if the change that needs to happen does not happen. Who or what am I? What is my place in the world? I need a big cause to believe in, but what cause is big enough to contain my idealism? Why do people say I am too big for my boots? Am I expecting too much from society? Is there something wrong with me? Why don't I fit in?

The self-questioning can go on endlessly, and there comes a time when a limit is reached. Idealism turns to despair, hope turns to cynicism, and the 'hidden greatness within me' collapses into turmoil and confusion. There is a *frustration of spiritual intent*. We are repressing a developmental process, and life won't stand for it.

A similar idea is found in the 'sayings of Jesus' in the Gnostic gospels. In the *Gospel of Thomas*, from 140 A.D., we read the following:

> If you bring forth that within yourselves,
> that which you have will save you.
> If you do not have that within yourselves,
> that which you do not have within you will kill you. (Saying 70; p.41)

This is a harsh and difficult truth, but the idea of something needing to be born within the self is as old as humanity. Ancient civilizations did not need psychology to tell them that the self is not a static thing but a dynamic process that has to give birth to forces beyond itself. The self is to act a midwife to a second self, and we cannot afford to block the second self or allow it to become stillborn.

HAZING AND TRIALS IN INDIGENOUS CULTURES

In tribal initiations, there are numerous methods used to enact the death of the first self. Hallucinogenic and mind-altering drugs are used to create an altered state of mind, and with it, the conviction that a change is taking place. This, of course, casts the problem of teenage drug addiction in a new light. There may be forces at work in the teenage use of drugs that our secular authorities know nothing about (Zoja, 1989). This is not to condone drug taking, but to suggest that dangerous habits in today's youth may be following ancient patterns, and we would do well to study this problem in a broader context.

Intoxicants have long been used in African and New Guinea initiations, and the mescaline-rich peyote is used in Mexican and American-Indian rituals. In some cultures, the initiate is led on a 'vision quest,' often accompanied by deprivations and trials. A common feature of initiation is to half-starve the initiate, or to frighten him or her with unearthly sounds, noises, and tribal dances. There is a 'rushing of forms,' sometimes referred to as 'hazing,' and often associated with totemic animals (Keen, 1994). Popular culture, rock videos, and film clips are fast, dizzying, and disorienting. Perhaps some of the fascination for these technical forms derives from a desire to collapse normal perception and turn the mind around.

In some Aboriginal rituals, the initiate is painted white and placed in a shallow grave, to signify the death of the self. Sometimes an eyetooth is knocked out, scars are made across the chest, and the ritual of circumcision is performed on boys, to signify the death of the natural man.

In this weakened state, the elders introduce the initiate to the sacred stories and mysteries of the community, and these are offered as a source of strength. Often the initiate is given a new name, to symbolize the emergence of a new identity, and he or she is re-introduced to the community as a different person.

These trials are painful, and the early Christian missionaries and anthropologists were often horrified by the rituals (Berndt, 1974). However, the transitions of life *are* painful, and it is better to ritualize the pain, and share it with the community, than to experience it in a solitary way. Organized rituals have the effect of containing pain, which otherwise might go on without closure. Today, without rituals, self-harming behaviors may go on indefinitely, and adolescence is lasting longer and starting earlier.

In tribal cultures, which could not afford the luxury of a long adolescence, with its rebelliousness, personal awkwardness and social alienation, the 'teenage' period was terminated by the decisive act of initiation. As an Aboriginal elder said to me, "For us, adolescence lasts 5 days – the time of the initiation. Before initiation he is a child, after initiation, he is an adult" (personal communication, June 2003). I should point out to the reader that in Aboriginal culture there is a strict protocol about gender and sacred knowledge. Since I am a male, I can only be spoken to in the context of male experience and men's business. If I show interest in the experience of females, Aboriginal elders will stop talking and see this as a violation of sacred knowledge and cultural taboo.

CUTTING PIERCING, TATTOOING

In many rituals, minor wounds or violations are inflicted upon the body. Young adults emerge from the initiation grounds with scarring across the chest, back, and body, with cuts and abrasions to the arms and legs, missing teeth, and circumcised genitals. According to Eliade (1957), such violations are outward signs that the human person, the mortal body, has been 'marked' by spirit and interrupted by another reality. We have been touched by eternity. The 'natural' is no longer innocent; the divine has scarred it.

This provides the archetypal background to a variety of modern practices found in youth culture. Many schools and colleges are reporting that teenagers are practicing self-mutilation. Young men and women are cutting themselves, using blades or knives to wound their limbs and bodies. Sometimes, hands and fingers are cut, and there is reported violation of the abdomen and thighs.

Less pathological, but within the same range of activities, are the popular habits of body piercing and tattooing. There is a desire to 'mark' the body, to announce that one has been 'touched' by something decisive. The body is no longer normal, no longer free of markings or imprints. The innocence of the body has been lost, and this has been sacrificed. Today we find rings, studs, and pins in nostrils, ears, tongues, eyebrows, navels and sundry other locations.

In his study of American youth culture and its 'irreverent' styles of spirituality, Tom Beaudoin (1998) writes:

> Like its related trend, tattooing, the permanent cut of body piercing is more than just teen folly. To pierce one's body is to leave a permanent mark of intense physical

118

experience, whether pleasurable or painful. The mark of indelible experience is…proof that something *marked me, something happened.* Contemporary youth are willing to have experience, to be profoundly marked, even cut, when religious institutions have not given them those opportunities. (pp. 77-78)

Beaudoin (1998) points out that safety pins are used in body piercings. 'A pin named *safety* – an artifact meant to avoid harming babies – becomes a social statement about harm and danger'. Young people sense that the world is not safe; we have not constructed the 'safe haven' that is supposed to protect us from the intrusions of the sacred. Something unsafe bears down on us, and it is not just the threat of external terrorism or violence; we are not protected from the incursions of the spirit. Contemporary fashions such as piercing and tattooing are acknowledging that something unnatural and unsafe makes its presence in our lives. We cannot remain innocent, but something else is at work, leaving its signature, its imprint, its cut on our bodies.

Beaudoin believes that contemporary youth perform these rituals consciously, as deliberate attempts at religious experience. My reading is that they are spontaneous acts of behavior. I am convinced that most teenagers are unaware of the religious significance of their actions. They just 'do' these things because they feel impelled to do them by an inner impulse. The fact that these ritualistic acts, such as cutting, binge drinking, and drug taking are pathological and harmful is itself the sign that they are unconscious. When religious acts are performed consciously they are never violent, demeaning, or pathological.

We need more than a response of disapproval or moral outrage to these practices. We can say that the cutting is bizarre and it should stop, or that the tattooing is in poor taste and it should stop. But youths are trying to mark the body, because there is an innate need to mark their passage from one state to another. A youth is driven to 'unnatural' acts because something 'unnatural' needs to happen in life. If this does not happen in the mind, the body is used as an outlet for unnatural activity. We might say that the less successful we are in changing the mind, the more likely we are to inflict pain on the body.

REBIRTH AND RENEWAL

Ritual death is followed by ritual rebirth. Here again the ancient cultures have the advantage over us, because it was made clear to the young person what they were being reborn to. The process of rebirth requires a cosmology or a sacred vision large enough to draw the inner spirit out of the person and to keep it held and stimulated. The cosmology acts like a magnet, drawing the second self out from its hiding place.

As this happens, personal isolation is overcome, because the spirit by definition links us with other people, other beings, and the world. When this occurs, healing takes place: the person stops harming himself and starts healing himself. Evolution has achieved its second birth, and anxiety and terror give way to equanimity and acceptance. Now the person knows who he or she is, and sees the vision that bestows meaning to all things, including his or her own suffering.

In tribal culture, it was the job of society to supply this vision for each individual. In our time, we have shrugged off the social religion as oppressive, and we say we want to find our own meaning. This gives us freedom of a kind, but it exposes us to dangers. We might not find a meaning which can draw out our spirit to begin the healing process. This requires trust, love, and surrender.

All along we had hoped for something tremendous to occur and, if we are unable to find it, rebirth cannot occur. Our ability to see truth and defend it becomes an existential requirement: our lives depend on it. It is hard to endure the death and suffering phase, but if we have hope in our hearts we can always look forward to what lies ahead. Hope is important psychologically and biologically; it enables us to endure difficulty with a positive attitude. Without a larger vision ahead of us, we are more likely to remain stuck in the death phase of our transformation.

At the climax of a ritual in central Australia, the elder moves forward to the initiate, and, showing him the sacred churinga, he says, "Here is your body, here is your second self" (Neumann, 1949, p. 289). There are parallels in all the world religions. Hinduism might refer to the second self as the Atman, which replaces the ego. Buddhism refers to the Buddha-self, which ousts the ego as the master of our fate. Or in Christianity, we have the witness of St Paul, who felt the sacred presence in his soul: "I live, yet not I but Christ lives within me" (Galatians 2: 20). Every sacred tradition has its own version of this transformation, which deposes the ego and gives honor to the highest value. When we live from that second self, we live properly.

The rites of passage are guarded with secrecy and taboo, because the process of transformation is central not only to the individual life, but to the community, whose spiritual existence is validated and revitalized by each new act of initiation (Keen, 1994). These rites can neither be trivialized nor made widely public or profaned, because so much is at stake, and the effectiveness of the rites is influenced by their mysterious or otherworldly character. The initiate must be made to feel a sense of awe and wonderment, a sense that he or she has been visited by an encounter with the numinous and transformed by a higher spiritual authority.

The world religions have systematized this sacred process which is found in its elemental form in tribal communities (Eliade, 1956). Christianity, Islam, Judaism, Hinduism, and Buddhism have their own codified and creedal understandings of this basic element of the spiritual life: the need to be born to a higher reality. In Christianity, these processes are expressed in baptism and confirmation, which are simultaneously inductions into the spiritual life and initiations into the community of the faithful. However, these potentially powerful and transformative rites have become so routine and automatic that the power of the spiritual transformation has seemingly been lost, or at least muted.

Among the Jews, we find the process of transformation expressed in the bar mitzvah or bat mitzvah, where the child symbolically dies, and in its place the adult self is born. This is a second birth, not of the flesh but of the spirit: the person matures in and through the spirit by learning the sacred texts, by internalizing the sacred law of the Torah, and by basing his or her new identity upon the spirit. The products of this second birth are maturity, a new sense of responsibility to others, respect for elders, and a faith in the reality of the sacred source that makes life possible. As with Christian rites, Jewish festivals can also be muted and disempowered by a routine or conventional awareness, and a merely mechanical repetition of events. It depends on the level of commitment of the family and community, and the passion and belief of the novice, as to whether these rites are effective or hollow.

Spiritual transformation cannot be guaranteed by the mechanical enactment of a ritual performance, which is why stealing ritual contents from one culture and handing them to another is ineffective. It is not the 'external' ritual that transforms the person, but his or her belief in the symbolic activity. Effectiveness must be seen as a combination of ritual action, community belief, and emotional conviction of the subject. Tribal communities cannot afford to have hollow rites, or to lose the intensity of their sacred ceremonies, because the livelihood and survival of the group depends upon the success of ritual in converting people from egotism to responsibility and community-mindedness.

WITHOUT WISDOM, THE PEOPLE PERISH

Today we live under enormous psychological pressure. Any culture without wisdom is living a lie, and eventually the lie is exposed. An Aboriginal man in Alice Springs once said to me, "You white fellows are a curious people, to us it looks like you are not initiated." He was saying that we still live, like infants, from the ego. The first self has not been broken, we have not given birth to the second.

But today Aboriginal society itself is racked by destruction. Since the trauma of European colonization, traditional culture and law has been undermined, and morbidity is prevalent in society, especially in young adults. In the Pitjantjatjara lands of the centre, I spoke with an *ngankari*, or spirit doctor, named Ilyatjari. Conversations with this remarkable man have already been recorded in the work of the American Jungian analyst Robert Bosnak (1996). I asked Ilyatjari about the high incidence of drug abuse among his people, and of the high rate of suicide. He said:

> There's too much concern about preventing suicide, and not enough about showing these boys how to die in ceremony. If we show them how to die, their living takes care of itself. (personal communication, June 1997)

He was suggesting that these young people might not be actually 'suicidal' at all. They are not unusual, pathological, aberrant, or wrong. They are simply in need of spiritual transformation in a time and place that does not understand such things. It is the culture or society that is aberrant or defective, because it fails to provide young people with the necessary rituals and ideas to allow the termination of the natural self and the emergence of a new personality.

In similar vein, Mircea Eliade (1957) writes, "In initiatory death...men die to something *that was not essential*; men die to the profane life" (p. 196). By this reckoning, it is not the individual who is mad or crazy, but society itself. Ilyatjari was saying that living outside sacred law is a dangerous state, and that the boys he was referring to were all detribalized and secularized. The key here is the spiritual responsibility of society for its own members: If we show them how to die in ceremony, that is, in symbol and in spirit, then their living will 'take care of itself.' It is an absence in society that brings us to moral insanity and self-mutilation, because the duty of care that was invested in our spiritual wellbeing has been abandoned by a 'modern' or 'enlightened' attitude. This was the voice of tradition casting judgment on the modern secular world.

A similar view was put to me by another Aboriginal lawman from the Kimberley region of the northwest country. David Mowaljarlai expressed his concern about the young men in the Kimberley who had succumbed to petrol or glue sniffing, known as 'chroming.' Mowaljarlai visited a hospital ward which was full of young men who had practiced chroming. He explained the situation this way, "All these boys, you see, lack ceremony. They haven't died in initiation. If you take away the sacred law, you take away their lives" (personal communication, November 1996). The Aboriginal men of high degree view the problem of self-destruction from the inside, not externally. They recognize that the human being is spiritual, and the spiritual core has needs, and if these are not attended to the results can be tragic. We need a spiritual goal, a pathway that can link us with truth. The only way to free the spirit is to think symbolically about the needs of the spirit. The way to stop us from killing ourselves is to teach people how to die in the spirit, so that we can be reborn in the spirit.

SYMBOLIC THINKING AS THE KEY TO REBIRTH

Jungian psychology uses a similar language to the spiritual discourse of Aboriginal culture. In his book *Suicide and the Soul*, James Hillman (1973) writes that when we are beset by suicidal ideation we have to ask a psychological question: what is it within me that wants to die? That question not only yields insight, but it also shifts something in the soul. The dark force is no longer against us, but it now works with us. Or rather, we are working with it to determine what change needs to occur.

In another work, Hillman (1976) makes a similar kind of statement:

> Everything the psyche presents is metaphorical. If you have images of suicide, there is some kind of movement toward the realm of death. It's an attempt to get to death in one way or another, or to leave some kind of thing that has been identified with as life, whether its body or world or family. (p. 146)

The psyche presents this urge as metaphorical, but it is not going to be experienced metaphorically by the person in great distress. That, of course, is the meaning of culture, or of 'ceremony,' as the Aboriginal view puts it. The purpose of culture is to provide metaphor and symbol for our inner urges, so that these urges do not have to be acted out. We are no longer at their mercy, because we have understood their meaning. There is a relevant saying from medieval alchemy: 'for he who has the symbol, the way is made easy.'

In the context of the need to think symbolically about spiritual death and rebirth, I am reminded of the encounter between Jesus and the rabbi Nicodemus, "I tell you the truth, no one can see the kingdom of God unless he is born again" (John 3: 3). Nicodemus asks: "How can a man be born when he is old? Surely he cannot enter a second time into his mother's womb to be born?" Jesus is astonished by this literal thinking, which leads Nicodemus to imagine that incest is the way to be reborn. Jesus repeats: "I tell you the truth, no one can enter the kingdom of God unless he is born of water and the Spirit. Flesh gives birth to flesh, but the Spirit gives birth to spirit." In other words, if we think in terms of the flesh, our thinking is literal, and we can only imagine rebirth as a return to the mother's womb. Symbolic thinking comes from the spirit, and this generates a new spiritual approach: hence "spirit gives birth to spirit."

Jesus admonishes Nicodemus for his literal cast of mind: "You should not be surprised at my saying, 'You must be born again.'" Jesus loses his patience: "What, are you Israel's teacher, and yet do you not understand these things?" (John 3: 10). Now, what would the voice of wisdom say today? Wouldn't it say: don't be surprised if you feel called to die? For something in you needs to die, so that something else can live.

What we can learn from the ancient wisdom of Palestine and Australia is that where there is symbolic understanding, then the spiritual aspect of our impulses can be realized. Where there is no symbolic understanding, the impulses that well up from the soul are wrongly interpreted, leading to ideas of incest or suicide. The impulses that drive us to transformation are powerful, and lethal if misinterpreted. There is almost nothing more practical, useful, or pragmatic than a spiritual wisdom that makes sense of the impulses that drive us from within.

I would like to end with some hints or clues about how to restore hope to our human situation.

TEN SUMMARY POINTS: ABOUT FOSTERING WISDOM IN A WORLD WITHOUT INITIATIONS

Question: What can adults do to counter the fatal impact of transitional impulses?

1. The importance of developing an awareness of the second self.
We can help foster an awareness of the reality of the second self in children and students, from the earliest age. If we grow up with the expectation that we have more than a single self, then the emergence of a second self might not catch us unawares or unprepared.

We have to counter the willful ignorance of society, which pretends that life is about 'number one,' that there is no second self, no transformation. This is a toxic environment in which to grow up, because the absence of wisdom leaves us helpless before the powerful transformational impulses, which can be fatal if not correctly interpreted. They are not calls to death, but calls to rebirth. If mishandled, they can be lethal.

From the earliest age, we need to look beyond the child's ego to the larger life that is already present within them. Despite their muddle or confusion, we need to hint all along that they are more than what meets the eye. There is a larger person waiting to break out, not just once or twice, but repeatedly in a series of ongoing transformations. It is healthy and vital to educate the young into a sense that life is large and mysterious, that things happen beyond our understanding.

2. *Finding a language that is not alienating.*
There is no point in using a language to describe this process or reality if it is alienating to the young. We need to find a language that speaks of spiritual journeying which is not too 'religious,' because so many young people are suspicious of religious language. We may need to find a 'secular spirituality' that is non-denominational, otherwise the young may see it as doctrinal, ideological, or coercive.
For instance, the language of first and second self is suitably suggestive but not overly religious; it also has a psychological aspect, which may appeal to the scientific spirit of the time.

3. *The birth of the new self is linked to pain.*
Indigenous traditions teach us that the birth of the second self is linked to pain. It cuts across and displaces the first self, and this is experienced as a violation or attack. However, the best way to reduce or delimit the pain is to go with the process, and allow the new self to appear.

We have to expect difficulty in life, despite the dangerous social message that life is about the avoidance of pain. If we learn to expect pain, we are more likely to endure it. It is a matter of finding the sacred in our woundedness, and in draining the profane from the pain.

For instance, drug taking or addictions, binge-drinking, chroming, self-mutilation, loud chaotic music, trance parties, tattooing, body piercing, risk-taking behaviors; all can be contextualized as initiatory impulses. All can be seen as profane attempts to attack the self, as a prelude to rebirth. But rebirth to what?

4. *The diversity of expressions in the process of rebirth.*
In each case, 'rebirth' will mean, and imply, different things to different people. There is no longer a standard formula, to be imposed by elders or society upon young adults. There are a variety of religions, cosmologies, spiritualities, causes, and ideas. But we have to encourage the young person to find his or her own way to one of these big ideas or causes, which then may act as a catalyst to renewal, reorientation, and rebirth.

Parents and teachers should try not to be too judgmental if the young person selects a big idea that does not appeal to their taste or background. For instance, a Christian parent might be alarmed if the child selects Buddhism as the vehicle for transformation; an atheist parent might be surprised if the child moves into charismatic Christianity; an industrialist might be upset if ecology or environmentalism is the larger concern, or a scientist might be alarmed if the child enters cosmology, kabbalah, or yoga.

The postmodern world is synonymous with diversity and plurality, and correct parenting at this crucial time of transition involves tolerance, suspension of disbelief, except perhaps where the interest is demonstrably harmful, i.e. an apocalyptic sect or a suicide cult. Parents and teachers should always be looking for initiatory signs in the experiences and interests of young people. The golden rule: never quash a large idea unless you can offer another one to replace it.

5. *Cultivating a sense of the specialness of every individual.*

The Greeks referred to the special essence of the individual as his or her 'daimon' (see chapter 12 for a more in depth discussion of the daimon). Living in harmony with the daimon gave rise to *eudaimonia*, a condition often translated as happiness or wellbeing. Today we might talk about relating to the 'true self' or 'inner self'. But no matter what we call it, relating to young people in such a way that we convey the recognition that they are potentially 'more' than they seem (more than their ego) can be liberating. Something deep inside is empowered by being seen, being noticed.

Recognition can be the key that frees the inner self that is inside, giving young people the permission to be more fully themselves. Recognition can act as midwife to the birth of the new self, and it can make the rebirth less traumatic because it has been anticipated. Again, the special talent or special interest may not accord with the parent's taste, and tact again is crucial.

6. *Adults, teachers, parents need to nurture the second self within ourselves.*

If we adults fail to see the potential greatness in ourselves, then children are less likely to respect or sense the greatness in them. We owe it to our children and students to cultivate a spiritual awareness in our own lives, and to tap the hidden potential that we sense below the surface of our first self. This is very hard to do in professional contexts, where role-play, social persona, and investment in our own seriousness, might mask the murmurings of the inner self.

But it is crucial for our own resilience, the resilience of our children, and the resilience of society as a whole. It is the one thing we can all do to build spiritual and social capital.

7. *Learning to read the soul's expressions in unusual phenomena.*

Cultivating a symbolic awareness is important, in addition to the moral judgment that teachers and responsible adults typically adopt toward young people. For instance, instead of showing revulsion toward body piercing, tattooing, we might interpret these acts symbolically. Instead of just saying no to drugs, drinking, or risk-taking behaviour, we might try to explore what impulse lies behind it. Instead of telling them to turn the music down, we might try to find out what the lyrics are saying.

8. *Learning to look for signs in dreams and imagination.*
Dreams usually express the processes of the inner self, in symbolic language that few of us can understand. It might be worthwhile for some of us to actually study the language of dreams and to be alert to signs of transformation or of struggles that are taking place in our children and ourselves.

9. *The importance of same-sex relationships across the generations.*
Indigenous cultures put a lot of emphasis on boys being initiated by older men, and girls by older women. We need to take this to heart today, to act as mentors for young people. The older person of the same sex has a particular kind of psychic power: he or she is like oneself, yet *other* than oneself. He or she is a mana figure: like yet unlike, similar but older and wiser. This may serve to activate the wisdom and maturity-generating powers within the young person's psyche.

10. *The recognition that forces at work in children are larger than us.*
Despite our best efforts to reach out to the child or student, there are forces at work in all our lives over which we can have little or no control. We live in a time of disruption and confusion, and this falls hardest on the young, who are the most vulnerable. As parents, we do our best, but we cannot control all that impacts on our children, as some of us know only too painfully. We must recognize, in our wisdom as elders and mentors, that there is a powerful force in every life, and a deep structure in every soul. They might be our offspring, and the fruits of our lives, but they have a sacred otherness that must be respected. In this disruptive time in history, there are forces at work that we are unable to control.

REFERENCES

Beaudoin, T. (1998). *Virtual faith: The irreverent spiritual quest of generation x.* San Francisco: Jossey-Bass.

Berndt, R. M. (1974). *Australian Aboriginal religion.* Leiden: Brill.

Bosnak, R. (1996). *Tracks in the wilderness of dreaming.* Boston: Delacorte Press.

Chilton Pearce, J. (2002). *The biology of transcendence: A blueprint of the human spirit.* Rochester, VT: Park Street Press.

Crick, F. (1994). *The astonishing hypothesis: The scientific search for the soul.* New York: Simon & Schuster.

Eckersley, R. (2004). *Well and good: How we feel and why it matters.* Text: Melbourne.

Eckhart, M. (1994). *Selected writings* (O. Davies, Trans.). London: Penguin.

Eliade, M. (1956). *Rites and symbols of initiation: The mysteries of birth and rebirth.* New York: Harper.

Eliade, M. (1957). *The sacred and the profane.* New York: Harcourt Brace & Company.

Jacobs, G. (2003). *The ancestral mind.* New York: Viking.

James, W. (1985). *The varieties of religious experience.* New York: Penguin. (Original work published 1902)

Jung, C. G. (1961). *Memories, dreams, reflections.* London: Harper Collins.

Hamilton T. K. & Schweitzer R. D. (2000). The cost of being perfect: perfection and suicidal ideation in university students. *Australian and NZ Journal of Psychiatry, 34,* 829-35.

Hay, D. & Nye, R. (1998). *The spirit of the child.* London: Fount.

Hillman, J. (1973). *Suicide and the soul.* New York: Harper & Row.

Hillman, J. (1976). Peaks and vales. In J. Needleman & D. Lewis (Eds.), *On the way to self knowledge.* New York: Alfred Knopf.

Keen, I. (1994). *Knowledge and secrecy in an aboriginal religion.* New York: Oxford University Press.

Moore, T. (1992). *Care of the soul.* New York: Harper Collins.

Mowaljarlai, D. (1993). *Yorro yorro: Everything standing up alive.* Broome: Magabala Books.

Neumann, E. (1973). *The origins and history of consciousness.* Princeton, NJ: Princeton University Press.

Orchard H. (Ed.). 2001: *Spirituality in health care contexts.* Philadelphia: Jessica Kingsley.

Otto, R. (1958). *The idea of the holy.* London: Oxford University Press. (Original work published 1923)

Peterson, E. (1997). *Subversive spirituality.* Grand Rapids: Eerdmans.

Roach, S. M. (1997). *Caring from the heart : The convergence of caring and spirituality.* New York: Paulist Press.

Rumbold, B. (Ed.). (2002). *Spirituality and palliative care: Social and pastoral perspectives.* Melbourne: Oxford University Press.

Stanner, W. E. H. (1989). *On Aboriginal religion.* Sydney: University of Sydney Press.

Swinton, J. (2001). *Spirituality and mental health care : Rediscovering a 'forgotten' dimension.* London: Kingsley.

Tacey, D. (1995). *Edge of the sacred.* Melbourne: Harper Collins.

Tacey, D. (2000). *ReEnchantment: The new Australian spirituality.* Sydney: Harper Collins.

Tacey, D. (2001). *Jung and the new age.* New York: Brunner-Routledge.

Tacey, D. (2004). *The Spirituality Revolution: The Emergence of Contemporary Spirituality.* New York: Brunner-Routledge.

Thompson, D. (1982). *Bora is like church: Aboriginal initiation ceremonies and the Christian church.* Darwin: Nungalinya Publications.

Thoresen, C. E. (1998). Spirituality, health, and science: The coming revival? In S. Roth-Roemer, S. E. Robinson Kurpius, & C. Carmin, (Eds.), *The emerging role of counseling psychology in health care* (pp. 409-431). New York: W.W. Norton.

Van Gennep, A. (1960). *The rites of passage.* Chicago: University of Chicago Press. (Original work published 1908)

Zoja, L. (1989). *Drugs, addiction and initiation: The modern search for ritual.* Boston: Sigo Press.

8

A Developmental Perspective on the God Image

Louis Hoffman, MAT, Ph.D.
Vanguard University of Southern California
Costa Mesa, California

A person's understanding of God is frequently underestimated as a rather simple reality. However, the manner people come to conceptualize God is anything but simple. It is much closer to the truth to state conceptions of God evolve out of one of the most complex relational matrixes known to human existence. Conceptions of other people develop in the context of a relationship where people communicate directly, watch the impact of their interaction, and relate as fellow finite beings who are also much more human than not. One can touch, taste, smell, and hear the other with whom she or he relates. This is not so with God. One cannot touch, taste, smell, or hear God; at the very least, one's communication with God is more intuitive and abstract.

A BASIS FOR KNOWING AND NOT KNOWING GOD

Paul Tillich (1951), one of most renowned theologians in American history, provides an important conceptual basis for approaching God with humility. Tillich makes the important distinction between an understanding of God from above, or in the realm of the infinite, and from below, the realm of the finite. This distinction portrays a transcendent reality of God (capital G) and a human conception of god (small g). The small 'g' god is the god of human understanding, which is a limited, finite understanding of God. In approaching any understanding of God, these human limitations must be accepted. Tillich states:

> the conception of revelation [of God] is approached from "below," from man in the situation of revelation, and not from "above," from the divine ground off revelation.

But after the meaning and actuality of revelation have been discussed, the question of the ground of revelation arises. (p. 155)

When approaching any conception of God, there is a need to acknowledge the inherent limitation of this conception.

Tillich's approach to understanding God and the revelation of God makes explicit the finite epistemology that necessarily limits humans. Even if the revelation of God to humans comes directly from God (the infinite), the understanding of that revelation is still human and finite. No revelation of God, no matter of direct, can be anything less than finite in the realm human understanding.

Finite epistemologies are never fully sufficient in and of themselves. The various human ways of knowing will always be less than perfect. As Barbour (1990, 2000) acknowledges, neither science nor religion can be seen as having an understanding so deeply rooted in truth as to claim a perfect epistemology. Any analysis of the history of religion and spirituality reflects numerous approaches to "knowing God" or, in other words, various epistemological approaches to understanding the infinite. As this chapter will further discuss, people tend to use different epistemologies to understand God. Furthermore, they may rely more heavily on particular epistemologies at different points of their spiritual and psychological development.

Another important development in Tillich's theology is the necessity of doubt for faith (Tillich, 1952; 1957). If people cannot know, then they must rely on faith. Faith, for Tillich, was not a mere belief and could never be seen as akin to knowledge. This place of faith (and doubt, thereof by necessity) is a place of terror which individuals try to escape by claims to know:

> Doubt is based on man's separation from the whole of reality, on his lack of universal participation, on the isolation of his individual self. So he tries to break out of this situation, to identify separation and self-relatedness. He flees from his freedom of asking and answering for himself to a situation in which no further questions can be asked and the answers to previous questions are imposed on him authoritatively. In order to avoid the risk of asking and doubting he surrenders the right to ask and to doubt. (1952, p. 49)

Tillich here explains the human need to know God in order to escape the terror of existence. The God of human understanding is not big enough to save people from these terrors. For this, one needs an infinite, transcendent God that cannot be fully known. Herein lies the necessity of faith in the presence of doubt.

The terror is vital in seeking to gain a deeper understanding of human conceptions of God. This terror serves as the basis for understanding God and the human condition. Existential philosophers, psychologists, and theologians discuss the terrible thing it is to be human.[1] Awareness of this, whether it be conscious or unconscious, is a driving force in a person's way of being. People seek to connect with something to save themselves from their finiteness. As Becker (1973) states, "Man cannot endure his own littleness unless he can translate it into meaningfulness on the largest possible level" (p.196).

This discussion of finiteness is not limited just to a discussion of finiteness of the human experience in the context of death. It refers to a broader conceptualization of finiteness in which death becomes the greatest symbol. Becker (1973), in his classic work *The Denial of Death*, presents one of the most penetrating analyses of death ever developed. The basis of Becker's thought was that the framework of Freud's theory was correct, but that there were essential errors. According to Becker, Freud's error was the reduction of people to biological drives, in particularly sex. Instead, Becker posits that death and the drive to avoid the reality of death serves as the basis of human existence.

People seek to overcome the reality of death by connecting with the heroic (Becker, 1973). Becker based his conception of the hero primarily off the work of Rank (1978). Yalom (1980) further developed this concept by postulating two ways that people escape the terror of death. The first escape is a belief in one's specialness. The implicit driving force here is the thought "because of my specialness I am not subject to the same laws of death everyone else is" or "because of my specialness or the special plan god has for me, God will not allow me to be harmed." A second way of escaping the terror of existence is through a belief in an ultimate rescuer, a belief which has some evident religious implications (Yalom, 1980). The ultimate rescuer who would save the individual from death would, at the very least, have some god-like qualities. This sounds similar to the first escape, that individuals will be saved by God because of some inherent specialness or a special plan god has for them, but there are some important process distinctions here. In the context of specialness, the reason for the act is something internally valuable in the person being saved. Essentially, this denial of death is a narcissistic process in which people believe there is something so special about them that they will not be subject to finiteness. The hero is internally based. In contrast, the case of the ultimate rescuer is more of a dependent process in which people wait for something or someone external to save the day. Here, the hero is externally based.

These two conceptions play out differently in conceptions of God. Those individuals subject to the specialness myth are less concerned with God because of their self-sufficiency. They see themselves on the same level and while they may recognize the important place of God, they also expect that God knows the important place they fill. Their view of God is more likely to be similar to their view of themselves. Those individuals subject to the ultimate rescuer myth are more likely to see God in terms of being a hero. Their view of God is more likely to be similar to significant people in their lives who have served in a hero role or projections of their need for the heroic.

---

[1] To avoid a frequent misunderstanding of existentialism, it is important to state here that many existentialists readily acknowledge that to be human is also a beautiful thing. For our discussion herein, the focus is on the part of human existence that is indeed terrifying.

One can see the heroic in a much broader conceptualization than pertaining only to death. As previously stated, death is the great symbol of human finiteness. Finiteness, however, is about much more than mortality. It also addresses the issue of human limitation, which then enters the realm of freedom, knowledge, meaning, and transcendence (both spiritual transcendence through connection with God, the Ground-of-being, and human and nature transcendence through connection with other people and nature). If Becker's conception of death is reinterpreted as death being symbolic of all realms of human finiteness, his work truly becomes a comprehensive existential masterpiece.

The companion volume to *The Denial of Death* was Becker's (1975) posthumous *Escape from Evil*, in which he builds on his conception of the heroic. Herein Becker states "man's natural and inevitable urge to deny mortality and achieve a heroic self-image are the root causes of human evil" (p. xvii). In other words, the basis of human evil is misguided attempts to overcome finiteness. This re-conceptualization places evil not at the opposite end of the continuum from good, but just one step to the right or one step to the left of that which is good. While a comprehensive discussion of evil is far beyond the scope of this chapter, it is important to acknowledge here that attempts to overcome one's finiteness can be seen as the true root of evil.

The implications of this are quite significant. Given that it is impossible for finite beings to completely know God, such claims to know what cannot be known create the potential for evil. Applied in a theological sense, attempts by finite humans to concretely define their understanding of God necessarily transform God into god, an act that, at a minimum, has the potential for evil. Any over moralistic or rigid approach to religion, spirituality, or other understanding of God could potentially fall into this category. The same danger occurs when symbols of faith or representations of God are turned into knowledge of God. Peter Gomes (1996) writes:

> The inherent risk in symbolism is that the symbol becomes a substitute for what it is meant to represent. The means becomes an end in itself, and the worship and devotion which the end requires, when devoted merely to the means, become a form of idolatry and an exercise in fraud. (p. 37)

The context of the above quote was in reference to what Gomes and others call "Bibliolatry," or turning the Bible (or other sacred texts) into God instead of representations of understanding sacred texts as God. In the current framework, the common debate of inerrancy or infallibility of scripture is irrelevant because all conceptualizations of scripture are interpreted through finite lenses.

A key implication of the discussion thus far is the value of using multiple epistemological lenses when approaching the Sacred. For many, this may seem problematic as conclusions about God or truth from one epistemological lens may directly contradict the conclusions of a different epistemological lens. What one knows of God aesthetically may not fit well with what one knows of God empirically or rationally. While seeming problematic, it should not be surprising for finite beings approaching the infinite. It is much more problematic and limiting to image God as fully accessible through a singular epistemology. Rather than privileging one epistemology over another in an attempt to concretely know God (and thus, turn God into god), the author of this chapter suggests that one approach such tensions and complexities with humility. Several definitions may also assist in developing an organizational framework to better understand these tensions and complexities.

THE GOD CONCEPT AND GOD IMAGE

Several writers have attempted to distinguish between differing levels of understanding and experiencing God (Lawrence, 1997; Moriarty, in press; Rizzuto, 1979; Spero, 1992). A fundamental distinction can be made between the *God Concept*, an intellectual, conceptual, or theological understanding of God (Lawrence, 1997), and the *God Image* an emotional understanding or experience of God (Lawrence, 1997; Moriarty, in press; Rizzuto, 1979).

The God Concept is the more straightforward definition. This level of understanding or experiencing God is largely rational and based upon what a person is taught about God. This cognitive understanding of God is heavily influenced by content learned from parents, spiritual leaders, books, friends, and religious experiences. The God Concept is largely a conscious phenomenon.

The God Image is more complex because of its emotional and experiential nature. This understanding of God is based primarily on process or experience and may be mostly unconscious. While one may debate from a psychoanalytic perspective the degree to which the God Image can become conscious, one would never conceive it as being fully conscious. Rizzuto (1979) and Spero (1992), in psychoanalytic and object relational perspectives, discuss the importance of early relationships with parents or significant early attachment figures on a person's emotional understanding of God. Many therapists and counselors are amazed by the similarities between the ways clients experience God and the way they experienced their parents. While there is little doubt of the importance of early parental relationships on the God Image, taking a more thorough examination of how the God Image develops is still important to consider.

The God Image and the God Concept are related processes or different aspects of a broader, more complex process. They develop parallel to each other through different aspects of the individual's experience. While the God Concept develops primarily by what a person is taught about God, the God Image develops through a relational process with parents and other significant authority or idealized figures. Classic interpretations of these processes have not adequately dealt with their inter-connectedness.

What one knows about God does influence how she or he experiences God. However, the limitation of the God Concept in influencing the God Image is comparable to the limitations of cognitive approaches to therapy. If cognitions do not contain some *experience*, they will be unable to touch the God Image. While cognitive approaches to therapy have revolutionized therapy in the eyes of many, they have been unable to fully solve the emotional dilemmas of human existence. Though a complete critique of cognitive therapy approaches is beyond the scope of this chapter, one important limitation has relevance for the current discussion. Although individuals can change their thoughts about a situation, this does not necessarily change their experience. Though thoughts can certainly influence emotions, they do not get at the full *emotional experience*. People can alter how they think and control how they feel about their parents, but this may not change their *experience of them*. This important distinction between the *experiencing of emotions* and the broader *emotional experience* should not be overlooked.

In a similar manner, changing one's thoughts of God does not necessarily change one's experience of God. If this were the case, mere education would resolve most God Image problems. However, as Thomas Moore (2002) has observed, religious studies departments are often a breeding ground for people who have fallen away from faith through the process of learning (Moore). Moore states that religious studies departments have ironically become one of the least religious departments at many universities. Learning about God or trying to *Know God* often creates the irresolvable crises of faith.

Cognitive approaches utilize a modernistic approach that downplays the phenomenological aspects of the human experience. Spirituality and faith, at their core, are phenomenological experiences, which generally necessitate a pre- or post-modern epistemology. Cognitive therapies base their approach to change on one realm of human experience hoping it will carryover to the others. Premodern approaches (pure mystical or cathartic approaches) utilize experience or emotion without the necessity of language (i.e. an understanding of the experience). Postmodern approaches, at their best, combine the modern and the premodern with the humility of the finite in the shadow of the infinite. This allows for change or growth to be holistic or "centered" through including both cognitive and experiential aspects of change. Applied to the God Concept, this is only one part of the God experience and cannot, in itself, change the whole.

Another important aspect of the relationship between the God Image and God Concept is discrepancies between these two constructs. When the God Image and the God Concept do not fit, this provides the basis for the formation of a spiritual neurosis with a guilt or shame basis. For example, if a person is taught that God is love, but experiences God as distant, the individual is likely to believe (unconsciously and/or consciously) that this discrepancy is due to something that is wrong with them (Moriarty, in press). Ideally, psychotherapy that embraces the spiritual dimensions of clients would assist them in understanding, recognizing, and working through these discrepancies. It is essential to understand each of the intrapsychic processes can become barriers to a genuine relationship with the infinite or transcendent. This bears similarity to what is discussed as working through the psychological to the spiritual in transpersonal psychology (Cortright, 1997; Wilber, 2000).

AVOIDING THE ERRORS OF REIFICATION

Reification is the process through which the abstract is made real or something believed to be real. Similarly, it could be stated that reification is a process by which *truth* is made into *Truth*. A common byproduct of reification is that the abstracted construct is assumed to be stagnant or non-fluid. Cobb and Griffin (1976) state, "process is fundamental...There are unchanging principles of process and abstract forms. But to be actual is to be a process. Anything which is not a process is an abstraction from process, not the full-fledged actuality" (p. 14). Some examples may help clarify.

Freud's id, ego, and super-ego are not actual constructs located somewhere in the human brain or even the mind. Rather, these refer to three processes that occur in the psyche. What Freud did was to create three abstractions (i.e., constructs) which refer to these processes. The danger is that once these abstractions were made, they were then reified to be seen as actual entities which are part of the self. This made Freud's theory unbelievable to some and served as the basis for others to turn the abstractions into a form of psychoanalytic fundamentalism. When an abstraction loses its abstractness, it is reified.

Stolorow and Atwood (1992) describe reification as essentially being a defense mechanism. In other words, reification is a psychological process that makes it easier to deal with the realities of existence and the world. Similar to the id, ego, and super ego, the God Concept and God Image are abstractions from process. By reifying them into actualities, they become distorted, but they also become easier to deal with. The essential point, which will be returned to later in the chapter, is that of the importance of recognizing that the God Image and God Concept are processes which continue to develop across an individual's life.

DEVELOPMENT OF THE GOD IMAGE:
AN EXISTENTIAL-ANTROPOLOGICAL PERSPECTIVE

The God Image emerges from multiple sources. The influence of parental relationships plays a primary role for many people. The psychoanalytic basis of this influence on the God Image is the transference process. People tend to experience God emotionally in the ways they experienced their parents. However, there are other factors that influence how the God Image develops.

Freud (1961) was a strong critic of religion and essentially saw religious belief as a sign of weakness. Despite this, he did see religion as having a functional purpose believing the average person was unable to survive without religion. Freud described both an intrapsychic need for God and the anthropological need for God (Freud, 1950; 1961; 1939). The intrapsychic need for God received more attention from contemporaries of Freud (Rizzuto 1979, 1994; Spero 1992) primarily through object relations theories.

Becker (1973) and Yalom's (1980) discussion of the hero from an existential perspective bears similarity to the psychoanalytic and object relations intrapsychic necessity of God. People are not able to survive the terrors of reality without some greater reason or meaning. A hero was created who would give meaning to the miserable human existence on earth while providing a hope for a better life after death for those who persevere. While the existential thinkers do an excellent job of discussing the intrapsychic need for God, the psychoanalytic and object relations thinkers (Freud, 1961; Rizzuto, 1979; Spero, 1992) provide an excellent foundation for understanding the psychological development of the God Image, albeit incomplete.

The problem with the pure object relations perspective of the development of the God Image is that it neglects the anthropological and cultural aspects. The God Image does not develop as an isolated intrapsychic process or experience. This would be to say it could never be a holistic or fully centered act. Rather, the God Image develops in a complex manner embracing intrapsychic, relational, anthropological, and cultural elements. Through integrating existential theory back to the God Image, it can once again become a more complete experience worthy of the courage of faith.

Several feminist writers provide some important critiques on how the cultural constructions of God have impacted women's experience of the Divine (Christ, 2003; Johnson, 1992; Keller, 1986). Acutely aware of how culture molds religion, these writers have helped recognize the sexism inherent in a large amount of religious thought. Hoffman (2004) also addressed other important diversity issues, including gender, race, and sexual orientation, influence the God Image. Through this recognition, it becomes increasingly possible to move beyond social constructions to less oppressive realities. However, a continued anthropological awareness in regard to the limitations of new constructions is necessary to prevent repeating old mistakes.

The anthropological necessity of God originated conceptually through the primeval father (Freud 1950, 1939; Rizzuto, 1979). Freud postulated that the people of that time overthrew and killed the authoritarian primeval father. They then realized their need for this father or hero figure. They created a totem, which eventually evolved to a god nearer to human form, to replace this father figure. This totem became an important authority figure. Religion, then, served the purpose of containing the problems of society through its moral rules. This God is a necessary evil that Freud believed would no longer be necessary with the development of science, which would replace religion.

These two processes, the intrapsychic and anthropological need for God, can be distinguished as a spiritual need for God (intrapsychic necessity) and a religious need for God (anthropological necessity). While useful for the development of theory, any such distinction is arbitrary and an oversimplification, as Tillich (1959) clearly points out in his distinction between a broad and narrow definition of religion. The distinction between the component of religion based on human construction (narrow) and the component of religion based on what Tillich refers to as ultimate concern (broad) remains important. The above noted religious need assumes this narrow definition of religion.

Myth, Anthropology, and the God Image

While Rizzuto (1979) focused primarily on this intrapsychic development, herein the author proposes that the anthropological necessity also bears influence on the development of the God Image through the development of religion and its pervasive impact both directly and indirectly upon the God Image. There is an interesting connection between this religious need for religion and the need for myth, as discussed by Rollo May (1991).

May's (1991) usage of myth is essentially comparable to Tillich's narrow definition of religion and will be used interchangeably hereafter. Myth is the attempt to organize, find, or create meaning in what often appears to be meaningless. Myth encapsulates the attempts of the finite to approach the infinite through the medium of language (i.e. theology, doctrines, moral codes, etc.). May states, "There can be no stronger proof of the impoverishment of our contemporary culture than the popular – though profoundly mistaken – definition of myth as falsehood" (p. 23). Myth is not something that is false, rather myth that which cannot be proven to be true.

May (1991) begins his book, *The Cry for Myth*, stating:

> I speak of the Cry for myths because I believe there is an urgency in the need for myth in our day. Many of the problems of our society, including cults and drug addiction, can be traced to the lack of myths which will give us as individuals the inner security we need in order to live adequately in our day. (p. 9)

Here it can be seen that Freud's critique of religion is not very different from May and Tillich's view of myth and religion (narrowly defined). The major difference is the intentions of their critiques and the latter authors allowing a place for a spiritual reality beyond religion. Freud made his critiques with the intention of promoting science's gradual overtaking and eradication of religion. May and Tillich made their critique in the service of promoting a *healthier* or more genuine religion.

Similarly, Nietzsche, another famous critic of religion, and in particular Christianity, was not so much critical of religion as he was of inauthentic or unchallenged religion (Kaufmann, 1974). His major critique was of Philistinism or Philistine morality (Kaufmann, 1974, Nietzsche, 1966). When read in context it can be seen that much of Nietzsche's attacks were not on spirituality (broadly defined religion), but rather on rigid religious systems (narrowly defined religion) to which people blindly conformed. In this light, it can be seen that Nietzsche was not so much an enemy of religion, but someone who challenged religion in its complacency. .

Freud, May, Tillich, and Nietzsche all share the criticism of religion's claim to be more than it is while not seeking to become more than it is. Too often religion becomes dissatisfied with its status as myth and seeks residency among the sciences and their claims on ultimate truth. However, postmodernism has taught us that even science's claims on truth are not what they are often made out to be (Barbour, 1990). A more important problem is that religion loses some of its power when it makes such grandiose claims. May (1991) states, "Whereas empirical language refers to objective facts, myth refers to the quintessence of human experience, the meaning and significance of human life. The whole person speaks to us, not just our brain" (p. 26). There is more power in myth (faith) than in science ('facts').

Similarly, Tillich argues that faith, which is the basis of religious *belief* or spirituality, necessitates doubt and courage to truly be faith (Tillich, 1952, 1955). Faith cannot be known, it must be embraced in the midst of the anxiety of the unknown.

Herein is where religion (narrowly defined) destroys religion (broadly defined), through its negation of faith with claims for knowledge. Some approaches to systematic theology even state followers are not to question, but just believe some assertions (see Pieper 1950-1953 for an example). Such statements, whether conveyed implicitly or explicitly, impact the experience of church members who participate in the corporate aspects of their church body. However, the questioning is not the basis of spiritual neurosis, but rather the fear or even the lack of it. Questioning what we don't know, contrary to what is often purported, can bring one closer to the transcendent by the release from self-aggrandized versions of faith. The narcissistic attempt to fit the infinite into the finite is the true neurosis. Furthermore, the degree to which one believes this has been accomplished reflects the severity of the neurosis.

EXPANDING INFLUENCES ON THE GOD IMAGE

The church body, as represented symbolically by its leaders and members, and ritually through its corporate practice, forms an experiential basis affecting the development of the God Image in a similar way to parental relationships. What parents tell their children about God forms a primary influence on the God Concept while how the child experiences their parents forms the primary basis for the God Image. Similarly, what the church tells members, particularly those young and immature in their faith, about God primarily influences their God Concept while the broader experience of the church primarily influences the God Image. So a church that teaches grace, but does not practice it, often has an influence upon its members in which a gap is built between the God Concept and God Image. This can create feelings of ambivalence, anxiety, guilt, and anger toward God and/or the church.

Much of this could be prevented or softened if the church presented itself more in terms of its finite reality. In other words, much of the spiritual neuroses of church members could be lessened if churches did a better job at acknowledging their limitations. Churches often become the symbol that has replaced that to which it was intended to point. In other words, the church becomes an idol, limiting individual church members' ability to seek that to which the church was intended to point. Talking about God as beyond, while acting as God, sends a conflicting message to church members, particularly the young and those most susceptible to influence. The explicit message is that there is a God beyond, but the implicit message is that the church is God. This explicit message primarily impacts the God Concept, while the implicit message impacts the God Image.

Several aspects of the church influence how the church is experienced. First, individual relationships with friends, leaders, and church officials all contribute to the broader *feel* of the church. In particularly, members of the church who may have been influential on introducing the individual to faith or the church may have a powerful impact. The style and feel of the corporate worship and the rituals, the theology, level of involvement with members, and many other aspects of the church will also have an influence.

This discussion highlights the experiential component of distortions in the God Image through religion and provides the basis for almost all other types of spiritual neuroses that affect the God Image. Experientially, this process along with the explicit and implicit messages distorts how a person experiences God through the church. The claims for truth and the negation of doubt and questioning allow for the content of belief to further impact the God Image in ways that could be prevented through a humbler epistemology of religion.

EPISTEMOLOGY AND THE CHURCH

Three primary epistemological approaches can be seen as represented in the discussion of psychology, science, religion, and spirituality. A premodern epistemology claims knowledge of ultimate truth through direct revelation from the bearer of Truth (the infinite). Religion frequently falls into this category. Modernistic epistemologies claim the ability to determine ultimate Truth through the usage of some human faculty such as reason, logic, or empiricism. Science is generally seen as a good example of a modernist epistemology.

Postmodernism is emerging as the current zeitgeist in most realms of thought including philosophy, education, politics, and even psychology and religion to a degree. However, these latter two fields seem to be the most resistant to the influences of postmodernism. While postmodernism is often referred to as a singular, united theory, a more accurate appraisal refers to the postmodern philosophies (Martin & Sugarman, 1999: Richards & Bergin, 1997). Within the postmodern approaches some similarities can be deduced. First, they all maintain we are unable to *Know Truth*. Second, they emphasize the importance of language and narratives on perceptions of reality. Third, they recognize various ways of knowing as valid or utilize a pluralistic epistemology.

Postmodern philosophies can be grouped into two major groups in relation to their stance on the existence of Ultimate Truth (Held, 1998; Martin & Sugarman, 1999). The first group, which are sometimes called the anti-realists, claim no Ultimate Truth exists. There is only relative, personal, or social truths which are created by people. This position necessarily either denies the existence of God or maintains God is fluid and changing, an idea contrary to classical theism (Hartshorne, 1948; 1984). The second group, the realists, maintains that an ultimate truth exists, however, people are unable to attain or Know this Truth. Any known truth is a personally or socially constructed truth. For the realists, God can exist as a non-fluid (or fluid) transcendent entity.

Postmodernism is often thought to be antithetical to religion. This is only the case if the basis of religion rests on the notion of Knowledge instead of faith. However, the realist/anti-realist distinction allows for differing understandings of God or the transcendent based upon the position taken. As stated, the anti-realist position would require any conception of God to be fluid or see God as something other than a being (i.e. being itself).

Christian theologians are generally resistant to seeing God as fluid, referring to God as constant and never-changing. However, Tillich's conception of God as the "Ground of Being," which allows God to become "being" instead of 'a being," could potentially account for the fluidity of God.[2]

The realist position allows for God through allowing for an Ultimate Truth. The claim is that we are unable to Know this Truth or we are unable to Know God. God as an unknowable Truth or Divine Mystery is the same as what Tillich and May argue for with their conceptions of religion and myth. The difference between the postmodern and the premodern or modern is that the latter claim the ability to Know religion if it truly exists. The different approaches to Christian Apologetics often make this same claim.

Churches and religious bodies, along with people in general, function in accordance with different epistemologies. Though one's epistemology is often unconscious and out of our awareness, epistemological statements and assumptions are made every day. These assumptions determine what to believe and what to trust. Frequently people will function with different epistemologies in different areas of their life. For example, Kuhn and Weinstock (2002) suggests people tend to function from more abstract, flexible epistemologies in the areas of the life where they are the most confident and comfortable. People are more likely to use a postmodern epistemology in areas in which they are more secure and more likely to use a premodern or modern epistemology in realms where they are less secure.

This may also be influenced by other contextual issues in a person's life. For example, a person may be more likely to be able to move into the abstract realms of faith and religious belief when they have other securities in their life. For example, if they have a good support system, particularly in the regards to their spiritual or religious belief, they are more likely to be able to explore the unknown aspect of faith. However, during tumultuous times, they may experience the need to rely on more concrete forms of religiosity.

The events of 9/11 provide a powerful example. Many people discussed how Americans tended to be more religious and church attendance increased following the attacks on the World Trade Centers and the Pentagon. However, it may be better explained that people were religious in a different manner. People needed a more concrete, secure religious belief to replace the false sense of security that used to be a part of American life. As Americans began to regain a sense of safety and security, most people returned to their previous ways of being religious.

The epistemology churches function from will influence the *feel* of the church and the experience of the church members. Churches functioning from a premodern or modern epistemological base are more likely to be rigid and authoritarian due to their claims of *knowing* Ultimate Truth. This often provides a sense of security because of the emphasis on the *known*. Churches functioning with a postmodern epistemological base are more likely to

---

[2] The "ground of being" is also a concept used in Buddhism (Hanh, 1998) which bears similarity to Tillich's conception.

have greater flexibility, fluidity, and humility in the face of the questions of knowing who or what is of God.

This is particularly interesting if looked at in the context of American culture along with some other western cultures. Americans tend to be very cautious about statements of opinion through clarifiers of "I think" or "it's just my opinion." In other cultures, the assumption implies that a statement is the opinion of the speaker without the clarifiers. In other words, there is an implied epistemological statement "in my opinion" that is a part of hermeneutics of some other cultures. When a person from a culture utilizing the implied "in my opinion" makes a statement to someone from American culture, there can often be a conflict that arises that is essentially a problem of hermeneutics or epistemology. The conflict often emerges from the American feeling as if the statement was arrogant or "too strong."

FOWLER'S STAGES OF FAITH AND THE GOD IMAGE

If, as this chapter purports, the God Image does change over time, then it becomes important to try to understand what factors influence this change. It should be evident by now that one of the factors which is likely to influence this ongoing development is the individual's relationships. How relationships change the God Image and which relationships are most influential in the process is still largely ambiguous and likely to be very complex. This is an important area for future theory and research as it has important implications for the therapy process.

However, some intrapsychic factors are also likely to have contributed to the change. Faith development is one important factor likely to have significant influence on the God Image. James Fowler's (1981) *Stages of Faith* contributed what is the most important contribution to faith development literature. According to Fowler, faith progresses from a "pre-stage" through six more formally developed stages. The first three of these stages, Intuitive-Projective Faith, Mythic-Literal Faith, and Synthetic-Conventional Faith, are closely related to age and cognitive abilities. Most people reach stage three by progressing through normal cognitive development. However, many people get stuck in stage three and don't progress beyond it.

Stage 3, Synthetic-Conventional Faith, remains heavily influenced by conformity to the group, authority figures, and other external influences (Fowler, 1981). Faith tends to be rather concrete and unchallenged. The individual in this stage is likely to be primarily unaware of their God Image, while focusing more on the God Concept. If the God Image and God Concept are in conflict, this will likely remain unconscious leading to guilt and anxiety. Any challenges to the God Concept would remain defended against. The God Concept is likely to remain fairly traditional and in agreement with the position or religious group the individual is affiliated with.

Fowler (1981) refers to stage 4 as Individuative-Reflective Faith. This period is marked by increasing turmoil in regards to spiritual issues. It could be seen as a transitional stage in which the individual is preparing for stages 5 and 6. Fowler warns that staying in this

141

stage too long can lead to cynicism and be destructive to faith. This is the stage where it is more likely that some awareness of the God Image may emerge. The individual is becoming increasingly aware of the complexities and ambiguities of spiritual life which allows them to experience some of what was previously repressed. At this stage, the God Concept begins to be deconstructed allowing movement toward a more genuine relationship with the Divine in the final stages.

Stages 5 and 6, Conjunctive Faith and Universalizing Faith, represent a more mature and solid faith (Fowler, 1981). The paradoxes which are a part of faith are tolerated and then valued as the individual forms a personal, internalized faith as opposed to the conformity prominent in stage 3. In this stage, the individual is able and willing to recognize the inconsistencies between the God Image and God Concept. Furthermore, these are not as threatening as they were in the previous stages. The individual is able to see more clearly that the God Image and the God Concept are not God, but only the individual's representations of God. While they may not be able to put this into words, the understanding of the distinction between thoughts, experiences, and the greater reality exists within the individual. In the purest form, the contents of faith have been removed leaving only faith. However, it is unlikely that this pure of faith can be achieved fully while the individual is still in their finite state.

There is a general progression from the known to the unknown, the concrete to the mysterious. It is not surprising that many of the authors in the new spirituality movements make frequent reference to the mystery when referring to the divine (Chopra, 1997; Johnson, 1992; Keen, 1994; Moore, 2002; O'Donohue, 1998). While the embracing of mystery and the unknown has often been feared in religious communities, it may be that there is more comfort and power in mystery than there ever was in the known.

There are a few important implications of faith development for clinical practice. First, the anxiety and fear associated with doubting is not necessarily the sign that something is wrong. It may be part of the spiritual growth process. Instead of trying to quickly remove the uncomfortable feelings, therapists can acknowledge the importance of helping the client understand what these feelings are about. Fowler (1981) emphasizes that the transition between stages is not comfortable. This is true of most development and growth. Taking away the discomfort, instead of being helpful, may actually be stifling the spiritual growth. However, it must be emphasized that this is not the therapist's decision to make. The client makes the decision, with the assistance of the therapist, to sit with these feelings or not. If the therapist is aware that the client's discomfort is due to the spiritual growth process, he or she may be able to help the client make a more informed decision.

Second, from a spiritual perspective, therapy that provides all the answers is not good therapy. Therapists who act as if they have all the answers may not always be that helpful to clients. Rather, if therapists can model for clients that the ability to be okay with anxiety and sit in the unknown, they can create a space for growth. The therapists are the bearers of hope, not answers, in this situation.

Finally, it can be important for therapists to be aware of where clients are in regards to their spiritual development. The type of intervention made should be informed by where the client is developmentally. Some interventions would be beneficial for a client in stage 3, but not in stage 5 or 6. For example, in stage 3, the client is holding on to a more concrete faith and trying to avoid ambiguity and paradox. Too much mystery, ambiguity, or paradox at this stage would be overwhelming and counterproductive. It can be best for the client to be able to ease into these. Furthermore, the therapist should always be aware of the other resources in the client's life. If a client does not have a good support system and has poor coping skills, it may be dangerous for them to journey too much into the unknown aspects of faith. It may be good to encourage the client to focus on the more secure aspects of their faith and put off the questioning until they are in a more secure place.

COURAGE, DOUBT, AND THE HEALTHY CHURCH

Tillich (1957) emphasizes the need for separation and participation in faith:

But faith would cease to be faith without separation – the opposite element [of participation]. He who has faith is separated from the object of his faith. Otherwise he would posses it. It would be a matter of immediate certainty and not of faith. (p. 100)

He further states, "There is no faith without participation!" (p. 100). Separation is the place of fear and anxiety. The Bible, as the primary religious text of Christianity, refers to separation from God as being that place where there is "weeping and gnashing of teeth." This is a place of terror. Yet, this is the reality of faith. Faith cannot posses; it cannot know. So faith necessitates doubt.

This doubt is not the terrible thing it is made out to be. Existential perspectives on painful emotions suggest that they are not as negative as they are often made out to be and serve a constructive purpose (May, 1977). Through developing a comfort with the different emotions, the experience of them changes. Anxiety is not so terrible. Sadness is not so miserable. Doubt is not so frightening. They are necessary.

May (1991) states there are two ways people have communicated throughout history. The first is the rational; the second is myth. Reason speaks to the cognitive realms, while myth speaks to the "whole person." Similarly, Tillich (1957) states:

Faith as ultimate concern is an act of the total personality. It happens in the center of the personal life and includes all its elements. Faith is the most centered act of the human mind. It is not a movement of a special section or a special function of man's total being. They all are united in the act of faith. (p. 4)

143

Myth, faith, and spirituality are complete in the gripping of the entirety, the essence of being. In *The Courage to Be*, Tillich (1952) discusses the dark side of this faith. In the face of faith which is unknown, it requires courage to embrace faith and being. This is the essence of faith – the courage to believe that which is unknown and embrace the anxiety and terror necessary to do so.

This is the intrapsychic process of the courage to be and the courage to believe. It is done in the face of anxiety. However, there is also an anthropology of the courage to be. People created religion (narrowly defined) because of the terror of living in faith. Religious institutions serve the purpose of alleviating anxiety through constructing and defending a truth claimed to be ultimate. If this religion allows for doubt, it has failed its purpose. But this is a religion of fear, not faith. The religion of faith is the religion of courage. The religion of faith is the religion so bold as to not answer all the questions and not take away the anxiety of faith.

Unfortunately, religious institutions of courage are not the common experience for most religious people in America. This is not to blame the religious institutions as they are generally providing that for which they were asked. Religious institutions far too often reduce the anxiety of its members and its own anxiety through power, control, and structure which reinforces the illusion of knowing. The courageous church or religious institution is the one willing to let people experience the anxiety that allows for the further development of faith. The courageous religious institution is the one which gives up its need for power, control, and structure in order to empower its members to faith.

WORKING WITH HUMILITY: PSYCHOTHERAPY AND THE GOD IMAGE

This chapter has demonstrated the complexity through which the God Image develops in the individual intrapsychically and anthropologically through culture. Even this remains to be an oversimplification of how the God Image comes into place. This chapter has shown the necessity of taking environment and culture along with the intrapsychic process into consideration when dealing with the God Image. Furthermore, it is hoped that it has been demonstrated that clinicians are walking on sacred ground with great human limitations anytime they are addressing the God Image in therapy. With this in mind, this topic must be approached humbly.

Part of the therapists job in working with client's God Image is role modeling this humility. If the therapist presents as the all-knowing spiritual figure, they will then further do damage to the client's God Image. Through acceptance of their own limitation in dealing with spiritual issues the therapist models humility in their approach to the infinite. They model acceptance of their own finiteness.

Therapists must also show humility when addressing institutional and cultural influences on the God Image. Clients often present with strong ties or strong reaction against these environmental factors. At times they will be protective of their church, even if it is detrimental to their mental health. If clinicians are unable to develop a relationship of trust and demonstrate proper respect for the client's church affiliation, they have not earned the honor of addressing issues related to the God Image. Furthermore, it *is not and should not be* the clinician's role to bring conflict between the client and their church. Ideally, an environment in which the client feels free to critically examine their church background will be established while maintaining connection with it. It can be dangerous to become too critical of the church as this may threaten the therapeutic alliance or coercively push the client away from their church.

Thomas Moore (2002) provides many examples of such a healthy church relationship. His stories demonstrate an ability to maintain connection with one's church roots through corporate, ritual, and social participation while not being limited by its influence. Spirituality is about being more than a church member and more than a person ascribing to a particular church doctrine. Spirituality is about the personal relationship of a finite being with the infinite or a transcendent reality. This relationship goes beyond theology, doctrine, and structure to embrace the *reality* of myth.

The true heroic is learning to live fully and courageously in the light of finiteness while fully embracing all its limitation and all its anxiety. The heroic is not, as Becker (1973, 1975) states, the overcoming of death or human limitation. It is the embracing of it. This interpretation of the heroic as conquering mortality and finite limitations is misguided. Therapists help clients achieve the heroic not through selling them a version of faith or religion that claims to be more than what it is. Rather, therapists help clients achieve the heroic by courageously embracing faith in the midst of the anxiety, terror, and beauty.

REFERENCES

Barbour, I. (1990). *Religion in an age of science*. San Francisco, CA: Harper.
Barbour, I. (2000). *When science meets religion*. San Francisco, CA: Harper.
Becker, E. (1973). *The denial of death*. New York: The Free Press.
Becker, E. (1975). *Escape from evil*. New York: The Free Press.
Chopra, D. (1997). *The path to love: Spiritual strategies for healing*. New York: Three Rivers Press.
Christ, C. P. (2003). *She who changes: Re-imaging the divine in the world*. New York: Palgrave Macmillian.
Cobb, J. B., Jr., & Griffin, D. R. (1976). *Process theology: An introductory exposition*. Louisville, KY: Westminster John Knox Press.
Cortright, , B. (1997). *Psychotherapy and spirit*. Albany, NY: State University of New York Press.
Fowler, J. W. (1981). *Stages of faith: The psychology of human development and the quest for meaning*. San Francisco, CA: HarperCollins.
Freud, S. (1939). *Moses and monotheism* (K. Jones, Trans.). New York: Alfred A. Knopf.

Freud, S. (1950). *Totem and taboo* (J. Strachey, Trans.). New York: W. W. Norton. (Original work published 1913)

Freud, S. (1961). *The future of an illusion* (J. Strachey, Trans.). New York: W. W. Norton. (Original work published 1927)

Gomes, P. J. (1996). *The good book.* New York: William Morrow and Company.

Hanh, T. N. (1998). *The heart of the Buddha's teaching.* New York: Broadway Books.

Hartshorne, C. (1948). *The divine relativity: A social conception of God.* New Haven, CT: Yale University Press.

Hartshorne, C. (1984). *Omnipotence and other theological mistakes.* Albany, NY: State University of New York.

Held, B. (1998). The many truths of postmodernist discourse. *Journal of Theoretical and Philosophical Psychology, 18,* 193-217.

Hoffman, L. (2004, October). *Cultural constructions of the God image and God concept: Implications for culture, psychology, and religion.* Paper presented at the joint meeting of the Society for the Scientific Study of Religion/Religious Research Association, Kansas City, MO.

Johnson, E. A. (1992). *She who is: The mystery of God in feminist theological discourse.* New York: Crossroad Herder.

Kaufmann, W. (1974). *Nietzsche: Philosopher, psychologist, antichrist.* Princeton, NJ: Princeton University Press.

Keen, S. (1994). *Hymns to an unknown God: Awakening the spirit in everyday life.* New York: Bantam.

Keller, C. (1986). *From a broken web: Separation, sexism, and self.* Boston, MA: Beacon.

Kuhn, D. & Weinstock, M. (2002). What is epistemological thinking and why does it matter? In B. K. Hofer & P. R. Pintrich (Eds.), *Personal epistemology: The psychology of beliefs about knowledge and knowing* (pp. 121-144). Mahwah, NJ: Lawrence Erlbaum Associates.

Lawrence, R. T. (1997). Measuring the image of God: The God image inventory and the God image scales. *The Journal of Psychology and Theology, 25,* 214-226.

Martin, J. & Sugarman, J. (1999). Psychology's reality debate: A "levels of reality" approach. *Journal of Theoretical and Philosophical Psychology, 19,* 177-194.

May, R. (1977). *The meaning of anxiety.* New York: W. W. Norton.

May, R. (1991). *The cry for myth.* New York: Delta.

Moore, T. (2002) *The soul's religion.* New York: Perennial.

Moriarty, G. L. (in press). *"Why is god always mad at me?" Understanding and changing how the depressed person experiences God.* Haworth Press.

Nietzsche, F. (1966). *Thus spoke Zarathustra* (W. Kaufmann, Trans.). New York: Penguin.

O'Donohue, J. (1998). *Anam Cara: A Celtic book of wisdom.* New York: HarperCollins.

Pieper, F. (1950-1953). *Christian dogmatics* (Vols. 1-3). St. Louis, MO: Concordia.

Richards, P. S. & Bergin, A. E. (2002). *A spiritual strategy for counseling and psychotherapy.* Washington, DC: American Psychological Association.

Rank, O. (1978). *Truth and reality*. (J. Taft, Trans.). New York: W. W. Norton & Company. (Original work published 1936)

Rizzuto, A. M. (1979). *The birth of the living God*. Chicago, IL: University of Chicago Press.

Rizzuto, A. M. (1994). The father and the child's representation of God: A developmental approach. In S. H. Cath, A. R. Gurwitt, & J. M. Ross (Eds.), *Father and child: Developmental and clinical perspectives* (pp. 357-381). Hillsdale, NJ: The Analytic Press.

Spero, M. H. (1992). *Religious objects as psychological structures*. Chicago, IL: University of Chicago Press.

Stolorow, R. D. & Atwood, G. E. (1992). *Contexts of being: The intersubjective foundations of psychological life*. Hillsdale, NJ: The Analytic Press.

Tillich, P. (1951). *Systematic theology* (Vol. 1). Chicago, IL: University of Chicago Press.

Tillich, P. (1952). *The courage to be*. New Haven, NY: Yale University Press.

Tillich, P. (1955). *Biblical religion and the search for ultimate reality*. Chicago, IL: University of Chicago Press.

Tillich, P. (1957). *Dynamics of faith*. New York: Harper & Row.

Tillich, P. (1959). *Theology and culture*. New York: Oxford University Press.

Wilber, K. (2000). *Integral psychology*. Boston, MA: Shambhala.

Yalom, I. (1980). *Existential psychotherapy*. New York: Basic Books.

Part III

Theory and Diversity

9

EXISTENTIAL AND TRANSPERSONAL SPIRITUALITY AND THE PERSONALITY

Daryl S. Paulson, Ph.D.
President and CEO
Bioscience Laboratories, Inc.
Bozeman, MT

Traditional religions - Christianity, Islam, Buddhism, Judaism, and Hinduism - have long been the bastion of exoteric spirituality for the bulk of humanity (Smart, 1989; Spiegelberg, 1956). For literally billions of human beings around the world, religion provides the basic meaning in their lives, the glue of their existence, and offers a set of guidelines about what is good and what is not. The majority of humanity describes spirituality in religious terms -- a belief system of a specific group, whose members enjoin specific contents and contexts laid down by a founder (Wulff, 1991). In this chapter, however, spiritual will refer to direct phenomenological *experience* which includes personal egoic experience but also goes beyond the ego (Scotton, 1996). Spirituality is also an awareness of a broader life meaning, extending beyond everyday matters and natural concerns. The term spiritual can be used developmentally in two different ways. First, it can refer to the highest, most inclusive developmental level of any or all intelligence categories (lines of development) a human being is capable of achieving (Gardiner, 1983, 1999). Second, spiritual can be referred to as a specific and unique line of human development unto itself (Fowler, 1987).

In modern industrialized nations, the quest for directly experiencing spiritual realms is not a high priority for the majority of humans. Personal and cultural defense mechanisms seem to obscure the need to challenge one's belief system. Most humans in modern cultures appear to be content with traditional religious practices and their ready-made belief systems. They merely plug themselves in, secure in the rules, roles, and taboos, to which a believer subscribes. The reward for subscription is entering paradise. But the need to confront one's religious beliefs becomes important when individuals have a close brush with death, confront a serious illness, or lose life's meaning. Apparently, it becomes increasingly difficult for cultural and personal defenses to contain the existential anxiety concerning meaning.

Religion and the spiritual aspects of life tend to be ignored as important contributors to health by both mainstream psychiatry and mainstream (behavioral) psychology. For example, in Kaplan and Sadock's (2000) *Comprehensive Textbook of Psychiatry*, a two-volume text comprising 3,344 pages, spiritual is not even indexed, religion is only cursorily listed, religious problems are accorded less than one page of discussion, and the majority of that was taken from the DSM-IV's description of spiritual problems. Transpersonal psychology (spiritual psychology) was provided but a one-page synopsis. But in spite of this plain oversight, membership in APA's Division 36 (Psychology of Religion) has increased steadily, and national polls repeatedly report that over 90% of Americans believe in God. Fortunately, a number of high quality books are appearing that present concepts of religiosity and spirituality. For example, Shafranske edited *Religion and the Clinical Practice of Psychology* (1996), an American Psychological Association-published book. Scotton, Chinen, and Battista edited the *Textbook of Transpersonal Psychiatry and Psychology* (1996), and Robert Frager and James Fadiman published *Personality & Personal Growth* (1998), which contains several chapters on spirituality. Finally, William Braud and Rosemarie Anderson have written *Transpersonal Research Methods for the Social Sciences* (1998), a sophisticated text on research methods designed to analyze and describe spiritual phenomena.

A main focus of this chapter will be existential spirituality. Here, one contacts and confronts *Being*, or the *ground of one's Being*, or more generally *what is*. Let us first look at organized religion in greater detail, examine science, followed by transpersonal psychology, and conclude with existential spirituality.

ORGANIZED RELIGION

In the majority of religious practices - Christian, Islam, Judaism, Buddhism, and Hinduism - mundane life is viewed as an obstacle to spiritual growth, particularly that in day-to-day living humans are tempted to breech the rules, roles, and taboos (Funk, 1996, 1982; Smart, 1989). At best, mundane life is seen as something to get through until salvation assures the rewards of paradise. One's personality is generally viewed as unclean, even worthless, and, in several religions, non-existent. But traditional religions across cultures benefit mundane life by reducing existential anxiety (the fear and trembling) of not knowing for sure what is (Wulff, 1991). Religions provide believers answers to this question of what is.

Over the centuries, organized religion has been a target of science, psychology, and political theory. For example, science has been in conflict with religion at least since Galileo was excommunicated for blasphemously stating the earth traveled around the sun. Many of the early scientists were burned at the stake for other such heresies. In more recent times, both Freud and Marx reduced God to merely an infantile Father figure, a hold-over from more primitive human times (Fromm, 1968). For them, the analogy that the child obeys the father, as the individual obeys God, was truth. A number of sociologists have reported that religious belief systems and their dogmas are merely surface structure phenomena (Merton, 1957; Newman, 1997). Their real importance lies deeper in human unconscious levels and interactions. For example, if a believer is asked what his/her religious practices bring, s/he might say something like salvation, by carrying out church rituals (surface structures). But at a deeper, unconscious level, s/he is involved in not only anxiety reduction strategies, but also in forging stronger intersubjective bonds between its members. This tends to lead to an increase of an individual's trust in and dependence on the religious group for emotional support (Peterson & Nisenholz, 1999).

In summary, although traditional religions help insulate an individual from existential anxiety, they prevent one from touching one's Being for an authentic spiritual connection. Phenomenologically, one does not encounter one's Being authentically by engaging in religious practices; rather, one obeys rules and shares rituals (Bugental, 1965; Zimmerman, 1981).

SCIENCE

Traditional religious practices provide meaning, direction, and purpose for the majority, but not for all. Many intellectuals in industrialized nations derive their spiritual meaning from science (Schneider & May, 1995). Science, with its ability to explain and even control aspects of the external world, brings to the psyche a sense of predictability. Predictability for a human equates to a feeling of control, and control reduces existential anxiety (Angyal, 1965; Fenichel, 1996; Shapiro & Astin, 1998). Additionally, if a phenomenon can be labeled, even if not explained, it still tends to provide individuals a feeling of control and well-being (Tart, 1986). In recent years, many have constructed a science-based form of religion, popularly referred to as deep ecology.

Ecology is essentially a systems view of the ways organisms and their physical environments (collectively known as the biosphere) exist and interact often in organism-benefiting ways (Odum, 1983). For example, before life could appear on the earth as we know it, certain geochemical cycles were required to be operating. In order for terrestrial life to establish a foothold out of the water, the hydrological cycle had to operate. Water from large bodies of fresh water and the oceans evaporate from the sun's heat. The atmosphere then holds that water and releases it as rain or snow throughout the terrestrial regions. There, a certain amount of that water evaporates from the sun's heat, but not all. Certain amounts are stored frozen, especially in the mountainous regions, until the seasonal heat melts it. Much of this water percolates through the sediments to flow into streams, rivers, and back to the large body of water where the cycle begins again. Other cycles important to life, including the sulphur cycle, the nitrogen cycle, and the O_2/CO_2 cycles, are driven by the hydrologic cycle. Finally, some of the water, essential to all living things, resides in the myriad life forms of the earth.

By studying ecology and other natural sciences nested within it (zoology, limnology, botany, and microbiology, as well as aspects of geology) one can clearly perceive a larger functional operating system which supports all our lives (Jantsh, 1980). Its mystery and its operation provide a sense of a universal intelligence at work, which promotes meaning. Ecology also tempers the staunch 19th century belief in Darwinism. One easily recognizes that Darwin's survival of the fittest (the strongest survive) is not the whole truth. While perhaps the strongest lion in a pride gets first servings from a kill, the lions are, themselves, at the upper end of the food chain, totally dependent upon the autotrophs (green, chlorophyl-containing plants), to produce food for the heterotrophs (gazelles, antelope, etc.) which feed on the plants, ultimately feeding the lions. Break the chain at the green plant level or heterotroph level, and no more lions.

Yet, as valuable as ecology is for meaning, it is limited to external, observable phenomena. One can witness manifestations of Being, discover intellectual meaning, but one cannot phenomenologically encounter one's source of Being through ecology. In fact, one can be reverent of objective ecological systems, but starve for real spiritual, subjective experiences (Emmons, 1999).

TRANSPERSONAL PSYCHOLOGY

Transpersonal psychology offers many humans the benefit of psychological growth with a spiritual undergirding. Transpersonal psychology studies the human need for and process of spiritual transformation and transcendence. Its main goal is to assist individuals in finding purpose beyond physical survival and sensual gratification (Vaughan, 1995a, 1995b). Its early roots were in Eastern philosophies, particularly Hindu Yoga practices and Buddhism, as well as from Maslow's influential work with peak experiences. Much of its initial interest to individuals evolved from experiences with altered states of consciousness, stemming from the wide-spread use of psychedelic drugs in the 1960s (Hastings, 1999).

Transpersonal psychology does not consist of a specific system, nor even several, but is an amalgam of the world's spiritual traditions blended with modern Western psychology's hard-earned knowledge. This has produced a variety of comprehensive models, which integrate the basement, depth psychologies (e.g., psychoanalysis) with the spiritual, height traditions. A number of theorists have offered highly original models of this integrative process (Assagioli, 1965; Cortright, 1997; Wade, 1996; Washburn, 1994, 1995), but none as comprehensive as that of Ken Wilber (Wilber, 1999, 2000). Because transpersonal psychology views a person as being both a spiritual being (a soul) and an egoic self, it bypasses the religious sublime and the earthly mundane thesis/antithesis argument (which tries to prove one is better than another) by integrating the two, creating a higher synthesis of both the egoic and spiritual selves.

Commonalities appear across different transpersonal theorists' models, which include (Cortright, 1997):

1. *One's basic nature is spiritual.* Hence, transpersonal psychology emphasizes the spiritual, but does not neglect the personal, and considers personal growth and exploration important.
2. *One's consciousness is multi-dimensional.* Several transpersonal perspectives exemplify this hypothesis. For example, Ken Wilber (1999, 2000) views consciousness as developing through various *stages*, existing in not only subjective consciousness, but in the physical, objective world as well (i.e., his quadrant model). Others emphasize multiple *states* of consciousness (Grof, 1975, 1985, 1988; Tart, 1975), including the near death experience states of consciousness (Paulson, 1999a; Ring, 1998).
3. *Human beings have valid urges toward seeking spirituality expressed as a search for wholeness.* The human hierarchical levels of need were initially discussed thoroughly by Maslow (1968), and no one has brought its importance to the fore more than Wilber (1999, 2000).
4. *Contacting a deeper source of wisdom and guidance within oneself is a major goal.* To contact the transpersonal Self -- the Soul, the real Self, the higher Self, Self, or whatever one labels it -- is a primary goal in transpersonal psychology. No one has emphasized its primacy more than have Roberto Assagioli (1965, 1973), the founder of Psychosynthesis, and the Neo-Assagiolians (e.g., Brown [1993], Firman & Gila [1997], and Whitmore [1991]).
5. *Human life is meaningful.* One's actions, joys, sorrows, and insights are significant to a person in a real way; they are not pointless or meaningless (Moustakas, 1956). Vicktor Frankl (1969), a Jewish psychiatrist interned in several Nazi death camps during World War II, demonstrated the critical importance that life-meaning has for a person. When one loses meaning, s/he dies.

In conclusion, transpersonal psychology has contributed significantly to understanding that a person is more than just a physical, emotional, and mental entity, and is, in fact, a Soul. But as valuable as this insight can be, there comes a point in many individuals' lives when they must authentically and phenomenologically know and encounter what is for themselves, through what I call existential spirituality.

EXISTENTIAL SPIRITUALITY

Existential spirituality has no set doctrines or procedures, for it consists of an authentic personal, subjective discovery of what is. By depending on theories and doctrines to explain what is, one will actually postpone confrontation with what is. In existential spirituality, one discovers what is on an intimately personal level. As previously stated, one does not generally venture into this psychic ground unless their personal and/or cultural life moorings have been disrupted. Disruption is common for those who face their own death, the death of a significant other, experiences chronic sickness, finds no meaning in their lives, or undergoes extensive psychotherapy, for example. Existential spirituality entails a quest for self-understanding, which, according to Heidegger (1962), allows one to become fully what one already is, a being who understands what it means to be. If a person exists in ways true to one's spiritual Being, one experiences the *Being* of things more profoundly than through manipulated concepts about *Being*.

Several common threads to experiencing Being emerge. The first is authenticity. That is, in discovering Being or what is, one becomes ever more what one is at one's core. In order to do this, however, one must allow whatever material is contained in the unconscious to emerge to consciousness. To consciously experience what has been banished to the unconscious is particularly painful, since there has usually been significant repression, suppression, and denial of emotionally-charged events (Washburn, 1994, 1995).

Additionally, all too often, and particularly in modern industrialized societies, humans become over-enculturated, with precise imprinted instructions on how to act the right way, go to the right places, and interact with the right people (May, 1953). While there is much positive to be said about this -- in fact, it is a need of both culture and society -- it is often overly restrictive for a person. To counteract this, one must learn to listen to one's own inner voice, not just the voice, the superego, of society, one's parents, or some other authority figure, in order to make authentic decisions, to act in one's own way, to be responsible for one's own actions, and to feel ever more in touch with one's real needs, wants, desires, and fears (Bugental, 1965; Maslow, 1971; Riesman et al., 1950).

A second component is that one begins to act in ever more congruent ways as s/he becomes more in touch with his/her needs, wants, desires, and fears (Peterson & Nisenholz, 1999). That is, one's phenomenological experience and one's actions become more self-consistent. As individuals become more responsible for their actions, they also become responsible for the impact of their actions on others, as well as on the environment (Vaughan, 1995b).

Tillich (1952) stated that spirituality is one's existential passion for the infinite, one's ultimate concern, and in order to find it one must unflinchingly ask oneself, "Does life have any real meaning? Is there an ultimate purpose of human existence?" These ultimate concerns have been reported to occupy a major position in the life of a person searching for spirituality (Emmons, 1999). How one answers these questions will greatly influence one's personal goals, well-being, happiness, sense of purpose, sense of Self, possibilities, and, of course, one' world view (Fingarette, 1963; Rowan, 1993).

Existential spirituality is not centered outside of oneself in the world but within oneself, in one's own Being (Van Kaam, 1966). It has little to do with one's academic knowledge, one's philosophical knowledge, or one's religious knowledge but, instead, it is centered in the core and totality of ones being as phenomenologically experienced (von Eckartsberg, 1998). It has little to do with special techniques, altered states of consciousness, spiritual rituals, or traditions (Firman & Gila, 1997). It has everything to do with getting to know oneself in greater depth and breadth (Hixon, 1989).

Authentic encounter with one's Self requires a committed, conscious relationship with oneself deepening to the very source of one's Being (Paulson, 1993). It requires searching one's deepest inner truth, no matter where that journey may lead, and it will, no doubt, wind through a variety of experiences (Arbuckle, 1975; Firman & Gila, 1997): the depths of traumatic pain, the heights of spiritual insight, unresolved childhood issues, denial around addictions and compulsions, the dynamics of the family system, the struggle with life values and choices, decisive social and political action, and the healing of relationships with self, others, and the world.

In seeking spiritual discovery, one is advised to begin the search where one is in one's life, instead of where one should be (Assagioli, 1965). Where one is in one's life depends upon one's inner values, beliefs, experiences, goals, and aspirations, as well as values shared within one's culture, concerning worldviews, meaning, and direction (Daniels & Horowitz, 1984).

In searching for one's own truth, one is also advised to pay due respect to the great ones (the Buddha, the Christ, Krishna, and the Prophet Mohammed) but acknowledge that one must find out for oneself what is (Chaudhuri, 1965). In this process, one reportedly experiences, often for the first time, what it feels like to be oneself authentically; down even to what one's arms, legs, and one's teeth feel like from within (Washburn, 1995). What one authentically feels and values about one's life becomes important in discovering positive meaning. It is important to note that one should seek to discover how s/he feels about this or that, not how s/he should feel (Paulson, 1993).

Another phenomenon often experienced by those searching for authenticity in Being is a critical examination of one's life philosophy and belief system. The question is not whether it is right or wrong, but whether it is useful and consistent with one's authentic insights. A key indicator of this is a person's ability to be self-sufficient, not relying on others to explain the meaning of things, but rather to find it within one's own psychospiritual processes (Anthony, et al., 1987).

It has also been reported that, as the encounter with Being progresses, one is metaphorically able to rest or let go into one's very being and to just be (Washburn, 1995). When issues surface to consciousness, a person is free to attend them or not, depending upon what s/he chooses to do. Over time, it appears that, as suppressed and repressed emotional issues are dealt with psychologically, genuine insights from one's deeper source of Being surface to consciousness making the entire introspective process deeply valuable and worthwhile (Boorstein, 1997; Paulson, 1999b; Washburn, 1994, 1995).

Let us now explore what the actual contact with Being is like for the experiencer. Direct confrontation with one's ultimate concerns and ultimate meaning in life generates huge amounts of existential anxiety for one does not know for certain what is, if s/he will find any positive meaning at all, or if s/he will be sent into a spiraling downward trajectory to meaninglessness and utter despair (Fingarette, 1963; Grof, 1975, 1985, 1988, 1998; Washburn, 1995). Metaphorically, many seekers report feeling as though they were alone in a snow blizzard or a thick dark fog, unable to see anything clearly, and unable to gain any sense of bearing (Metzner, 1998). This anxiety is not mere tension; it is total gut-wrenching and all-consuming terror and confusion (Washburn, 1995). There appears to be nowhere to go for escape, for the cultural defenses are broken, as are one's personal defenses. There is no ready-made belief system to subscribe to now, only confrontation of the Ground which appears to threaten absolute non-being (Washburn, 1995).

This period of existential anxiety has been called the dark night of the Soul and the night sea journey, for one is not only alone, but all is unknown (Campbell, 1971). Predominant feelings reported are that one is on some dark planet somewhere in a dark corner of the universe where one is utterly alone, where there is no one to know how one feels or that one even existed (Angyal, 1965). One's meaning, direction, and purpose evaporate. Nothing makes sense. All appears to be lost. Yet continue one must (Campbell, 1968).

Raw courage is needed to continue, since this is a period of no exit; one knows s/he cannot go back to former ways of being, but feels s/he cannot go forward either (Campbell, 1968; Grof, 1985). One can only continue the struggle. It is at this point where traditional existential encounters stop. That is, one must face death and destruction alone, and one is alone, in a meaningless world, except for the meaning one gives it. Yet in this aloneness, one is free to choose the way one is.

Traditional existentialists did not go far enough in exploring this encounter with Being. A surprising number of individuals I have studied find that, within this apparent chaos and aloneness, a deeper, a more solidly grounded Self emerges (Paulson, 1993, 1994). This Self knows things for sure. Individuals experiencing this Self perceive their day-to-day egoic self as being a part of this larger Self (Paulson, 1993; Whitmore, 1991). This Self, while not generally interpreted as the Ground of Being in any absolute sense, is perceived to be a direct link to, as well as a part of it. In fact, many individuals no longer feel a need to contact the Absolute ground of Being, once they discover this aspect of themselves. They feel connected enough with what is through this Self sense to provide not only relief from groundlessness, but also an existential *knowing* of what is. That knowing is sufficient to not only bringing meaning into their lives, but to literally infusing their lives with it.

When one has contacted the deeper Self, s/he finds that there are no set spiritual goals which must be pursued, directions to follow, or techniques to use (Paulson, 1993; Whitmore, 1991). There is, however, a growing ability to experience this Self directly as one's own Being (Brown, 1993). This Self is not a symbol of oneself, but a constantly emerging 'Being-ness' of oneself (Paulson, 1993).

This deeper Self is not perceived by the person as emotionally needy, controlling, directing, judgmental, or self-righteous. In fact, an overwhelming majority of subjects studied report that this Self-sense seems not to care if one even listens to its voice (Paulson, 1995). But those who do hear its soft, friendly, accepting voice find it loud and clear in revealing truth.

This Self obeys no tradition, set of rules, roles, or taboos, nor does it make them for the personality. It is creative, authentic, and wise, knowing what troubles the individual, even before s/he asks (Assagioli, 1965). To many this sense of Self appears as an other while at the same time as oneself (Vaughan, 2000). At no time has it been explained as an it, but rather, as what Martin Buber termed, a "thou" (Buber, 1958; Firman, 1996).

Contact with this Self is truly a spiritual event in that, through this connection, one intuits egoically that *everything* is as it should be (Paulson, 1995). All appears to be perfect in its imperfection. Like the Japanese aesthetic term, Wabi Sabi, it enables the egoically-centered person to appreciate the deep beauty of ordinary existence (Rivera, 1997).

Yet there are individuals who do not discover a deeper Self. Research conducted by the author has revealed that they feel themselves touching their *Source of Being*, which they generally state is a life-giving mystery, a rejuvenation, or energy infusor beyond any Self-sense, yet not separate (Paulson, 1999c). By merely becoming aware of that mystery directly they feel grounded and solid within their lives. It is like being fed or supplied nourishment from the river or spring of life.

BEING IN HE WORLD

The majority of individuals studied who phenomenologically have touched their greater depths as a Self, or as Being beyond a Self, find the experience, while satisfying, incomplete (Paulson, 1999b). These individuals are not so immersed in their personal issues that they cannot express their spiritual insights through creative, as well as practical contributions to others, to humanity, and even to the external world; often through their life's work. They seem to genuinely care about others and are even enlivened by others' successes, as if they were their own (Washburn, 1995). In providing service to others, they generally feel no need of personal recognition; to be able to help is enough.

Just as inner courage was needed to encounter their Being, the courage to carry out Being insights into the external world is now a priority (Paulson, 1999b). To pursue these new behaviors in spite of one's fears concerning being singled out, being visible, and even being rejected, requires not only a high level, but a persistent level, of courage. For example, after their encounter with Being, individuals often find they do not fit in with their peers any more. The things they used to do, the places they went, as well as the people with whom they liked sharing these things, are no longer enjoyable. Even though they feel connected to the Universal Mystery, it is often a lonely time, requiring courage to begin anew, to live in accord with a new-found inner truth (Paulson, 1999b).

Living by one's convictions comes at a price. It cannot be free from negative repercussions. Those who walk away from a toxic job, leave a bad marriage, or stand up for what they believe often pay with pain, loss of profession or profit, and, sometimes, even the loss of their lives.

Take the case of Dietrich Bonhoeffer, a Germany Lutheran theologian who was living safely outside of Hitler's Nazi Germany and its reign of terror in the late 1930s (Paulson, 1999a). He returned to Germany to live in accord with his spiritual truth and humanitarian love by openly resisting the oppression and the systematic extermination of the Jews, Gypsies, Communists, and other inferior people. He could not ignore the inhumane Nazi actions, as did most organized religious groups, to avoid Hitler's wrath. Dietrich was true to his inner source of Being which enabled him to stand and defend that which he believed. He was executed in 1945 which was, for him, the cost of discipleship. For Bonhoeffer, courage was to live authentically in *this* life, expressing his soul insights and serving humanity openly, justly, and with dignity, not awaiting his reward in a future life.

As Roberto Assagioli wrote in *The Act of Will* (1973),

at times when danger threatens to paralyze us, suddenly, from the mysterious depths of our being, surges an unsuspected strength, enabling us to place a firm foot on the edge of the precipice and confront an aggressor calmly and resolutely, standing by our convictions at all costs. (p. 8)

Finally, to be and act as oneself also, at times, requires self-sacrifice. Consider the case of Gary and Mary Jane Chauncey and their 11-year-old daughter Andrea, a victim of cerebral palsy. The Chauncey family were passengers on an Amtrack train that crashed into a river while crossing a bridge hit and weakened by a river barge. As the railroad passenger car was sinking, the parents managed to push Andrea out through a broken window to rescuers, but at the expense of their lives.

Interestingly enough, research has shown that spirituality, as perceived by the experiencer, is not merely a state of feeling good or blissful, but a realization to the core of one's Being that one is an integral part of the web of life, as one is in Being. Finding the courage to be oneself can enable one to forgive others for failing to understand and even respect them. It also allows one to forgive all humanity for its senseless cruelties imposed upon those who do not fit in.

EXISTENTIAL SPIRITUALITY AS A RITE OF PASSAGE

While there are no directions on the wall or protocol steps in the spiritual process one must follow in the discovering of Being, there is a general viewing frame which seems to be useful to many individuals who have been studied (Paulson, 1994). This perspective greatly assists the seeker in dealing with an unknown circumstance over an unknown period of time (Campbell, 1968; Feinstein & Krippner, 1988; Paulson, 1994; Vaughan, 1995; Walsh, 1990). It is that of viewing the path to the discovery of Being as a rite of passage or an initiatory rite. Charles Taylor (1989) argues that without a framework or horizon to orient oneself in life, one is essentially adrift and disoriented. Viewing frames are absolutely necessary for humans, according to Taylor. A rite of passage perspective provides such a frame.

In Western contemporary society, individuals lack processes which aid in finding meaning in various life transitions. While puberty, high school, and/or college graduation, marriage and retirement are certainly rites of passage, each carrying some implicit psychological meaning, they are, for the most part, superficial social conventions. Yet research suggests that reframing these into a personal rite of passage can be extremely helpful for the egoic self in successfully dealing with life transitions (Feinstein & Krippner, 1988; Paulson, 1994; Walsh, 1990). Reframing the search for what is as a rite of passage can act as a compass when one is lost within his/her own psychospiritual processes. It can enable one to step back psychologically to reorient oneself.

Based upon Joseph Campbell's (1968) research, as well as research with Vietnam veterans (Paulson, 1994), a rite of passage traditionally has three sequential, invariant stages:

161

1. The separation phase, or call to adventure
2. The initiation phase, and
3. The return phase.

The separation phase occurs when the old ways of living no longer work. A person no longer wants to live in what Heidegger (1962) called "the inauthentic, everyday self." S/he wants something more. There seems to be a call for a different life path for this individual. Yet the person knows not what to do, where to go, or whom to see. This is a time James Hillman (1996) termed a call:

> There is more in a human life than our theories allow. Sooner or later, something seems to call us onto a particular path. You may remember this "something" as a single moment in childhood when an urge came out of nowhere, a fascination... like an annunciation: This is what I must do. (p. 3)

This is a time when one tries out new ways of being to replace those which do not work for him/her in navigating life any longer. One feels stuck and often asks oneself over and over: Is this all there is? The normal satisfactions of eating well, playing well, and making love well no longer work.

One might be drawn to new age practices, search through traditional religions, or even be drawn to psychotherapy. But in the end, one knows all too well s/he must make this journey alone (Paulson, 1994). As one begins the journey by accepting the call, one knows, metaphorically, s/he cannot go back to a former way of being. The only way available is to press on, no matter where it leads. Like Dante in the Divine Comedy having lost his way in life, s/he must travel through hell before enjoying the fruits of heaven.

Thus begins the second stage, the initiation. It is a process of deconstructing construct after construct until the individual is untethered from his/her former world (Paulson, 1994). Now nothing appears familiar and there is no ground to get a solid footing (Washburn, 1995). Everything appears to be in ruin. As we have previously discussed, this is an incredibly difficult period for the individual. Yet, by perceiving it as a *necessary life transition period*, through which one is only passing, is anxiety-reducing in itself (Bridges, 1980; Paulson, 1994). The old, inauthentic ways of being do not work and new ways of being are not yet known, but as one persists in confronting one's Ground of Being, ultimately, a positive, meaningful breakthrough is achieved (Washburn, 1995). As we have discussed, achieving that breakthrough to a clear, direct connection with the Being requires that one work through layers of repressed, suppressed, and denied, highly emotionally-charged material. Behind that material, finally, there comes a feeling, of a *knowing*, of finding *home*, finding Self, finding meaning, purpose, and direction.

The return stage of existential spirituality is sharing one's direct insights and channeling one's behavior into one's calling (Hillman, 1996). This is a period of not only integrating the new discoveries from confrontation with Being in the initiation period, but also of expressing them throughout one's entire life field.

CONCLUSION

In the end, if humans are to find authentic spirituality, spirituality beyond cognitive constructs and shared belief systems, they will have to encounter phenomenologically *what is* directly. This, of course, is an extremely stressful period of life, but one which can ultimately provide one a solid foothold or grounding in Being. The process requires courage, and such courage requires one to step out of the safety of their familiar dogmas, policies, and group biases to discover for oneself what is true, what is right, what is just, and what is. As Vivekanada (1953) stated, most of us have searched for life's spiritual meaning in temples, in churches, in science, in medicine, on earth, in heaven, and even hell. But, in the end, often in despair, we come back to ourselves, where the whole search began, and find that the spirituality we have searched for outside of ourselves, abides within us. It is our own authentic Self, our Source Being, which was always there waiting to welcome us home.

REFERENCES

Alexander, C. & Langer, G. (Eds.). (1990). *Higher stages of human development.* New York: Oxford University Press.

Angyal, A. (1965). *Neurosis and treatment.* New York: John Wiley.

Anthony, D., Ecker, B., & Wilber, K. (1987). *Spiritual choices.* New York: Paragon.

Arbuckle, D. S. (1975). *Counseling and psychotherapy* (3rd ed.). Boston: Allyn & Bacon.

Assagioli, R. (1965). *Psychosynthesis.* New York: Hobbs-Dorman.

Assagioli, R. (1973). *The act of will.* New York: Viking.

Boorstein, S. (1997). *Clinical studies in transpersonal psychology.* Albany: State University of New York Press.

Braud, W. & Anderson, R. (1998). *Transpersonal research methods for the social sciences.* Thousand Oaks, CA: Sage Publishing.

Bridges, W. (1980). *Transitions.* Menlo Park, CA: Addison-Wesley.

Brown, M. (1993). *Growing whole.* New York: Harper-Collins.

Buber, M. (1958). *I and thou.* (2nd ed.). New York: Scribner.

Bugental, J. F. T. (1965). *The search for authenticity.* New York: Holt, Rhinehart, & Winston.

Campbell, J. (1968). *The hero with a thousand faces.* Princeton, NJ: Princeton University Press.

Campbell, J. (1971). *The portable Jung.* New York: Viking.

Chaudhuri, H. (1965). *Integral yoga.* London: George Allen & Unwin, Ltd.

Cortright, B. (1997). *Psychotherapy and spirit.* Albany: State University of New York Press.

Daniels, V. & Horowitz, L. J. (1984). *Being and caring* (2nd ed.). Mountain View, CA: Mayfield Publishing.

Emmons, R. A. (1999). *The psychology of ultimate concerns*. New York: Guilford Press.

Feinstein, D. & Krippner, S. (1988). *Personal mythology*. Los Angeles: Tarcher.

Fenichel, O. (1996). *The psychoanalytic theory of neurosis.* (50th anniversary ed.). New York: Norton.

Fingarette, H. (1963). *The self in transformation*. New York: Basic.

Firman, J. & Gila, A. (1997). *The primal wound*. Albany: State University of New York Press.

Firman, J. (1996). *Self and self-realization*. Palo Alto, CA: Psychosynthesis Palo Alto.

Fowler, J. (1981). *Stages of faith*. San Francisco: Harper & Row.

Frager, R. & Fadiman, J. (1998). *Personality & personal growth* (4th ed.). New York: Longman.

Frankl, V. (1969). *Man's search for meaning*. New York: World Publishing.

Fromm, E. (1968). *Revolution of hope*. New York: Harper-Row.

Funk, R. W. (1982). *Parables and presence*. Philadelphia: Fortress Press.

Funk, R. W. (1996). *Honest to Jesus*. New York: Harper-Collins.

Gardiner, H. (1983). *Frames of mind*. New York: Basic Books.

Gardiner, H. (1999). *Intelligence reframed*. New York: Basic Books.

Grof, S. (1975). *LSD Psychotherapy*. Albany: State University of New York Press.

Grof, S. (1985). *Beyond the brain*. Albany: State University of New York Press.

Grof, S. (1988). *The adventure of self-discovery*. Albany: State University of New York Press.

Grof, S. (1998). *The cosmic game*. Albany: State University of New York Press.

Hastings, A. (1999). Transpersonal psychology: The fourth face. In D. Moss (Ed.), *Humanistic and transpersonal psychology*. Westport, CT: Greenwood Press.

Heidegger, M. (1962). *Being and time*. New York: Harper & Row.

Hillman, J. (1996). *The soul's code*. New York: Random House.

Hixon, L. (1989). *Coming home*. Los Angeles, Tarcher.

Jantsch, E. (1980). *The self-organizing universe*. New York: Pergamon.

Maslow, A. (1968). *Toward a psychology of being.* (2nd ed.). Princeton: Von Nostrand.

Maslow, A. (1971). *The further reaches of human nature*. New York: Viking.

May, R. (1953). *Man's search for himself*. New York: Norton.

Merton, R. K. (1957). *Social theory and social structure*. Glencoe, IL: Free Press.

Metzner, R. (1998). *The unfolding self*. Novato, CA: Origin Press.

Moustakas, C. E. (1956). *The self*. New York: Harper & Brothers.

Newman, D. M. (1997). *Sociology*. Thousand Oaks, CA: Sage Publishing.

Paulson, D. S. (1993). Authentic integral living: The search for the real self. *Journal of the American Academy of Psychotherapists, 30,* 58-65.

Paulson, D. S. (1994). *Walking the point*. Plantation, FL: Distinctive Publishing.

Paulson, D. S. (1995). Integration of esoteric and transpersonal psychologies. *Journal of Esoteric Psychology, 9,* 118-131.

Paulson, D. S. (1999a). The near death experience: an integration of cultural, spiritual, and physical perspectives. *Journal of Near Death Studies, 18,* 13-25.

Paulson, D. S. (1999b). Courage to be oneself. *Journal of the American Academy of Psychotherapists, 35,* 56-58.

Paulson, D. S. (1999c). Is where we are going where we want to be? *Journal of Esoteric Psychology, 8,* 1-15.

Odum, E. P. (1983). *Basic ecology.* Philadelphia: Saunders.

Peterson, J. V. & Nisenholz, B. (1999). *Orientation to counseling* (4th ed.). Boston: Allyn & Bacon.

Riesman, D., Glazer, N. & Denny, R. (1950). *The lonely crowd.* New Haven, CT: Yale University Press.

Ring, K. (1998). *Lessons from the light.* New York: Insights.

Rivera, F. G. (1997). *Suiseki.* Berkeley: Stone Bridge Press.

Rowan, J. (1993). *The transpersonal.* New York: Routledge.

Sadock, B. J. & Sadock, V. A. (2000). *Kaplans and sadock's comprehensive of psychiatry* (7th ed.). Philadelphia: Lippincott, Wilkens & Wilkens.

Schneider, K. J. & May, R. (1995). *The psychology of existence.* New York: McGraw-Hill.

Scotton, B. W. (1996). Introduction and definition of transpersonal psychiatry. In B. W. Scotton, A. B. Chinen, & J. R. Battista (Eds.). *Textbook of transpersonal psychiatry and psychology.* (pp. 39-51). New York: Basic.

Shafranske, E. P. (1996). *Religion and the clinical practice of psychology.* Washington, DC: American Psychological Association.

Shapiro, Jr., D. H. & Astin, J. (1998). *Control therapy.* New York: John Wiley.

Sinnott, J. D. (1994). The relationship of postformal thought, adult learning, and lifespan development. In J. D. Sinnott (Ed.). *Interdisciplinary handbook of adult lifespan learning.* (pp. 90-104). Westport, CT: Greenwood.

Smart, N. (1989). *The world's religions.* Cambridge, UK: University of Cambridge Press.

Spiegelberg, F. (1956). *Living religions of the world.* Englewood Cliffs, NJ: Prentice-Hall.

Tart, C. (1975). *Transpersonal psychologies.* New York: Harper-Row.

Tart, C. (1986). *Waking up.* Boston: Shambhala.

Taylor, C. (1989). *Sources of the self.* Cambridge, MA: Harvard Press.

Tillich, P. (1952). *The courage to be.* New Haven, CT: Yale University Press.

Van Kaam, A. (1966). *Existential foundations of psychology.* Pittsburg: Duquesne University.

Vaughan, F. (1995a). *The inward arc.* (2nd ed.). Nevada City, CA: Blue Dolphin Publishing.

Vaughan, F. (1995b). *Shadows of the sacred.* Wheaton, IL: Theosophical Publishing House.

Vaughan, F. (2000). *Personal communications.* Mill Valley, CA.

Vivekananda. (1953). *Vivekananda: The yogas and other works.* New York: Rama Krishna-Vivekananda Center.

Von Eckartsburg, R. (1998). Introducing existential-phenomenological psychology. In R. Valle (Ed.). *Phenomenological Inquiry in psychology.* New York: Plenum Press.

Wade, J. (1996). *Changes of mind.* Albany: State University of New York Press.

Walsh, R. (1990). *The spirit of shamanism.* Los Angeles: Tarcher.

Washburn, M. (1995). *The ego and the dynamic ground.* (2nd ed.). Albany: State University of New York Press.

Washburn, M. (1994). *Transpersonal psychology in psychoanalytic perspective.* Albany: State University of New York Press.

Whitmore, D. (1991). *Psychosynthesis counseling in action.* Newbury Park, CA: Sage Publishing.

Wilber, K. (1999). *The collected works of Ken Wilber: Vols. 1-4.* Boston: Shambhala Press.

Wilber, K. (2000). *The collected works of Ken Wilber: Vols. 5-9.* Boston: Shambhala Press.

Wulff, D. M. (1991). *Psychology of religion.* New York: John Wiley & Sons.

Zimmerman, M. E. (1981). *Eclipse of the self.* Athens, OH: Ohio University Press.

10

TRANSCENDENCE AND IMMINENCE IN PSYCHOTHERAPY[1]

Richard H. Cox, Ph.D., M.D., D.Min.
Provost
Colorado School of Professional Psychology
Colorado Springs, CO

Psychology has become an idol of this age. Psychological terms have become common household jargon. Everything seems to be measured by the yardstick of the psychological model of development. Education, industry, politics, law enforcement, and, indeed, even the church now teaches, follows, and reckons with a psychological definition of what should be the norm. In the short time since Freud, an ethic stronger than that of the Puritans has taken over. Religion no longer primarily speaks to the issues of faith and life, but rather has adapted to the cultural mode of psychology.

The "psychological revolution" of religion was in full swing by the late fifties and early sixties in the United States. Churches were conducting group meetings (therapy), "touchy-feely," and "tell- all" sessions, and a new kind of "group forgiveness" following this new form of group confession was bestowed. "In recent years, a romantic haze has developed around the word *psychology*. The church has become just as vulnerable to this gimmick as any other institution" (Cox, 1966). In a day of waning church attendance and the recent "God is Dead" movement of that time, methods for revitalizing the Church were very welcome.

Psychology had proven its value by that time. Psychological knowledge and methodology had improved the educational component of the Church, a sound basis for pastoral counseling had been established, missionary selection had been improved, and

---

[1] This was original published in the American Journal of Psychotherapy, Volume 51, 1997.

seminaries were seeing the value of looking at the overall psychological make-up on candidates for the ministry.

As often happens with new knowledge, the application of this field of human behavior took on a zeal and power of its own. Psychological methods and ideas became driving forces, and problems arose of an entirely new kind. "Neuroses are often created which are more pathological than those with which parishioners began" (Cox, 1968). The message and method of *psychology* was being mistaken for the message and method of *religion*.

The thrust of this article is not to detract from either religion or psychology, but to state that *they are not the same and that one cannot replace the other*. It speaks specifically to the issue of religion, the religious, and the institutions of the religious, in an attempt to question the validity of utilizing the language and method of imminence to convey and accomplish the message of transcendence.

IMMINENCE

The language of imminence is the language of the here and now, i.e. that which is apt to happen unpredictably at any time. It is the language of the age. *The Cambridge International Dictionary of English* (1995) gives the following definition: "Imminence, that which is likely to happen soon...the imminence of an attack made us all nervous." The term is usually used in a negative context. Although psychology is not necessarily negative, it certainly emphasizes the reality of the here-and-now, deals with that which is apt to happen, speaks of predictable behavior, and in its most prevalent form allows little if any room for faith and hope of the religious sort. When *psychology* speaks of hope, it is speaking of faith in humanity. When *religion* speaks of hope, it is speaking of faith in the transcendent. "Faith is the state of being ultimately concerned: the dynamics of faith are the dynamics of man's ultimate concern" (Tillich, 1957, p. 1) Tillich reminds us that man not only has all the concerns of every other living creatures, but also "has spiritual concerns – cognitive, aesthetic, social, political" (Tillich, 1957, p. 1).

TRANSCENDENCE

Transcendence is to rise above, go beyond, experience more than the here and now could predict or anticipate. In spite of the message, method, and language of psychology often being that of the imminent, psychotherapy, although rooted in psychology, strives to attain the transcendent. The "worried well" along with the most psychotic person seeks, and are often able to find, hope and emotional relief that far exceeds the imminence of the language and methods of psychology.

The Church has not gone out of the religion business, however, it could be argued that in many circles it has gone into the psychology-of-religion business, or even the religion-of-psychology business. Psychology has proven to be a most persuasive, socially acceptable manipulation of the human mind; yet, as a basis for "faith and life," it has tremendous shortcomings.

Every age in human history promotes a coveted image for all people. The eminent psychoanalyst Erick H. Erickson is helpful to us in understanding this concept. He speaks of "generativity" as second to the highest form for human living. He asserts that "ego integrity vs. stagnation" was the eighth or highest age of life. In this "age," he reached for, and embraces transcendence when he states, "healthy children will not fear life if their elders have integrity enough not to fear death" (Erickson, 1950). Erickson was attempting to establish a goal beyond the imminent. He had already established that "hope is both the earliest and the most indispensable virtue inherent in the state of being alive" (Erickson, 1964). Generativity is defined by Erikson as "establishing and guiding the next generation...is meant to include productivity and creativity" (Erickson, 1950). When Erickson's "generativity" is coupled with his concept of "ego integrity" and built upon the primary foundation of hope and trust, we approach a next step, which we can legitimately called the transcendent.

We must not buy imminence as a form of spirituality. Imminence is devoid of faith, and by definition awaits negativity. Imminence awaits the worst and expects bad things to happen. Most psychological methods and tools are based on the assumption that we can by such tools change human destiny. Imminence speaks of the here-and-now and awaits the troubles and failures that occur simply by existing as a human being. Imminence is the harbinger of anxiety.

The religious view must by definition be based on faith and hope and, therefore, transcendence. The ultimate human form is therefore not the "generative" person, or even the "ego integrity" person, but the "transcendent" person. To transcend is to "go beyond the limits of, to transcend the limits of common thought" (*Random House Dictionary of the English Language*, 1967). Within the definitions of "imminence" and "transcendence," we see clearly why religion and psychology are mutual friends and mutual enemies.

The person of "faith" cannot be bogged down by "imminence," which expects disaster. The believer in "imminence" cannot understand that which is known only to "transcendence." According to the Bible, "faith is the assurance of things hoped for, the conviction of things not seen" (Holy Bible, RSV, Heb.11:1). Transcendence is the harbinger of hope.

It is interesting to note that both "imminence" and "transcendence" are based on *belief.* The assumption of psychology is that its principles are based in knowledge, even *scientific knowledge.* There are many parts of psychology which are indeed based on laboratory findings and solid empirical research. Most of psychology which deals with human behavior; however, is based on observation, phenomenological understandings, and clinical experience. Our "norms" are the result of acceptable statistical samples which establish that which is *normal, i.e., average.* This definition can easily accept "imminence" as a base of operation, since man certainly seems to gravitate to the norm, or the mean of any statistical measure. However, "transcendence" is the ability to rise above the norm, the belief that man can achieve a state of mind and resultant life style that is grounded in the extra-ordinary, the "not yet seen but believed."

One of the basic principles of all psychotherapy, whether spoken or not, is to give a person *hope*. The "generative person" established something to work toward, i.e., "actualization" of his/her full potential (Maslow, A., 1968). However, the energy for that journey is left to the innate abilities and creative potential of the individual. The "transcendent person" has all which is human available *plus* the energies of hope, faith, and a belief in powers greater than him/herself. Alcoholics Anonymous recognized many years ago that a psychology of imminence was insufficient to provide the tools to deal with addiction; therefore, its founders adopted a creed based on transcendence. Step two of their Twelve-Step Program states, "Came to believe that a Power greater than ourselves could restore us to sanity" (Alcoholics Anonymous, 1952). They recognized that when the end product is based only in the here and now, their program would not work. Goleman (1995), in his recent book *Emotional Intelligence*, discusses hope as part of *The Master Attitude*, "having hope means that one will not give in to overwhelming anxiety, a defeatist attitude, or depression in the face of difficult challenges or setbacks" (p. 86).

This is where religion enters the picture. It is where ethereal hope finds a pragmatic *modus operandi*. It is where psychotherapy and religion meet. It is where psychotherapy and religion joined together become a gestalt, a product greater than the sum of its parts. It is where psychotherapy is able to transcend human understanding and offer human growth beyond human expectation. Psychotherapy of this sort provides a stage upon which the problems of life may be both acted out and *resolved*. A psychotherapy of hope, by itself, frequently allows patients to understand themselves and why they behave in a certain way, but is not able to actually change the behavior. Without an ongoing experience in the "transcendent," anything else is only "imminent" and is a dead-end street.

When religion and psychotherapy unite, we have a combination of reality based behavior and an energy for adaptation, growth, and change which is not rooted in negativism and is transcendent. It transcends not only the norm, but goes beyond that which has been measured, therefore, has no norm.

RELIGIOUS AND SPIRITUAL CRISIS

The crisis in Western culture is a religious one. The understanding of human development, human behavior and the knowledge of how to motivate change are valuable tools for anyone, religious or not. The question is how to utilize basic knowledge without adopting the basic assumptions upon which that knowledge was built, and the premises of belief which that knowledge espouses. The question remains: is it possible to combine religious values with psychological knowledge? The answer to this question is "yes."

Long before there was a discipline called "psychology," its principles were employed within the church and throughout the world and that continues to be done to be done today. Long before Freud and his predecessors, even before we knew the knowledge of human behavior was "psychological," the knowledge and results of that knowledge were used. The greater question has not to do with the knowledge, but the value base of a given psychological framework and the tools which develop out of that knowledge base.

Confession, a discipline of the Roman Catholic Church, based on a theology of its own, is a good example. The Protestant Church, which disavowed confession as a religious discipline, resurrected confession under the guise of "growth groups" in the late 1950's. It resurrected "forgiveness" by offering "psychological acceptance." The results of confession, a dimension being sought by many persons, was missing in the Protestant Church. Psychology, which understands isolation, guilt, and abandonment, was instrumental in bringing back that missing element, although not called confession and not offered within a theological framework. Long before psychologists recognized the need for forgiveness, the Church had seen the results of persons who through confession found a way to "start over" and "transcend" their past. Religion and psychology have a long history of working together.

Many psychologists started their formal training in theology, then combined it with psychology. Such was the case with Carl Rogers, Rollo May, and this author. Others, such as Paul Tillich, remained in theology and brought to us incredible psychological insights. These persons and many others have shown that it may not matter so much which discipline is considered primary. When psychology and religion are combined, a new discipline results which is greater than either by itself.

Rogers (1959), illustrates the value of this fact in his concept of "unconditional positive regard." Here we have a concept that in and of itself is totally alien to human nature, i.e., gives other persons love regardless of who they are or what they have done. This concept by any definition is not an ordinary human characteristic. He draws upon the transcendent to enable the imminent. Rogers began his studies at Union Theological Seminary then transferred to study psychology at Columbia University. Many persons have found institutionalized theology devoid of the human element. Many persons have found institutionalized theology devoid of the human element. Like him, many persons who have studied both psychology and theology have found a meaningful combination of these two incredibly powerful disciplines.

By the same token, there are many psychotherapists who have been disappointed in the "imminence" of psychology and who then attend theological studies to find hope, faith, and transcendence. The high incidence of persons who start with one discipline then go on to study the other emphasizes the value and possibilities available to the therapist when both disciplines are embraced.

Psychology is the language of *human behavior*. Religion is the language of *being human*. To confuse these facts is to expect things that cannot be. Psychology talks about what we *have done*. Religion speaks to what *we can do*. Psychology recognizes what we *are*, while religion looks at what we can *become*.

In the language of human behavior, life takes on a very anemic hue at best. Human behavior, even our own, is not that uplifting and worthy of reward. Theological language allows for a more colorful picture with a hope to live "above the ordinary" and not settle back into the "average." However, just as psychology by itself, when speaking of *human behavior,* can have a hollow ring, religion, likewise, can and often does have a very hollow ring of a "pie in the sky" mentality.

The transcendent person lives within the bounds of imminence, while actualizing her/his potential and reaching beyond the here and now with both belief and method which are more than earthbound. There is no necessity to become "otherworldly" and lose touch with day-to-day reality. To recognize both reality in the here-and-now and the reality of that which is based in belief is not an easy task. Psychotherapy cannot be effective without both. The ability to instill a faith in oneself beyond the reality of one's current behavior is an art that only skilled, personally transcending therapists have. To speak only of human behavior within the old cliché of "picking up yourself by your own bootstraps" is both a "put down" and an untruth. Most patients would have long ago "picked themselves up" if they could have done so. They would not be prone to spend time and money if their own "bootstraps" had been sufficient. Hence, to put forth that argument is to only further exaggerate their sense of low self-esteem.

Virtually all psychotherapists utilize deeply rooted religious concepts in their work. They speak of catharsis, i.e., confession, acceptance, i.e., forgiveness; and of empathy, i.e., love. They connect with many other basically theological ideologies. They speak of "human potential," as if we knew apart from a value base what that is. Some would argue that this takes us back to a philosophical/theological debate as to the depravity or divinity of the human being. Perhaps, but more useful is the discussion that whatever we are and do, it is possible to become something greater and perform better. This concept apart from a spiritual, value base is meaningless. Psychotherapists instinctively, and by training and experience know this to be true. As a result, psychotherapists offer their assistance in helping patients to *change.* Herbert Benson (1996), noted author of *The Relaxation Response,* states in *Timeless Healing:* "The sound of a doctor's voice, the words he or she chooses, the hope he or she can instill, and the time required to develop a good doctor-patient conversation promote health in ways many doctors and most insurers underestimate today" (p. 252).

PSYCHOTHERAPIST AS AGENT

The psychotherapist as *change agent* must be examined in detail. It is important to see the psychotherapist as *an agent,* which is "a person authorized by another to act on his behalf" (Random House Dictionary of the English Language, 1967). There are many inherent assumptions, possibilities and dangers in being an agent.

Rarely, if ever, does a patient know what he/she is doing when allowing a therapist to act as an agent. Further, psychotherapists are not trained to fully understand the huge responsibility that becoming an agent entails. Most therapists see their task as helping to change certain behaviors or certain specific ways of thinking. This is to take a rather shallow view of the human being. We cannot be separated into segments, i.e., things we do and things we think. The human is an entity: body, mind, and spirit. To treat one part is to treat all parts.

172

To ignore one part is to ignore all parts. It has often been promulgated that if a psychotherapist has differing views on a given subject, that subject should be either ignored or dealt with "neutrally." Illustrative of this is the very issue of religion. Many psychotherapy trainers would teach that one should not "push your religious views onto a patient", or for instance, if the therapist's views on abortion, right to life, euthanasia, and other controversial topics differ, they should be kept to oneself. Some would even suggest that the patient should be transferred to a therapist whose views are more compatible.

This approach seems to be naive. To transfer a patient because of differing views on one subject, does not guarantee agreement on other subjects between the new therapist and the patient. Even if one finds a therapist who agrees on the "basic" issue, it is likely that many other issues will arise upon which they do not agree. Further, differing opinions do not make for mental health or mental illness. To fragment the message from the messenger is also not possible in a psychotherapist. In psychotherapy the messenger is the message. A therapist who has begun the journey of transcending gives that message and even large differences in belief matter only slightly. The therapist who is enmeshed in the imminence of life attempts to make each item complete, perfect, and present thought systems as shiny, finished products. None of us are that accomplished.

As an agent for change, we do not determine the changes. It is easy for a psychotherapist to honestly believe that he/she is treating, for instance, a phobia. Sometimes we forget that we are treating a *person with a phobia*. As such, the phobia becomes secondary to the person. The patient may have presented with a phobia because the *real problem* was too painful, or altogether unknown. Dealing with the phobia as the true and only problem may well be a disservice to the patient. Phobias are no doubt excellent illustrations of being caught in the imminent. There is no sense of transcendence in a phobia. To treat the phobia instead of the whole person is to have both the therapist and the patient caught in the imminent. This perhaps explains why so many patients are successfully treated for one phobia only to find another. The phobia is not the problem. Being caught in the imminent is the problem.

The transcendent psychotherapist is *personally* in the *process* of transcending, always an unfinished, but continuing to be finished product. This message is clear to all who come into contact with that therapist, whether patient or not. Herein lies another important message. Psychotherapists do not develop techniques for patients. They develop styles of life, communication, and energy that are more vibrant and living. The psychotherapist who works within the concept of techniques tends to obscure the individual patient and treat only "*the problem.*" We teach students various skills. We teach them to diagnose personalities and to treat *problems*. We do so because we do not know how to teach students to *transcend*. Fortunately, many therapists learn the process of transcending and are able to communicate such to their patients.

Skills are very deceptive. We teach certain methods for dealing with various "*human behavior*" problems; therapeutic techniques that apply to specific mental illness problems. We are once more reminded that the fundamental problem that underlies all human problems is the fear of death. In his stellar work *The Denial of Death*, Ernest Becker (1973) states "that death is man's peculiar and greatest anxiety" (p. 70). From the earliest philosophers and theologians thorough the most thoughtful psychologists and psychoanalysts, we cannot escape this most primal of all human terrors.

Students learn these techniques, yet, in supervision, the senior clinician is confronted with "why didn't it work?" It did not work because patients are immune to techniques. They are only open to transcending spirits who are able to rise above the technique. For instance, the only person who ever truly utilized the Rogerian method was Carl Rogers and in that method, Dr. Rogers, as a person, was there far more than his method. Learning methods and techniques does not make a psychotherapist. Utilizing methods and techniques as foundations allows the student to transcend the tool and become a transcending therapist whose technique becomes an extension of oneself.

The transcending personhood of the psychotherapist is the key. The listening, sensing, feeling, responding, essence of the person comes through when skill and methods fail. The human is not a machine and the therapist is not a mechanic. Much has been written about the uniqueness of the therapeutic relationship. Not so much has been written about the uniqueness of the therapist.

As an *agent for change*, what is the change? Is the change attempted that which the patient requests? Is the change attempted that which the therapist deems best? Is the change that comes about the result of "following the flow" and waiting to see what happens? As an agent for change, what is the responsibility for the therapist who has been assigned by the patient as an agent to act upon the patient's behalf, even if the patient does not know what to request?

> For many decades most psychotherapists have tried to deny the effects of their personal belief systems upon their clients...studies suggest the need to examine how the psychotherapist's practice is affected by his personal beliefs, but we touch upon some very sensitive areas, when we raise questions concerning the effects of religious commitment upon professional practice. (Clement & Warren, 1973, p. 422)

It seems so blatantly absurd that we should question the effect of any part of the psychotherapist upon patients from whom such honesty is expected. Herein lies the necessity for the mature psychotherapist to be a person who is diligently traveling the journey of transcendence. We can only share that which we have, and we can share all of what we have, both the imminence (i.e., our own anxieties), and the transcendency (i.e., our faith and hopes). Patients frequently "read" the therapist better than the therapist "reads" the patient. The patient knows whether our "intervention" is a phony technique or if it emanates from a deeply spiritual person who may not know the answers, but does know the right questions.

Transcendence and imminence are not simply linguistic terms. They are ways of thinking, styles of living, types of maturity, and the bases for development into a whole person. Understanding transcendence as a psychotherapist is being part of the whole structure, and being able to invite others into that wholeness, rather than getting bogged down in why certain techniques do or do not work.

With the many changes coming about in the over-all health care system, it will be easy to become caught up in how to deal with patients quickly and how to develop techniques that will bring about rapid changes. This may be the most destructive move yet in the field of human services. It is important that we keep our sense of transcendence and not sell out to the imminent.

The stage upon which psychotherapy takes place will also give deep meaning to the patient. It will be difficult to communicate transcendence when therapy is limited to certain conditions that must be treated within so many sessions, and the use of only certain techniques are recognized. The psychotherapist will inevitably be caught in one of the most ultimate of all paradoxes involving the imminent and the transcendent, namely, how to *really care for someone* with faith and hope, while at the same time bound to an imminent, here-and-now, time frame, cost frame, diagnosis frame, treatment frame and termination of treatment frame. How to be a transcendent psychotherapist in a world of forced imminence will continue to be our challenge.

SUMMARY

Psychotherapists who become bogged down in the language and behavior of the imminent are by definition unable to move themselves and/or their clients/patients to the creative and fulfilling level of the transcendent. To be "generative" and to become "integrative" in the Erikson tradition is laudable, albeit insufficient. That which one integrates and that which one generates is fulfilling only if it transcends the human dilemma of the here-and-now.

The necessity of rethinking the task of the psychotherapist has never been more important than today in the shadow of what appears to be the most dramatic change in the practice of Western medicine and mental health.

The intent of this discussion is not to detract from either religion or psychotherapy, but to emphasize that they are not the same and cannot replace each other. Attempts through the years to do so have brought about gross confusion in the roles of each as regards wholeness of the mind.

Psychotherapists who are able to become transcending within their own experience are likely to move beyond the barriers of the age and bring a hope to others, which exceeds methods and technology.

REFERENCES

Alcoholics Anonymous. (1952) *Twelve steps and twelve traditions*. Alcoholics Anonymous Publishing.

Becker, E. (1973). *The denial of death*. New York: Free Press.

Benson, H. (1996). *Timeless healing*. New York: Scribner.

Clement, P. & Warren, N. T. (1973). In R. H. Cox (Ed.), *Religious systems and psychotherapy* (pp. 417-426). Springfield, IL: Charles C. Thomas.

Cox, R. H. (1966). Pseudopsychology and the church. *Christianity Today, 10*.

Cox, R. H. (1968). The being real neurosis. *Christian Century, 85*, 10.

Erickson, E. H. (1950). *Childhood and society*. New York: Norton.

Erikson, E. H. (1964). *Insight and responsibility*. New York: Norton.

Goleman, D. (1995). *Emotional intelligence*. New York: Bantam Books.

Lowry, R. J. (1973). *Dominance, self-esteem, self-actualization: germinal papers of A. H. Maslow*. Monterey, CA.: Brooks/Cole.

Maslow, A. (1968). *Toward a psychology of being*. New York: Van Norstrand.

Rogers, C. R. (1959). A theory of therapy, personality and interpersonal relationships, as developed in the client-centered framework. In S. Koch (Ed.), *Psychology: A study of a science*. New York: McGraw Hill.

Tillich, P. (1957). *Dynamics of faith*. New York: Harper and Row.

11

ANOMALIES IN SPIRITUALITY, HEALTH, AND HEALING[1]

Richard H. Cox, Ph.D., M.D., D.Min.
Provost
Colorado School of Professional Psychology
Colorado Springs, CO

The term "anomalous" refers to that which differs from the common or the norm. Nowhere has the "norm" been more emphasized than in psychology, however, some branches of psychology, particularly the humanistic groups, have emphasized the validity of individual experience regardless of how anomalous it may be. Main stream psychology has tended to consider experiences outside the norm as "abnormal" rather than anomalous. Frequently, the statistical data which were the basis for such judgments were the abnormal or at least the anomalous experiences of the researcher. However, psychology has prided itself on being scientific even when it was not and allowed statistics, however anomalous they may have been, to provide an aura of proof.

This is an interesting phenomenon since psychology is the study of the individual in all the uniqueness and individuation of the human. Sociology is the study of group behavior based upon mores and folkways, whereas psychology has traditionally been focused on the individual and individual behavior, yet psychology has at times allowed itself to be hampered by applying pseudo-statistical norms of groups to the individual. The norm by definition is that center point against which both ends of the spectrum are measured.

---

[1] An earlier version of this chapter was presented at the American Psychological Association Annual Convention in San Francisco, CA, August 24, 2001.

If we use this pseudo-scientific approach we cannot entertain any validity for the varieties of anomalous spiritual experience. Such statistics tend to invalidate our own observations, personal experiences, and the very individuation that psychology stands for.

In truth, every experience is anomalous in that each us experience that which is similar to the experiences of others, but never the same. The spiritual dimension in human experience is particularly unique in that our individual spiritual experiences are often not even similar to others, let alone the same. Most, if not all of us, have experiences of a spiritual nature that we do not share with others; sometimes out of individual privacy, at other times because there are no words to adequately describe them, and at other times out of concern that others will disbelieve or ridicule us. These experiences are not abnormal, nor are they actually anomalous since we have no measure against which to say they differ from those that could be considered normal and ordinary.

In cultures where freedom exists to share such experiences, strange, unusual, mystical, magical, and even the miraculous is considered normal and ordinary. In those cultures experiences are looked upon as a blessing, a special treatment from God, and highly desirable. Experiences which in our culture is considered paranormal, and at times even abnormal, are in many cultures recognized not only as the norm but extra-normal and to be greatly desired. There are segments of religious groups in the United States that would also testify to this phenomenon; notably groups that seek glossalalia and other charismatic manifestations. Those in such assemblies who cannot speak in tongues, see visions, have out-of-the-body experiences, and perform spiritual healings are seen as lacking in spirituality and lacking the special gifts of God.

When traveling in third world countries I found persons speaking freely about highly individualized spiritual experiences, dreams, angelic and demonic visitations, mystical messages, and miraculous happenings, and the rest of the community listened with respect and even envy. There was no consideration that such anomalous experiences were in any way abnormal. The freedom for persons experiencing the anomalous to discuss this openly and the acceptance of such persons, and their experiences even within organized religious groups, was particularly striking. Many denominational and religious organizations that condemned such experiences in the United States were accepting of those experiences in third world culture. When asking denominational leaders about this seeming discrepancy, they were quick to state that they had to allow for the cultural influence until their followers were as enlightened as we are in the United States!

Our society, which is full of highly organized religious groups, may have learned something from third world culture about respecting individual experiences of a spiritual nature. With the influx of more and more persons into the United States from all over the world, there is an observable increase in the recognition and acceptance of anomalous spiritual experience, both inside and outside of organized religion. In spite of creeds and statements of faith, even organized religion has come to admit that we do not have a commonly accepted measure of spiritual experiences, therefore it is impossible to judge what

178

is anomalous as being "good" or "bad." It is only possible to respect and accept the experiences of others regardless of how different they may be from our own.

In recent years there has been an observable emergence of non-denominational and independent Protestant and Roman Catholic congregations in our country. These congregations do not typically have any denominational ties and thrive on the anomalous experiences of their members. They eschew traditional stereotypes and concretized worship patterns and seek the unusual in what they refer to as manifestations of the spirit. While psychology has remained diagnostic and tied to descriptive patterns of behavior and assumed mental health, these religious communities believe that anomalies in both faith and behavior are normal and desirable. Psychology's attempt to diagnose behavior according to presumed social acceptance has kept it from serving many of these populations. Since these groups do not claim to have a measurable guide for individual spiritual experience; visions and other parapsychological behavior assumed to be aberrant in other sectors of society are less likely to be judged as abnormal. They are considered to be valid even though they are unique and outside of most other person's experience. Not everyone in the congregation need have the same or even similar experiences. The validity of any experience is gauged only against one's claim to its anomalous authenticity. Although doubtless there is danger in this model, it may be no more destructive than the communities that deny the personal experience unless it fits a norm.

It is quite interesting that the Freudian basis for analytic psychology was rooted in dreams - i.e., anomalous spiritual experiences. This is even interesting when one considers the interpretation of dreams; a practice that had been ascribed to soothsayers and practitioners of the occult.

What we do have are commonly accepted societal folkways and mores against which we measure externalized behavior. However, behavior that would be considered aberrant in one society is highly encouraged in another. The increased interest among Western psychologists in spirituality and psychology is in a large part due to our shrinking world and the influx of immigrants from countries other than Western Europe into the United States. Eastern thought, pagan ideologies, mystical and magical thinking, all sorts of the "occult," and variations on every world religion along with the combination of pieces of various religious systems have invaded our thinking. Rather than calling many new practices "religions," it may be preferable to call them religious systems since they are to a greater or lesser degree systematized but may not have the creeds, bureaucracy, and formalized guidelines of commonly recognized religions. The religious systems themselves, as well as their members, are manifestations of the growing interest and acceptance of an anomalous spiritual awakening in our culture.

When we review written history of the world we see that every hundred years or so there is a major resurgence of interest in things spiritual and a wide variety of what might be termed anomalous spiritual experience. The great revivals in Protestant history, the upheavals and reorganizations within the Roman Catholic Church, interest in and the practice of the occult, witchcraft, and even Satan worship have distinctive patterns of emergence and disappearance at various intervals in the Western world.

Franz Delitzsch in 1890 published, *A System of Biblical Psychology* and, of course, our own William James published his *Varieties of Religious Experience* in 1902. We have therefore a theologian, Delitzsch, writing about psychology and a psychologist/physician, James, writing about religion. Their interest in what might be called the anomalous in both religion and psychology is obvious. Now at the turn of a new century we have a renewed interest in psychology and psychiatry in religion and a tremendous amount of attention from theologians in psychology. The turn of interest however this time appears more related to what is termed spirituality than religion. There is a plethora of books in every bookstore relating to spirituality. We might ask, "what prompts our 21st century interest?"

There are doubtless many reasons. Major among them, from my point of view is the recognized and universal nature of modern day angst, demanding answers, asking for relief, and searching for hope. Both organized religion and professional mental health movements have come to admit impotence in dealing with the problems of our age. As a result, permission has been granted to seek other avenues of gratification and anxiety reduction. The vast number of traditional and emerging psychological methods attests to our inability to find one that works for all people.

Disaffection with formalized religions, disappointment within traditional Western organized faiths, the influence of Eastern thought upon Western thinking, an infusion of literally hundreds of religions into the United States, and an increased acceptance of the occult are some of the reasons that anomalous experience has come to be more accepted. These are also some of the reasons that the most religious systems have become confusing and unacceptable to the ordinary layperson.

Recently while writing two book manuscripts and three chapters for books on religion and psychology, the author interviewed hundreds of persons in regard to their personal thoughts on religious experience and found them to be truly anomalous. Although many persons verbally gave allegiance to a specific religion, few of them were willing to ascribe to the "system" of that religion but rather admitted to highly individualistic thinking while externally appearing to be in conformity with some sort of socially accepted practice. My data are anecdotal, observational, and interpretive, therefore, they can claim no statistical validity of any kind. The proof of anomalous experience defies statistics except to validate that such experiences reliably occur.

While there are many areas of anomalous spiritual experience, there are three areas that I wish to briefly discuss in this paper. First, is the *diagnostic*. We have traditionally referred to psychosomatic and somatopsychic as areas for mind/body connection. We have done so as if one were the light bulb and the other the electrical source with no switch in between connecting the two. While rejecting the mind/body split and claiming a holistic view of the human, most of psychology has gone on its merry way practicing as Cartesians. This Cartesian mind/body dichotomy is not only implausible but impossible. Whether the mind is producing dysfunction in the body or the body producing dysfunction in the mind there must be an intervening variable - that variable is the spiritual nature of the human being.

Some persons with similar mental dysfunction do not develop organic impairment and likewise others with similar physical disorders do not develop mental disorders. What is the difference? The difference is found in the highly individualized unique nature of the switch, the connection between the mind and the body. The switch is the anomalous spiritual experience of the person. The difficulty with our diagnostic practice of human behavior is that we do not have a good handle on how each of us in our highly individualistic ways deal with our own anomalous experiences. We do not know how as individuals we develop methods of integrating, separating, organizing, accepting, and denying experience.

As well as attempting to find out how the mind can heal the body, and how the body can heal the mind, we need to spend more time on trying to find out how individual anomalous spiritual experience determines our unique individualized methods for maintaining what we each perceive as homeostasis. After all, health is that state of homeostasis that requires a perfect balance of thought, physiology and spirit.

The second is the treatment of *human behavior*. Paying attention to the counselee's spiritual experience is far more common in most of today's therapies and among more of today's therapists than in previous years. However, most of this attention is directed toward methods or techniques. Techniques and methods do not adequately communicate spiritual experience. Spiritual experiences cannot be utilized as tools or techniques since every experience is anomalous and cannot be fully shared between the counselor and the counselee. Further, we still adhere to a diagnostic manual, developed largely by medicine and described in sociological terms for treatment plans. As a result, we tend to discount the internal, anomalous experience of the patient in favor of describing and labeling the behavior. Schizophrenics learned long ago that the fastest way to gain discharge from treatment was to learn the vocabulary of the therapist and to keep their anomalous experiences secret. When the patient used the same language as the therapist, the doctor believed that the patient had gained insight and could be discharged. They had gained insight but sometimes far from the insight the doctor thought they had gained. They learned that if they wanted to live in their own world they would have to share only experiences and language that their doctor accepted. We still do the same thing. Dealing with behavior always tends to be judged by our own anomalous experience therefore become either normal or abnormal as measured by our own definition of normalcy. We might do well to discard the term "treatment" in favor of some more user-friendly and honest term such as "interaction," "communication," or "relational-influence," however, what then would happen to third-party pay?

We also have many religious practitioners today utilizing more psychology than religion. In so doing, while denying such, they tacitly admit to the impotence of their religious methods and the validity of every individual's anomalous experience. It is my contention that the inappropriate mixture of religion into psychology and the ineffective introduction of psychology into religion forces persons seeking personal wholeness into more and more individualized and secretive anomalous experience.

In order to recognize, give respect, and utilize anomalous spiritual experience in dealing with human behavior we must pay less attention to the label and the disorder and more attention to the ability of the seeker to share and develop anomalous experiences with the helper. In this regard, Rogers and others who helped to develop Humanistic Psychology were right. The movement toward the medicalization of psychology and its dependence upon insurance reimbursement has pushed treatment into a corner that is going to be hard to get out of.

The third area of my discussion has to do with *the therapist*. The Westernized method of establishing a profession is to prove the efficacy of the profession's armamentarium. The emphasis needs to be on validating the efficacy of the persons who work within that profession, not the validity of the tools. Nowhere is this more needed than in psychology. We have hundreds of methods, most of which claim to do the same thing. There has been little attention paid to the development of the person who aspires to become a healer. In the early days of the professional school of psychology movement, personal growth courses and personal therapy were required. With a few exceptions, most schools and universities no longer emphasize this dimension of training. As a result, we produce technicians with methods rather than persons who are healers and are capable of sorting through the morass of techniques and methods to enhance their own person as they assist in healing others.

The anomalous experience of the therapist must be re-visited with emphasis upon personal transcendence. Attention must be paid to the existential nature of development within the therapist and concern with the immanent rather than the imminent. These two words differ only by one letter, imm-a-nent instead of imm- i -nent but immanent speaks to that which is within, indwelling, inherent, and taking place in our inner-person, while imminent speaks to that which is usually negative, can happen at any moment and is often overwhelming and foreboding (Cox, 2001; 2002).

This author is convinced after conducting the hundreds of informal interviews mentioned earlier, that psychologists must:

1) Find ways to understand and accept the anomalous experiences of the seeker,
2) Stop useless diagnostic mental exercises, and
3) Concentrate upon finding the spiritual core within ourselves as healers that will allow us to meet those we would help at the spiritual switchboard of their lives rather than at that which we:
    a) mistakenly perceive as the etiology of their problem,
    b) inaccurately label as their problem,
    c) deceptively believe is the way to cure their problem, and as a result,
    d) dangerously validate our misperceptions as our success.

REFERENCES

Cox, R. H. (Ed.). (1973). *Religious systems and psychotherapy*. Springfield, IL: Chase
    Thomas.

Cox, R. H. (2001). *Issues of the soul*. Sanford, FL.: Synchronicity Press

Cox, R. H. (2002). *The sacrament of psychology*. Sanford, FL.: InSync Press

Delitzsch, F. (1855). *A system of Biblical psychology*. Edinburgh. T.& T. Clark

12

PSYCHOTHERAPY, EVIL, AND THE DAIMONIC: TOWARD A SECULAR SPIRITUAL PSYCHOLOGY

Stephen A. Diamond, Ph.D.
Center for Existential Depth Psychology
Los Angeles, CA

RELIGION, SECULAR SPIRITUALITY, AND PSYCHOLOGY

For the past few decades or so we are witnessing a fascinating phenomenon still on the upswing: what could be called the "spiritualization" of psychology. Surprisingly to some, swelling numbers of psychologists and other mental health professionals--with the notable exception of most psychiatrists, who, in their mundane medical emphasis on biology, genetics, neurochemistry and psychopharmacology, have generally grown increasingly materialistic in their mechanistic *Weltanschauung*-- are concerning themselves with what was not long ago the nebulous, lofty, non-scientific, strictly *verboten* territory tread primarily by the priesthood, pastoral counselor, philosopher and theologian. This reborn interest in spirituality is sweeping the psychological landscape, evidenced by a virtual tidal wave of papers, books, and even graduate training programs geared toward synthesizing the study of psychology with spirituality. The once exclusively religious subject of "soul" has been prominently taken up in numerous psychologically-oriented texts, both scholarly and popular. All of which begs the questions: From whence springs this postmodern obsession with all things spiritual? What is it's individual and collective significance? And what might the mixed blessings and curses of this popular movement mean to the future of psychology and psychotherapy?

184

First, the enigmatic term "spirituality" demands definition--a daunting task indeed. If we were to conduct a random poll of the American public, most respondents would probably tell us that spirituality has something to do with religion. Many of these individuals would be quick to distinguish between the two, however, asserting that "spirituality" is a generic term connoting a certain eclecticism and independence from the dogmatic doctrines of organized religion. A majority would likely relate how they came to reject the organized religion into which they were indoctrinated during childhood, how they no longer found their traditional religious practices personally meaningful. And curiously, while some of our interviewees would admit to atheism or even agnosticism, a liberal number would insist that while no longer "religious" in the traditional sense, they still strongly consider themselves to be "spiritual" in their relationship to both god and humanity, typically having adopted a hodge-podge of custom-tailored, time-honored practices and beliefs from the considerable collective smorgasbord of world religions and spiritual traditions. "I am spiritual," they might assert, "not religious." But just what exactly would they mean by this proclamation? As is often the case, defining a difficult, complex, and indistinct term such as "spirituality" requires some simultaneous statement addressing what it is not, since myriad misconceptions about spirituality abound.

Let us consider the psychology of religion. Religion is conceived, created, and perpetuated by virtually every culture throughout history to provide meaning, comfort, and succorance in the face of the stark, disturbing, existential facts of life: suffering, meaninglessness, isolation, limitation, finitude, and ultimately, death. The impressive longevity and tenacity of religion in human affairs attests to its efficacy in this regard. Religion can further be understood as a means of seeking to acknowledge, comprehend, and honor the "numinous" aspects of life: fate; destiny; the sense of mystery; wonder, beauty, or awe; the forces of nature; the perception of some intelligent and loving grand design in the universe; the organic interconnectedness of all things; the relative insignificance of the personal ego; and the ineffable yet transformative experience of oneness with the cosmos and its creator. Religion may be viewed as a type of psychologically valuable mythology, and vice-versa: we will always need some way of consciously reflecting on the reality of evil and making sense of it. This is the main function of enduring, archetypal myths and symbols such as god, devils, and demons. Without these pragmatic intellectual props--which are really divine gifts inherently rooted in the human psyche--it would be doubly difficult to live very long in a world so thoroughly riddled with suffering and evil. Like the Greek hero Perseus confronting the petrifying gorgon, Medusa, with the aid of a polished shield provided by Athena, people cannot gaze too directly into the terrifying, repulsive aspect of life without some shielding reflective mechanism or mythological filter, be it philosophy, theology, science, or psychology. Religion serves this innate protective purpose for the vulnerable human psyche: it buffers and deflects the devastating impact of radical evil, and imbues it--and life--with spiritual significance.

On the negative side, religion, as Freud critically observed, can be a means of dogmatically avoiding or denying the primal realities of existence and refusing to accept full responsibility for oneself, one's thoughts, desires and feelings, and one's own actions. This misguided, infantilizing, illusory, rigid form of religiosity, frequently found in spiritual fundamentalism, can be exceedingly dangerous, since it engenders the psychological projection of both power and evil onto some external entity, be it God, Satan, demons or one's demonized enemies. Projecting our deepest fears, darkest impulses, least acceptable, negative qualities, and most despicable, malicious motivations onto another person, an organization, a religious or ethnic group, a country, a gender, or an entire race--we hate them. By scapegoating or demonizing the "other," we imagine them less human, and hence, easier to despise, defame, and, if need be, even to kill. Such a grossly irresponsible, immature, and unconscious attitude toward humanity is the antithesis of spirituality or any genuine religiosity. Few theologians today would deny that, throughout history, organized religion has itself been the divisive source of many evils, from the Crucifixion to the Inquisition to the recent rash of international terrorism promulgated with religious fervor in the holy name of Allah.

Still, it must be admitted that Freud's decidedly anti-religious system of psychoanalysis sprang in part from the repressed religiosity of an assimilated Jew residing in a predominantly anti-Semitic Austria. Psychoanalysis was, in effect, Freud's unconscious replacement for organized religion, his own meaning-making mythological system, stemming from his suppressed spirituality--though he strove consciously to exclude mysticism, metaphysics, or spirituality from psychoanalysis at all costs, including the pharisaical excommunication of Carl Jung and his secular spiritual psychology from the orthodox (then, almost exclusively Jewish) psychoanalytic establishment. Freud, setting the tone for decades to come, deeply feared the credibility-compromising contamination of his new and controversial "science" of psychoanalysis by spirituality--whether Jewish or Gentile--which he pejoratively referred to as "the black mud of occultism." It is noteworthy, however, that despite his conscious rejection of spirituality, Freud was quite a superstitious person in certain areas, suggesting an unconscious--and therefore, underdeveloped, primitive and immature--latent spiritual complex at play.

Organized religion or theology has, of course, always concerned itself primarily with the spiritual (immaterial) rather than the material world. *Secularity* is generally understood to be the antonym of *spirituality*, connoting the worldly, pagan, mundane, temporal side of life, as opposed to the sacred, incorporeal, eternal side. So for some, juxtaposing these two terms may seem contradictory. But a different definition of secularity applies here: that which is *secular* does not identify itself overtly with any specific religious organization, dogma or doctrine and has no direct relationship to the church, synagogue, etc. *Secular spirituality* addresses *both* the so-called secular (e.g., mundane) and spiritual (metaphysical) planes of existence without deeming them mutually exclusive. In this sense, a secular spirituality can, independent of any particular religious indoctrination or theological preconceptions, phenomenologically focus upon the inner, interior realm of hard-to-quantify feelings, cognitions, intuitions, images, perceptions, and experience. Subjectivity is the sacred subject of spirituality, as opposed to science, which worships objectivity. Secular spirituality likewise takes seriously the irrational, invisible, insubstantial, ethereal yet nonetheless palpable forces in human existence, often referred to traditionally as god, gods, angels, spirits or demons.

DEVILS, DEMONS, AND THE DAIMONIC: SPIRITUALITY AND THE PSYCHOLOGY OF EVIL

Despite their elusive, amorphous, ambiguous nature, these mist-enshrouded metaphysical forces, *daimons* as the ancient Greeks called them (*daemon* being the Roman spelling), possess immense power to influence psyche and behavior. Indeed, these *daimons* are fully capable of taking possession of a person, both positively and negatively. Any secular spirituality worth its salt must take seriously the mystifying phenomenon of *possession*, in both its negative and positive manifestations. For instance, there has long been an archetypal connection linking creativity--and religion or spirituality--with the positive transforming phenomenon of *daimonic possession*. Jungian analyst M. Esther Harding (1973) writes:

> In such experiences of inspiration and rapture the poets of all times have felt themselves to be filled with a divine influx...For a short space of time such an individual feels himself to be made whole through *submitting* to possession of his being by a power greater than himself...There is no doubt that life is renewed through contact with these instinctive depths, dangerous though such a contact [can be]...Individuals who have had such experiences assert that they attained a sense of redemption...through such a consummation of union with the daemonic force, which they conceived of as God. (pp. 152-154)

Spirituality is certainly not all sweetness and light. Most postmodern spiritual dilettantes dare not deal with the dark, shadowy side of themselves or others: our devils and demons, our innate capacity for evil. They avoid these "negative" aspects, this dark, destructive side of the daimonic, like the plague. Instead, they are fascinated with the pure symbolic polar opposite of demons--namely *angels*--indeed, obsessed with them, if the glut of books, magazine articles and television specials on this subject are any indication. Regrettably, modern day angels (meaning *messengers*) have today become blandly emblematic only of the good, positive or creative aspects of the daimonic. But like Cupid, their cherubic posterboy, those beloved angels are actually *daimons*, embodying the positive qualities of those so deeply despised demons. Traditional Native American shamans or medicine men, on the other hand, acknowledged not only the light but also the darker visage of these *spiritus familiares* or "helping spirits" they called the "winged ones." When heeded and taken seriously, these wise, angelic energies would prove helpful; but if ignored, they turned demonic and destructive. So spirituality, secular or religious, is a serious enterprise with potentially perilous consequences. For all who dare venture into the true "spiritual" realm--the passionate, shadowy domain of the daimons--must be psychologically and emotionally prepared to meet the metaphorical dark deities, forces, powers or spirits, abandoning all hope, as Dante forewarned, of finding only friendly, benign or benevolent ones. Many seekers, alas, are not. Herein lies a common recipe for spiritual disaster.

So-called *demonic possession*, the negative version of the possession syndrome, despite its notorious destructiveness, exemplifies dramatically the undeniable power of the spirit world and its undying hold upon even the sophisticated twenty-first century psyche. According to some recent polls, despite their burgeoning rejection of organized religion in general, more than two-thirds of the citizens in the United States believe in the existence of the Devil. How to interpret this resurgent popularity of Mephistopheles in America? Permit me to propose at least a partial reply to this question: Americans need desperately, now more than ever, to better understand, constructively relate to, and meaningfully communicate about the perennial problem of evil without simply turning a blind eye to it or projecting it defensively onto our perceived enemies. Lacking adequate language or alternative conceptual myths, many return regressively to that archaic and archetypal symbolic personification of evil--the devil. Indeed, most religions include some conception or idea of the devil. Why? While religion has various sources and cultural significance, one common, archetypal purpose spans across cultures: religion or spirituality is a traditional system developed and refined over millennia to help the individual and group cope with and make sense of the universal reality of evil.

Evil has always been a subject relegated primarily to theology and philosophy. But in the late twentieth-century, the encounter with evil shifted significantly from the church, mosque, synagogue, or philosopher's analysis to the psychologist's consulting room. The vexing problem of evil stands defiantly at the crucial nexus between religion, spirituality, and psychology. Psychologically speaking, the controversial term "evil" has been closely associated with hostility and hatred, and the undeniably destructive aspects of anger, rage, and violence. But, due to its deeply rooted theological and religious or spiritual connotations, most mental health professionals feel uneasy using this judgmental language in describing malevolent human behavior. Nonetheless, as Liliane Frey-Rohn (1967), another Jungian analyst, rightly remarks,

> evil is a phenomenon that exists and has always existed only in the human world. Animals know nothing of it. But there is no form of religion, of ethics, or of community life in which it is not important. What is more, we need to discriminate between evil and good in our daily life with others, and as psychologists in our professional work. And yet it is difficult to give a precise definition of what we mean psychologically by these terms. (p. 153)

While a preoccupation with the perplexing problem of evil is not new to psychology--it is certainly timely, especially in our increasingly violent and volatile post-9/11 world. Sigmund Freud first wrestled with this confounding phenomenon, as have several other psychologists and psychiatrists since, most notably Carl Jung, Rollo May, and, more recently, M. Scott Peck. Freud's ultimate solution took the mythological (but not religious or spiritual) form of an evil "death instinct" (Thanatos) doing eternal battle with a good "life instinct" (Eros), with evil ever dominating this tragic duel. Freud's former collaborator and protégé, C.G. Jung, parted ways with Freud in a few fundamental areas, not the least of which was the importance of religion and its proper place in psychotherapeutic treatment. Jung felt that religiosity has archetypal roots in the human psyche, and that, for some, it still satisfies an elemental need for spiritual meaning. Indeed, Jung would, whenever possible, encourage his patients to return to their religious roots. But he also recognized that for many, organized religion had lost its significance and spiritual caché, and that, for them, there was no going back. Nonetheless, they too were still starving for spiritual sustenance, for some religious mythology to make life more meaningful and suffering (or evil) more bearable.

Drawing on Nietzsche's existential philosophy, Jung introduced the "shadow" into the psychological lexicon in order to offer disillusioned patients an alternative paradigm or myth for addressing and constructively coming to terms with the traditionally religious notions of evil and the devil in a way which their organized religion no longer could. Jung insisted that, unlike the devil, the shadow can also be a positive (indeed an essential) spiritual force in people's lives. Disciple Liliane Frey-Rohn points out that,

> Bringing the shadow to consciousness is a psychological problem of the highest moral significance. It demands that the individual hold himself accountable not only for what happens to him, but also for what he projects...Without the conscious inclusion of the shadow in daily life there cannot be a positive relationship to other people, or to the creative sources in the soul; there cannot be an individual relationship to the Divine. (p. 175-176)

Similarly, a generation later and across the Atlantic, American existential psychologist and neo-Freudian psychoanalyst Rollo May, himself a former Protestant pastor, asserted that here in this country, we comprehend little of evil's true nature, and are thus pitifully ill-prepared to deal with it, essentially echoing Jung's (1963) stern warning:

> Evil has become a determinant reality. It can no longer be dismissed from the world by a circumlocution. We must learn to handle it, since it is here to stay. How we can live with it without terrible consequences cannot for the present be conceived. (p. 123)

Following the lead of his mentor and friend, theologian and émigré from Nazi Germany, Paul Tillich, (see May's 1973 reminiscence of this relationship, re-published as *Paulus: Tillich as Spiritual Teacher*) May introduced the myth of the *daimonic* as an alternative secular paradigm radically designed (not unlike Jung's concept of the "shadow") to rival the "devil," that traditional Judeo-Christian symbol and personification of cosmic evil. With his background in both theology and psychology, May too, like Freud and Jung, felt that the traditional notion of the devil lends itself excessively to psychological projection and an unhealthy relinquishing of personal responsibility for evil. The daimonic, writes Rollo May (1969), eight years after Jung's death,

> is the urge in every being to affirm itself, assert itself, perpetuate and increase itself. The daimonic becomes evil when it usurps the total self without regard to the integration of that self, or to the unique forms and desires of others and their need for integration. It then appears as excessive aggression, hostility, cruelty--the things about ourselves which horrify us most, and which we repress whenever we can or, more likely, project on others. But these are the reverse side of the same assertion which empowers our creativity. All life is a flux between these two aspects of the daimonic. (p. 123)

M. Scott Peck, an American psychiatrist whose writing has been compared to May's by some, has no formal theological training but is nonetheless notably non-secular in his approach: Peck's psychology focuses mainly on the spiritual/theological domain; his religious belief system is conventionally Christian. Peck (1983) draws a distinction, however, between *human* evil and *demonic* evil. He sees human evil as a "specific form of mental illness," a chronic, insidious sort of "malignant narcissism." Peck, quite traditionally, believes demonic evil, however, to be supernatural in origin, a direct product of "possession by minor demons" or by Satan, for which exorcism is the essential treatment. For Peck and most Christians in general, the "demonic" is purely negative, a power so vile it can only be exorcised, expelled, and excluded from consciousness; it has no redeeming qualities and is unworthy of redemption.

While I disagree with Peck's denominational literalism and fundamental negativism regarding the demonic, he deserves credit for having had the courage to tackle the taboo subject of evil in psychiatry and psychology. Indeed, exorcism (and its age old secular variants, such as shamanism) is probably the primeval prototype of modern psychotherapy. The practice of exorcism--which has also seen a renascence in recent times--is anchored in the equally ancient idea of *demonology*: The victim's problem is due to evil spirits that have penetrated and violently possessed his or her body. The exorcist seeks to expel the invading evil from the mind and body of the sufferer. Much the same may be said about twenty-first-century psychotherapists! As Rollo May (1940), whose trail-blazing book *The Springs of Creative Living: A Study of Human Nature and God* presaged today's spiritual psychology, elsewhere observes:

> Therapists belong to a strange profession. It is partly religion. Since the time of Paracelsus in the Renaissance the physician--and afterward the psychiatrist and psychological therapist--has taken on the mantle of the priest. We cannot deny that we who are therapists deal with people's moral and spiritual questions and that we fill the role of father [or mother]-confessor as part of our armamentarium, as shown in Freud's position behind and unseen by the person confessing. (May, 1991, p. 151)

From time immemorial, devils and demons have been seen as the source and personification of evil. Freud (1938) suggests that native peoples projected their hostility onto imaginary demons. Moreover, he considered it

> quite possible that the whole conception of demons was derived from the extremely important relation to the dead...nothing testifies so much to the influence of mourning on the origin of belief in demons as the fact that demons were always taken to be the spirits of persons not long dead. (p. 848)

Historically, demons served at least partly, it seems, as scapegoats and repositories for all sorts of unacceptable, threatening human impulses and emotions, especially surrounding the inescapable, dreadful fact of death. But the now popular, singularly negative view of demons reinforced by Peck's religious perspective is simplistic and psychologically unsophisticated. For Freud further informs us that demons, though feared at first by our forebears, were also positively instrumental in the mourning process. Once confronted and emotionally assimilated by the mourners, these very same despised evil demons were theretofore "revered as ancestors and appealed to for help in times of distress." (1938, p. 858)

Referring to the medieval idea of the "daemonic" (the Latin spelling), C.G. Jung (1971) declares:

> Demons are nothing other than intruders from the unconscious, spontaneous irruptions of the unconscious complexes into the continuity of the conscious process. Complexes are comparable to demons which fitfully harass our thought and actions; hence in antiquity and the Middle Ages acute neurotic disturbances were conceived as possession. (p. 109)

Indeed, prior to the seventeenth-century philosophical revelations of René Descartes, which later gave rise to scientific objectivism, it was commonly believed that an emotional disorder or insanity was literally the work of demons, who in their winged travels would inhabit the unwitting body (or brain) of the unfortunate sufferer. This imagery of invasive flying entities with supernatural powers can still be seen in such euphemisms for insanity as "having bats in the belfry," and in the paranoid patient's certainty of being influenced by aliens in flying saucers.

Jung's (1963) life-long exploration of the powerful, archetypal forces of the unconscious led him to conclude they

> possess a specific energy which causes or compels definite modes of behavior or impulses; that is, they may under certain circumstances have a possessive or obsessive force (numinosity!). The conception of them as *daimonia* is therefore quite in accord with their nature. (p. 347)

Along similar lines, Rollo May (1969) points out that our modern word *demon* derives from the classical Greek idea of the *daimon*, which provides the basis for his mythological model of the daimonic:

> The daimonic is *any natural function which has the power to take over the whole person.* Sex and eros, anger and rage, and the craving for power are examples. The daimonic can be either creative or destructive and is normally both. When this power goes awry, and one element usurps control over the total personality, we have 'daimon possession,' the traditional name through history for psychosis. The daimonic is obviously not an entity but refers to a fundamental, archetypal function of human experience--an existential reality. (p. 121)

The genesis of the idea of the "daimon"--pronounced "di-mone"--is decidedly difficult to pin down. Empedocles, the fifth-century B.C., pre-Socratic Greek philosopher, employed this term in describing the *psyche* or *soul*. To be even more precise, Empedocles identified *daimon* with *self*. While some classical scholars say that the term "daimon" was used by writers such as Homer, Hesiod, and Plato as a synonym for the word *theos*, or *god*, others point to a definite distinction between these terms: the term "daimon" referred to something indeterminate, invisible, incorporeal, amorphous, and unknown, a purely spiritual reality, whereas "theos" was the personification of a god, such as Zeus or Apollo. The daimon was that divine, mediating spiritual power that impelled one's actions and determined one's destiny. It was, in the judgment of most scholars, inborn and immortal, embodying all innate talents, tendencies (both positive and negative) and natural abilities. Indeed, one's daimon manifested as a sort of fateful "soul" or spirit spurring one on toward good or evil.

According to another of Jung's followers, Marie-Louise Von Franz (1981), "in pre-Hellenic Greece the demons, as in Egypt, were part of a nameless collectivity." (p. 36) This is the way that May, too, conceives of the daimonic: as an essentially undifferentiated, impersonal, primal force of nature. For the early Greeks, the daimon was both evil and creative; it was the source of destruction as well as spiritual guidance, much like those primitive demons described by Freud. The word *daimon* was sometimes used by Plato as a synonym for *theos* or god; and mighty Eros was also a daimon.

Daimons were potentially both good and evil, constructive and destructive, depending upon how the person would relate to them. But later on in history, reports May (1969) during

> the Hellenistic and Christian eras, the dualistic split between the good and evil side of the daimon became more pronounced. We now have a celestial population separated into two camps--devils and angels, the former on the side of their leader, Satan, and the latter allied to God. Though such developments are never fully rationalized, there

must have existed in those days the expectation that with this split it would be easier for man to face and conquer the devil. (pp. 136-137)

Western religion, with its anachronistic doctrines of the devil and the demonic, has failed to provide postmodern adherents with a psychologically meaningful apprehension of the perennial problem of evil. For most Judeo-Christians, the devil has been diminished to a lifeless concept lacking the kind of religious authority it once so widely enjoyed. Indeed, for some, Satan has become a sign--no longer a vital, true symbol--of a rejected, unscientific, superstitious religious system. Nevertheless, the problem of personal and collective evil appears with alarming regularity in our daily newspapers and nightly television news. Evil, it seems, is everywhere--most visibly in the form of pathological anger and rage, hostility, vicious interpersonal savagery, and so-called senseless violence. Violence has become the secular evil of our times (see, for example, Diamond, 2002; "Violence as Secular Evil: Forensic Evaluation and Treatment of Violent Offenders from the Viewpoint of Existential Depth Psychology"). Rollo May (1969) defines violence as

the daimonic gone awry. It is "demon possession" in its starkest form. Our age is one of transition, in which the normal channels for utilizing the daimonic are denied; and such ages tend to be times when the daimonic is expressed in its most destructive form. (p. 130)

These turbulent times force us to come face-to-face with the ugly reality of evil. For lack of a more psychologically accurate, integrating, and meaningful myth, some seize upon the timeworn symbol of the devil to express their disturbing encounter with the destructive side of the daimonic. The reappearance of such an archaic symbol can be accompanied by a morbid fascination with the devil and demonology, as evidenced by the proliferation of Satanic cults. In my estimation, this troubling contemporary trend toward Satanism is a tragically misdirected, desperate attempt by spiritually bereft individuals to come to terms with evil and their anxiety about it via the defense mechanism of identification--a type of identification with the aggressor--and to re-establish their lost connection to the transpersonal realm. But pursuit of these otherwise legitimate spiritual goals by engaging in perverse, destructive--sometimes deadly--behavior bespeaks the devilish dilemma that presently plagues society. The problem resides in the obsolete split between good and evil promulgated for millennia by most religions, a rigid dualism that views the daimonic as evil, and evil only. This is precisely the same misconception we find perpetuated in M. Scott Peck's religiously-based spiritual psychology.

Correcting this conundrum calls for a new or renewed secular conception of that realm of reality represented by the devil, one which can also include the creative side of this elemental power. For the devil holds truly what Jung called a *coincidentia oppositorum*. Indeed, the word *devil,* explains May (1969), comes from the Greek word *diabolos*; "diabolic" is the term in contemporary English. *Diabolos*, interestingly enough, literally means "to tear apart" (*dia-bollein*). Now it is fascinating to note that this diabolic is the antonym of "symbolic." The latter comes from *sym-bollein*, which means "to throw together," to unite. There lie in these words tremendous implications with respect to an ontology of good and evil. The symbolic is that which draws together, ties, integrates the individual in himself and with his group; the diabolic, incontrast, is that which disintegrates and tears apart. Both of these are present in the daimonic. (p. 138)

Like May's transcendent paradigm of the daimonic, Jung's unifying notion of the shadow serves to reconcile the sundering contradictions imposed upon us by the existential conflict of opposites. Facing and assimilating our shadow forces the recognition of a totality of being consisting of both good and evil, rational and irrational, masculine and feminine, as well as conscious and unconscious polarities. When the classic psychological concepts of the *shadow* and the *daimonic* are juxtaposed, one is left with the distinct impression that the secular spiritual psychologies of both Jung and May seek to convey the same essential truths about human existence. In my judgment, Jung's well-known doctrine of the *shadow* and May's less familiar (but more than equally serviceable) paradigm of the *daimonic* pave the way toward a more progressive, secular psychology of evil and, therefore, of spirituality.

DISCERNMENT, EUDAIMONISM, AND SECULAR SPIRITUAL PSYCHOLOGY

Since the time of Freud, the Greek term "psyche" has been erroneously used merely to connote the "mind," comprised of ego, id and superego, including both consciousness and the unconscious. Consequently, contemporary psychology has widely come to be reductively seen as the study of cognitive, conative and affective processes, and human behavior in general. But the classical meaning of psychology and psychiatry's etymological root word, *psyche*, symbolized by the delicately beautiful butterfly, actually means *spirit*, *soul*, or simply *life*. And life can never be simplistically reduced to cognitions, affects or behavior. The spirit or soul must also be taken into account. *Psychology and psychotherapy are being rightfully recognized and redefined by some today as the study and healing (or therapy) of the human soul or spirit.* Indeed, Freud (1928) himself referred on at least one occasion to future depth psychologists as "curers of souls."

By the time I started studying psychology and practicing psychotherapy in the mid-1970's, spirituality--spurred simultaneously by its massive suppression in secular American society as well as by the eye-opening, "mind-altering" psychedelic drug "trips" of the late 1960's--began surfacing as the pressing issue that most preoccupied my peers. The Woodstock generation, having already been sexually liberated, now sought spiritual liberation. There was an exuberant spirit of self-exploration and self-discovery, leading many (later to be pejoratively dubbed the "me" generation) not only to new or "alternative" types of therapies, but toward Eastern philosophy and religion. This generation was searching for something more in life than the bland materialism for which most of our parents had seemingly settled. We were seeking god, meaning, spirituality--though most of us, in our youthful naiveté, knew little or nothing about true spirituality. This "flower-power" brand of so-called spirituality was a one-sided, "blissed out" affair in which all "negative" impulses, thoughts or emotions like jealously, envy, anger or rage were judged "unspiritual" or "anti-spiritual," and hence, suppressed as anathema to the spiritual journey. We aspired to be "good," "mellow," "enlightened" men and women, without malice. But such childish attitudes unwittingly tend to deny the daimonic. Even now, decades later, this fundamental confusion regarding spirituality persists, not only among "boomers," but in subsequent generations and American culture at large.

Today's nominal spiritual leaders are no less susceptible to this sort of *pseudospirituality*: an ego-driven, narcissistic pretense, a mere mistaken caricature of what we in our culture conceive to be spirituality. Overly moralistic, arrogant, rigid, dogmatic religious or spiritual teachers who deny their own daimonic impulsions--hence, inevitably falling prey to them--exemplify Nietzsche's assertion that when daimonic emotions such as anger, rage or resentment are chronically repressed, they manifest indirectly in spiritual pretentiousness. In addition to denying the sexual component of the daimonic, there is also the traditional belief among such self-righteous poseurs and their followers that religious or spiritual or enlightened people are never personally aggressive. Hate, resentment, rage, anger and so forth are considered "unspiritual" feelings which must be "transcended" rather than consciously acknowledged and accepted. Such holier-than-thou, high-minded "spirituality" tends to hold the daimonic in contempt, deeming it despicable, diabolic, unholy and irretrievably evil.

If we sincerely aspire to be spiritual, we must start by learning to practice the fine art of *discernment*. To *discern*--derived in part from the Latin verb *cernere*, "to sift"--means "to separate, distinguish between; . . . to detect or discover with other senses than vision. . . That [which] is hidden or obscure" (Webster, 1986, p. 644); and to distinguish or sort out the differences between qualities like good and evil, right and wrong, constructive and destructive. Discernment first requires insight: the capacity to see within ourselves. Insight allows us to become aware--sometimes painfully so--of our rich and complex inner life. It is the capacity to perceive and comprehend not only our covert motivations, but the true nature of being, in both its positive and negative aspects. Consciousness is the hard-won consequence of insight, and the irreplaceable key to discerning and constructively interacting with the daimonic. The primary factor determining whether the daimonic will be expressed positively or negatively is the introverted, psychospiritual practice of discernment, traditionally associated with meditation.[1] Some basic form of secular or spiritual meditation

---

[1] This is why some type of meditation can be a very helpful, if not indispensable, component of any secular spiritual psychology. While discernment naturally takes place as part and parcel of the psychotherapeutic process itself, I recommend augmenting psychotherapy with secular meditation whenever possible, and often briefly provide some rudimentary instruction in generic, time-honored meditation techniques to interested patients.

can be a quite useful, if not indispensable, adjunct to psychotherapy. While discernment naturally occurs as part and parcel of the psychotherapeutic process, augmenting psychotherapy with meditation whenever warranted further facilitates the development of discernment.

In his book *Discernment: A Study in Ecstasy and Evil*, theologian Morton Kelsey (1978) comments that unconsciousness, as Jung has said,

> is evil *par excellence,* the primal human sin, and it is the moral duty of each of us to become as conscious as we can, to differentiate [i.e., to discern] good from evil as best we can, and to deal with evil rather than acting in its bondage. (p. 101)

Discernment is a process which takes place in the arena of *intentionality*. To discern one's intentionality is to discover--as opposed to rationally deciding--what one truly wants, rather than what one thinks one wants, feels one wants, or even what one wants to want. Intentionality underpins--and frequently undermines--conscious intention because it takes into consideration the inherent organic wisdom within, including that of the body. It is only at the level of intentionality, rather than intention, that we can manage the daimons with integrity. In this context, *integrity can be defined as dealing with the daimonic in ways which coincide with the innermost dictates of one's sense of self and one's truest intentionality.* Consciously discerning our intentionality, and choosing our actions and reactions accordingly, conforms with one of the most mystic admonitions attributed to Jesus of Nazareth: "Man, if thou knowest what thou doest, thou art blessed; but if thou knowest not, thou art accursed and a transgressor of the law." (Luke 6:4)

Another key spiritual principle in the practice of any secular psychotherapy is that of "catharsis." Catharsis is commonly (though inaccurately) understood today as solely connoting emotional "release" and therapeutic "_expression" of pent-up, previously suppressed or repressed affects like anger, rage or crying. The English word *catharsis* comes from the Greek *katharsis*, whose root means "to clean or purify," and implies any affective purification or purgation that brings about a spiritual renewal or therapeutic release from tension and conflict. The conception of catharsis as purgation can be found in Dante's early fourteenth-century masterpiece, the *Divine Comedy,* wherein Dante and his spiritual guide, Virgil, descend into the Stygian depths of Hell, their subsequent ascent to Heaven being possible only by way of Purgatory. Psychologically, purgatory can be compared to part of the psychotherapeutic or cathartic process, the conscious confronting and confessional purging of our disturbing devils and demons. "The 'Inferno'--or hell--consists," says Rollo May (1991):

> of suffering and endless torment that produces no change in the soul that endures it and is imposed from without. But in the "Purgatorio" suffering is temporary, a means of purification, and is eagerly embraced by the soul's own will. Both must be traversed before arriving at the celestial "Paradiso." (p. 162)

196

Dante evidently understood the difference between unconscious and conscious suffering. As C.G. Jung keenly observed, neurosis is refusal to suffer consciously. The daimonic cannot be circumnavigated, side-stepped, or spiritually transcended, rendering the journey through one's own personal heart of darkness unnecessary--much as we might wish it possible. This is one of the subtle perils of the "transpersonal psychology" movement and "spiritual psychology" in general: seekers drawn to mysticism, metaphysics, and New Age spiritualism tend to naively believe they can attain to Paradiso directly, conveniently forgoing the dirty, deflating work of first facing their personal demons on the mundane, gritty, earth-bound level rather than leaping to the transcendent, spiritual or transpersonal plane. But dealing with the daimonic brooks no shortcuts, an inescapable fact that every twenty-first-century psychotherapist must eventually face.

As for the crucial matter of catharsis or "cure" in psychotherapy, May (1991), contradicting conventional mainstream medical model mentality, reminds us:

> [O]ur task is not to "cure" people. . . . Our task is to be guide, friend, and interpreter to persons on their journey through their private hells and purgatories. . . . All through history it is true that only by going through hell does one have any chance of reaching heaven. (pp. 165-166)

In somewhat more Buddhistic terms, May's important point is that the psychotherapist must not be overly *attached* to or *desirous* regarding the final outcome or goal of treatment, endeavoring mainly to be as present and empathetic as possible to the patient's subjective suffering--and it's inherent spiritual value. In my own clinical experience, it is only by moving through this suffering consciously, willingly, and developing a more philosophical or spiritual stance toward it, that patients approximate anything close to a "cure" in psychotherapy.

Secular spirituality can be characterized by psychological growth, creativity, and emotional maturation. In this sense, spirituality--specifically authentic spirituality--is the antithesis of pseudoinnocence. Spirituality entails the capacity to see life as it is--wholly, including the existential realities of evil, suffering and the daimonic--and to love life nonetheless. This *amor fati*, as Friedrich Nietzsche phrased it, is a spiritual achievement of the highest magnitude. Indeed, *secular spirituality can fundamentally be defined as a capacity to love the daimonic.* "For God," Diotima tells Socrates, "mingles not with man; but through a spirit [daimon] all the intercourse and converse of god with man, whether awake or asleep, is carried on. The wisdom which understands this is spiritual." (Plato, 1953, p. 117)

Secular spirituality is also inextricably connected to creativity--and vice versa. Spirituality is a creative response to the problem of existence. It signifies a positive approach to life--and to death. Creativity is a profound spiritual solution to the problem of existence, though not necessarily a religious one. Ludwig von Beethoven, for example, was a deeply troubled genius, who, in his maturity, writes biographer J.W.N. Sullivan (1960), had come to realize that his creative energy, which he at one time opposed to his destiny, in reality owed its very life to that destiny. It is not merely that he believed that the price was worth paying; he came to see it as necessary that a price should be paid. To be willing to suffer in order to create is one thing; to realize that one's creation necessitates one's suffering, that suffering is one of the greatest of God's gifts, is almost to reach a mystical solution of the problem of evil... (p. 155)

The exquisite presence of this assenting attitude toward life is plainly palpable in Beethoven's last string quartets, composed joyfully just before his death, despite his total deafness, isolation and intense physical suffering. Clearly, he had arrived at some sublime conciliation with his demons, with his difficult, tragic, lonely life, and with death. Beethoven had become a *eudaimonic* man.

Eudaimonism always implies a conscious, spiritual development, wherein the daimonic is acknowledged, accepted and constructively integrated into the lifestyle and personality. A eudaimonic genius like Beethoven utilizes his or her art to meet, accept and assimilate the daimonic, a process from which we all could learn more about living creatively and spiritually. For each of us faces essentially the same task: To assertively and constructively affirm ourselves and our lives; to muster the requisite courage to confront existence and to accept--even embrace--life on its own terms, including our own and others' intrinsic daimonic tendencies. Such an acceptance requires the conscious recognition of *being* as ineluctably incorporating *non-being*-- in all its demonic, noxious, negative, multifarious forms forever threatening the annihilation, degradation, defeat or death of the individual. As existential theologian Paul Tillich pithily put it, "The self is stronger the more non-being it can take into itself." (as quoted in R. May, 1988, p. 83) Eudaimonism, if truth be told, is the ultimate goal of secular spiritual psychology, one which goes far beyond mere symptom reduction, crisis intervention, mood stabilization, or cognitive-behavioral "anger management."

Another vivid illustration of eudaimonism is provided by the great Greek playwright Sophocles in *Oedipus at Colonus*. In this lesser studied sequel to *Oedipus the King (Oedipus Rex),* Sophocles presents a now venerable Oedipus who has finally learned to live with his demons which had decades ago driven him toward the fiery murder of his father and impassioned marriage to his mother--but not in the sense of having suppressed them or the daimonic in general. His eudaimonism does not consist of unadulterated absolution, lightness and love, though loving and gracious he has surely become. He is, at the same time, still able to get angry when necessary, passionately standing up for himself and those he loves. "His sharp and violent temper," writes Rollo May (1991),

present at the crossroads where he killed his father years [before]...Is still much in evidence in this last drama, unsubdued by suffering or maturity. The fact that Sophocles does not see fit to remove or even soften Oedipus' aggression and anger-- the fact, that is, that the "aggression" and the "angry affects" are not the "flaws" he has old Oedipus get over--...illustrate[s]...that...[his] maturity is not at all a renouncing of [daimonic] passion to come to terms with society, not a learning to live "in accord with the reality requirements of civilization." It is Oedipus' reconciliation with himself, with the special people he loves, and with the...[spiritual] meaning of his life. (p. 85)

May's perceptive commentary brings to mind a frustrated meditation practitioner who sought the advice of a Buddhist monk: "I have been meditating for thirty years--and I'm still angry!" This epitomizes the dilemma of so many spiritual seekers today: they desire to deny, destroy or eradicate the daimonic, making this their spiritual mission. But such a goal is futile, and creates only frustration--and more anger. The daimonic can never be eliminated, but only acknowledged and consciously integrated into the self-system. In this regard, perhaps Freud's seemingly cynical remark that the goal of psychoanalysis is to transform neurotic misery into common unhappiness makes more sense: rather than merely reflecting his fundamental pessimism about the human condition, Freud, who suffered excruciatingly from oral cancer during his final fifteen years, recognized deeply and personally the need for courageous acceptance of physical and emotional suffering and the high price we pay for trying to avoid or deny life's tragic reality. Nowhere in religious literature is this spiritual principle of accepting life's suffering and acceding to one's divine destiny more dramatically, movingly and elegantly illustrated than in the Crucifixion.

The aged Oedipus found a way to forgive himself for his sins, while at the same time taking commensurate responsibility for his destructive unconscious behavior and its fateful consequences. Sophocles, a creative genius who penned this play in his own old age, offers us what may be a splendid self-portrait of the process of spiritual and psychological growth evolving slowly, over time, from dysdaimonia to eudaimonia. Long-suffering Oedipus at last comes to terms with his own daimonic tendencies. He has become a daimonic man, a genuinely spiritual person. Authentic spirituality is not simply about being "good" or "loving"; it is about being real, balanced, conscious, whole and humbly respectful of the vast and mysterious realm of the "unknown," what we psychologists call the "unconscious," and what theologians call "God." As Carl Jung once controversially quipped, "I would rather be whole than good." Paradoxically, the precious byproduct of this acknowledgement, integration and acceptance of the daimonic and the capacity for evil in ourselves, is the highly-prized spiritual quality of compassion toward others.

Jung too, like Oedipus, was a daimonic man, and, like Beethoven and Sophocles, in his maturity, a eudaimonic genius. Jung's creativity as a psychologist was prodigious. His psychology is undoubtedly a secular spiritual psychology, really the progenitor of spiritually-based psychology. Indeed, Jung is the preeminent forerunner and pioneer of the present intersection and intercourse between psychology and spirituality. As already indicated, Jung was extraordinarily erudite and had been exposed to and indelibly influenced by the classical idea of the daimonic: he refers to it frequently throughout his prolific writings, and clearly wished to capture and assimilate its vitally equivocal quality in his own paradoxical myth of the "shadow." As the son of a Swiss parson, Jung was steeped in the Protestant mythos, had fully partaken and digested the rich symbolism of Catholicism, and intensively studied several other great religious and philosophical systems. However, he preferred to employ the relatively banal--and therefore, more rational, less sensationalistic--terms "the shadow" and "the unconscious," as he once said, "knowing that I might equally well speak of 'God' or 'daimon,'...When I do use such mythic language, I am aware that 'mana,' 'daimon,' and 'God' are synonyms for the unconscious" (Jung, 1963, pp. 336-337). By Jung's own admission, terms such as "the shadow" or "the unconscious" were "coined for scientific purposes, and [are] far better suited to dispassionate observation which makes no metaphysical claims than are the transcendental concepts, which are controversial and therefore tend to breed fanaticism" (p. 336).

Still, there is no question that Jung, who suppressed his religiosity as a young physician, became, in the latter half of his life, a deeply spiritual person. (For more on Jung's psychospiritual development and metamorphosis into a eudaimonic man, see Diamond, 1999.) Nor can there be any doubt that his system of psychotherapy (Analytical Psychology) is a secular spiritual path for those individuals for whom organized, traditional religion has lost meaning. But it must be duly noted that Jung's spiritual awakening and development had a dreadful dark side, in the form of a lengthy and life-threatening "creative illness": after his acrimonious falling out with Freud, Jung suffered through several years of depression, disorientation, and quasi-psychotic symptomatology before finding his way out of (or "through" as he would say) his labyrinth, his "dark night of the soul," and, during that process, developing his own secular spirituality. And this is not only part of what came up from the depths to devastate Jung personally during his perilous mid-life *nekyia*, but also what is subsequently convulsing collective Western culture: the intensifying eruptions of severe psychopathology, anger, rage and violence flowing from the stifled archetypal need for spirituality accompanying a prolonged period of spiritual latency. Violence in such a sustained spiritual vacuum serves for some as a secular substitute for spirituality, evoking a temporary loss of voluntary control; self-transcendence; an abrupt breaking down of ego boundaries; a sudden surrender to animal instinct; and engendering a direct and sometimes purposely sought *participation mystique* in the daimonic powers of nature -- phenomena which frequently occur during sexual orgasm and certain ecstatic states invited and valued by traditional religious rituals. Indeed, much of today's epidemic violence--the secular evil of our times--can be viewed as a perverted expression of existential rage arising from frustration of the innate quest for spiritual meaning, often manifesting, as in the tragic case of contemporary terroristic religious fanatics, as a misguided, fundamentalist and sometimes savage form of pseudospirituality.

CONCLUSION

Psychotherapy stands at a critical crossroad. In its heyday, during the mid-to-latter twentieth-century, psychotherapy was touted by some as tantamount to "religion for the previously irreligious." But the practice and profession of psychotherapy has been in sharp decline of late, particularly due to increasing medicalization and overuse of psychopharmacological agents, it's recent movement away from its roots in depth psychology toward a supposedly more scientific and quantifiable (but, in actuality, woefully inadequate) cognitive-behavioral orientation, and the decimating effects of so-called "managed care," which, due mostly to monetary considerations, permits only psychological treatment that is deemed "medically necessary."

Moreover, psychotherapy is being gradually devalued and denigrated as a relevant treatment modality, not only by insurance companies, but by the general public, many of whom, in search of a "quick fix," are turning to ostensibly more "spiritual" approaches to solving their problems, such as consulting sundry psychics, gurus, intuitive healers, clairvoyants and other self-proclaimed "spiritual teachers." Unfortunately, the overwhelming majority of these "spiritualists" have no formal training in psychology or psychiatry, the lack of which sorely impoverishes their practices, and tend to harbor sometimes strange, even bizarre conceptions of spirituality. Yet, they are presented with many of the identical symptoms, signs, and syndromes to which highly trained mental health professionals typically minister: anger, rage, depression, malaise, anxiety, discouragement, nihilism, meaninglessness, alienation, and not infrequently, personality disorders and latent or outright psychosis. This is a potentially harmful and wholly unacceptable state of affairs.

If it is to survive and thrive for a second century, the struggling enterprise of psychotherapy must constructively respond to these formidable challenges to its continued existence. Psychotherapy must boldly redefine itself to incorporate secular spirituality in order to adequately and competently meet the demands of the collective culture. Refusal to accept and embrace psychotherapy's destiny to become a secular spiritual psychology will prove catastrophic for both practitioners and consumers. Perhaps Sigmund Freud in some ways predicted our present predicament in 1928 when he wrote to his friend, Swiss clergyman Oskar Pfister, regarding the future of psychoanalysis, "I should like to hand it over to a profession which does not yet exist, a profession of *lay* curers of souls who need not be [medical] doctors and should not be priests." (1972, p. 404) At all events, even such a specialized secular spiritual psychology as first envisioned by Freud, developed by Jung, May and others, and described in some detail in the foregoing pages, must nonetheless continue to be regulated and require specific minimal academic and clinical training if it wishes to competently and responsibly minister to the suffering souls and psyches of the needful public.

In the final analysis, the fundamental task of a secular spiritual psychology is to redeem (rather than cast out or exorcise) our devils and demons. It is inevitably both a psychological and spiritual venture. Psychotherapy such as this is one way of coming to terms with the daimonic. By bravely voicing our inner "demons"--symbolizing those unconscious tendencies we most fear, flee from, and hence, are obsessed or haunted by--we transmute them into helpful spiritual allies, in the form of newly liberated, life-giving psychic energy, for use in constructive activity. During this process, the strange paradox that many artists and spiritual savants embrace is discovered: that same devil so righteously run from and rejected turns out to be the redemptive source of vitality, creativity, and authentic spirituality.

REFERENCES

Diamond, S. A. (1990). The psychology of evil. *The San Francisco Jung Institute Library Journal*, 9, 5-26.

Diamond, S. A. (1991). Redeeming our devils and demons. In J. Abrams and C. Zweig (Eds.), *Meeting the shadow: The hidden power of the dark side of human nature* (pp. 180-186). New York: Tarcher/Putnam. .

Diamond, S. A. (1996). *Anger, madness, and the daimonic: The psychological genesis of violence, evil, and creativity.* Albany, NY: SUNY Press.

Diamond, S. A. (1999). Jung's angry genius. *The San Francisco Jung Institute Library Journal, 17(4),* 5-18.

Diamond, S. A. (2002). Violence as secular evil: Forensic evaluation and treatment of violent offenders from the viewpoint of existential depth psychology. *Journal of Applied Psychoanalytic Studies, 5*(1), 21-45.

Freud, S. (1938). Totem and taboo. In A.A. Brill (Trans.& Ed.), *The basic writings of Sigmund Freud,* New York: The Modern Library, pp. 807-930. (Original work published 1913)

Frey-Rohn, L. (1967). Evil from the psychological point of view. In R. Manheim & H. Nagel (Trans.) Curatorium of the C.G. Jung Institute, Zurich (Eds.) *Evil (pp.5-48).* Evanston, Ill: Northwestern University Press.

Harding, M.E. (1973). *Psychic energy: Its source and transformation.* Princeton, NJ: Princeton University Press.

Jung, C.G. (1963). *Memories, dreams, reflections.* (R. C. Winsgton trans). New York: Pantheon Books.

Jung, C.G. (1971). *Psychological types.* In R.F.C. Hull (Trans.) & H. Read, M. Fordham, G. Adler, and W. McGuire (Eds.), *The collected works of C.G. Jung,* Vol. 6, Princeton, NJ: Princeton University Press.

Kelsey, M. (1978). *Discernment: A study in ecstasy and evil.* New York: Paulist Press.

May, R. (1940). *The springs of creative living: A study of human nature and god.* New York: Abington-Cokesbury Press.

May, R. (1953). *Man's search for himself.* New York: W.W. Norton.

May, R. (1969) *Love and will.* New York: W.W. Norton.

May, R. (1988*). Paulus: Tillich as spiritual teacher* (Rev. ed.). Dallas, TX: Saybrook Publishing.

Peck, M.S. (1983). *People of the lie: The hope for healing human evil.* New York: Simon & Schuster.

Plato (1953). *Symposium.* In B. Jowett (Trans.), (Rev. ed.). *Plato: Euthyphro, Crito, Apology, and Symposium.* Chicago: Henry Regnery Co.

Schur, M. (1972). *Freud: Living and dying.* New York: International Universities Press.

Sullivan, J.W.N. (1960). *Beethoven: His spiritual development.* New York: Vintage Books.

Von Franz, M.L. (1981). Daimons and the inner companions. In *Parabola* 6 (4).

Webster, D. (1986). *Webster's third new international dictionary.* Springfield, MA: Merriam-Webster Inc.

13

SPIRITUALITY ACROSS CULTURES, RELIGIONS, AND ETHNICITIES

Stanley Krippner, Ph.D.
Saybrook Graduate School and Research Center
San Francisco, CA

The inclusion of spirituality in health care is an uncommon practice in industrialized nations, but it once permeated all forms of medicine and counseling. The word "spiritual" can be used to describe those aspects of human behavior and experience that reflect an alleged transcendent intelligence or process that inspires devotion and directs behavior. The spiritual dimension of living is evident among human beings whenever there is an awareness of a broader life meaning that goes beyond the immediacy of everyday expediency and material concerns. Muslims, Christians, and Jews consider prayer a spiritual exercise that enables them to establish contact with Allah, God, or Jehovah. Buddhists, Taoists, and Hindus speak of spiritual development obtained by engaging in such practices as yoga, meditation, and the martial arts. Secular humanists often use the word "spiritual" to refer to those noble, admirable, and altruistic human traits brought about by social betterment. Most secular humanists disregard or deny the existence of a Divine Being but still may refer to humankind's highest moral and ethical motives and actions as "spiritual." Members of an indigenous tribe may claim to receive messages from the "spirit world," a realm of existence that is not immediately apparent but which is thought to direct important life decisions and activities.

The California State Psychological Association Task Force on Spirituality and Psychotherapy adopted a definition of "spirituality" that is quite similar: "It has been said that spirituality is the 'courage to look within and trust.' What is seen and what is trusted appears to be a deep sense of belonging, of wholeness, of connectedness, and of the openness to the infinite." When 1,400 California clinical psychologists were asked by mail whether or not they felt that spirituality was relevant in their personal lives and their clinical work, 406 responded. Although the majority answered positively, fewer affirmed the personal relevance of spirituality than of the population in general. Behavioral psychologists were the least likely to affirm the relevance of spirituality in psychological therapy while Jungian analysts were the most likely. Those therapists who felt that spirituality was relevant to their personal lives were the most likely to use it in their clinical practice (Shafranske, 1984).

Some psychologists of religion have proposed the term "primary religious experience" as a non-ideological term to refer to profound spiritual experiences that contrast with trivial, shallow, undisciplined encounters. Nevertheless, "spiritual" is not necessarily a synonym for "religious" because a religion is an institutionalized body of believers who accept a common set of beliefs, practices, and rituals regarding spiritual concerns and issues. Nevertheless, people who have internalized these beliefs and practices, and who claim to have direct experiences with what they consider "sacred," are generally "spiritual" (Krippner & Welch, 1992, pp. 5, 122; Walsh, 1999, p. 3). In addition, many people are "spiritual" without being "religious" in the sense of participating in organized religion. It follows that one can be "religious" without being "spiritual" -- many members of religious institutions perform the necessary rituals and accept its creed (at least superficially), but their ethics, morals, and opportunities for day-by-day practice of their religion do not match their professed beliefs.

Modern Western biomedicine, nursing, social work, counseling, and psychological therapy address themselves to a person's physical, mental, emotional, and social problems but rarely to one's spiritual concerns. Nor are most practitioners aware of cultural and ethnic differences in spiritual perspectives. Many health care professionals are embarrassed and speechless when a patient or client asks them, "But doctor, what does it all mean?" The closer people in need of professional help move toward a consideration of such spiritual issues as the fear of death, the feeling of loneliness, and the lack of meaning in their lives, the less likely it is that they can find professional workers who can be of assistance.

In considering spirituality across cultures, religions, and ethnicities, a few additional definitions are in order. The term "culture" refers to the explicit and implicit patterns of human behavior acquired and transmitted by signs and symbols, including their embodiments in specific languages and institutions, customs and folkways, values and laws, arts and crafts, tools and weapons, and other artifacts. There are hundreds of "cultures" in the world, and even more "sub-cultures" -- cultural groups that live within the geographical parameters of the predominant culture, sharing many of its attributes. Some of these subcultures are "ethnic groups," the term "ethnicities" refers to culturally defined groupings of people, based on common languages, customs, and/or religious affiliations. Some writers ascribe biological markers to various ethnic groups, even though current anthropological thinking holds that "races" as objectively existing biological entities do not exist (e.g., Richards, 1997, p. x).

Commentators use the term "Muslim" to refer to members of a religion, the term "Arab" to refer to an ethnic group, and the term "Palestinian" to refer to a cultural group.

Many Muslims are neither Arabs nor Palestinians, most Arabs are not Palestinians, and some Palestinians are not Muslims. In 1997, I visited the recently organized Palestinian Museum near Jericho, which portrayed the cultural legacy of Palestinians over the centuries, hoping to help lay the groundwork for the establishment of a Palestinian state. In the meantime, large states, such as Russia, consist of several ethnicities, many of which have their own cultures, religions, and languages. In the United States, there is a general American culture, but many subcultures that represent various ethnic and/or religious groupings. The dozens of ethnic and religious wars marking the end of the 20th century reflect the desire of various cultural groups to break away from the predominant state and form their own political entity. Militants in such groups as the Tamils, the Kurds, the Tibetans, and the Basques would agree that they are members of a "culture" but would not consider themselves members of a "subculture," claiming that they do not share common values or customs with their "oppressors." In addition, they would prefer the word "nation" for "culture," representing their struggle to become "nation-states." There are several Native American "nations" living within the United States, with various degrees of autonomy over the management of their internal issues and concerns. It can be correctly observed that the political world of the 21st century is a world of countries or states, not tribes or nations (Tarling, 1998, p. vii).

TYPES OF SPIRITUAL PRACTIONERS

"Society," an additional term that needs to be introduced into this discourse, refers to a closely integrated group of people held together by mutual dependence and in which there is a division of labor. Nations, states, and cultures are all "societies," but comprise larger numbers of people than those to whom the term is typically applied. Michael Winkelman (1992) studied the records of religious and magical practices in 47 different societies. The documentary evidence from these societies revealed that the religious and magical practitioners interacted with those human experiences that could be thought of as "spiritual." They claimed to have access to spiritual entities (e.g., deities, ghosts, spirits) as they directed the society's spiritual activities (e.g., sacred rituals and ceremonies). These practitioners were felt to employ special powers (e.g., casting spells, bestowing blessings, exorcising demons) that allowed them to influence the course of human affairs or natural phenomena in ways not possible by other members of their social group.

Winkelman found remarkable similarities among these groups, especially regarding the manner in which the nature and role of spiritual practitioners changed as their society became more complex. For example, shamans were found only in groups with no formal social classes. No shamans were observed in agricultural societies; rather, their presence was typical of hunting and gathering tribes and fishing societies. The Creek, Crow, and Kiman were among the Native American societies that awarded considerable power and prestige to the shamans in their midst. Shamanism is a term used to describe a variety of techniques that socially sanctioned practitioners use to regulate their attention, obtaining information not ordinarily available, which is used to help and to heal members of the community.

Once the society became sedentary and began to practice agriculture, social stratification took place. In addition to the division of labor, political and economic divisions occurred. Priests or priestesses emerged, taking charge of the group's religious rituals. The shaman's power and status were reduced. According to Winkelman, the term "shaman/healer" (or *shamanic* healer) is a more accurate description of this practitioner because healing became his or her major function. The role of the shamanic healer became specialized and formalized; official initiation ceremonies and training procedures became more common. Political development beyond the level of the local community was observed in almost all the societies in which priests were present. The Jivaros in South America and the Ibo tribe in western Africa are among the groups in which priests were assigned a healing function. Priests also served healing functions in Japanese Buddhist and Kurd Dervish groups. In the contemporary world there are healing ministries of Christian clergymen, clergywomen, and priests, as well as religious shrines where healings purportedly occur.

Political integration became even more complex with the appearance of judicial, military, and legislative institutions. As the competition between (and within) these groups took place, the malevolent practitioner (sorcerer or witch), appeared. Originally it was shamans who cast hexes and spells on tribal enemies; these functions were taken over by the sorcerer and, for a price, were often directed against members of one's own social group. Potions and charms became the province of witches and their associates. The shamanic healer's scope of activity was now reduced not only by priests but by sorcerers and/or witches as well. There were sorcerers among the Aztecs and witches among the Navahos.

Further political complexities and continued dependence on agriculture became associated with the development of another practitioner, the spiritist, diviner, or medium, such as those found among the Eurasian Kazakhs. At one time the shaman's repertoire had included talking with spirits; later, mediums began to specialize in this feat, "incorporating" the spirits and allowing them to speak and act through their voice and body. At this point, the shaman's role had been dispersed to the extent that the only functions remaining were such specialized healing capacities as the performing of healing songs and dances, dispensing herbal medicines, bone-setting and surgery, and the diagnosing of disease. Altered states of consciousness were rarely present, although they once had played an important role in the work of shamans and shamanic healers. Winkelman referred to these practitioners as "healers" (or *shamanistic* healers). Shamanistic healers no longer carried out most of the shamanic functions but reflected the shamans' intent because they held the healing of one's spirit in high regard.

Both shamanic and shamanistic healers emphasized spiritual aspects of the healing process. Furthermore, shamanic healers still maintained a commitment to their community that was a central element of shamanism, and often engaged in practices to alter their consciousness and enter the world of spirits. Shamanistic healers, on the other hand, were more involved in individual work than community work. Further, altered states of consciousness and journeying to the spirit world were not an essential element of their healing work as was true of shamans.

One might say that shamanic healers are one step removed from shamanism and that shamanistic healers are two steps removed from these roots. Winkelman's classification system was found to be remarkably accurate when cross-societal comparisons were made. Shamans were found in societies with no formal classes. With only two exceptions, shamans never were found in tribal groups displaying an administrative political organization beyond the local level. No shamans were found in sedentary societies where the nomadic way of life was absent. Of course, Winkelman's classification system breaks down when applied to the contemporary scene. Modern-day witches are rarely malevolent practitioners; indeed, they seem to resemble shamanic or shamanistic healers and have little in common with contemporary sorcerers, some of whom espouse an allegiance to satanic or demonic practices.

WORLDVIEWS AND MODELS

Underlying the procedures of each of these practitioners was an explicit or implicit model of healing that arranged, structured, and systematized the practitioner's beliefs and assumptions. For example, the allopathic biomedical model holds that physicians confer the "sick role" on certain people who are then treated in an attempt to restore their health. Care by physicians and nurses, diagnosis, medication, surgery, hospitalization, and visits to the physician's office all occur on the basis of this model. An obvious benefit of the "sick role" is that patients are relieved from the stress involved in carrying out their regular activities and meeting their ordinary obligations. On the other hand, taking the "sick role" too seriously often deprives patients of the opportunity to engage in self-healing and play a significant role in their recovery.

There are models of healing that differ considerably from the allopathic biomedical model. Allopaths assume that a large dose of medicine is generally stronger than a small dose. Homeopaths believe that a highly diluted solution of medicine is more powerful than an undiluted solution. Allopaths assume that the patient must be physically present for treatment. Practitioners of radionics and radiesthesia believe in "subtle energies" and operate from a different worldview, treating many of their clients at a distance. The allopathic biomedical model is discontinuous; people are either ill and need treatment, or they are well and do not need to be treated. The Chinese medical model is continuous; people exist on a spectrum of wellness, and require treatment to keep from becoming seriously ill.

In general, allopathic physicians can not be considered shamanistic healers because they do not deal with their patients' spiritual needs. There are exceptions; I have met a number of allopathic practitioners who are aware of the spiritual dimensions of their patients' lives, and who engage in spiritual counseling, discussing the meaning and value of life with their patients. Some talk about the possibility of life after death; others pray with their patients before sending them for radiation treatment or to the operating room. On the other hand, spirituality is an essential part of the shamanic healing model and permeates each of its dimensions; spirituality is also an integral part of the healing models of native priests and mediums. Often referred to as "indigenous healers," "native healers," or "traditional healers," these practitioners handle the health care needs of some 70 per cent of the current world population (Mahler, 1977).

SYMBOLISM AND SPIRITUAL TREATMENTS

Signs, concrete representations of something else, and symbols, images that represent something more complex, are central elements of cultures. Numbers, letters, and directional marks are signs; mandalas, totem poles, and abstract stone formations are symbols. An understanding of a culture's spiritual signs and symbols is essential to mental health practitioners who intend to relieve distress and facilitative recovery in settings different than their own.

For example, the central element in Navaho healing ceremonies is the "sand painting," a symbolic design created in the soil by the tribe's spiritual healers. This painting represents the spiritual and physical landscapes in which the clients and their sicknesses exist. At the same time, the sand painting is felt to portray the cause of the disease and the meaning of the procedure that has been chosen by the practitioner for its cure. Several other tribes in the American Southwest use sand paintings in their healing ceremonies. Stones, plants, and sacred objects often are placed inside the painting; relationships among the elements are symbolized by the colored sand. The sand figures may be clouds, snakes, or whatever is needed to portray the path of the sickness as it proceeds through time and space. Dangers and hazards have their place in the matrix as well; if they have been the cause of a misfortune or ailment, attention must be paid to them to alleviate the ensuing distress.

Chanting and holding a community vigil are typical procedures that bring all the elements of a sand painting together. Indisposed people then become aware of the relationship between their sickness and the rest of their life. Usually they are surrounded by their friends, neighbors, and relatives who sing and pray for a recovery (Grossinger, 1982). The Navaho apprenticeship is complex and lengthy. For example, there are ten basic ceremonial chants in the Navaho tradition and it might take years to learn just one of them. A chant consists of hundreds of songs; some chants are preceded by various purification rites, others are accompanied by the construction of a sand painting, and a few extend over several nights (Sandner, 1979).

The anthropologist Claude Levi-Strauss (1955) has proposed that the kind of logic developed by tribal people is as rigorous and complete as that of modern scientists. Both use signs and symbols in highly sophisticated ways, but the mode of expression and application differs. For example, the cultural myths of pre-Columbian Mexican and Central American societies not only were comprehensive guides to daily conduct but also provided an explanation for the mysteries of the universe. Each mythological episode can be interpreted in several ways according to the context and the listener's understanding. The symbols used are manipulated with such economy that each serves a wide range of philosophical and religious ideas. Quetzalcoatl was the "feathered serpent" (who symbolized the transformation of matter

209

into spirit), as well as the god of the winds, the Lord of Dawn, the spirit of the sacred ocelot (a fierce jungle cat), the last king of the Toltecs, and (following the Spanish conquest) Jesus Christ.

The Christian cross, often used in healing ceremonies, is a symbol of Christ's crucifixion. In Buddhism, the Buddha is often symbolized by a white elephant, the six-pointed Star of David symbolizes Judaism, and the swastika was a sacred symbol in Hinduism, in the Eastern Orthodox Church, and among the Maya in Central America as well as the Navajos, long before its utilization by the Nazis in the 20th century (Panati, 1996).

THE SPIRITUAL COMPONENT OF HEALING MODELS

For several decades, social and behavioral scientists have been collecting data that reflect the wide variety of humankind's healing systems. Sicknesses and injuries are universal experiences, but each society implicitly or explicitly classifies them as to cause and cure. In addition, each individual has a belief system, or personal myth, that provides an explanation of how he or she can maintain health and overcome illness.

These personal myths include the spiritual dimension if the social context is supportive. For example, Mexican-American curanderos and curanderas often attribute an illness to an agent whose existence must be taken on faith because it can not be detected with medical instruments. The *mal ojo* or "evil eye" has no place in allopathic biomedicine but curanderismo's spiritual practitioners claim it is caused by a person staring intently at someone else, usually with envy or desire. It is often treated by forming three crosses on the victim's body with an egg while the practitioner recites the Apostle's Creed. An Apache disease, *nitsch*, results from the neglect of nature entities. If an Apache does not properly salute an owl, he or she may suffer from heart palpitations, anxiety, sweating, and shaking. Shamanic prayers and songs are needed to treat this illness which, it is believed, can lead to suicide if it is not carefully managed.

The psychiatrist and psychologist Jerome Frank conjectured that the first healing model was built around the prehistoric belief that the etiology of illness was either supernatural (e.g., possession by a malevolent spirit) or magical (e.g., the result of a sorcerer's curse). Treatment consisted of appropriate rituals that supposedly undid or neutralized the cause. These rituals typically required the active participation not only of the sufferer but also family and community members. Spirits were felt to facilitate the healing process (Frank & Frank, 1991).

Some perceived causes and cures were seen to operate from the world of nature, utilizing herbs, exercises, and fasts. When shamanic healers and shamanistic healers coexisted within the same tribal group, the former usually directed spiritual healing procedures while the latter took charge of naturalistic remedies. For example, curanderos and curanderas believe that only certain people have the ability, gift, or *don* to work intensively on the spiritual level. They also believe that this distinction is one of degree rather than kind. The shaman or medium can receive spirit communications but, in their absence, a curandero, curandera, or other practitioner can treat spiritual problems, such as the *mal ojo* or various hexes (Trotter & Chavira, 1981, pp. 144-145).

The allopathic model of healing and indigenous models of healing are both comprehensive, yet each presents its adherents with a very different worldview. The native models are spiritual, because they demonstrate an awareness of a broader life meaning that transcends the immediacy of everyday physical expediency, as well as an "other worldly" transcendent reality that interfaces with ordinary reality. An individual allopathic practitioner might work spiritual aspects into his or her worldview and medical practice, but this effort is not intrinsic to the Western biomedical model as it is widely taught and promulgated. Spirituality, however, is part and parcel of shamanism and of curanderismo; either model of healing would change radically if it were to lose its spiritual components.

These diversities are important because they allow the differentiation between "disease" and "illness." "Disease" is conceptualized here as a mechanical difficulty of the body resulting from injury, infection, or inadequate diet or sanitation. "Illness" is a broader term incorporating social constructs that imply dysfunctional behaviors, mood disorders, or inappropriate thoughts and feelings. These behaviors, moods, thoughts, and feelings can accompany an injury, infection, or imbalance, or can exist without them. Thus one can speak of a "diseased brain" rather than an "ill brain," but of "mental illness" rather than of "mental disease." Cassell (1979) goes so far as to claim that allopathic biomedicine treats disease but not illness; "physicians are trained to practice a technological medicine in which disease is their sole concern and in which technology is their only weapon" (p. 18).

CONTRASTING MODELS OF HEALING

A cross-cultural comparison of healing models can be made using a 12-faceted model proposed by Miriam Siegler and Humphry Osmond (1974). In the social and behavioral sciences, a "model" is an explicit or implicit explanatory structure that underlies a set of organized group behaviors. Their use in science attempts to improve understanding of the process they represent. Models have been constructed to describe human conflict, competition, and cooperation. Models have been proposed to explain mental illness, personality dynamics, and family interactions. For the purposes of this chapter, the Siegler/Osmond model has been modified making it applicable to both "biological" and "psychological" disorders, although non-Western traditions usually do not differentiate between the two, because spiritual principles pervade both.

The Kallawaya healing tradition of the South American Andes, which is both spiritual in nature and non-allopathic in theory, illustrates the use of this model (Krippner, 1999). The author visited Bolivia in 1996 and observed several Kallawaya practitioners working with their clients. Because a spiritual outlook is at the core of their work, and because altered states of consciousness are not a central part of their practice, they would qualify as shamanistic healers, using the Winkelman classification system. The Siegler and Osmond model was a useful framework for understanding the practices I observed.

1. Among the Kallawaya, *diagnosis* is as important as treatment. A client's body is seen as the microcosm of the natural environment. It is the task of the healer to make an accurate diagnosis, and my interviews revealed several different methods. An initial decision must be made as to whether or not the client should be referred to an allopathic physician; I was told it was a common practice for referrals to go in both directions as some physicians send clients to Kallawaya healers. A final decision involves whether the sickness is treatable by the person doing the diagnosis or if another Kallawaya healer should be consulted. After making the first decision, and before making the second decision, the practitioner must determine the problem.

A common diagnostic tool is the "casting" of coca leaves in which the healer holds several leaves high above his or her head, dropping them on to the ground or a ceremonial *mesa* (i.e., a fabric that purportedly has spiritual powers, and on which various objects are displayed). Each aspect of the leaf is instructive. e.g., the side of the leaf exposed, the orientation of the leaf, its resemblance to the Christian cross, its relative location to other leaves. I witnessed a "casting" and noticed that the healer chewed coca leaves to attain a spiritual "unity" with the plant, allowing the information to "flow" from the diagnostic leaves to the healer.

One practitioner told me that he takes a client's pulse (at the heart, left arm, and right arm) and blood pressure, and makes direct observations of the tongue, eyes, breath, urine, and feces. Irregular pulse is an immediate sign of spiritual disharmony. The color of the tongue and iris are observed carefully as well as the dilation of the client's pupil.

According to another practitioner, a common folk method of diagnosis utilizes a guinea pig. The procedure begins with tying the guinea pig to the client's stomach or kidney area. A coca leaf preparation is placed over the head of the client followed by a joint prayer affirming belief in the procedure. The guinea pig is removed and cut open so that its internal organs can be observed. Any anomaly of these internal organs is regarded as a representation of the client's illness. A small lesion in the animal's lung is most serious as it indicates a terminal illness on the part of the client. This procedure did not originate with the Kallawaya, but is used by some practitioners.

Another folk tradition that is taken seriously by some Kallawaya healers is the examination of the client's side for small scars that resemble puncture marks. These marks, in combination with certain behavioral symptoms, indicate an invasive illness, marked by high temperatures, brought on by sorcery or *kharisiri*. The marks indicate evil spirits have entered the clients' body, usually near the liver, to steal their fatty tissue. These malevolent spirits can take the form of human beings referred to as *karikari*; they live on fat and usually strike when their victims are not fully aware, such as when they are intoxicated (Bastien, 1992, p. 71).

One practitioner explained that he uses clients' dreams for diagnostic purposes because they represent one's own spirit communicating with the body. Nightmares may predict serious health problems; an important decision might be made on the basis of a dream, such as postponing a trip. One person's dreams might even be an omen of things to come for the entire community.

Regardless of the diagnosis, it is important that the practitioner and client come to an agreement. Family members often are present when the diagnosis is announced and are often given tasks to perform. The clients and their families are fully informed and are advised to share the diagnosis with the entire community--except in the case of *kharisiri* which the practitioner might treat privately so as to not alarm the client. In general, liver, stomach, and respiratory problems are the most commonly diagnosed sicknesses, but Kallawaya healers also diagnose and treat most of the conditions, both physical and psychological, familiar to allopathic biomedicine. In addition, they work with spiritual problems such as *susto*, the loss of one's *haio* (i.e., spirit), often conceptualized as a vital fluid that animates each human being. The author was told that each person has a major and a minor spirit, and maintaining harmony between them is a crucial life task.

2. *Etiology*, or cause of the illness, is seen as a disintegration of harmony between the clients and their community and/or natural environment, except in cases where there is a direct supernatural intervention (as in *kharisiri*. *Susto* has several possible etiologies, e.g., sorcery, traumas or shocks, an inclement wind that captures a baby's spirit (which is why the birth process occurs indoors). Sometimes it is the major *haio* that is lost, and sometime the minor *haio*; in either instance, the individual is thrown out of balance.

3. The *client's behavior* provides important clues for diagnosis and treatment. Crying and screaming may be signs of *susto*. The symptoms of *susto* vary, but include depression, anxiety, laziness, loss of appetite, shaking, fever, nausea, hearing noises in the ears, and passing gas. Folk tradition in the Andes defines a sick person operationally, as someone who is unable to work.

4. *Treatment* is highly individualized but the importance of a balanced diet to prevent sickness is emphasized. One practitioner told me that he advises his clients to "eat food from the area and during its season;" some fruits may be eaten for medical purposes before they are fully ripe. The Kallawaya healers employ more than one thousand medicinal plants, about one third of which have demonstrated their effectiveness by Western biomedical standards, and another third of which have been judged to be "likely" effective (Bastien, 1992, p. 47). These plants are divided according to the three distinct "weathers" which Pachamama (Earth Mother) and Tataente (Father Sun) have given to their earth children or *ayllu*, namely hot, mild, and cold.

When a guinea pig is dissected for diagnostic purposes, a plaster made of copal incense is placed on the lesioned area of the animal; this is thought to lead to the healing of the client's internal problems. Another procedure is to tie a living guinea pig to the dysfunctional area of the client, e.g., near a kidney; the animal is thought to "rescue" the client's organ by "absorbing" the illness. My informants told me that few contemporary Kallawaya practitioners use these folk procedures. Nevertheless, some of them are still utilized to treat *susto*, for example, burning incense, using the Christian rosary, and making offerings in the four directions of the compass.

Coca plays a major role in many of the healing procedures because the plant is thought to grow between the world of human beings and world of the spirits. A coca and quinine mixture has been used to treat malaria, as Kallawaya healers tell the story, during the digging of the Panama Canal, a triumph that brought them to world-wide attention. The fungus of corn or bananas produces a substance similar to penicillin that is used for local infections. More serious infections are treated by a preparation similar to tetramycin yielded by fermented soil; this preparation is also used for ulcerated skin and chronic illnesses.

Kallawaya medicine generally is accompanied by rituals involving prayers, amulets, and *mesas* on which objects are arranged that symbolize the client's journey from sickness to health. Llama fetuses are commonly used in the preparation of mesas because the llama is a sacred animal. Amulets are placed on the *mesa* or worn around the client's neck, giving him or her confidence and spiritual power, especially when a client complains of some type of deprivation. Different amulets represent health, love, wealth, or equilibrium with Pachamama and Tataente. *Mesas* are often used to prevent sickness or imbalance, sometimes for the entire community. When *mesas* represent offerings to the spirit world, they are burned after their utilization.

One practitioner itemized the symbols he frequently uses for his *mesas*--coca leaves, religious figurines, "gold" or "silver" bread (*pan de oro*) or *pan de plato*, alcohol, eggs, white flowers, and llama fetuses. A *suyo* is a call to the llama fetus for its healing power. If a llama fetus is not available, he may use a pig or sheep fetus.

Herbal preparations usually are ingested but occasionally are used in conjunction with a "steam box;" the naked client enters the receptacle filled with steam created from the medicinal mixture. The active ingredients of the herbs are said to enter the pores of the client at the same time as the sweat cleanses the toxins. The author observed a client in one of these steam boxes in the Tambillo Hospital on the outskirts of La Paz. In addition to the steam boxes and their cleansing therapy, the hospital was replete with hundreds of Kallawaya herbal preparations, all carefully prescribed, measured, and given to clients with explanatory procedures. There is an armamentarium of procedures that do not involve herbs. For example, healing songs are used, especially for treating insomnia, and dances may be used to renew the client's supply of energy..

5. *Prognosis*, or anticipated outcome, is dependent on a number of factors--the sickness itself, its severity, and the cooperation of clients and their families. The confidence and the faith of the client are key factors because herbal treatment is a slow process that requires a great deal of patience. Belief is felt to activate the self-healing mechanisms that are fundamental to recovery.

6. *Premature death or suicide* may result if the treatment does not work, or if the client's condition can not be successfully treated. There are few suicides among the Kallawaya, as this act would bring dishonor to their families. Death at the end of one's life is a natural process that can be prepared for and confronted with valor. After death, one or both of one's spirits rejoins Pachamama. Some Kallawaya practitioners think that reincarnation is possible, but others are skeptical.

7. The *institutional setting* depends on the client's mobility; if the client can not go to the healer, the healer will go to the client. Female Kallawaya practitioners typically do not

leave their homes, thus their clients must come to them. In La Paz, there are clinics where clients can visit a Kallawaya practitioner. The *function of the institution* is for diagnosis and treatment regardless of its location but the client's preference usually is home visitation, far from the influence of hostile spirits and unfamiliar surroundings and near to familiar animals, plants, and land. Hospitals are dreaded, in part because the color white is associated with the death and burial of infants.

8. The *institutional personnel* involved among the Kallawaya represent various skills and functions. *Herbalarios* collect plants; *yerbateros* prepare plants; *curanderos* apply the herbs and other medicines; *yatiris* (also known as *amautas*) are spiritual healers; *partidas* are midwives. Over time, Kallawaya practitioners began to perform more than one function, hence many of these traditional divisions have become less rigid. Nevertheless, all practitioners take a spiritual perspective on healing, mediating between the environment and the client (and, in some cases, the community-at-large).

9. In the Kallawaya system, *clients' priority* is that of treatment, and they assume the *role* of cooperating with the practitioner. They have the *right* to receive effective treatment and to receive an alternative treatment if the first one is not effective, as well as the *responsibility* to take a role in preventing sickness. The client also has the *responsibility* of informing the community of his or her diagnosis.

10. The major *priority of the client's family* is to obtain diagnosis and treatment for its indisposed family members. The family takes on the *role* of providing emotional support for the client, maintaining his or her faith, as well as being of practical assistance, e.g., giving clients their medicinal herbs. The family has the *right* to receive an accurate and honest diagnosis (with the exception of instances of sorcery). Family members are informed of the client's progress or deterioration, as would be the case if the condition is incurable, e.g., AIDS-related conditions, terminal cancer.

11. The Kallawaya *society's right* is to maintain a spiritual environment that exists in harmony with nature. Prevention is an important goal of the Kallawaya system; any disequilibrium deserves immediate attention. In rare cases, the community has the *right* to expel members who endanger the society's balance. A society's *responsibility* is to support clients by bringing them food, money, music, and anything else that may enhance their faith and their motivation to recover; this community process is referred to as *ayni*. A festive ceremony for offering group assistance is referred to as a *preste* and is frequently used to treat *susto*.   Society places a high *priority* on the availability of healing practitioners for its members. There is a vigorous attempt to train students to become effective practitioners. It is the duty of the eldest son of a healer to become a healer himself, and the boy will spend some 14 years in preparation before he will be allowed to assist his mentor. Some informants told me that all male children are obligated to study Kallawaya healing practices, and many girls are admitted to the training programs as well. They must first learn how to plant, irrigate, and harvest medicinal plants. They are taught to identify herbs by their sight and smell. Animals, such as llamas, must be cared for. When a healer returns from a professional excursion, his or

her family assumes the responsibility of having more medicinal plants ready; when in training, the eldest son has most of the responsibility for this collection and preparation.

Once the aspiring practitioner has completed the 14 years of preparation, he or she will assume the position of apprentice, often traveling with his or her mentor to assist in healing rituals. As he or she turns 23, he or she is considered of age to become a healer; several Kallawaya practitioners gather to examine their students' fund of knowledge and skills with oral questions. Only those who demonstrate adequate proficiency will be sanctioned by the community as healers and allowed to practice.

Kallawaya society also plays the *role* of obeying traditional spiritual laws so that its people will maintain balance, and will be protected from plagues and epidemics. They have the *right* to evaluate practitioners according to how well they perform the *role* expected of them based on availability, accessibility, dependability, and effectiveness. As a result, the community recognizes various ranks of herbal skills, and frugal peasants depend upon word-of-mouth to discover which healers are superior.

12. The *goal* of the Kallawaya model is to maintain and restore the harmonious relationship of community members, the community as a whole, and the natural environment. The Kallawaya practitioner needs to assure the availability of medicinal plants and proficient healers who are conversant with health, sickness, the natural realm, and the world of spirits. Prevention involves the practice of moderation in daily life, and the maintenance of trust among members of the community.

THE ALLOPATHIC BIOMEDICAL MODEL

The allopathic biomedical model stands in sharp contrast to the Kallawaya model. *Diagnosis* is usually made by the physician. It follows logical procedures that may be carried out with or without input from the patient; it rarely asks for extensive input from the family, and almost never involves input from the client's community. *Etiology* is considered to be natural rather than supernatural.

The *patient's behavior* is connected to the diagnosis through symptoms (the patient's reported experiences) and the results of examinations of the patient's body. The treatment of symptoms sometimes proceeds in the absence of a known etiology. For example, a physician will often prescribe medication to lower a patient's fever before identifying the cause of the fever.

Treatment is usually medicinal or surgical. It is specific for each disease, but when a diagnosis is unclear, it may proceed by trial and error. Treatment is oriented toward specific objectives and is adjusted to the response of the patient.

Prognosis is based on diagnosis. The physician will discuss such matters as the chances of recovery, the probable length of time needed for recovery, and the chances of a relapse. The physician offers hope but often can not promise a cure. *Premature death* is seen as a failure of the diagnostic and treatment system, or simply as the inevitable result of a serious disease that is unresponsive to the best treatment currently available. *Suicide* typically is seen as an extreme outcome of a psychiatric disturbance.

The *function of the institution*, whether it is the physician's office or a hospital, is to provide care for patients. Some physicians are based at a hospital while others may work at an office. *Personnel* in the allopathic medical system include physicians (who treat the patients), nurses (who assist physicians in caring for the patients), and various rehabilitationists (who teach patients how to regain lost or damaged bodily functions). These personnel are subject to formal regulative and licensure procedures to maintain standards of quality.

The allopathic medical model holds that *patients have the right* to assume the "sick role." While assuming this *role*, they can receive care and are not expected to assume their ordinary responsibilities. Patients have the *responsibility* to obey their physician, nurse, and/or rehabilitationist. They have the *right* to be protected against incompetent practitioners.

The patient's *family has the priority* to seek help. Family members also have the *right* to sympathy and to receive information about the patient's condition and progress. Their *role* is to cooperate with the medical personnel in carrying out the treatment. The patient's *society has a high priority* to be protected from ill people who are a danger to others. Its *role* is to provide medical care in one form or another.

The *goal* of this model is to treat patients for illness. Allopaths attempt to restore patients to the greatest degree of functioning possible, and if not, to prevent the illness from getting worse. A secondary goal is the accumulation of medical knowledge so that more diseases can be cured and so that treatment can become increasingly effective.

Peasants in Bolivia, as well as those in other parts of the developing world, recognize the advantages of allopathic medicine. Yet they are often wary of how biomedicine can be used as a political instrument to discriminate against ethnic groups and socioeconomic classes, as well as to create dependent relations with the industrialized countries who supply (and profit from) allopathic medicines and implements. In this way, the contrast of the Kallawaya model with the allopathic biomedicine enters what has been called the "postmodern dialogue" (Gergen, 1991). Some of the Kallawaya practitioners I interviewed contrasted "official" medicine (i.e., biomedicine) with "traditional" medicine (i.e., herbal preparations), noting that the latter has had to struggle for legitimacy against powerful forces. This represents what postmodernists refer to as the ongoing conflict between "privilege" and "other." Kallawaya practitioners, representing the postmodern "other," attempt, against formidable odds, to preserve the Andean way of living with its emphasis on balance, harmony, and the notion that "people are the fruit of what they eat."

THE TRADITIONAL ISLAMIC MODEL

This model can be applied to any sophisticated healing practice. For example, I encountered the traditional Islamic healing model during a field trip to Morocco in 1998. This can be summarized, following the Siegler and Osmond model:

1. Etiology is based on the "humors"; there are two types of sickness--of the heart and of the body.
2. Diagnosis is both directed to internal and external examination.
3. The client's behavior is observed; unusual cravings are symptomatic of a disorder.
4. Treatment can be natural, spiritual, or both; specific methods include "cupping" the afflicted area, prescribing dates, honey, and herbs, and exorcism for cases of "demonic possession"; a *zekr* (repeating the 99 attributes of Allah) is often performed by the client.
5. Prognosis depends on how well the client follows instructions.
6. The role of client is to follow instructions and to prevent a recurrence of the problem.
7. The role of family is to feed the ailing client, and so help in prevention.
8. The role of community is to make qualified practitioners available, and to visit the sick.
9. Premature death is especially adverse if it comes before the client performs the required pilgrimage; suicide is a sin.
10. Institutional settings include hospitals and clinics.
11. Practitioners include *hakims* (spiritual healers), *sheiks* (spiritual advisors), herbalists, surgeons, veterinarians, orthopedists, and exorcists; often, their functions overlap.
12. The goal of this model holds that the art of Islamic medicine is concerned with the preservation of good health, combating disease, and restoring health to the sick (McDonald, 1909). Sufism, the mystical aspect of Islam, adds that healing must help clients attain a state where their system functions harmoniously with the universe. People are cosmic beings as well as social and biological beings (Arasteh & Sheikh, 1989, pp. 166-167).

Using the Winkelman classification system, some of the Islamic practitioners (e.g., *hakims*, herbalists) could be considered shamanistic healers, while others (e.g., *sheiks*, exorcists) could be classified as priests. Still others, such as the surgeons, orthopedists, and veterinarians, fall outside of Winkelman's system, although they all operate from a spiritual base, frequently invoking the Koran as well as the Sufi literature.

SPIRITUAL HEALING, COUNSELING, AND PSYCHOLOGICAL THERAPY

According to the United Nations World Health Organization (WHO), over 70% of the world's population relies on non-allopathic systems of healing (Mahler, 1977). The World Health Organization (WHO) has initiated a program that prepares native healing practitioners to serve as health auxiliaries. Halfdan Mahler, when he was the Director-General of WHO, stated:

> traditional healers who practice today in virtually every country of the world should not be overlooked...Such traditional healers and local midwives can, at a very moderate expense, be trained to the level where they can provide adequate and acceptable health care under suitable supervision...The age-old arts of the herbalists too must be tapped. Many of the plants familiar to the 'wise-woman' or the 'witch-doctor' really do have the healing powers that tradition attaches to them...Let us not be in any doubt: modern medicine has a great deal still to learn from the collector of herbs. (p. 3)

Mahler concluded that the utilization of native health care providers "may seem very disagreeable to some policy makers, but if the solution is the right one to help people, we should have the courage to insist that this is the best policy in the long run" (p. 3).

Many Native American healing practitioners had integrated the discoveries of allopathic medicine into their approaches long before the World Health Organization took its position. The Navaho Indians, for example, divide illnesses into categories that require treatment from different specialists. "Lightning sickness" and "lizard illness" are considered best treated by Navaho practitioners; tuberculosis and appendicitis are best treated by allopathic physicians. Snakebites can be treated by either type of professional. Pima Indians regard snakebites as untreatable, but refer many types of what they call "wandering sickness" to Western-trained physicians.

The influence of Native American healers can be seen in some of the practices of the Spiritual Emergence Network, organized by Christina Grof and Stanislav Grof (1990). They were assisted by several therapists who had an understanding of such phenomena as purported spirit communication (by means of "channeling," "visitations," etc.), unusual mental imagery (visions, voices, etc.), shifts in body sensations (out-of-body experiences, stigmata, etc.), religious experience (encounters with Jesus Christ, the Buddha, etc.), and mystical experience ("dissolving" into the cosmos or into "ineffable love"). The Network's purpose is to offer a process where persons undergoing spiritual transformation can find support and guidance to enable them to work through and then integrate their experiences.

The Grofs have cited 10 varieties of spiritual crises that conventional counselors and psychological therapists could easily diagnose as psychosis, prescribing isolation and medication instead of the counseling and networking provided by the Spiritual Emergence Network. None of these crises would be unfamiliar to the bulk of native healers, but they fall outside the parameters of Western culture, which sees them as "emergencies" rather than as a potential emergence of a new level of spiritual development:

1. *The shamanistic crisis.* In these instances, individuals experience episodes closely resemble shamanic "calls" and "initiations," e.g., images of physical and

emotional torture, death and dismemberment, resurrection and rebirth; feelings of being "connected" with animals, plants, and elemental forms of nature; attempts to create rituals that resemble tribal ceremonies.

2. *The "kundalini" awakening.* In these cases, individuals experience intense sensations of "energy" and "heat" streaming up the spinal column. This is usually associated with violent shaking, twisting, and spasmodic movements. There may be images of brilliant light, of spiritual entities, and/or internally perceived sounds.

3. *Episodes of "unitive consciousness."* These experiences often have a sacred quality. People report "merging with Cosmic Energy," with "universal consciousness," or with God.

4. *Episodes of "cosmic combat."* Individuals who report these experiences often speak of feeling like a "battlefield" where a war is transpiring between good and evil, light and darkness, life and death. They may be preoccupied with death themes (ritual killing, sacrifice, martyrdom), the afterlife, or the problem of opposites (male and female, passivity and action).

5. *The crises of "psychic opening."* These reports may contain dramatic references to out-of-body experiences, telepathy, clairvoyance, precognition, psychokinesis, or to uncanny coincidences. The latter, often called "synchronicity," may link inner and outer reality -- dreams to waking life events, visions to everyday life.

6. "Past life" experiences. These reports usually take the form of detailed life events taking place in other historical periods and/or other countries. They are typically accompanied by powerful emotions and physical sensations, and are recalled as "memories." There is a convincing sense of personally remembering and reliving something that one had personally experienced.

7. Communication with spirit guides. These reports concern entities who seem to show interest in the person who has had the experience, assuming the position of a teacher, counselor, protector, or giver of information. Sometimes this information is "channeled" and an individual "transmits" messages from a purported external source, either by involuntarily speaking or writing them. Often an individual sees or hears (or even feels or smells) the alleged spirits, but sometimes they simply manifest themselves through the "channeling" process.

8. Experiences of being "possessed" by negative entities. This is one of the most serious "spiritual emergencies" because the behavior of the individual may alter radically to reflect the character of the "low spirit," "demon," or "intruder" who has purportedly taken over the individual's psyche and/or body.

9. Experiences with "aliens" or "unidentified flying objects." These reports describe moving lights that have an uncanny quality, sometimes in the form of aircraft. There may be reported abductions by the "aliens" who command these aircraft, usually with claims of physical examinations, sexual interactions, or scientific experiments carried out by the "aliens."

10. "Near-death" experiences. People reporting near-death experiences often witness a review of their entire life in a short period of time. They may find themselves moving through a "tunnel" toward a transcendental realm, sometimes being welcomed by deceased friends and relatives. Occasionally they report traveling toward a fearful, "hellish" domain. Near-death experiences frequently lead to spiritual emergencies because they challenge the belief system of the person experiencing them. On the other hand, a "heavenly" near-death experience might result in peace of mind, personal growth, and enhanced spirituality.

These 10 spiritual crises have been conceptualized much differently in the past, especially by Western religious and psychiatric institutions. The Roman Catholic Church's manual on exorcism lists many of them as signs that a person has been possessed by satanic forces, for example "the facility of divulging future and hidden events" is considered potentially demonic (Karpel, 1975). More recently, a client's claims of such abilities have been labelled "magical thinking," or considered to be symptoms of emotional disturbance by many conventional psychiatrists (American Psychiatric Association, 1980). Neither of these stances recognizes the potential for growth inherent in a spiritual crisis.

In an attempt to inform counselors and psychological therapists that these, and other, unusual experiences are not necessarily pathological, Cardena, Lynn, and Krippner (2000) edited a book covering several types of "anomalous experiences." Our basic goal in compiling the chapters of this book was to draw attention to a number of meaningful human experiences too long neglected, ignored, or even derided. These experiences are examples of what postmodernists refer to as "the other," phenomena that have fallen between the cracks of the structures built by contemporary psychologists, or in some cases thrown out of the house once it had been built! In writing these chapters, the intent was not to debate the veridicality or "reality" of anomalous experiences, but focused on the nature of the descriptive reports and how these accounts could inform psychological therapists, counselors, psychiatrists, and related professionals desiring to be informed about the full range of the human condition. The book was prepared in the spirit of William James' "radical empiricism" which extended the boundaries of scientific investigation to the totality of human experience (James, 1902/1985, p. xxiv).

"CULTURE-BOUND SYNDROMES"

The fourth edition of the Diagnostic and Statistical Manual of the American Psychiatric Association (DSM-IV; American Psychiatric Association, 1994) has attempted to enhance its universal validity not only with a brief mention of "dissociative trance disorder" but with a supplemental category of "religious or spiritual problem" and a glossary of "culture-bound syndromes." Roberto Lewis-Ferna'ndez and Arthur Kleinman (1995) admit that this aspect of DSM-IV is the "main clinical development in current cultural psychiatry in North America" (p. 437), even though they judge the overall attempt to have been less than successful (p. 439). Why do Lewis-Ferna'ndez and Kleinman judge the DSM-IV so harshly? They point out that there are many cross-cultural limitations in DSM-IV. For example, the Hopi identify five distinct indigenous categories related to "depression," only one of which shares significant parameters with DSM-IV's depressive disorders. Such disorders as those involving eating behavior and sexual behavior "show such pervasive Western cultural determinants that they cannot, as presently formulated, be compared across different cultures" (p. 437). Along with *anorexia nervosa* and "chronic fatigue syndrome," they consider dissociation identity disorder (DID) to be a Western "culture-bound disorder" despite some enthusiasts' claims that it is ubiquitous around the globe (e.g., Kluft, 1996, p. 338). They also identify two dozen culture-specific illness categories omitted by DSM-IV, and fault it for not advocating a systematic review of a client's cultural background, gender, and age, the role of the cultural context in the expression and evaluation of symptoms and dysfunctions, and the effect that cultural differences may have on the clinical encounter.

"Culture-bound syndromes" can be described as those psychopathologies that carry the marks of a specific culture and that are closely associated with the social context of the individual (Marti'nez-Taboas, 1995). These syndromes express the client's internal conflicts in particular ways, taking as their foundation the expectations and beliefs of the client's culture. When discussing dissociative identity disorder (i.e., DID, formerly multiple personality disorder), he makes no definitive judgment on whether it is "culture-bound," but makes the case that cultures where it occurs (a) have not been able to protect its children from abuse and other stressors and (b) have placed too heavy a value on the unique, autonomous, and individual aspects of self-identity (pp. 174-175). It could be added that cultures where DID is identified and treated (c) emphasize logic, reason, and self-control as the only viable decision-making processes; (d) devalue or pathologize unusual reports such as "out-of-body," "near-death," "past-life," and "telepathic" experiences; and (e) contain mental health practitioners who, in general, depreciate the importance of spiritual experiences, e.g., being "born again," having a "mystical union" with the Divine.

The identification and demystification of Western "culture-bound syndromes" permits a similar deconstruction for non-Western disorders. For example, *amok, latah, piblpktoq,* and *vimbuza* are all classified by DSM-IV as "dissociative disorders not otherwise specified" that are "dissociative trance disorders...not a normal part of a broadly accepted collective cultural or religious practice" (pp. 490-491). But these disorders are exhibitionistic in nature, are not always considered "illnesses" by their families, and may be deceptive maneuvers in marital conflicts (Bartholomew, 1995, p. 40).

Lewis-Ferna'ndez and Kleinman (1995) were disappointed that DSM-IV did not include more information about similarities and dissimilarities in dissociative disorders across cultures. Even so, this author believes the DSM-IV makes a valiant attempt to establish some common characteristics such as "narrowing of awareness of immediate surroundings or stereotyped behaviors or movements that are experienced as being beyond one's control." "Dissociative trance disorder" is described as involving "replacement of the customary sense of personal identity by a new identity, attributed to the influence of a spirit, power, deity, or other person, and associated with stereotyped 'involuntary' movements or amnesia" (pp. 490-491). This parallels Erika Bourguignon's (1973) anthropological description of "possession" which the author has found useful in visits to indigenous healers and their clients. Other examples given by DSM-IV include *bebaian* in Indonesia and *ataque de nervios* in Latin America. Lewis-Ferna'ndez (1992) has added "blacking out" among Bahamnians and *indisposition* among Haitians, each of which are characterized by "high rates of distress and impairment" (p. 302). Gilbert Rouget (1985), noting that many subtleties have been lost in the casual use of indigenous spiritual concepts by Western psychotherapists, has described several different types of possession. He notes that (a) voluntary and involuntary possession contrast both behaviorally and phenomenologically; (b) many "possession states" are not single states at all but have distinct phases; and (c) being possessed by one deity may produce very different reactions than being possessed by a different deity.

Lewis-Ferna'ndez (1992, p. 303) has identified another problem regarding the DSM-IV categories: they are based mainly on the presence of symptoms or descriptive indicators, and only secondarily on contextual considerations. Most indigenous classification systems distinguish health from distress at least as much on the basis of contextual characteristics as on descriptive ones; the difference between what Bourguignon would call "trance," "possession," or "possession trance" would depend on what is considered appropriate in a particular setting, the relationships between the people involved, the nature and status of the person having the experience, the human interactions occurring at the time of the manifestation, and the possible factors that provoked the condition.

In contrast, DSM-IV categories have been a contextual. For example, in 1996 I learned of a 70-year-old Native American woman who had been diagnosed as schizophrenic because she had answered affirmatively when a psychiatrist asked if she heard voices. The psychiatrist had not inquired as to whether this was part of her culture as a Native American where part of her life style was to listen to the earth's messages for signs sent by a higher power. This woman was hospitalized as a result of this diagnosis, remaining in the hospital until her inner voices told her what measures to take in order to obtain a release (Breasure, 1996). Both "out-of-body" experiences and auditory hallucinations are clinical indicators of DID's core symptoms, but they could also be indicators of some types of shamanic journeying or mystical experience, or simply as an indicator of someone who is highly hypnotizable, suggestible, or prone to fantasy.

If the cultural, religious, and ethnic context is taken seriously, not all *ataque de nervios* would be considered tantamount to trance and possession disorders (Lewis-Ferna'ndez, 1992). The "possession syndromes" in India are quite different from the *ataques* of Puerto Rico although both might be placed in the same DSM-IV category. Most *ataques* are characterized by an involuntary narrowing of awareness of the environment, associated with shaking or convulsive movements, hyperventilation, screaming, agitation, and culminating in collapse. After the acute event, sufferers may complain of partial or total amnesia for the episode. In the "possession syndrome" in India, on the other hand, an individual begins to speak and behave in a manner consistent with an alternate identity, easily recognized by members of that person's community as that of a spirit or deity. Typically, special requests are solicited by the possessing entity, such as cessation of abuse or an improvement in marital relations, followed by bursts of agitation or aggression if these requests are not met (Lewis-Ferna'ndez, 1994). Both phenomena qualify as dissociative events, but the former resembles Bourguignon's "trance" category while the latter is closer to her categories of "possession" or, if voluntary, to "possession trance."

TREATING SPIRITUAL CRISES

The counselor or psychological therapist, who recognizes the importance of spiritual issues, must realize that some spiritual experiences have psychotic features. David Lukoff states (1985) that "differentiating psychotic from spiritual experience is not easy" (p. 155). The task requires familiarity with psychopathological perspectives as well as the religious, cultural, and ethnic background of the client. In treating these individuals, Lukoff has used creative writing and painting, as well as other therapeutic modalities. In working with a client (diagnosed as suffering from "manic psychosis") who claimed that he had been abducted by space aliens, Lukoff (1988) tried to understand the client's underlying personal mythology and its accompanying metaphors. Eventually, the client was able to understand his mythic framework as well, and communicated it in art and writing that was of such a high quality that it was displayed and published. Even though the client insisted that he actually had been abducted, he lost his preoccupation with the incident and was able to get on with his life.

Psychological therapists and counselors dealing with spiritual crises have several critical decisions to make. They need to determine whether the experience has psychotic components. They need to decide whether the crisis is basically an *emergency* which has little growth potential, a spiritual *emergence* in which the client may gain something of value if the crisis is well handled, or whether it is an *emergency* that can lead to spiritual *emergence*. A recurring issue is whether the reported experience (e.g., abduction by aliens, possession by a demonic entity, recalling episodes from a past life) is metaphors for an internal process, a trauma that has been forgotten, or whether it should be taken literally. Sometimes a therapist can be non-judgmental about the issue; I have interviewed therapists who claim to have successfully used hypnotically-elicited "past-life" reports in the treatment of phobias (e.g., unreasonable fears such as an anxiety about heights or a dread of spiders). Some of them frankly tell their clients that they take a neutral position on the "reality" of these "past-life" reports, but that they usually find them effective in reducing or eliminating the phobic problem.

In addition, I have discussed these issues with several practitioners working with individuals who have reported abduction by aliens or satanic ritual abuse. Many of them told me that they believe these claims often are metaphors for their clients' earlier physical or sexual abuse. The actual event is too threatening to be accepted, and a disguised account of the abuse is perceived as less potentially harmful than other responses, e.g., a dissociation from the incident (which could lead to a dissociative disorder; Powers, 1994) or a repression of the incident (which could result in psychosomatic problems; Wickramasekera, 1994).

DIVERSITY IN 12-STEP PROGRAMS

One of the best-known therapeutic programs that emphasizes a spiritual dimension is Alcoholics Anonymous (AA). The psychiatrist Ruth Fox (1958) once declared, "The best therapy of all in alcoholism I believe to be Alcoholics Anonymous, and every patient is urged to associate himself with this group" (p. 8). In 1989, a survey of AA members was conducted, concluding that the U.S. membership was about 750,000 of whom 29% had been able to complete at least five years of sobriety; some critics point out that controlled studies to justify this statement are lacking (Bufe, 1991). Most studies of AA's effectiveness have found that greater involvement in AA activities could modestly predict reduced alcohol consumption (Emerick, Tonigan, Montgomery, & Little, 1993). Again, the existing research has been criticized for methodological flaws (Tonigan & Hiller-Sturmhofel, 1994).

Nevertheless, many individuals claim to have derived great benefit from AA. Founded in 1935 by two alcoholics, a stockbroker and a surgeon, AA relies on a spiritual approach, calling upon a "Higher Power greater than ourselves." The chief ingredients of AA's Twelve Steps to recovery are moral and spiritual, progressing from "admission" that one is an alcoholic, to "submission" to the Higher Power, to "restitution" and reciprocal forgiveness, and finally to "construction," which includes maintaining a spiritual approach to life and assisting others who are still suffering. AA's suggested prayer is, "God, I offer myself to Thee to build with me and to do with me as Thou wilt." The Twelve Steps are worked through by each alcoholic in consultation with a sponsor (typically a recovering alcoholic who has spent considerable time in the program).

The Twelve Step program has been followed by other self-help groups who feel they are addicted to narcotics, sexual indulgence, food, and a variety of other substances and behaviors. It is not without its critics; the use of the Twelve Step program for individuals displaying promiscuous sexual behavior has been called into question. Critics have charged that using the addiction model in hypersexuality simplifies a complex issue, focuses on symptoms rather than causes, and reinforces repressive ideas of human sexual behavior (Avasthi, 1990).

Working in another area of human distress, a team of therapists applied the Twelve Step program to Vietnam veterans suffering from post-traumatic stress disorder. The therapists asked 68 combat veterans to complete a questionnaire and rank 78 different disturbing experiences on a 10-point scale. The most frequently mentioned experiences were accidentally killing other Americans, seeing close friends killed, seeing Americans killed, placing Americans in body bags, seeing atrocities committed against Americans, and holding friends as they were dying.

These experiences produced feelings of guilt among many veterans, for example, guilt about having taken a human life, guilt about being part of a morally corrupt society, guilt about having lost prior moral values as they began to freely kill and commit atrocities, and guilt about discovering that killing people was often thrilling and empowering. This unresolved guilt was found to be a source of self-destructive attitudes and behavior, a remorse perpetuated by the veterans' inability to control violent thoughts and urges. Some even felt guilty that they had become the instrument of evil forces, bargaining with demonic forces to gain feelings of omnipotence over death. One veteran recalled a fear that he had given in to the devil through a pledge that he would do anything if he were to be saved (Brende & McDonald, 1989).

This therapeutic team, working at a Veterans Administration medical center, integrated such AA principles into their program as interdependency of group members, conceptualizing recovery as a process rather than a cure, educating veterans to lead a meaningful life, and depending on a Higher Power to assist their recovery. The discussion and sharing of traumatic emotions and memories was encouraged to help the veterans work through their post-traumatic stress symptoms. The Twelve Steps were rephrased to deal directly with the veterans' stress, guilt, and alienation:

1. We acknowledge that we have become essentially powerless to live meaningful lives. Hence we hope to discover the presence of a "Good Higher Power" who can help.
2. We recognize that our lives have little or no meaning, hence we seek a purpose in having survived and open our minds to a "Good Higher Power" to show us that purpose.
3. We seek the capacity to trust not only friends and professionals who wish to help us, but God (as individually understood) who seeks our well-being.
4. We make a searching self-inventory of both negative and positive traits, acknowledging both those traits to someone we trust and to God (as individually interpreted), accepting those that are positive and asking for help to change those that are negative.
5. We acknowledge our rage toward God and those we believe abandoned or betrayed us, and hope to understand the other sources of our continuing anger. We seek, with the help of those we trust and a "Good Higher Power," to control destructive rage and channel anger constructively.
6. We seek to relinquish the "wall" around our feelings, with help from those we trust, and from God. With their help, we face the fear and withstand the terrifying moments we feel during day and night.
7. We face our guilty secrets, revealing them to someone we trust and to God from whom we seek and accept forgiveness and help to forgive ourselves.
8. We seek to grieve friends and loved ones who died and the death of parts of ourselves -- our youth and innocence. We face these painful memories with the comfort of those we trust and our "Good Higher Power," and are thankful that our tears can heal our sorrows.

9. We reveal to someone we trust and a "Good Higher Power" all suicidal plans and wishes and seek, with help, to replace them with a commitment to life.
10. We acknowledge to a "Good Higher Power," to another person, and to ourselves all those whom we continue to hate. We seek to relinquish our revengeful wishes and seek to be a channel for forgiveness that flows from a "Good Higher Power" to those we have hated.
11. We seek to discover who we are and why we are here, not only from those who wish to help us, but from a "Good Higher Power," so that we may find a personal relationship with God and seek God's direction for our lives.
12. We commit ourselves to those whose love we have taken for granted, help those who have suffered as we have suffered, and seek God's strength to love those we have not been able to love.

The psychotherapeutic team reported that only about 10% of the veterans rejected the program, usually because they did not want "God forced upon them." Those who participated were able to reduce their violent urges, self-destructive behaviors, and guilt, while enhancing the positive aspects of their self-identities. Despite this success, "the Veterans Administration was cautious -- even hostile -- towards any [spiritual] program...But we found that these men were more likely to sustain their recovery when involved in a spiritual group similar to that found in Alcoholics Anonymous" (p. 339). In 1989, the author was told that this psychotherapeutic team had been terminated from this Veterans Administration hospital because of their incorporation of spiritual counseling into their work, despite the positive and long-lasting results they obtained.

Like the small number of veterans who opted out of this study, not every recovering alcoholic is comfortable with AA's appeal to a Higher Power. Some of these people have founded the Secular Organization for Sobriety (SOS) which appeals to atheists and agnostics who believe they gain self-esteem by crediting themselves rather than God (Christopher, 1988). SOS and AA share a reliance on group processes to encourage sobriety, and one AA member stated, "SOS has made the group their 'higher power.' I don't have a problem with that, if it works" (Robertson, 1988).

In the United States there are at least 10 million problem drinkers or alcoholics; AA reaches no more than two million of them, indicating that there is room for alternate approaches. This framework does not translate easily in all religious perspectives. For example, to make the prayer meaningful to her purposes, a Buddhist revised it to read, "Force of rhythm and meaning moving through all things including me,...I offer myself to you" (Collett, 1988, p. 48).

The termination of the spiritually-oriented psychotherapeutic team from a Veterans Administration hospital, despite the effectiveness of their adaptation of a Twelve Step program, demonstrates the resistance that exists in many U.S. bureaucracies to this type of approach. The objection would be understandable if the program had been religious, because of the principle of separation of church and state. Nonetheless, the AA is not a church, nor is it church-affiliated.

A far more controversial approach to traumatized Vietnam veterans has been used by Fawn Journeyhawk, a Shawnee-Mandan shamanic healer. In Journeyhawk's model of healing, the treatment of disease is "medicine work" while the treatment of mental illness is "warrior work." When working with veterans, she will adopt her warrior stance, making "shamanic journeys" to Vietnam, accompanied by her "power animals." Once there, Journeyhawk asks the dead victims of her American clients to forgive them and release whatever hexes they have placed upon them (Krippner & Welch, 1992, pp. 56-59).

Another alternative treatment model for Vietnam veterans has been developed by the Olympia Institute, which uses Taoist movement exercises and Native American sweat lodges, vision quests, and medicine circles to "empower" its clients. In so doing, the Institute attempts to deconstruct the term "post-traumatic stress disorder," pointing out that violent experiences, "inner voices," and alternative states of consciousness have always been a part of the human repertoire; native practitioners in varied times and places have emphasized understanding and integration, rather than disapproval and medication, in helping people deal with these experiences (Krippner & Colodzin, 1989). Needless to say, the biomedical bureaucracy in the United States has taken no interest in the work of Journeyhawk or the Olympia Institute!

POSTMODERN RAPPROCHEMENTS

In the late 1970s, the philosopher Jean-Francois Lyotard was commissioned by the Council of Universities of Quebec to undertake a study on the state of knowledge in the Western world. His report, published in English in 1984, was titled *The Postmodern Condition* and concluded that all modern systems of knowledge, including science, had been supported by some "metanarrative" or "grand discourse." His examples included Christianity's story of God's will being enacted on Earth, the Enlightenment's intellectual story of rational progress, and the Marxists' political story of class conflict and revolution.

Lyotard concluded that these metanarratives usually suppress differences in order to legitimate their own vision of reality, and described the emerging "postmodern" perspective as one of incredulity and skepticism toward all metanarratives. Technically speaking, "postmodernity" refers to the postmodern era or condition while "postmodernism" refers to the various schools, movements, and perspectives that postmodernity has engendered (Gergen, 1991). One does not have to be a postmodernist to acknowledge that postmodernity is upon us. As Anderson (1996) has observed, "postmodernisms will come and go, but postmodernity -- the postmodern condition -- will still be here" (p. 7). This postmodern condition recognizes the breakdown of both premodern (e.g., religion) and modern (e.g., science) institutions as arbiters of "absolute truth." Yet, one may recognize the advent of postmodernity without celebrating it, ignoring our collective human situation on this planet.

The philosopher W.T. Anderson (1996) has identified the "four corners of the postmodern world" as (a) The replacement of "found" identity by "made" identity that is constructed from many cultural sources; (b) The understanding that moral and ethical judgments are made on the basis of socially constructed cultural worldviews; (c) The emphasis on improvisation, variation, parody, and playfulness in art and culture; and (d) The awareness that borders of all kinds are social constructions of reality that can be crossed, erased, and reconstructed.

The rapprochment of counseling, psychological therapy, and allopathic biomedicine with non-Western alternative and complementary treatment programs touches base with these four corners because they are constructed from many cultural sources, construct their moral and ethical judgments on a societal basis, improvise their treatments depending on the needs of the client, and cross ethnic, religious, and cultural boundaries with ease to fulfill their mission. In the spirit of postmodern thought, H.W. Reese (1997) has deconstructed the term "spirituality," offering a postmodern definition. For him, "spirituality" is the consistency of actual action with a belief (p. 29); in Biblical terms, this definition reminds me of the "word made flesh."

CURANDERISMO AND SPIRITISM

The advent of postmodernity has threatened both strict advocates of premodern and modern worldviews. Dogmatic religious advocates speak of "culture wars" and biomedical purists rally against "medical fraud." Admittedly, there are excesses which are causes for concern, but in the meantime, curanderos, curanderas, mediums, and spiritists provide a health resource in their communities, and have incorporated allopathic data about bacteria and viruses into their list of agents that can cause sickness. Although they are rarely consulted by hospitals, physicians, or therapists in the United States, in Cuba many curanderas have been given a two-month training course, then awarded positions as educators and assistants to personnel working in the health centers (Navarro, 1972). Two curanderos were placed on the staff of a California mental health center as "consultants," but there was so much opposition their title was changed to "religious specialist" (Torrey, 1986, p. 153).

Other instances of cooperation have been reported. Jerold Kreisman (1975) has described two cases involving Mexican-American schizophrenic patients in which conventional psychotherapy was seriously stalled until treatment was adopted to conform appropriately to the curanderismo model. In one case, the client was told she might have been "bewitched." She responded with great relief, discussed pertinent portions of her life that she previously had kept secret, and improved to the extent that she was released from the hospital as an out-patient. In the other case, the client felt she had been "hexed"; when the hospital began to treat her within the parameters of this belief system, she responded well and returned to work. Richard Warner (1977) cites a Mexican-American woman who believed in witchcraft and "soul loss" to illustrate the value of operating within the belief system of the client. When treated by a combination of home visits, family therapy, and medication, within the curanderismo framework, her delusions ceased and she regained her usual mood, working ability, sexual activity, and sleep patterns. She was still happy and active a year later.

Spiritism has been used as a supplementary healing system in New York City community mental health centers for several years. Alan Harwood (1977), an anthropologist, found both African and European spiritistic influences among New York Puerto Ricans, the former more apparent in Santeria, the latter in Espiritismo or Mesa Blanca ("White Table"). Mesa Blanca mediums tend to communicate with "intranquil" and "protector" spirits as they sit around a table covered with a white cloth, while Santeria mediums believe that they are able to contact the more exalted levels of the spirit world. Some mediums combine the traditions, as contact with both the "lower" and the "higher" spirits are needed for different aspects of healing. Harwood instituted a collaborative program at a neighborhood health center in the Bronx, New York, where he educated health practitioners on how to work more effectively with Puerto Rican clients; among his suggestions was cooperation with the local spiritistic practitioners.

Another program in the Bronx was instituted by Pedro Ruiz (Ruiz & Langrod, 1976), who facilitated informal collaboration with spiritistic practitioners. Mental health professionals were encouraged to visit the *centros* where the mediums worked. These mediums were invited to the Lincoln Community Mental Health Center so that professionals could observe their work. From this beginning, exchanges developed that often involved cooperation in working with the same client, giving new status to these practitioners.In both the Harwood and the Ruiz programs, those ailments attributed to spiritual causes by the local Puerto Rican community were typically referred to spiritists, e.g., insomnia, nightmares, suicidal urges, loss of memory, and bizarre mood changes. Other problems, such as insanity and seizures, were held to be due to both spiritual and physical causes. Harwood found that the use of mediums as a mental health resource tended to allow clients to conceptualize their illness as a rite of passage, moving them from one level of social status to another. Allopathic biomedicine and Western-oriented psychological therapy typically neglect these possibilities of transition, despite their potential creativity and therapeutic usefulness.

A successful project designed to facilitate collaboration between Western psychological therapy and spiritism has been initiated in several Puerto Rican community mental health centers. In 1979, the author visited a center in Cayey, Puerto Rico, observing that mediums and health professionals had been meeting twice a week over a 3-year period. The first week was devoted to lectures by representatives from both groups. The second week focused on case conferences where both groups gave their input in regard to clients seen at the center. From this point on, the spiritistic practitioners were accepted as members of a team that typically included a physician, a psychologist, and a social worker. Sometimes a psychiatrist was available for consultation as well. When asked about the use of dreams in psychological therapy and counseling; it was told that spiritists would use them to identify the client's helping spirits while the Western-oriented therapists would use them to understand the client's conflicts and problems. These two purposes are not contradictory, and both practitioners were able to use dream recall advantageously.

A research study by Joan Koss-Chioino (1992) concluded that the spiritists were highly motivated and committed to their work. It was also noted that spiritistic therapy was more emotionally charged than Western psychological therapy and that spiritism utilized rituals and herbal remedies. Clients were urged to accentuate their spiritual development; sessions often focused on the meaning of life and the individual's connection to God and to the cosmos. The client's family often was called in, and advice was freely given. The Western-trained therapists also gave advice but it pertained to the practical aspects of the case rather than to the spiritual dimensions of a client's life.

Koss-Chioino (1992) described a client who was seen by both psychiatric and spiritist practitioners. When brought to the center, she was given medication for her depression and visual hallucinations. The spiritist brought in four colleagues who allegedly exorcised eight malevolent spirits. Despite the seriousness of the case at the outset, the client was discharged a week later and resumed her classes at secretarial school. The two types of practitioners had worked cooperatively, addressing themselves to various aspects of the client's belief system.

Koss-Chioino (1992) was surprised to discover that the mental health professionals frequently sought out spiritistic counseling themselves. One psychologist consulted with a spiritist during his divorce proceedings and was given instructions on how to contact his spirit guides to help him win his court battles. With the help of spiritistic practices, the psychologist worked through his problems in forming close relationships and eventually married again. He reported that spiritism had been far more effective in his case than any type of psychotherapy he had previously received.

Koss-Chioino (1992) later followed up clients who had received Western psychotherapeutic treatment in Puerto Rico and compared them with the clients of spiritistic healers, finding that the latter group reported greater improvement. Clients who visited spiritists (some 60% of all Puerto Ricans she questioned) also had higher expectations; this factor might have influenced the outcome. Koss-Chioino noted that spiritistic healers did somewhat better than the therapists in treating mood and behavioral complaints, while therapists were deemed more successful with clients complaining of disordered thinking.

NATIVE AMERICAN PRACTIONERS

In the southwest United States, Navaho practitioners are often allowed to enter hospitals to work with Native American patients, where they frequently rely on the use of herbs and healing chants. In 1969, a U. S. National Institute of Mental Health grant was awarded to finance the training of Navaho shamanic healers at Rough Rock, Arizona, so that the tradition would not be lost. The purpose of the training program was to teach apprentice medicine men and women the intricate Navaho healing ceremonies and techniques in order to preserve and propagate these procedures for the well-being of the Navaho people (Topper, 1987). These rituals are based on a worldview that sees personality as a totality, as a part of a family, and as inseparable from the tribe. Navaho medicine is not only dedicated to restoring

231

the health and harmony of the individual, but to restore family ecology, and any aspects of the tribe that have become disharmonious with nature.

Several other tribes have moved toward making their mental health services more relevant to their cultural needs. In the early 1970s, several Papago Indians were recruited and trained as mental health workers by the University of Arizona department of psychology in Tucson. The Papago Indian client expects his or her therapist or healer to play an active role during the healing session and to make suggestions freely (Torrey, 1986, pp. 177-178).

In 1987, an Arizona rancher was paid $4,140 by the Crime Victim Foundation to reimburse him for 69 sheep that he gave a Navaho medicine man as payment for his services; the Foundation stated that "culturally speaking, a traditional medicine ceremony is just as valid as going to your local physician" (Krippner & Welch, 1992, pp. 224-226). In Ontario, Canada, the provincial government approved the hiring of an Ojibwa medicine man for a rural mental health program for American Indians. In Alaska, mental health services are trying to revive the traditional role of the shaman to assist with such problems as alcoholism, alienation, and chronic depression.

Voss (1999) has taken a critical look at social work literature that views Native Americans as a "problem group," failing to recognize the contributions that tribal and shamanic-based traditions can make in shaping social work theory, practice, and policy. Using the Lakota Sioux as an example, Voss points out the centrality of tribalism, which emphasized the importance of kinship bonds and the interconnectedness of all life, as well as the spiritual role of shamans in fostering individual and community health and well-being. These two paths can restore *wicozani* (i.e., health) and enhance *wo'wa'bleza* (i.e., understanding) among peoples. The Lakota sense of self is permeable, and can cross boundaries to include the natural world and other people; detached, autonomous individuals without these connections are viewed as flawed and misguided.

For the Lakota Sioux, harmony, happiness, and health can be fostered by ceremonial practices, and moral practices. Traditional Lakota Sioux philosophy sees abuse, rejection, and neglect as affecting the child's *nagi* (i.e., soul), often causing it to detach from the body, resulting in "soul loss." In these instances, it is necessary for a shaman to find the child's *nagi* and bring it back. Other shamanic procedures (e.g., the sweat lodge, vision quests) lead to empowerment, regeneration, synergy, and inner healing. Voss provides examples of social services and treatment centers for alcoholism that have incorporated Native American practitioners and perspectives with beneficial results, concluding that social work lacks the insight of shamanism that all beings, human as well as nonhuman, are personal, powerful, and deserving of respect.

Nonetheless, the services of traditional healers have not always been welcomed. In 1985, the author met Denny Thong, an Indonesian psychiatrist who had organized the Bangli Mental Hospital, the first psychiatric facility on the island of Bali. One of his innovations was the introduction of a "family ward," where patients could request that a family member live with them, cook for them, and take an active role in their treatment. Shamans and other native healers were permitted to examine and treat the patient, on the family's request. Despite the success of this program in reducing the time a patient spent at the hospital, the opposition was persistent and intense. Thong was accused of dabbling in "superstition" and the "occult," and was transferred to another island in 1987 (Thong, 1993).

CLARIFYING SPIRITUAL ISSUES

This chapter has described a typology of spiritual healers, proposed a model suitable for cross-cultural comparison of healing systems, delivered a critique of the DSM-IV's attempts to bridge cultures and ethnicities, examined Twelve Step programs as an example of a spiritual self-help program, and provided examples of rapprochement between systems from a postmodern perspective. My investigation of various healing models has convinced me that it would be foolish to abandon what is of value in allopathic biomedicine and Western-oriented counseling and psychological therapy. There is abundant evidence that these procedures can be practical and powerful, especially as carried out by competent, caring practitioners. However, I have also observed an emergence of support for the position that Western medicine and therapy has neglected the spiritual aspects of healing to their peril. Allopathic practitioners and conventional therapists need to integrate a concern for the spiritual aspects of life into their practice, and collaborate with indigenous healers in those areas of the world where Western practitioners are virtually absent or are regarded with suspicion.

An example of this application was provided by Charlene Westgate (1996), whose summary of pertinent literature on "spiritual wellness" identified four dimensions including (a) meaning and purpose in life, (b) intrinsic values, (c) transcendent beliefs and experiences, and (d) community relationships. In the 16 empirical studies located by Westgate, 9 yielded statistically significant results demonstrating lower levels of depression in individuals who manifested one or more of these four dimensions. Of special interest to students of cultures, religions, and ethnicities was the fourth dimension; Westgate noted that "the spiritually well person also lives in the community -- praying, chanting, worshiping, or meditating with others. This community not only provides a sense of shared values and identity but also offers mutual support and an avenue for community outreach" (p. 33). In commenting on young members of African American churches in the United States, Aimee Howd (1999) observed, "There's something about a faith community that seems to make a difference in their lives and that seems to be the church" (p. 18).

It is apparent that psychological therapists and counselors need to be aware of the spiritual backgrounds of their clients in multicultural societies, such as the United States. There is ample evidence that, in general, individuals with internalized spiritual and religious values score higher on measures of mental health than those who consider themselves non-religious, those who only give lip service to religious values, or those whose religious commitment takes the form of adherence to fanatical cults or uncompromising belief systems. A great deal of this value appears to emanate from the social support and community activities generated by fellow believers and participants (Justice, 1987). Other research data indicate that religiously-oriented people have higher scores on tests of mental health than do non-religiously oriented individuals (Wulff, 1991).

Koenig (1999) surveyed the research literature, concluding that the thoughts and actions of religious orientation seem to enhance health. Individuals who attend religious services at least once a week live longer than those who go less often, even after such factors as alcohol consumption and social support are parceled out. As they grow older, those who worship weekly are more likely to live on their own and be free of disabilities. High blood pressure and heart attacks are less common, hospitalization is less frequent, and when religiously-oriented people are hospitalized they return home more quickly. Another survey was conducted by David Larson and Susan Larson (1994) who claimed to find a robust association between spirituality and both physical and mental health.

These data refute debunkers (e.g., Ellis & Yeager, 1989) who claim that religious beliefs, spiritual practices, and transcendent experiences endanger one's mental health. But more to the point is Sloan and Powell (1999), who claim such variables as age, gender, education, ethnicity, and socioeconomic status have not been given adequate consideration in most of the studies. In addition, the living situations of the groups studied prevent them from engaging in such lifestyle behaviors as smoking, alcohol consumption, and psychosocial stress, making it difficult to draw conclusions regarding causation. Sloan and Powell conclude in cautioning that it is not yet time to promote faith as a part of medical treatments. However, they continue to suggest there is a middle ground between rejecting faith and including faith as a part of treatment that calls for further examination.

Given that this territory is "uncharted," what position should psychological therapists and counselors take in regard to spiritual issues with their clients? It is my opinion that mental health practitioners need to have well thought-through opinions of their own, and to inform clients of those opinions if the therapeutic situation requires it. Therapists need to collaborate with clients in considering alternative actions on spiritual issues, and help them to realize the likely consequences of their actions. The final decision, however, is the responsibility of the client. The expertise of the therapist needs to shape the course of therapy, and this includes helping clients formulate a set of values, morals, and ethics that will guide them through life. Such critical life issues as abortion, birth control, sexual practices, competitive business activities, and participation in military service are some on which therapists and clients might disagree, or which might cause the therapist to bring in a member of the clergy as a co-counselor. In any event, it is the client's growth toward autonomy and mature functioning that is the goal of therapy, not the conversion of the client to the therapist's worldview or religious orientation. Thoughtful position papers on spiritual issues in psychological therapy, counseling, and medicine have been prepared by A.E. Bergin (1991), Frances Vaughan (1991), Charlene Westgate (1996), and Richard Wilkinson (1992).

Frank Barron (1963) has concluded that religion, at its best,

> is not a dogma, not a set of forever-prescribed particularities, not static abstraction at all, but a formative process with faith as its foundation and vision as its goal -- faith

in the intelligibility and order of the universe, leading through necessary difficulties of interpretation and changing meanings to moments of spiritual integration which are themselves transient. (p. 169)

Siang-Yang Tan (1999) advises that "religion in psychological therapy is a crucial part of the clinical practice of psychology, because it deals with a significant dimension of human diversity as well as treats the whole person, focusing particularly on the often neglected spiritual aspect of human functioning" (p. 5). African American churches, representing some 20 million members, exemplify this treatment of the "whole person"; most congregations are active in providing community services ranging from child care to substance abuse prevention (Howd, 1999).

In the meantime, Thomas Szasz (1990) wryly comments that humankind is plagued by the fear of diversity, a fear that expresses itself in an insistence on monotheism, monogamy, and monomedicine. No one culture or ethnic group has a right to impose its concepts of disease, illness, etiology, or treatment upon another culture or ethnic group. The only possible exception would be if a scientifically validated discovery is made in one society that could be beneficial in another society. Even so, that discovery should be displayed, explained, but not imposed.

In the early 20th century, the mental hospitals in the southern part of the United States were filled with pellagra victims. They suffered from diarrhea, skin inflammations, and -- as the disease progressed -- psychotic episodes. Eventually it was discovered that the disease resulted from poor nutrition and that vitamin C was an effective treatment. Thousands of patients who had shown severe emotional disturbances were given vitamin C and improved to the degree that they could be released. Western cultures are justified in sharing these kinds of data with other cultures and encouraging them to take appropriate action.

Moreover, there is no need to romanticize indigenous healers and native healing practices. Linnea Smith, after practicing medicine in remote areas of the Amazon for several years, observed that traditional healers in the Yagua tribe "don't really believe in or understand germ theory" and often will not avail themselves of Western medicinal treatment even when it is free of charge. Smith reflected, "I don't like to see people dying, especially from diseases that re treatable. But...people have to make their own choices" (in Denison, 1999, p. 37).

Dogmatic religious positions often block interfaces between allopathic treatment and that of traditional healers. In the Lincoln Community Health Center program originated by Pedro Luiz, formal rather than informal cooperation with the spiritists was blocked. A major factor was the opposition of the Roman Catholic Church, which claimed that spiritism was the work of the devil (Torrey, 1986). Denny Thong's "family ward" in Bali was eliminated by medical bureaucrats who felt that the incorporation of traditional healers was an affront to Indonesia's attempt to burnish its image as a modern state. Szasz' identification of the hegemony of "monotheism" and "monomedicine" rings true, even in an era of postmodernity.

The ways in which spirituality manifests itself will differ from culture to culture. At its best, spiritual experience can be an impetus for growth, development, and the expression of a person's or a group's full capacity for love and service. In one survey, the individuals who reported having had deep "mystical" experiences scored higher than any other group on a standard test of psychological well-being (Greeley, 1975). At its worst, however, spiritual experience can lead to rigid, self-righteous attitudes and the persecution of those whose beliefs and behaviors deviate from a particular dogma or creed. The doctrines of some Western and non-Western religious groups oppose allopathic biomedical care; several cases have been documented where patients, including children, have died because of this harsh dictum (Brenneman, 1990). For example, a husband and wife who were members of the Faith Tabernacle Congregation sect refused to call a physician on two occasions when their children fell ill, claiming that disease comes from the devil and that only God can cure illness. Both children died (Dowell, 1997).

Over the years, the author has observed and studied native healing practitioners on six continents and has observed how the models of health and healing adhered to by these indigenous healers pay special attention to spirituality and spiritual issues. Spirituality implies awareness of broader life meanings that transcend the immediacy of everyday life. If allopathic biomedicine, counseling, and conventional psychological therapy could participate in this awareness, health care in North America would more closely reflect the wholeness and integrity of individuals as well as the meaningfulness of interactions with their families and their societies.

In Tantric Buddhism, truth is said to find its most practical expression in terms of healing. As allopathic biomedicine and Western psychological therapy continue to explore the complexities of the healing process, they may also discover that its structure can accommodate the spiritual dimension. Indeed, that dimension may well lead to the unfolding of awe and the flowering of wonder that will enhance the scope of contemporary medicine, psychological therapy, and counseling and revitalize their quest.

REFERENCES

American Psychiatric Association. (1980). *Diagnostic and Statistical Manual of Mental Disorders* (3rd ed.). Washington, DC: American Psychiatric Association.

American Psychiatric Association. (1994). *Diagnostic and Statistical Manual of Mental Disorders* (4th ed.). Washington, DC: American Psychiatric Association.

Anderson, W.T. (1996). Introduction: What's going on here? In W.T. Anderson (Ed.), *The Truth about truth: De-confusing and re-constructing the postmodern world* (pp. 1-11). New York: Jeremy P. Tarcher/G.P. Putnam's Sons.

Arasteh, A.R., & Sheikh, A.A. (1989). Sufism: The way to universal self. In A.A. Sheikh & K.S. Sheikh (Eds.), *Eastern and Western approaches to healing* (pp. 146-179). New York: John Wiley & Sons.

Avasthi, S. (1990, September 1). Sex addiction: Pros and cons of 12 Step treatment fuel controversy. *Guidepost*, 1, 20-21.

Barron, F.X. (1963). *Creativity and psychological health: Origins of personal vitality and creative freedom*. Princeton, NJ: D. Van Nostrand.

Bartholomew, R.E. (1995, November/December). Culture-bound syndromes as fakery. *Skeptical Inquirer*, 36-41.

Bastien, J.W. (1987). *Healers of the Andes*. Salt Lake City: University of Utah Press.

Bastien, J.W. (1992). *Drum and stethoscope*. Salt Lake City: University of Utah Press.

Bergin, A.E. (1991). Values and religious issues in psychotherapy and mental health. *American Psychologist, 46*, 394-403.

Bourguignon, E. (1973). *Religion, altered states of consciousness, and social change*. Columbus, OH: Ohio State University Press.

Breasure, J. (1996, March). The mind, body and soul connection. *Counseling Today*, p. 5.

Brende, J., & McDonald, E. (1989). Post-traumatic spiritual alienation and recovery in Vietnam combat veterans. *Spirituality Today, 41*, 319-340.

Brenneman, R.J. (1990). *Deadly blessings: Faith healing on trial*. Buffalo, NY: Prometheus Books.

Bufe, C. (1991). *Alcoholics Anonymous: Cult or cure?* San Francisco: Sharpe Press.

Cardena, E., Lynn, S. J., & Krippner, S. (Eds.). (2000). *Varieties of anomalous experience*. Washington, DC: American Psychological Association Press.

Cassell, E.J. (1979). *The healer's art*. Middlesex, England: Penguin Books.

Christopher, J. (1988). *How to stay sober without religion*. Buffalo, NY: Prometheus Books.

Collett, L. (1988, July/August). "Step by step." *Mother Jones*, pp. 42-46, 48.

Denison, N. (1999, Winter). Medicine and metaphysics. *On Wisconsin*, p. 37.

Dowell, W. (1997, May 5). Her dying prayers. *Time*, p. 66.

Ellis, A., & Yeager, R. J. (1989). *Why some therapies don't work -- the dangers of transpersonal psychology*. Buffalo, NY: Prometheus Books.

Emerick, C.D., Tonigan, J.S., Montgomery, J., & Little, L. (1993). Alcoholics Anonymous: What is currently known? In B.S. McReady & W.R. Miller (Eds.), *Research on Alcoholics Anonymous: Opportunities and alternatives* (pp. 41-76). New Bruswick, NJ: Rutgers Center of Alcohol Studies.

Fox, R. (1958). Antabuse as an adjunct to psychotherapy in alcoholism. *New York State Journal of Medicine, 58*, 2-9.

Frank, J.D., & Frank. J.B. (1991). *Persuasion and healing* (3rd ed.). Baltimore: Johns Hopkins University Press.

Gergen, K.J. (1991). *The saturated self: Dilemmas of identity in contemporary life*. New York: Basic Books.

Greeley, A.M. (1975). *The sociology of the paranormal: A reconnaissance*. Beverly Hills, CA: Sage Publications.

Grof, C., & Grof, S. (1990). *The stormy search for the self*. Los Angeles: J.P. Tarcher.

Grossinger, R. (1982). *Planet medicine: From Stone Age shamanism to post-industrial healing* (Rev. ed.). Boulder, CO: Shambhala.

Harwood, A. (1977). *RX: Spiritist as needed: A study of a Puerto Rican community mental health resource.* New York: John Wiley and Sons.

Howd, A. (1999, October 18). The black church in the inner city. *Insight,* pp. 18-19, 39.

James, W. (1985). *The varieties of religious experience: A study in human nature.* New York: Penguin Books. (Original work published 1902)

Justice, B. (1987). *Who gets sick: Thinking and health.* Houston, TX: Peak Press.

Karpel, C. (1975). *The rite of exorcism.* New York: Berkley.

Kluft, R.P. (1996). Dissociative identity disorder. In L.K. Michelson & W.J. Ray (Eds.), *Handbook of dissociation: Theoretical, empirical, and clinical perspectives* (pp. 337-366). New York: Plenum Press.

Koenig, H.G. (1999). *The healing power of faith: Science explores medicine's last great frontier.* New York: Simon & Schuster.

Koss-Chioino, J. (1992). *Women as healers, women as patients: Mental health care & traditional healing in Puerto Rico.* Boulder, CO: Westview Press.

Kreisman, J. J. (1975). The *curandero's* apprentice: A therapeutic integration of folk and medical healing. *American Journal of Psychiatry, 132,* 81-83.

Krippner, S. (1999). Common aspects of traditional healing systems across cultures. In *Essentials of complementary and alternative medicine* (pp. 181-199). Baltimore: Lippincott Williams & Wilkins.

Krippner, S., & Colodzin, B. (1989). Multi-cultural methods of treating Vietnam veterans with post traumatic stress disorder. *International Journal of Psychosomatics, 36,* 79-85.

Krippner, S., & Welch, P. (1992). *Spiritual dimensions of healing: From native shamanism to contemporary health care.* New York: Irvington Publishers.

Larson, D.B., & Larson, S. (1994). *The forgotten factor in physical and mental health: What does the research show?* Rockville, MD: National Institute for Healthcare Research.

Levi-Strauss, C. (1955). The structural study of myth. *Journal of American Folklore, 78,* 428-444.

Lewis-Ferna'ndez, R. (1992). The proposed DSM-IV trance and possession disorder category: Potential risks and benefits. *Transcultural Psychiatric Research Review, 29,* 301-317.

Lewis-Ferna'ndez, R. (1994). Culture and dissociation: A comparison of *ataque de nervios* Among Puerto Ricans and possession syndrome in India. In D. Spiegel (Ed.), *Dissociation: Culture ,mind, body* (pp. 123-167). Washington, DC: American Psychiatric Press.

Lewis-Ferna'ndez, R., & Kleinman, A. (1995). Cultural psychiatry: Theoretical, clinical, and research issues. *Cultural Psychiatry, 18,* 433-448.

Lukoff, D. (1985). Diagnosis of mystical experiences with psychotic features. *Journal of Transpersonal Psychology, 17,* 155-181.

Lukoff, D. (1988). Transpersonal perspectives on manic psychosis, creative, visionary, and mystical states. *Journal of Transpersonal Psychology, 20*, 111-139.

Lyotard, J.F. (1984). The postmodern condition: A report on knowledge. (G. Bennington & B. Massumi, Trans.) Minneapolis: University of Minnesota Press.

Mahler, H. (1977, November). The staff of Aesculapius. *World Health*, p. 3.

Marti'nez-Taboas, A. (1995). *Multiple personality: A Hispanic perspective.* San Juan, Puerto Rico: Puente.

McDonald, D.B. (1909). *The religious life and attitude in Islam.* Chicago: University of Chicago Press.

Navarro, V. (1972). Health, health services and health planning in Cuba. *International Journal of Health Services, 2*, 397-431.

Panati, C. (1996). *Sacred origins of profound things: The stories behind the rites and rituals of the world's religions.* New York: Penguin.

Powers, S. (1994). Dissociation in alleged extraterrestrial abductees. *Dissociation, 7*, 44-50.

Reese, H.W. (1997). Spirituality, belief, and action. *Journal of Mind and Behavior, 18*, 29-51.

Richards, G. (1997). *"Race," racism and psychology: Toward a reflexive history.* New York: Routledge.

Robertson, M. (1988, May 25). Sobriety without the hand of God. *San Francisco Chronicle*, pp. B3, B5.

Rouget, G. (1985). *Music and trance: A theory of the relations between music and possession* (B. Biebuyck, Trans.). Chicago: University of Chicago Press. (Original work published 1980)

Ruiz, P., & Langrod, J. (1976). The role of folk healers in community mental health. *Community Mental Health Journal, 12*, 392-398.

Sandner, D. (1979). *Navajo symbols of healing.* New York: Harcourt, Brace, Jovanovich.

Shafranske, E.P. (1984). Factors associated with the perception of spirituality in psychotherapy. *Journal of Transpersonal Psychology, 16*, 231-241.

Siegler, M., & Osmond, H. (1974). *Models of madness, models of healing.* New York: Macmillan.

Sloan, R.P., & Powell, B.T. (1999). Religion, spirituality, and medicine. *The Lancet, 353*, 664-667.

Szasz, T. (1990). *The untamed tongue: A dissenting dictionary.* San Francisco: Laissez Faire Books.

Tan, S.-Y. (1999, Fall). Religion in psychological therapy. *Psychology of Religion Newsletter: American Psychological Association Division 36*, pp. 1-7.

Tarling, N. (1998). *Nations and states of southeast Asia.* New York: Cambridge University Press.

Thong, D., with Carpenter, B., & Krippner, S. (1993). *A psychiatrist in paradise: Treating Mental illness in Bali.* Bangkok: White Lotus Press.

Tonigan, J.S., & Hiller-Sturmhofel, S. (1994). Alcholics Anonymous: Who benefits? *Alcohol Health & Research World, 18*, 308-309.

Topper, M. D. (1987). The traditional Navajo medicine man: Therapist, counselor, and community leader. *Journal of Psychoanalytic Anthropology, 10*, 217-249.

Torrey, E.F. (1986). *Witchdoctors and psychiatrists.* New York: Harper and Row.

Trotter, R.T., III, & Chavira, J.A. (1981). *Curanderismo: Mexican American folk healing.* Athens: University of Georgia Press.

Vaughan, F. (1991). Spiritual issues in psychotherapy. *Journal of Transpersonal Psychology, 23,* 105-119.

Voss, R.W. (1999). Tribal and shamanic social work practice: A Lakota perspective. *Social Work, 44,* 228-241.

Walsh, R. (1999). *Essential spirituality.* New York: John Wiley & Sons.

Warner, R. (1977). Witchcraft and soul loss. *Hospital and Community Psychiatry, 28,* 686-690.

Westgate, C.E. (1996). Spiritual wellness and depression. *Journal of Counseling and Development, 75,* 26-35.

Wickramasekera, I. (1994). Somatic to psychological symptoms and information transfer from implicit to explicit memory: A controlled case study with predictions from the high risk model of threat perception. *Dissociation, 7,* 153-166.

Wilkinson, R.S. (1992, October). Spirituality and medicine. *Townsend Letter for Doctors,* pp. 834-837.

Winkelman, M.J. (1992). *Shamans, priests and witches: A cross-cultural study of magico religious practitioners.* Tempe, AZ: University of Arizona.

Wulff, D.N. (1991). *Psychology of religion: Classic and contemporary views.* New York: John Wiley & Sons.

Part IV

Application

14

VALUES AS THE BASIS FOR SPIRITUAL INTERVENTION

Billy B. Sharp, M. Div., Ed.D.
Retired Minister and Psychology
Springfield, MO

This chapter will primarily address spirituality in the context of an individual's endeavors to change his life. The need to change may be motivated by a desire to solve problems that are causing difficulty, or perhaps the person may want to live a different lifestyle because of changes in age and circumstances.

From this perspective, spirituality is one concept that can be used to describe the person's being. It is assumed the state of being involves the total person and the spirit is not an entity separate and apart from the psyche and soma, a distinction that is often made. By this definition, every person is a spiritual person. The spiritual dimension encompasses all of life and may have nothing to do with the person's specific religious beliefs or lack thereof.

Using this definition of spirituality, an intervention implies that something is introduced from outside the person that will impact the total being – the spirit. It also implies that all needs, beliefs, attitudes, and values one currently has are spiritual. Any behavior of the individual has a spiritual component. This perspective may well fly in the face of more commonly accepted beliefs because it maintains that evil, or bad, as well as good is a vital part of spirituality. This notion becomes more complex when evil is confronted in everyday life. If one is to change, to improve, what can be done about the evil components of spirituality? Is it possible to rid the person of this evil, or can a "management system" be introduced to motivate the person to choose good over evil? Would such management alter the dynamics of spirituality, although the evil remains present?

This approach implies that a person will always be in a state of tension, or what some might refer to as stress. Opposing forces that are ever present will always be at odds with each other. The expectation that life can be developed to a stage where there is no tension and there is complete peace is a magical concept. The magical belief can cause social problems and/or mental illness. Since man has this magical belief and continues to experience tension and stress, the belief is that if one can predict and control the future, security and blissful peace will be the consequence.

A MAGICAL APPROACH TO CREATING AN "IMPOSSIBLE SPIRITUALITY"

The best summary of this subject that I have seen is in Ernest Becker's book, *Escape from Evil*. People at the very base of their nature are animal. As with all animals, they must be fed. Thus, as a constant part of human endeavor is the struggle to feed himself or herself. From experience:

> man has come…to identify disease and death as the two principal ends of the human condition…man is cursed with a burden that no other animal has to bear; he is conscious that his own end is inevitable, that his stomach will die. (Becker p.2-3)

Becker makes the point that a part of spirituality is the human desire to live and make a difference. He continues by pointing out that all cultures have the same goal: "to raise man above nature, to assure them that in some ways their lives count…" (Becker p.4). At the very heart of man's spirituality struggle is his need to be immortal and his abiding fear that he isn't. Or, if some can be immortal and others cannot, he may not be among the chosen.

CONTROLLING THE FUTURE

A.M. Hocart states: "The object of ritual is to secure full life and to escape from evil." (in Becker, 1973, p.6) Here again is the unrealistic effort to control nature and create a non-tension state of peace. The desire is to in some magical way change the basic spiritual characteristics of being human.

In order to place a long period of history in perspective regarding people's unrealistic effort to alter nature, and thus human spirituality, included below is a rather long quote from Becker:

> As I see it, the history of mankind divides into two great periods: the first one existed from time immortal until roughly the Renaissance or Enlightenment, and it was characterized by the ritualist view of nature. The second period began with the advent of the modern machine age and the domination of the scientific method and world view. In both periods men wanted to control life and death, but in the first period they had to rely on a non-machine

244

technology to do it: ritual is actually a pre-industrial technique of manufacture; it doesn't exactly create new things, Hocart says, but it transfers the power of life and it renovates nature. But how can we have a technique of manufacture without machinery? Precisely by building a ritual altar and making that the locus of the transfer and renewal of life power. (p. 8)

Becker (1975) continues:

Unable to take down, repair, and put together again the actual machinery [of the world] when it goes wrong, [the ritualist]...takes to pieces and rebuilds their form by means of the [ritual] sacrifice." (Becker p.8)

Interestingly, we call those ancient ritual acts "magic" because we don't believe they worked. Our rituals, or more specifically our technologies, we call "scientific" because we believe they work.

But there seems to be another basic human need to consider when we are working with spirituality and change, and that is how we organize our societies as well as our spiritual lives. Hocart explains the profound dualism in which we live in the real world of human ambitions and hopes:

Perhaps it's a law of nature, but that is not sufficient to explain the dual organization...nor does it explain the curious interaction of the moieties: in fact it is their interaction which must explain the dual dimension; for men divide themselves into two groups in order that they may impart life to one another, that they may intermarry, compete with one another, make offerings to one another, and do to one another whatever is required by their prosperity. (Becker p. 10-11)

Life from this perspective seems to "fit" into a rather complex overlapping and inter-relating system made up of various components and needs. Only those parts that relate to our effort to change spiritually will be considered here.

Our society is the seat of the culture in which we live. Hocart and Becker have pointed out that there will be at least two parts to the society. Culture, by definition, is designed to alter the functioning of nature. The unique spiritual need of humans causes them to deny themselves and desperately grasp for a godly nature. Living under these circumstances leaves one in a constant state of tension struggling with opposing forces in a universe that he or she truly tries desperately to control so that they can live forever in peace. Therefore, when one is "psychologically troubled" there is a narrowing down of perception so that the person will not feel totally overwhelmed and hopeless. The goal is to find a magical solution to the problem. Historically people have worked diligently in an effort to conceptualize life so that problems give it meaning. Solutions answer problems. Many of these solutions are limited to one discipline and make little or no effort to address the troubling situation from a broader perspective that we have labeled "spirituality". Perhaps a wider perspective can help.

COMMENTS ON PSYCHOTHERPAY

Generally, when individuals seek psychological help there are one or more specific problems they wish to solve. Their magic has not worked. When asked the reason for seeking help, a problem will be presented. Almost without exception, when asked what desire, wish, expectation, or goal has created the problem, the person has not thought about the problem in relationship to a goal. In other words, an isolated experience of reality is usually not considered a problem with which one needs help. It is when the reality experience is related to an expectation (or goal) that the gap, or distance, between the two is identified as a problem. A simple example would be the person who is earning $8.00 an hour and is able to manage. The $8.00 an hour job creates a psychological problem when the person desires to earn $15.00 an hour. Therefore, to understand a presenting problem three elements must be considered:

1. the reality experience
2. the desired, or expected state
3. the perceived difference between the two

This approach illustrates the multi-nature of the spirit. It is what makes people human.

The next step in the process of change is to explore, and perhaps understand, what is behind the presented problems. Usually, a "presented problem" is not strongly resistant to some change. The situation behind the presented problem may be much more difficult for the person to change. Again, an example may assist with understanding. Consider the spouse who was abused as a child and is currently involved in an abusive marital relationship. The individual presents the problem of abuse and the expectation that it stop. Although this has been going on for 15 years, the spouse remains in the relationship. After a period of therapy it is revealed that the person is fearful to be responsible for herself. She stated, "I am afraid I can't make it on my own. I don't know that I could even provide food and shelter." Regardless of how difficult the situation, a childish need for security is the controlling emotional priority. This underlying problem is usually only revealed when the person feels there is a solution to the problem. The first focus in therapy is generally more effective when related to the initially presented problem. That is the crack in the defense that provides a working path for intervention.

From a spirituality perspective, it is important to remember that people by nature are always in conflict and that every step along the path of change requires a decision – whether to hang on to the known past or to step into the unknown future. A constant battle between experience and faith characterizes the dynamics of spirituality. The question is, "will the true being emerge based on courage or will growth stop blocked by fear?"

As we consider change, and in many instances drastic change, we might do well to consider some insights provided by Eric Hoffer (1963) in his classic little book, *The Ordeal of Change*. His impression is that no one really likes change. "It is not only as Dostoyevsky put it that taking a new step, uttering a new word is what people fear most." (Hoffer p.3) He continues to point out that action is the most obvious way to gain confidence. How often in therapeutic situations have we heard the statement, "it sounds good but I am afraid to act." Speaking of the Europeans that came to this country Hoffer said:

> They were misfits in every sense of the word, and ideal material for a revolutionary explosion. But they had a vast continent at their disposal, and fabulous opportunities for self-advancement, and an environment which held self-reliance and individual enterprise in high esteem... They tamed and mastered a continent in an incredibly short time. (Hoffer p.5)

Perhaps Hoffer's following insights apply even more directly to people forced into change without a vital and positive imbalance among the forces rumbling about in their souls – during a time when their spirituality is under siege.

> Things are different when people subjected to drastic change find only meager opportunities for action or when they cannot, or are not allowed to, attain self-confidence and self-esteem by individual pursuits. In this case, the hunger for confidence, for worth, and for balance directs itself toward the attainment of substitutes. The substitute for self-confidence is faith; the substitute for self-esteem is pride; and the substitute for individual balance is fusion with others into a compact group.
>
> It needs no underlining that this reaching out for substitutes means trouble...we can never have enough of what we don't want. (Hoffer p.5)

Hoffer, although not directly addressing psychotherapy and spirituality, provides great insight into the dynamics of change that will alter the spirituality of an individual.

Isn't it true that most who seek psychological or spiritual help to solve problems consider themselves misfits in some way – they live in the wrong place; are in the wrong marriage; need to change jobs, etc? Interestingly, the "misfit" can change more in a positive way when opportunity is obvious. How many of the helping professions deliberately include in the change process an early step to develop possible opportunities – to make choices obvious. This is a vital component that is frequently ignored. It is especially important since the fearful person, loaded with anxiety, has narrowed his perspective in an effort to wall off the invasion of stresses that seem unmanageable. Unfortunately, the same wall that stops stress also blocks perceived opportunity.

If the opportunities are not existent, or are seen as too meager, Hoffer points out that the person will develop substitutes and those substitutes mean trouble. As he says, we can never get enough of the substitutes. Psychologists frequently refer to what he calls substitutes as a form of defense. As defenses fail, anxiety intensifies. This leads to the development of other defenses that are designed to keep the basic problems intact and that life, even though miserable, will remain predictable. The troubled person digs the psychological hole deeper and the conflict of the soul creates more suffering.

THE PROCESS OF CHANGE

As has been stated, the individual will present one or more problems at the beginning of therapy. These problems are open to change but do not represent the more basic or core problems. However, in therapy it is necessary to start where there is a crack in the defense. The goals creating the problems can be evaluated for purposes of intervention by viewing them through a filter that is formed by Maslow's hierarchy of needs. The level of need will provide clues to the type of intervention that may be acceptable to altering the dynamics of a person's spirituality. More will be said about this later in the chapter.

If an individual's presenting problem is one caused by deficiency in basic needs, any effort to skip a solution to this problem and move to a higher need will usually fail. The caregiver also needs to be aware of what the person in need considers a solution to the problem. A common situation where confusion is seen in this area is with the homeless. What one person may consider a "home" another may not. In a spiritual sense one represents the world to himself or herself and then responds to those representations. Any change in those representations, and thus the self-image, can impact the spiritual dynamics. If the change is too severe, or too quick, the person may resist to avoid the anxiety caused by sudden change. A recent TV show presented some of the lives of people who had won large sums of money in the lottery. In most instances the winnings had not produced the blissful life that the winners had expected.

Stated simply, solutions to presented problems need to be agreed upon by the therapist and patient. The level of need must be considered. The pace of change requires constant consideration. Fearful people do in fact resist and refuse "good things." A person who has learned how to live a limited life on welfare may be terrified to get a job that he might lose at any moment - welfare provides security; and a job is not necessarily secure.

For people who are living at the very basic levels of life, if a spiritual dynamic is changed, it may be necessary to allow enough time for that change to be integrated into one's lifestyle before other changes are attempted. The spiritual dynamic is different for each individual. In an effort to understand how individuals view their lives, some case histories are included.

FEAR OF FLYING SOLVES GREATER PROBLEM

Tom[1] was in his middle 40's. He arrived for his counseling appointment neatly dressed in casual clothes. He was nervous during the first few minutes of the session. When asked what problem motivated him to make the appointment, his reply was direct and simple: "I want to be able to fly in an airplane and I can't." When asked to elaborate on his answer he continued: "Several years ago I was out of town making sales calls in another city. The day I was scheduled to return home I got up early and bought the daily paper to read while having breakfast. The front-page story, with pictures, was about a commercial airplane crash the night before. Just reading the story and looking at the pictures caused great anxiety. However, I was able to go to the airport and board my plane. After a few minutes in the air the pilot announced we had a mechanical problem and would return to the airport. I could feel the panic in my entire body. My mind raced with thoughts about dying. We were only on the ground for a few minutes and we took off again. It was all I could do to hold it together until we arrived home. I haven't been on an airplane since."

After filling in a few more details he answered some questions, "Have you made any effort to fly since that time?"

"A couple of times. Once I got medication from my doctor. That didn't help. I couldn't get on the plane. Another time I went through a brief group program to overcome the fear of flying. No luck."

"You said this fear developed several years ago and you have not flown since. Why are you so determined to overcome this fear and start flying again now? From your description it seems you have managed to live O.K. for several years without flying." "In the last two or three years my life has changed."

"How?"

"I have two children and a wife who likes to keep up with the Jones'. The kids are now teenagers and it requires much more money to support them. Especially because one is going to college next year. My wife is demanding a larger house and a new car."

"What do two children and a demanding wife have to do with your needing to fly?" "I have been a commissioned salesman all my career. Just working within a day's drive I can keep a roof over our heads and food on the table, but to support these new demands requires that I work a larger territory and use my time more efficiently. Specifically, keeping my family happy has become more important to me than holding on to my fear of flying."

"Tom, have there been other times in your life that you can recall that things were tough and you experienced a lot of anxiety. Perhaps you felt forced to make decisions you didn't want to make?"

"You bet. Those were tough times too."

"Are you willing to talk about those times?"

---

[1] All names and identities have been altered to conceal the identity of the clients.

"Well, it isn't difficult for me to remember. It was during the time that I developed the fear of flying. Those were tough days."

"Please be more specific and provide details that will help me understand the situation."

"Well, it requires that I talk briefly about my childhood and growing up. My family was on the low end of the scale financially and socially. I have an older sister. From my parents' perspective she could do nothing wrong. Even when she made a mistake they called it a learning experience. If that were not enough, because of her beauty and brains she was well accepted in school. In contrast I could never do anything right according to my parents. I can remember as a child that I felt like an outsider in my own home. School was difficult for me. With much effort I finally finished high school. With my poor grades, college was not an option. After numerous jobs, I fell into a sales job. It seemed like just what I needed. The hours were my own. I was not confined. I did not have to be around the same people on a regular basis. If things were tense at home the job was an excuse to stay away. During the time that the fear developed my wife was putting pressure on me to be with the family more. She actually talked to my boss. He said I could have a job in the home office. It was high anxiety. The fear of flying, although it isn't logical, seemed like a solution to a lot of problems."

FEAR AND GRACE NOWHERE TO BE FOUND

Neil was in his late 50's. By his own description his life was "a mess" and had been for years. He grew up in a lower class, blue-collar neighborhood. His father moved from job to job to support the family. Formal education had little value in his home. As a result he dropped out of high school and joined the Navy. After several years he decided the naval life was not for him. He had a plan to eat and sleep but there was little satisfaction. Because of his limited education and poor motivation promotions were few and there was little hope that his situation would change.

After his separation from the Navy he returned home to the old neighborhood, although he knew he did not want to stay there. He started looking for a good job and had little success. He worked at part-time jobs to earn a little money. He became bored and in a depressed, bored state met a young woman in a similar situation. After a few dates she suggested marriage might solve some of their problems. He accepted. Rather than solving problems, new ones were created. For almost ten years they stayed in a marriage that was made up of boring, low paying jobs during the day, nights of arguing, and long periods of depression. Finally, as he said, he got lucky and found a better paying, more permanent job. Even though there were two children by now, he decided to get a divorce. It was not a friendly divorce and following the divorce he rarely saw his former wife and children. She kept the children from seeing him and made sure they knew how irresponsible he was and what a tramp he had become. He did manage to keep the job and actually got several promotions, but his personal life was in shambles. He had woman after woman. He could no longer remember how many he had slept with. Relationships were one continuous blur for him.

One night, "half drunk and depressed", he committed a foolish felony. He was caught, convicted, and sent to prison. He found himself truly alone. No one visited or contacted him. His children would not admit that they even knew him. The depression became worse and he truly did not care whether he lived or died. In this severely depressed state he served his term. When he was released he couldn't find a job and was placed on disability. He doesn't know how it happened but he found another woman and married her. She had a house and he moved in. Again he walked into trouble rather than escaping it. As with his first wife, they kept a troubled relationship together for several years. Problems surfaced again as a result of the felony and she divorced him, giving him two weeks to leave the house. At this time he made an unexpected decision. He decided to live as a homeless person. In a real sense he saw it as a challenge, as well as an escape from a life that he thought of as a total failure. Yet, this strange decision seemed to release a creativity that he had not experienced for many years, if ever.

He got an old car with back seats that folded down. This created a space long enough for him to stretch out and sleep. He acquired a warm sleeping bag and found safe places where he could park and spend the night. Even more amazing to those who knew him, he went to the local community college, passed the GED and enrolled in college courses. Since he was on welfare, certain benefits were available to him, one being membership in the local "Y". He joined the "Y" and this provided a locker for some of his clothes and a place to shower and shave. He rented a self-storage unit and kept his larger possessions in carefully organized and marked boxes. The college had a lounge with a microwave oven. There he could cook to eat.

Neil said he felt more successful than at any time in his life. He kept his appointments, made good grades, and kept himself neat and clean. He actually developed hope that he might get a job, but the felony record limited his opportunities. One of the most interesting changes was his interest in what he called "the philosophy of life." He was especially interested in guilt, forgiveness and grace.

ARE THE JUST REWARDED?

Maggie not only asked this question often, she said she actually lived with it almost constantly. Although she tried not to think about it too much, another constant question was "why me?" From her perspective, she was convinced that bad things do in fact happen to good people. As she said, "I try to be the best I can be."

Maggie was in her early 30's, although she said she felt much older at times because of the struggles she had experienced. Early in life she lived in an upper class neighborhood in a large house. Her mother was a member of the local society. Her father was a successful executive with a large corporation. To her life seemed secure and good. As she looked back, she realized there were problems that did not mean much to someone her age. At age 14 her

251

life literally came apart. Her father was fired because of alcoholism and poor performance. She was told their life style was based on a house of cards. They were deeply in debt with no way to pay those debts. They quickly lost the house, the cars, everything. Her parents divorced. And, for reasons she never understood her mother took her younger sister, and Maggie was told she would have to find some other place to live. At age 14 with no life management skills she was on her own. At this point, one of the good things in life happened to her. The parents of one of her friends invited her to come and stay with them. She moved in, got a job for some spending money, and stayed to finish high school. She discovered during this period how creative she could be and how much emotional strength she had. Not only did she finish high school but over a period of several years she earned a college degree. She went to class part time and worked part time. Her father continued to drink and was frequently homeless. She described him as living in a magical world. He truly believed that something magical would happen and he would go back to the good life with a good job. She said it was pathetic. Even in his homeless state he wore a tie saying he needed to be ready for a job interview at anytime. However, each time he contacted her he just needed a little money to tide him over. He could make her feel terribly guilty.

Her mother remarried and rarely contacted her. She remains uncertain as to the cause of the broken relationship with her mother. She has re-established a relationship with her sister and as much as possible they support each other.

Maggie decided she wanted to teach at a higher level so she returned to graduate school. Again, problems dogged her existence. She became seriously ill and couldn't get the kind of health insurance she needed. She was dating a man who could claim her as a dependent. They established a marriage of convenience. She continued in graduate school but the question of "why me" sounded more loudly than ever. She wanted to know if goodness was ever rewarded and if so, how.

Each of these situations relates to an individual's purpose, beliefs, attitudes, needs, values and thus, spirituality. To understand the relations requires a closer look at some of the specifics.

PURPOSE AND MISSION

During the last twenty or so years, an interesting development has taken place in the business and educational communities. It has become popular, in some instances demanded, that businesses and organizations have mission statements. What caused these organizations to adopt a tradition from the religious communities is not clear. There are speculations about the reasons but no specifically agreed upon answers. However, this situation creates another question. Will the next development be for such organizations to create creeds that specify values, beliefs, and attitudes?

These questions about mission, purpose, beliefs, attitudes, and values were especially interesting to Henry, a very successful businessman. He was at the stage in life where he said he needed to give something back to society but he didn't know how. He had tried serving on not-for-profit boards and didn't find this satisfying. He was generous with financial gifts to a number of charities but after several years of giving he said his gifts seemed to make no difference.

Henry, only half-joking, said maybe he needed to write a personal mission statement. At one point, he said maybe he should make a list entitled, "This is what I believe". He was searching for a process that would enable him to define his desires more specifically and pursue those goals using techniques that would work for him. It was clear to him that if he had a larger purpose in life other than what he had accomplished, he had no idea what it was. Life to him was somewhat meaningful when he was doing what he knew how to do – making money in business. But making money was no longer enough. One of the things he decided to do was to conduct a weekly training group for young business people. He found this rewarding but continued to be frustrated because he wanted to do more. But what was the more to be?

MORE ABOUT SPIRITUAL INTERVENTION

Each of these persons, Neil, Maggie, Tom, and Henry, who came for help, was experiencing spiritual stress. Each was struggling to re-organize their spiritual dynamic. They didn't talk in those terms because the concept to them was foreign. To them, they had psychological problems. Henry had shifted his focus slightly when considering the writing of a creed that included beliefs. Tom couldn't get on an airplane and needed to fly. Initially, he saw his problem as not getting on the airplane. It was only after some exploration that he realized he had a need that was motivating him, and also caused him fear. He stopped short of thinking of this situation as a spiritual concern.

Neil's problems had to do with basic living. Where would he get money? How and where would he sleep? How would he provide for his food needs? What about showering and shaving? The result was that he was amazingly creative about solving those problems. They were the result of his immediate goals and current situation. Although he was pleased that he could solve these problems, his psychological frustration continued. In his discussion about such things as forgiveness, guilt, and grace he knew he was off target because the frustration continued but he didn't know what to do about it. As he said, "I don't have a clue about the deeper meaning of my life and know of no way to find out what I need to know." For him it was a spiritual question without an answer.

Maggie truly felt life had dealt her a dirty hand and continued to do so. She could easily list some of her presenting problems: continuing financial challenges; anger at her mother and father; guilt about the anger; trying to get rid of her dependent father; feeling trapped by an illness, and a culture that made no allowances for those who were different.

Although she frequently didn't like how she did it, she did manage to deal well with reality. The problems that were so frustrating to her were not the practical ones, but were the spiritual ones that give life meaning and purpose. She felt there was a wall between her and a meaningful life. She continued to ask, "why me and where is justice?"

Henry's frustration was different in a sense. All of his basic needs had long since been fulfilled. He could not explain why he was not satisfied. He wondered why he couldn't just take his money and with his family go enjoy himself. He could rationalize that he had already done a lot for society. He had created many jobs that supported workers and their families; he had been generous with his money and time; and he considered himself to be a good person. Yet, there was a nagging feeling that there should be something else.

MASLOW'S HIERARCHY OF NEEDS

Abraham Maslow (1954) became interested in what motivates people and through his research observed that people's motivation changed according to their situations and their perceptions. However, one constant seemed to be that a normal, or healthy, person wanted to be some place where they weren't asked to be something different than what they were. In an effort to explain this inspirational dissatisfaction he developed a hierarchy of needs. One first had to fulfill basic needs before moving to a higher order of needs. The level at which a person functioned was partially a matter of personal perception.

Basic needs include having food and shelter. It is interesting to note that in our case studies all four people perceived themselves to have these basic needs fulfilled, although an outsider's observance might well question that perception in the cases of Neil and Maggie. But from their point of view more energy was devoted to fulfilling needs of a higher order.

Since perception plays such a major role in establishing the level of need that is predominant in a person's life, in doing counseling or consulting it is necessary to have the client establish the need level that is primary. For example, although Maggie had practically no savings account, she had provided food and shelter since she was 14 and was confident that regardless of the situation she could continue to do so. She had the ability to focus on survival no matter what situation she found herself in. Tom, on the other hand, found himself overly influenced by what he thought others wanted or expected. As much as he feared flying he was willing to try to change because of his wife and children. In this instance he needed to belong so much that he wanted to try and do what he thought might literally cause him to die. He did not understand his conflicts, was unable to deal with them in an emotionally mature way, but felt that his anxiety was so great that something needed to change. For years Tom had been dealing with life by creating and maintaining a psychological problem. Until recently, Tom would have been classified as neurotic. Currently he would be classified as having a phobic reaction to flying. This explanation is provided because Ernest Becker in his classic book, The Denial of Death makes statements that are helpful to understand and appreciate Tom's position.

Almost without exception, when a person seeks help to solve a problem he expects some type of intervention. Some expectations are realistic, others magical. The help seeker usually expresses an opinion about what type of person he desires as a therapist. This would not be true if the treatment were required – as court ordered.

Even though the troubled person may exercise some choice, it would be rare indeed for someone to tell a caregiver that he or she wishes help with his spiritual life by using techniques based on values. If an approach is to alter spirituality from a values perspective, the process must be introduced by the caregiver, regardless of his specific profession. It will probably be necessary to begin with a more traditional therapy and move gradually toward a "spiritual intervention" based on values.

It might be helpful to realize that a perceived problem generally is a solution to a greater problem that one may not be ready to face. As one patient said, "please don't take my chosen problem away." To understand this conflict more clearly let us turn to Ernest Becker's (1973) classic book, *The Denial of Death*:

> When we say neurosis represents the truth of life we again mean that life is an overwhelming problem for an animal free of instinct. The individual has to protect himself against the world, and he can only do this as any other animal would: by narrowing down the world, shutting off experience, developing an obliviousness both to the terrors of the world and to his own anxieties. Otherwise he would be crippled for action. We cannot repeat too often the great lessons of Freudian psychology: that repression is normal self-protection and creative self-restriction – in a real sense, man's natural substitute for instinct... the 'normal' man bites off what he can chew and digest of life and no more. In other words, men aren't built to be gods, to take in the whole world: they are built like other creatures, to take in the piece of ground in front of their noses... But as soon as a man lifts his nose from the ground and starts sniffing at eternal problems like life and death, the meaning of a rose or a star cluster – then he is in trouble. Kierkegaard said 'men tranquilize themselves with the trivial' – and so they can lead normal lives. (pp. 177-178)

Becker goes on to say "that the essence of normality is the refusal of reality" (p. 178)

A CLOSER LOOK AT LIFE STOPPING ANXIETIES

Although Tom, Neil, and Maggie could discuss their situations in logical, traditionally acceptable terms, each knew there was something wrong. In a sense this wrongness was a result of forces outside themselves. They sensed that life was either stopped or being lived at a slow pace. Yet, they believed that something beyond them had to happen to open the door to a different and future life. Were they correct? For an answer let's quote again from Becker's book:

> It must be clear that the despair and anguish of which the patient complains is not the result of such symptoms but rather are the reason for their

255

existence. It is in fact these very symptoms that shield him from the torment of the profound contradictions that lie at the heart of human existence. The particular phobia or obsession is the very means by which man…eases the burden of his life's tasks… is able to assuage His sense of insignificance…Thus, neurotic symptoms serve to reduce and narrow – to magically transform the world so that he may be distracted from his concerns of death, guilt, and meaninglessness. The neurotic preoccupied with his symptom is led to believe that his central task is one of confrontation with his particular obsession or phobia. In a sense his neurosis allows him to take control of his destiny – to transform the whole of life's meaning into the simplified meaning emanating from his self-created world. (p. 181)

Another insight from Becker can be helpful.

To live is to engage in experience at least partly on the terms of the experience itself. One has to stick his neck out in the action without any guarantees about satisfaction or safety. One never knows how it will come out or how silly he will look, but the neurotic type wants these guarantees. He doesn't want to risk his self-image. Rank calls this very aptly the 'self-willed over- valuation of self' whereby the neurotic tries to cheat nature. He won't pay the price that nature wants of him: to age, fall ill or be injured, and die. Instead of living experience he ideates it; instead of arranging it in action he works it all out in his head. (p.183)

FROM ANXIETY BASED IDEATION TO VALUE DIRECTED ACTION

One of the assumptions on which this intervention approach is based is that a positive spirituality will enable a person to manage the fear of the unknown. One crippled by anxiety will hold to the past regardless of how miserable the consequences are. A person of faith will take action and see the unknown as opportunity, not a world filled with emotional and spiritual land mines. Yet, faith alone will not enable a person to move out of daydreams and into a challenging and exciting unknown. A person who has never explored and experienced positive spirituality needs direction and a system of action that provides guidelines by which to live.

A DEFINITION OF THOSE WHO WALK WITHCOURAGE IN THE LAND OF FAITH

There are numerous approaches that could be used to define the person who is living with courage within what some would call the spiritual self. One professional who has done extensive research regarding the psychology of optimal experience is Mihaly

Csikszentmihalyi. The material included in this paper is found in his national bestseller, *Flow*.

The Autotelic Self: A Summary

> The difference between someone who enjoys life and someone who is overwhelmed by it is a product of a combination of such external factors and the way a person has come to interpret them – that is, whether he sees challenges as threats or as opportunities for action...A person who is never bored, seldom anxious, involved with what goes on, and in flow most of the time may be said to have an autotelic self...For an autotelic person, the primary goals emerge from experience evaluated in consciousness, and therefore from the self proper. (Csikszentmihalyi, 1991)

Csikszentmihalyi says the rules for developing such a self are simple and come directly from the flow model:

> 1. Setting goals. To be able to experience flow, one must have clear goals to strive for...Selecting a goal is related to the recognition of challenge...As soon as the goals and challenges define a system of action, they in turn suggest the skills necessary to operate within it...One of the basic differences between a person with an autotelic self and one without it is that the former knows that it is she who has chosen whatever goal she is pursuing.
> 2. Becoming immersed in the activity – After choosing a system of action, a person with an autotelic personality grows deeply involved with whatever he is doing...he invests attention in the task at hand. To do so successfully, one must learn to balance the opportunities for action with the skills one possesses."
> 3. Paying attention to what is happening. Concentration leads to involvement, which can only be maintained by constant input of attention... Having an autotelic self implies the ability to sustain involvement.
> 4. Learning to enjoy immediate experience...one must develop skills that stretch capacities, that make one become more than what one is... The necessity to develop increasingly refined skills to sustain enjoyment is what lies behind the evolution of culture. (pp. 209-213)

MOVING FROM WHERE ONE IS TO WHERE ONE WISHES TO BE

Each person will have different goals that create their own challenges and require different skills. Just as each person will have different goals, he will also start at a different place along the journey of change. Current practice indicates that the starting point can be placed in one of two broad categories.

The first category is the troubled person category. The person is hampered by anxiety and has narrowed life down to a survival mode. These are the people who come for clinical help and in most instances "a treatment plan" is based on a clinical diagnosis. As one person said, "the task is to keep the ship afloat." The caregiver for those in this category is usually clinically trained.

The second category is comprised of people who are functioning adequately or better and wish to live a life full of optional experiences. They are seeking enhancement. They know what they want but do not know how to get there. These people seek assistance from a variety of sources – peers, ministers, psychologists, and professional coaches.

Because each individual starts the change journey at a different point, a method to conceptualize that point can be helpful. One method to identify the "state of the person" is to use the hierarchy of need theory developed by Maslow. Much detail of this theory can be found in two books by Dr. Maslow: *Motivation and Personality* (1954) and *The Farther Reaches of Human Nature* (19 72).

It can now be seen that the change process that can impact the spiritual aspect of life can be divided into three broad phases:

1. Establishing where a person begins
2. Defining where a person wishes to go
3. Developing an action plan to move from one point to another

MOVING FROM ONE POINT TO ANOTHER

This approach uses values for spiritual intervention. In most instances values are considered in the context of needs, beliefs, and attitudes. Experience has shown it is difficult for a person to alter his values. Beliefs frequently change based on experience. Attitudes may alter if a group of beliefs are altered. However, at the core of one's life are their values, which are developed early in life and reinforced often.

The Allpart-Vermon Value Scale is divided into six groups: religious, social, political, economic, theoretical, and esthetic (Rokeach, 1960). There are techniques that can be used to place the values of an individual according to priority. There are also "teaching techniques" that can be used to influence the power of a value or, perhaps in some cases to alter values.

The valuing processes presented here were developed by Louis Raths, Merrill Harmin, and Sidney B. Simon. The book from which the information is taken is Values and Teaching.

The criteria of values is as follows: having been freely chosen, having been chosen among alternative, having been chosen after due reflection, having been prized and cherished, having been publicly affirmed, having been incorporated into actual behavior, and having been repeated in one's life style.

The characteristic can be explored with a series of questions in the process of values clarification and change. The process can become complex and may require a guide and others who can give both realistic and positive feedback to the person endeavoring to develop a more positive or constructive aspect of their spirit. Needless to say, the process guide can be more effective if they are in touch with their own values and spirituality.

SUMMARY

A person's spirit involves the total person. It contains both good and bad drives and requires constant "management and improvement" if it is to have a positive impact on the person and their surroundings. It is assumed that there is a relationship between the current concept of health and positive spirituality. Thus, as one becomes healthier one also becomes more spiritual. There are many approaches to life style changes. This paper presents one that uses a valuing process to intervene in spirituality.

The process in format is simple. In practice it becomes more complex because of the concepts that need to be understood and the change techniques that need to be applied. Most simply stated the approach has three parts:

1. Know where you are
2. Know where you want to go
3. Develop an action plan to get there

Values are frequently considered along with beliefs and attitudes. In this context, values are at the core of one's spirituality (being). Beliefs are on the outskirts of the being. Attitudes are formed by a cluster of beliefs. Values are enduring and difficult to change. An attitude is also difficult to change but can be altered more readily than values. Beliefs are numerous and are the shirting sands of one's spirituality. Thus beliefs are changed frequently.

These relationships are reflected in the expressions we hear and say every day. For example, if we listen carefully, we will hear such expressions as; "I don't believe that!" "That couldn't be true;" "I think she is jealous;" Each of these can be seen as statements of beliefs. A belief can be changed with an experience. One man told me he believed all people drove on the right side of the road all the time. That was before a person crossed the centerline and hit him head-on. One experience altered this belief.

Generally speaking, a person's attitude is referred to in one of two ways. The person either has a positive or negative attitude. In order for the person to change, it is required that a number of beliefs change. This requires numerous experiences that occur over a long period of time. Many techniques have been developed through the years to change a person's attitude from negative to positive. A famous book in this area is entitled *The Power of Positive Thinking*, by Norman Vincent Peale (1952).

Core values are far less obvious than beliefs and attitudes. Values are few in number and very important to a person. The values are enduring – they have staying power. An example is honesty. It is not unusual to discover that when honesty is not present in a relationship, neither is trust. Without trust, a relationship is always in question.

From the above perspective, it is not difficult to see that only rarely in an intervention process is a value question approached first and directly. The road to value clarification and change goes through beliefs and attitudes. This approach is especially significant when related to spirituality, or a person's overall being. In some theories values are placed into larger categories such as religious, social, political, and economic.

More information about Neil will assist in seeing value intervention in action. Even though much of Neil's trouble was caused by the felony he committed, he frequently talked about honesty and his concern for others. However, he was unable to relate these values to his own past behavior. He was able to see relationships between his actions and beliefs. He was convinced that at the root of many of his problems was the belief that he developed in childhood that he was "no good." He frequently talked about this belief. As strange as it may seem, the belief gradually changed as he slept in his car, showered at the "Y," and studied for his GED. He was able to build his self-esteem by "starting where he was." As one success was built on another, his negative attitude was altered. He called it changing glasses to look at the world. He was aware that it was the same world but he saw it differently. With the change in his beliefs and attitude came his interest in what he called a "philosophy of life." As he discovered this philosophy it was possible to explore and clarify some of his values. As mentioned before, honesty was very important to him. Based on this value he made the decision to "come clean" with his children and work toward establishing a relationship with them. This was no easy process for him because they didn't believe him. This effort created a "long look" at his feelings of guilt and need to forgive and be forgiven. Insight was slow. Actions changed every so slowly. Gradually he felt a spiritual presence in his life – "I feel like a human being."

For him doubts, fears and conflicts were still present but he was able to focus on the positive and pursue his selected goals and "not be driven by the evil within me." For him, values were clarified rather than altered.

You will recall that Maggie had two burning questions, "why me?" and "are the *just* ever rewarded?" Although these questions were paramount in Maggie's mind, what motivated her to seek help was the powerful burden of guilt she felt. She was very angry with her father and yet felt guilty that she did not help him every time he requested it. Her deeper thoughts were that he deserved what had happened to him. He could have done something about his drinking. "He didn't and ended up in the gutter." She did the best she could for herself and she frequently tried to help him. Yet, the real life struggle continued and the guilt mounted.

After several months of therapy, in a session late one afternoon, Maggie became very quiet, got up and looked out the window. Finally, she turned and asked, "Am I trying to be God? Am I trying to do something that I am not capable of doing?" Then she asked, "What causes guilt like mine?" She was asked, "Do you think you have over-estimated your power?" After a long pause she answered a soft, "Yes. My beliefs are wrong, aren't they?" This insight freed her to explore what was really important to her. She realized that she had to value herself because she couldn't do what she was trying to do. She had to let go of her father. In the letting go, the guilt was gone and the anger reduced. She accepted that to value herself was not selfish. Little by little she was able to see her life as it was, and also what it possibly could be. She referred to this break-through experience as "spiritual." It resulted from changes of beliefs and clarification of values.

A person's spirit involves the total person. This spirit contains both good and bad characteristics. Spiritual insight cycles in and out of conflict and requires constant attention and management. The challenge is to focus on the good and see life in a positive and realistic way. By "managing" beliefs, attitudes, values, and actions, spirituality is enhanced and life is lived with a feeling of meaning and the ability to make constructive contributions to a society at large.

REFERENCES

Becker, E. (1973). *The denial of death*. New York: The Free Press.
Becker, E. (1975). *Escape from evil*. New York: The Free Press.
Csikszemtmikalyi, M. (1991). *Flow*. New York: Harper & Row.
Hoffer, E. (1963). *The ordeal of change*. New York: Harper & Row.
Maslow, A. H. (1954) *Motivation and personality*. New York: Harper & Row.
Maslow, A. H. (1972) *The farthest reaches of human nature*. New York: Penguin.
Peale, N. V. (1952). *The power of positive thinking*. New York: Prentice-Hall.
Rokeach, M. (1960). *The open and closed mind*. New York: Basic Books.

15

PRACTICAL APPLICATION OF SPIRITUALITY IN THE PRACTICE OF PSYCHOLOGY

Clarence M. Leung, Ph.D.
Private Practice,
Azusa, CA

Louis R. Hoffman, Ph.D.
Vanguard University of Southern California
Costa Mesa, California

Religion has been an integral part of human history. Long before the inauguration of psychology as a scientific study of mental processes and behaviors people engaged in various types of monotheistic or polytheistic worships for thousands of years. In every culture, there is recognition of the existence of higher being(s), and myriad of folklores contain theistic contents. While some religions, such as Buddhism, Christianity, Hinduism, Judaism, and Muslim, are more institutionalized, popular, and traditional than others, indigenous theistic worships exist in every corner of human civilization and communities. In fact, one can hardly find an ethnic group that does not have any religious belief or practice, and any chronicle of human history would be incomplete if it does not account for the pervasive influence of religion. Religion is observed by different segments of the society in numerous ways for a variety of reasons. Individuals appeal to the Divine for atonement of transgressions, blessings, comfort, fulfillment of personal wishes, protection, and restoration of justice. Families practice religion to honor their ancestors and to preserve familial and cultural heritages. Political parties endorse religion to ensure order, conformity, and national unity. All in all, religion has been a significant constituent of human cultures.

In the United States, many people embrace religion in their lives. The majority of Americans are neither atheistic nor agnostic. Interviews conducted by the Gallup Poll in the past forty years show a steady trend indicating that over 90% of Americans believe in God and report some religious preference (Larson, Pattison, Blazer, Omran, & Kaplan, 1986; Princeton Religion Research Center, 1996). The terrorist attack on World Trade Center on September 11th, 2001 is a vivid example of the prevailing religious inclination underlying the American culture. Following the World Trade Center crisis, millions of people flocked to churches to pray for peace and to seek mental tranquility. Some of them perceive an apocalyptic urge to be at peace with God, while others rediscover the merit of their faith in the midst of national or even global calamities. Increasingly, more and more individuals attend or participate in religious activities on a regular basis, as evidenced by the rising numbers of church attendance and membership in recent decades. It is estimated that more than 40% attend religious services at least once a week, and more than 20% consider their religious beliefs a vital part in their lives (Princeton Religion Research Center, 1996). These statistics reveal a progressive endorsement of religion in American culture, particularly during times of heightened stress, tragedies, and major losses.

Undeniably, religion is a reliable source of comfort, hope, and inspiration. It provides meaning and purpose to life, helps people make sense of their suffering, and empowers people to endure even the most challenging circumstances. Religious involvement is also linked to positive physical and mental health. Research studies consistently find that active religious involvement promotes primary and secondary prevention of physical and psychological impairment. For instance, frequent church attendance is negatively correlated with immune system deficiency (Koenig, Cohen, George, Hays, Larson, & Blazer, 1997). People who consistently participate in religious activities and communities may delay the onset of physical disability (Idler & Kasl, 1997) and may reduce the mortality rate by 25% (Strawbridge, Cohen, Shema, & Kaplan, 1997). Religious involvement may also safeguard mental health. Individuals who actively exercise their beliefs are less likely to engage in risky behavior and lifestyle, such as substance abuse, domestic violence, promiscuity, and criminal activities. They tend to have stable marriages, healthy lifestyles, and supportive social relationships. They also experience greater well-being, higher life satisfaction, and less anxiety than their counterpart (Spilka, 1986). Needless to say, there are also negative effects associated with religion, particularly among religious groups that are repressive, controlling, insular, and prejudicial.

Religion is not a haven that shields people from all kinds of predicaments on earth either. Humans are bound to have problems. Whether they are religious or not, people from all walks of life are confronted with daily stresses. From mundane concerns to philosophical conundrums, from clannish disputes to national crises, from individual quandaries to communal impasses, from ordinary plights to moral dilemmas, and from medical afflictions to mental anguishes, life presents to its inhabitants, religious or non-religious alike, a variety of challenges. When challenges become overwhelming, people may seek psychological services in their coping. In particular, individuals who are struggling with theological issues alongside with their psychological predicaments may prefer to see therapists who can relate to their specific needs (Rose, Westefeld, & Ansley, 2001). While clerical staffs are available for religious/spiritual consultation, religious individuals who are wrestling with personal matters such as abortion, extramarital affairs, homosexuality, loss or questioning of faith, problems associated with conversion to a new belief, or substance abuse may prefer discussing these issues with mental health practitioners to disclosing them to a clergy.

The demand for mental health practitioners with spiritual and religious experience, interests, or background is undeniable. However, the response to this call is generally lukewarm, if not apathetic. For instance, less than one third of practitioners in the field responded in a survey stating that they would incorporate religious matters as a part of their treatment plan (Bergin & Jensen, 1990). In general practitioners are skeptical in discussing religious issues in therapy; many are reluctant to explore or address religious topics with their clients. Even when religious issues are brought up in the session, practitioners may tend to be oblivious about the subject matter. Some may downplay its significance in clients' lives. Some may become uncomfortable or evasive in engaging the client in such discourse. Some may redirect the focus to psychological issues. Others may feel uncertain how to address religious matters with clients. It is not common that clients' religious concerns are regarded as rightful topics in therapy. The resistance toward religion led to studies examining the rationales underlying the skepticism across mental health disciplines.

There are two main reasons that account for the general exclusion of spiritual and religious issues from psychotherapy. First, religion has been poorly represented in various ways in the academia. The emphasis of science as a "dominating source of truth" in the academic world has left little room for the development of subjectivism, mentalism, and phenomenalism as an authentic and substantiative approach for knowledge (Bergin, 1980). Specifically, empiricism and its derivative, behaviorism, have become the benchmark for the psychology profession for a large part of the twentieth century. As a result of the accentuation of empirical principles and methodologies, the colloquial phrase, "seeing is believing," epitomizes the mentality of most scholars. Social scientists, therefore, devote much academic effort primarily in quantitative research than in qualitative studies. Sadly, religion has lost its voice as a legitimate source of truth in the academic realm, and its jurisdiction is confined in ecclesiastical settings. This segregation of religion has minimized opportunities for integrative research in secular universities. Furthering the paucity of integrative religious studies in the academia is the vilification against religion by prominent leaders in the psychology profession. Religion has been viewed by renowned psychologists as antithetical to emotional health, and professional bias against religion is evidenced elsewhere in scholarly journals. For instance, Freud (1961) viewed religion as a harmful illusion and an impediment of growth for the individual and society. Ellis (1986) equated emotional disturbances with irrational religious beliefs. This denunciation of religion has stalled the advancement of psychological studies on religious variables. For many decades, many editors of psychological journals have shunned from publishing research that has religious orientation. Of the few extant religious studies in the psychiatric literature, the bulk of them display skewed sampling error or focus on psychopathological or neurotic use of religion in the psychiatric population (Larson, Pattison, Blazer, Omran, & Kaplan, 1986), thereby partially and slantingly presenting findings that perpetuate professional ignorance and bias. It s not surprising, therefore, that many mental health practitioners consider religious matters irrelevant in their treatment plans or feel uneasy or awkward in dealing with religious clients or religious materials in therapy.

Second, practitioners' hesitancy in handling religious materials in psychotherapy may plausibly be attributed to the inadequate training they receive in graduate schools. While diversity is a virtue that is highly appreciated in mental health professions, religion as a viable area of diversity training in graduate psychology programs have been neglected (Hawkins & Bullock, 1995). Additionally, admission to clinical psychology programs is more stringent for students with active religious affiliation than for individuals without much religious background (Gartner, 1986). A review of the American Psychological Association accredited clinical psychology program directory indicates that only a few graduate programs offer religious or integrative studies. A national survey conducted among training directors of the Association of Psychology Internship Centers (APIC) in 1990-91 showed that all respondents did not receive formal training on religious/spiritual matters in their graduate studies (Lannert, 1991). The neglect in training is not only common in the profession of psychology. To the best of our knowledge, many medical schools do not teach their residents how to handle religious patients. It is not until recently that the Templeton Foundation, and other charitable institutes alike, provides financial incentives for medical schools to include spirituality in their curriculum that more medical schools have begun to train prospective physicians about spirituality and religious issues. However, such financial incentive has rarely been made available to graduate psychology programs. Without proper training, supervision, and consultation in handling religious matters in therapy, practitioners are inclined to address religious concerns based on their personal convictions and knowledge, thereby raising ethical questions on professional competency (Lannert, 1991).

A religiously disinclined clinical approach may inevitably set off skepticism toward counseling among religious clients. Despite their interest in discussing religious matters in counseling, religiously inclined clients are concerned how they would be treated in counseling or how secular clinicians may respond to their religious belief. Fear of being misunderstood, ignored, or even ridiculed makes it difficult for these clients to seek counseling services or to initiate any religious topic in counseling. Some of them are concerned that their religious faith may be undermined and that their values may converge to that of their therapist. Some clergies hesitate in referring their parishioners to mental health professionals worrying their parishioners may be led astray. In fact, a few pastors related to us that they simply do not trust mental health practitioners and, therefore, would not make any referral to clinicians because of negative experiences they have had in which the religious values of their parishioners clashed with the secular morals of clinicians. These ministers added that some of their parishioners who sought counseling services were more confused about and even forsook their religious beliefs, their religious roles, and the religious values that they used to embrace.

The religious communities are under-served. The need to acquaint practitioners with respect to treating religious/spiritual clients is immense. Certainly, there are practitioners who would like to reach out to the religious communities and who are eager to counsel religious/spiritual clients but have not had many opportunities to be familiar with the subject matter. With this group of audience in mind, we gather our thoughts and present the following discussion: differences between religion and spirituality, ways to distinguish religious/spiritual experience from psychopathology, the religiosity and ethical consideration of practitioners, treatment, and training issues.

DISTINCTIONS BETWEEN RELIGION AND SPIRITUALITY

The definitions of and distinctions between religion and spirituality abound numerously in the literature. The recent dedication of two issues of *The Journal of Psychology and Theology* (Hall & McMinn, 2000; 2001) and one issue of the *American Psychologist* (Anderson, 2003) to theoretical and empirical studies in Christian spirituality accentuates the importance and relevance of the subject matters in Christian communities. Some authors, such as David Tacey (1997, 2004) have chosen to focus more on spirituality than religion. A variety of perspectives can be perused even within the chapters of this book. Despite the increase in recent attention given to the topic, clarity of basic definitions is still lacking. This is plausibly due to the fact that definitions of religion and spirituality are likely influenced by personal beliefs and values. As a result, theoretical differences of opinions may persist regardless of the progressive elucidation of these constructs through empirical efforts. The limitations that we have addressed do not render attempts of defining religion and spirituality as futile. Instead, it affirms the essentiality of addressing definitions consistently in the literature. While this may not lead to greater accordance on definitions, it may clarify the conceptual disparity among differing perspectives and prevents inaccurate application of concepts.

Both religion and spirituality can be perceived as the two sides of the same coin. Religion, as a concept, is related to the structural aspects of a belief system. It is commonly viewed as structured, organized, and, at times, rigid. Religion involves the behavioral and the ritualistic aspects (e.g. church attendance, ceremonies, sacraments, prayer, personal devotions, etc.) of worship. Spirituality, on the other hand, refers to the abstract and transcendent aspects of a belief system. It is often conceived of in loose terms and has been frequently associated with mystical experiences, intense emotions, and meaningfulness.

While religion and spirituality can be conceptually distinguished in this manner, it should be noted that this is not an orthogonal distinction. There is a necessary connection between and overlap within these concepts. Religion must impact spirituality by its nature, and spirituality must influence religion by its nature. It is not possible to be religious, but not spiritual or spiritual, but not religious. This distinction may help us identify various meaningful aspects of a belief system. For instance, if a person is religious, but not very spiritual, this may be a problem in itself. In this case it would imply that one is adhering to a religious system, but the religious affiliation has little impact on the emotional life, thereby invalidating one's religiosity. Conversely being spiritual without being very religious may indicate that the person is pursuing experiential or the sentimental aspect of any numinous acquaintance that is not grounded in a belief system. As mentioned earlier, these extremes may not be feasible. However, it is of concern if the cognitive/intellectual portions of faith (religion) have limited impact on the emotional/transcendent aspects (spirituality). It should also be noted that adhering to a particular religious system does not indicate resolution of spiritual issues. Contrarily, adherence to a religious system can be a barrier to working through spiritual issues if the religious system does not promote personal exploration of these issues.

Several reviews of the literature have found some consistent patterns between religion and mental health (Koenig, McCullough, & Larson, 2001). Among these reviews, the extrinsic and intrinsic concepts of religion introduced by Allport are deemed the most empirically useful (Gorsuch, 1988). Extrinsic religiosity, the instrumental aspect of religion used in the service of other goals and needs, has been consistently found to have negative associations with mental health. On the other hand, intrinsic religiosity, the religious practice that serves as its own end or goal, has been found to have a positive relationship with psychological well-being. However, it should be noted that the specific content of the intrinsic beliefs should be taken into consideration. If a legalistic concept is integrated into the core belief system, the result may not be positive. Contrarily, if a grace-centered viewpoint is integrated into the core belief system, the consequence may be constructive. This may also be a point of tension between religiosity and spirituality. Extrinsic religiosity has the legalistic connotation while spirituality is more holistic as it encompasses both intrinsic and extrinsic religiosity. In sum, the aforementioned distinctions between religion and spirituality may be helpful to some clients. Some sees the need for conceptual clarification, while others care less of the distinction between these constructs. All in all, how religion and spirituality are perceived and experienced may become clinical issues in counseling.

RELIGION, PSYCHOLOGY, AND PSYCHOPATHOLOGY

Religious issues may emerge in a variety of ways in psychotherapy. Oftentimes clients ask if the therapist is religious during the early stages of therapy. Clients may talk about religion as a way of coping with their problems or talk about their feelings toward God. They may discuss their church in connection with their support system. Other issues, such as existential quest for the meaning of life, inquires of human suffering or theodicy, fear of mortality, struggles between good and evil, clarification of religious values, moral dilemmas, sentiments of guilt, inability to forgive, problematic relationships with clergy and parishioners, and church scandals, are common topics in therapy (Grame, Tortorici, Healey, Dillingham, & Winkelblaur, 1999). It should be noted that spiritual issues may be manifest or latent, conscious or unconscious, and, therefore, may not be easily identifiable. Regardless of how spiritual matters are presented in therapy, they often emerge in connection with quests for meaning or ultimate purposes in life (Frankl, 2000). For Frankl, personal meaning is inherently tied to religiosity, and the challenge for clinicians is to help the client construct meaning that has perpetual values. This is by no means a simple task, as religious, spiritual, and mental health issues can be interwoven in the life of the psychologically distressed.

How do practitioners differentiate religious/spiritual experience from hallucinations, delusions, or psychotic disorders? The discernment between religious, spiritual, and psychological issues can be arduous even for the religiously trained mental health professional. Some religious beliefs appear delusional without an understanding of their context. For instance, intense religious experience could appear to be a psychotic process to the unfamiliar observer. The drastic changes associated with the conversion experience, glossolalia, or compulsive praying may appear to be pathological. It is, therefore, imperative to have some exposure to the various beliefs systems in order to make such distinctions. Before such distinctions are made, clinicians should avoid any a priori assumption of mental disorder based on the report of a single incidence of personal inspiration, and they need to look into the context of the whole lives of clients to determine whether the personal mystical experience presented has a psychopathological origin or is a religious inspiration (Koltko, 1990). Gathering a thorough religious history may help account for some religious experiences that mimic pathology. Additionally, mystical experiences that enhance social isolation, or exacerbate other functioning, are likely pathological in nature (Bullis, 1996, cited in Northcut, 2000). The mental health professional may, at times, require a consultation with a religious professional from that tradition or need to research a belief system to ascertain whether the belief is pathological. Clinicians that ignore religious issues are susceptible in making diagnostic errors. A more productive approach would be to consult with a religious professional or clergy from within the client's belief system. This supplement to treatment is far too often overlooked. At times, when the belief is rooted deeper within the religious system, this consultation may not be adequate. However, if the clergy is respectfully consulted as a colleague, then this may open the door to new avenues of helping the client work through these spiritual stumbling blocks in an ethical manner.

Spirituality can be either beneficial or detrimental toward psychological wellbeing. Clinicians should not assume that religion/spirituality is beneficial or destructive solely by virtue of their presence. Particular ways of being religious or modes of religiosity may have beneficial impacts on mental health while others may have destructive effects (Koenig, et al, 2001; Meissner, 1996). Pargament (1997) suggests several ways in which religion can be used to facilitate coping. Post (1998) discusses the ethical imperative of utilizing religious beliefs as a means of hope. Chamberlain and Hall (2000) accentuate the healing aspects of prayer. Koenig, McCullough, and Larson (2001) review the benefits of social support associated with being involved with organized religion. On the other hand, there are detrimental aspects of religious belief, too. Gartner (1996) reports that religion has generally been found to be associated with authoritarianism, dogmatism, intolerance of ambiguity, suggestibility, and dependence. There are other negative ways in which religious belief are utilized. For example, it is common in many Christian belief systems to place great importance on God's will. While there can be beneficial aspects associated with this perspective, it can lead to an avoidance of personal responsibility. It is also plausible that reliance on God may result in passivity in important areas. Clinicians may need to help clients explore their religious commitment with respect to their functioning in other aspects of life.

Religious beliefs may lead to excessive self-blame and self-derogation. Clients who have compartmentalized their lives may be unaware of internal conflicts among their spiritual beliefs, their worldview, and their behaviors. For example, a person may believe their problems in life are the result of personal sin or not having enough faith. This may lead to doubt or shame further complicate their current well-being. Along similar lines, distorted images of God may lead to excessive fear and anxiety in some individuals. This can be partially due to the anthropomorphic aspects of religious belief. Many of our current and past relationships with people can lead to distortions in our view of God. For example, growing up with parents who are very rigid can lead to perceptions of God as punitive. A therapeutic goal for these clients may involve helping them integrate spiritual, religious, worldview, and behavioral aspects of self.

RELIGIOSITY AND EHTICS OF PRACTIONERS

Research looking at the religious beliefs of psychologists and other mental health professionals has been subject to more varied results (Shafranske, 1996; Shafranske & Malony, 1991). Most research prior to Shafranske and Malony's consistently found psychologists to be much less religious than the general population. In a survey conducted among mental health practitioners, clinical psychologists are considered the least religiously involved cohort as compared to marriage and family therapists, clinical social workers, and psychiatrists (Bergin & Jensen, 1990). However, Shafranske and Malony found that psychologists were not as irreligious as previously thought. They do, however, tend to be religious in different ways than the general population. This difference can be seen as reflecting the difference between being spiritual and being religious. Psychologists appear to be more likely to endorse beliefs that are less dependent upon the traditional religious systems. In other words, they tend to focus more on spirituality than religion.

While psychologists still are one of the professions most likely to respond as "none" to the question of religious preference, they generally do see religion as important in the lives of their clients. Despite this, most therapists do not feel they are adequately trained to deal with religious issues in therapy. Psychologists generally view religion as a controversial area that they cannot deal with adequately and effectively. This leads us to the first of many important ethical issues in dealing with spiritual issues in psychotherapy. The current trend toward viewing people from a holistic perspective seems to mandate that therapists include religion, like culture, as a viable part of the client's life. To do less would be to view the client as less than a whole person. Does this mean that all therapists should explicitly deal with spiritual issues in therapy or that all therapists should use religious techniques? The answer to the question is a resounding "no." Instead, a strong distinction should be made between exploring religious issues and treating spiritual issues. Additionally, therapists need to be aware of their limitations and the spiritual implications of their interventions.

The full meaning of this statement requires further exploration. There is an important distinction between exploring and treating spiritual issues. Exploring religious issues is taking a more passive approach. This can be viewed as a form of value clarification in which the therapist is helping the client explore and clarify their beliefs. Therapists should be aware of the religious and spiritual implications of their interventions while exploring these issues. For example, various religious traditions interpret issues relating to freedom and personal responsibility differently. Some Christian traditions will attribute certain areas of responsibility to God's will. Psychologists, conversely, tend to focus on personal responsibility as being the individual's. This issue should be dealt with in a sensitive manner to help maximize personal responsibility while not judging or attempting to change the individual's belief about the role of God's will. A therapist's emphasis solely on the individual's responsibility can have spiritual implications for the person's view of God's role in their life. The denial of the divine involvement in a client's life, directly or indirectly, by the therapist may be interpreted by the spiritual client as denying the existence of God or as defiance against the Divine.

Therapists must be aware of how they represent themselves in regards to both spiritual issues and expertise. It is their responsibility to engage in marketing promotions in an ethical and truthful manner. Two labels do not make an integrated whole. In other words, just because someone is a Christian and a psychologist does not make one a Christian Psychologist, lest there will be Christian electrician, Christian architect, Christian accountant, and so on. It is our opinion that these classifications should be more thoroughly governed. For example, one should not be able to call themselves a Christian psychologist without specialized training in working with religious issues in therapy.

Therapists need to be aware of their own limitations in treating spiritual issues. Certain interventions that may involve the integration of psychological techniques with spirituality are best left to those with formal training in these areas. Therapists using an explicit means of dealing with religious issues in therapy should have formal training and/or appropriate supervision in dealing with these issues. Some areas may be best left to spiritual or religious professionals. For example, many of the rituals that are a part of a specific religious tradition ought to be performed by clergies. This is true even for those who have academic training in both realms. For instance, a person who is both a priest and a psychologist needs to keep appropriate boundaries between these two roles.

CREATIN THE ECOLOGY OF RELIGIO-THERAPEUTIC ENVIRONMENT

Professionals interested in treating religious/spiritual clients may want to cultivate a therapeutic environment that opens to and encourages any exploration and discussion of religious/spiritual issues. In order to acclimatize in such a setting, they should be exposed to relevant important issues that contain spiritual implications. One of these important issues is thanatology, the study of death or the meaning of death. Thanatology has important implications for spiritual clients. While all clinicians should be familiar with death issues in therapy, there are some unique aspects of this issue with spiritual clients. Abi-Hashem (1999) purports that grief or loss often leads to spiritual and/or existential crises. Therapists do a great disservice to their clients if they are unable to help them work through the spiritual aspects of loss that may include anger at God and questioning of God's sovereignty or existence. Similarly, many clients wrestle with trying to reconcile suffering and evil in the world with the reality of a God of love. Forgiveness is another topic that clinicians must be able to deal with in working with spiritually motivated clients. This topic is fundamental to human wellbeing but has historically been poorly understood and utilized in the field of psychology. A recent edited book by McCullough, Pargament, and Thorsesen (2000) in addition to an increase in recent journal articles, is helping to reconcile this problem.

The exposure to these different complex issues is only part of the process of becoming able to help people wrestle with these issues in the therapy context. It is important for clinicians to wrestle with these issues themselves. Additionally, it is important that clinicians are able to reconcile their own spiritual beliefs, worldview, epistemology, and conception of human nature. For example, how does the Christian humanistic therapist reconcile their view of human nature with original sin? How does the psychodynamic therapist integrate their perspective on the role of instincts with concepts such as free will and predestination? These obtuse issues don't offer easy answers, and the clinician should not be expected to have a definitive answer to these issues. However, if a clinician is unable to reconcile their spiritual beliefs with the therapeutic orientation their ability to constructively help client work through these issues may be compromised. An integrated theoretical base is necessary to help clinician prevent their own issues from interfering with their ability to help their clients. This does not mean clinician should try to convince their client of their beliefs, but that they should have enough personal insight to allow themselves to see the client's issues clearly.

Religious or spiritual themes may overtly or covertly emerge in psychotherapy. The timing of their emergence may depend on the therapeutic relationship between the practitioner and the client. To the extent that clients feel safe in the session, the discussion of religious/spiritual content may come up in therapy without much therapeutic solicitation. Whereas the probability of being ridiculed is detected in the ambience of the session, the quest for consultation on religious/spiritual matters may be thwarted. Additionally, clients' pace in introducing religious/spiritual topics in therapy also needs to be considered. Practitioners need to be mindful of the fact that seeking professional help on religious matters in therapy may inherently involve demoralization or an acknowledgement of inadequacy (Garfield, 1978). Some clients may consider seeking therapy as a denial of their religious belief; if they were able to live their religion as they suppose to, they would not need professional assistance. Some clients may feel uncomfortable and threatened engaging in prolonged religious/spiritual discussion because of the inherent ambiguity and complexity of the subject matter (Northcut, 2000). Therefore, practitioners need to proceed gently and respectfully in sessions, availing the time and space for clients to make personal decisions of when, what, and how to present their religious materials in therapy. Premature questioning or confrontation of religious beliefs, particularly without a solid therapeutic relationship, may come across as judgmental and may adversely impact the client's faith (Northcut, 2000; White, 1987).

Assessment

Incorporating an assessment of clients' religious/spiritual background and experience as an integral part of the intake is important. An assessment of the client's religious/spiritual history serves several objectives (Northcut, 2000). The act of assessment validates religion as an important part of the client's life. Information gathered may help practitioners identify whether the client's religion/spirituality is a potential coping resource. It may also allow practitioners to determine whether client's beliefs negatively affect current functioning, and thereby providing directions for therapeutic intervention. Bowman (1989) indicates that obtaining a religious history, prior to working with religious issues in therapy, during the intake interview is essential, as "the religious background of the patient and the attitudes and practices of her parents will yield information about the emotional tone of her childhood religious experiences and any connection between religion and abuse" (p. 234). Specifically, Bowman maintains the following information should be gathered during the intake:

a) the client's current denominational affiliation;
b) any past and recent changes in denominational affiliation, and reasons of these changes;
c) any experience of religious training;
d) the frequency of the client's participation in religious activities during childhood;
e) the client's perception about the parent's religious beliefs and practices; and
f) the client's opinion regarding God, prayer, and religious/spiritual rituals.

Other questions that may be added in the intake include:

a) What positive or negative experiences with religion or spirituality have you had in the past?
b) What importance does religion/spirituality have for you today?
c) What type of religious behaviors or spiritual practices do you engage in today? What attitudes do you have about these behaviors? Why are they performed?

272

d) Has religion/spirituality been helpful in the past when dealing with stressful life situations or events? To what extent is religion/spirituality being used for such purposes today?

e) Is a supreme being part of your spirituality? If so, how do you view that supreme being? Angry? Concerned? Loving? Punishing? Distant? Uninterested? Uninvolved? (Northcut, 2000, p. 161)

Additionally, information about clients' personal relationships with God, about their perception of how God thinks of and treats them, and about their sentiments for the Divine are helpful (Grame, Tortoric, Healey, Dillingham, and Winklebaur, 1999). Inquiries of such would not only yield data regarding the client's relational experience with God, but also afford a glimpse of the parent-child relationship as God symbolizes the parental figure in the client's world (Bowman, 1989).

Treatment

Treatment approaches vary among practitioners with different theological and clinical orientations. Two of them are presented here. Koltko (1990) offers five guidelines for practitioners who treat clients with religious beliefs. First, practitioners do not attempt to alter religious beliefs, values, and practices that were adopted and handed down by generations of believers. These normative religious traditions are endorsed by many individuals and are believed to have historic significance and adaptive values. Any tampering may inevitably invoke strong reactions and may recoil any therapeutic intervention. Second, it is clinically prudent to utilize information about the client's religion as a backdrop. The knowledge of clients' belief and the awareness of any personal meaning that clients attach to their religion may enable practitioners to effectively relate to clients' experience and their therapeutic issues. Third, practitioners should pay attention to the belief issues brought up by clients' subgroup within the religion. Fourth, regardless of how inactive, passive, perfunctory, or even disaffiliative clients appear toward their religion, they may still have "active issues" with respect to their belief. Practitioners may want to examine the inconsistent patterns of presenting information to determine whether they are clinically relevant to the problems that lead the client to seek therapy. Finally, practitioners need to decorously utilize the adaptive and curative power inherent in clients' belief to optimize clients' functioning. As previously discussed, religion can both be a source of support and a source of maladaptation depending on how it is being applied (Spilka, 986). If religious issues become impediments to clients' functioning, clinicians are behooved to seek the intrinsic healing power of clients' beliefs to bear on the presenting complaint.

Northcut (2000) adopts the conceptual framework of Kelley (1996) and White and Epston (1990) and proposes a unique narrative approach that combines the general philosophy of constructivism and psychodynamic theories. Briefly defined here, constructivism can be viewed as a meaning-making process through which practitioners assist clients in constructing meaning from emerging religious/spiritual issues in therapy. Psychodynamic theories are useful for its explanation of the present in terms of the past development and influence. Northcut's narrative approach has several features, two of which, namely the deconstruction and reconstruction stages, are adopted for the present discussion.

The deconstruction stage encompasses several components including listening to the clients' story, externalizing the problem, and deconstructing the dominant story. The "listening to the clients' story" component involves an initial inquiry of the client's religious/spiritual background and experience. This is the inquiry process in which practitioners gather information to determine whether religion/spirituality has a positive or negative impact on clients' life, whether religion/spirituality could be a coping resource, and whether pastoral staff should be included in the intervention process. Practitioners may follow the questions listed in the assessment section to facilitate clients' narration of their religious/spiritual background and experience.

The narrative process allows clients to step back and review their beliefs. By externalizing their problems, clients distance themselves from a part of their life that may evoke vehement sentimental reactions or distressful recollections. It is as if they are viewing a part of their lives as a bystander. From the ego psychological perspective, clients' capability in forming life narratives may help reinforce the observing aspect of their ego. From the practitioners' point of view, examining the patterns in which clients construct their stores may allow clinicians to understand clients' internal struggles and their viewpoint about religion and spirituality. Hypotheses that formed during clients' narration may aid later discussion and subsequent intervention.

The next step is to deconstruct clients' stories. As clients tell their stories, it is not difficult for practitioners to identify themes that emerge from their narrative. These themes usually are meaningful and have implications to clients' functioning. Cornett (1988, p. 21, cited in Northcut, 2000) describes six spiritual elements that may emerge in treatment: meaning in life, values, mortality, organization of the universe, suffering, and transcendence.

1) Meaning in life – Does the client worry s/he has missed out on the meaning of life? Is s/he having difficulty creating a personal meaning in life?
2) Values – Are there conflicts between the client's temperaments and/or experience and his or her values?
3) Mortality – Does the client fear death or struggle with the physical finiteness of life?
4) Organization of the universe – Does the client operate under the belief that some type of God or supreme being controls the universe?
5) Suffering – Does the client believe suffering is supposed to bring you closer to God or to a mystical experience? Is s/he questioning "Why do bad things happen to good people?"
6) Transcendence – Is the client questioning what happens after death? Is there something "larger than Life?"

Other themes that could be identified in clients' stories include family secrets, myths, and rituals. Exploring their meaning in relationship to religious/spiritual issues may facilitate the treatment process. In choosing a relevant theme for discussion, practitioners need to observe clients' confirming and disconfirming verbal and nonverbal cues. Interpretation, intervention, and hypothesis testing may be intermittently conducted to ensure clients and practitioners work compatibly on issues that are the core of clinical concerns.

The reconstruction stage of treatment consists of several components. In essence, reconstruction involves a sensible clinical impression, strategy planning, and an improvement of capabilities. After working with clients in the deconstruction stage for some time, practitioners should have developed some clinical impression regarding clients' ego functioning, such as reality testing, judgment, impulse control, social relationship, and capacity for intimacy. This clinical impression may enable practitioners to formulate strategies in mobilizing clients' strengths so as to augment their vulnerabilities. The objective is to "bring out existing but dormant abilities in the client such that the client can grow in desired ways" (Saari, 1999, p. 10, cited in Northcut, 2000). Practitioners may choose strategies that are appropriate and pertinent in the course of treatment. However, strict adherence to prescriptive or linear formats is not encouraged.

Reconstruction also involves reviewing with clients their therapeutic goals. Following the discussion in the deconstruction stage, both practitioners and clients should have some ideas whether certain aspects of clients' beliefs are affirmative or hurtful. Practitioners may help clients consider ways in which religious issues are supportive in the accomplishment of treatment goals. They may also help their clients assess the extent in which religious matters impede the therapeutic process. In this phase both practitioners and clients may come to realize the religious issues they have been working on are beyond the scope of treatment. If this is the case, consultation or referral to religious communities may need to be arranged.

Reviewing clients' narratives is also an integral part of the reconstruction process. As practitioners are able to determine both the overt role of religion/spirituality in treatment and the themes that emerge in clients' narratives, they may proceed to reflect and articulate these themes. Concurrently, practitioners should monitor clients' reactions to the recapitulation of their religious/spiritual problems and struggles. If on target, the reflective therapeutic language may trigger a variety of affective responses, ranging from a sigh of relief knowing that they are being understood to an outpouring of despondent sobbing validating the pain that has been hurting.

Non-thematic religious/spiritual topics may need to be reviewed in the reconstruction stage as well. These are the issues that cannot be elucidated by the thematic content, including the variations or contradictions in the narrative. These discrepancies may skip out of the cognizance of the client but may have significant clinical importance. Uncovering them may prove to be therapeutic. Practitioners may assist clients in exploring the implications of these discrepancies and in determining any action that needs to be taken with respect to them.

Techniques

Practitioners may help religious clients become more cognizant of the religious/spiritual issues that they are struggling by encouraging them to practice a variety of exercises. Bullis (1996, cited in Northcut, 2000) suggests two exercises, a spiritual genogram and a timeline, which can be used in observing the impact of religious/spiritual beliefs and practices on the client's live. As commonly known among practitioners, a genogram is a visual representation of a person's family tree depicted in geometric figures, lines, and words. Similarly, a spiritual genogram is used to describe one's spiritual heritage. It can identify people, places, ideas, and experiences that make up one's current spiritual identity. Following the construction of a spiritual genogram, the client should be able to answer the following questions:

1) Who were the most significant persons and what were the most significant events in my spiritual development?
2) How have they affected my spiritual growth and development?
3) How have I changed my spiritual stance in the past five years?
4) Was there one particular experience (or experiences) that had a lasting spiritual impact on me?
5) What are the current spiritual ideas, books, authors, persons, or events most important to me? (p. 34-35)

The second exercise is constructing a timeline. The technique is simple. Clients are asked to draw a line on which the client chronologically marks the significant spiritual events and experiences from the beginning up to the current stage of their spiritual development. The timeline is useful in placing the client's spiritual journey in perspective over time. The following questions may help clients gain insight after they complete the timeline:

1) How long have I been on a conscious spiritual journey?
2) Did my spiritual journey begin from my deliberate effort or did it begin from a spontaneous, unplanned event?
3) Have there been large gaps in my spiritual growth and development or has my spiritual growth been regular and consistent?
4) Have I changed my spiritual outlook or position since my childhood upbringing? If so, how? (p. 35)

Transference

Transference issues may inevitably surface in therapy. Displacement of anger is one of the negative transferences that is commonly observed in sessions. Clients may project their relational experience of God onto practitioners. They may blame God for failing to protect them or may accuse God for acquiescently allowing bad things to happen to them, especially when they sequence of perceived natural order (e.g. people die young) is violated. They may

276

lash out their anger against the practitioner as if they are protesting to the Divine. Despite the unpleasant sentiment transpired in the session, negative transferences provide a rich context for therapeutic interventions. Analyses of transferences may help uncover the latent meanings of disguised communications or unresolved conflicts. The essential task of practitioners is to facilitate the exploration of these meanings either through their active interpretation or by directly encouraging the client to elaborate upon them so that clients may regain hope in their suffering or restore a genuine perspective of God and ultimately of themselves (Tortorici, 1993).

Countertransference

Countertransference may undermine the practitioner's efforts in relating to and understanding the clients' experience. Humphries (1982) comments that the projection of practitioners' unresolved religious conflicts in sessions is counterproductive and may have an adverse impact on clients, albeit this kind of countertransference is largely unintentional. Practitioners attitude toward religion/spirituality may inadvertently convey in therapy. Therapists whose religious beliefs are different from that of the client may attempt to rectify or change their client's belief to their ways of thinking, particularly in situations where practitioners have a negative view toward a specific sect or denomination (Lannert, 1991). When their efforts are in vain, they may interpret the client's religious convictions as a defensive or resistance to treatment.

On the other hand, shared religious beliefs do not necessarily avert countertransference. Northcut (2000) indicates several ways in which similar religious beliefs may interfere with the therapeutic process. First, similar religious beliefs may mislead both the client and the practitioner to assume that they know what each other is talking about, thereby minimizing opportunities of therapeutic inquiries and exploration. Second, practitioners may find it difficult to maintain professional boundaries and to avoid dual relationship if their clients come from the same religious affiliation or belong to the same denomination. Third, practitioners may overidentify with the struggles of the client by "vicariously gratifying personal fantasies through exploiting clients' 'sinful experience'...or by assuming clients who are theologically similar are the most psychologically mature and therefore healthier" (p. 160). Additionally, therapeutic processes can be compromised when the client feel "obligated" to respond in certain ways so as to "disarm" the theologically compatible practitioner. By and large, the boundary of countertransference may not be conspicuous. Practitioners need to be respectful and sensitive to the client's religious beliefs and experience, empowering clients to make their own autonomous religious choices and guarding against any temptation to impose their religious values on their clients.

Therapists with limited experience or training in religious issues may not be apt to recognize the unconscious spiritual material or may feel uncomfortable interpreting it. Yalom (1980) suggests therapists who have not worked through their issues with the death or who have worked through it only at a superficial level often miss the thanatotic issue when presented by clients. The same would appear to be true with religion. Therapists who are troubled with their own spiritual issues are likely to avoid these issues with clients or feel uncomfortable in dealing with them in the clinical setting. This does not mean that therapists need to have resolved all the problems with spirituality, however, it is important for them to achieve some level of comfort with spiritual issues if they are to help their clients address these same issues.

TRAINING ISSUES

The lack of training in the area of religious issues in psychotherapy complicates the ability to deal appropriately with religious issues. Despite the emergence of new higher quality research and theory of high quality on religious/spiritual issues in psychotherapy, few psychology students and professionals are aware of their presence. Bowen (1998) introduced a proposal for various levels of material to be included in training models for mental health professionals. The first level is the foundational or essential material that is for all mental health professionals. Included in the essential material is general information about the relationship of religion/spirituality and mental health, along with learning how to gather and interpret a client's religious/spiritual history. As part of the basic interface between spirituality and mental health, the first training level also includes "history, ethical issues, research, definitions, and the traditions and beliefs of major world religions" (p. 370). We would add to Bowen's essential material by including training in how to help clients explore spiritual issues in a non-obtrusive manner.

Bowen's (1998) second level includes important material. These she considers to be a high priority for training, but non-essential. Included here are the differential diagnoses of spiritual, religious, and psychological material, ethical considerations in response to religious issues, and a review of the scientific literature on the relationship between religion/spirituality and mental health. Bowen's final category, helpful material, includes the psychodynamics of religion and spiritual development. A fourth category, labeled specialized material, could be added to Bowen's model. This would include training in specialized spiritual-based interventions. This could include training such as Tan's (1987; 1996) cognitive-behavioral approach to dealing with religious issues, Pargament's (1997) religious coping based interventions, or Moriarty's (2001) God Image applications.

Quality training is foundational for dealing with religious issues in psychotherapy. We maintain that Bowen's essential materials should be required as a training minimum for mental health professionals. The second and third levels of training should be offered at all doctoral level training programs, if not required. Finally, the specialized training should be limited to being offered at programs that are committed in developing a quality specialized track. Additionally, religious issues should be dealt with on a routine basis in other coursework as a part of a commitment to diversity training.

Books and journals are also helpful training materials for clinicians who want to self-educate themselves regarding religious/spiritual issues in therapy. Publications such as *When Bad Things Happen to Good People* (Kushner, 1981), the *Revelation of God in Human Suffering* (Oates, 1959), *Forgive and Forget* (Smedes, 1996), *Where is God When It Hurts* (Yancey, 1990), *The Wounded Healer* (Nouwen, 1972), *A Grace Disguised* (Sittser, 1995) and *How Good Do We Have to Be?* (Kushner, 1996) are edifying resources. Jones and Butman's (1991) book, entitled *Modern Psychotherapies: A Comprehensive Christian Appraisal*, reviews and critiques the various theoretical approaches to therapy in accordance with Christian values. Allan Bergin and his colleagues have long argued that we live in an age where we can no longer live under the illusion that therapy is able to remain objective or value-free (see Bergin, Payne & Richards, 1996). In light of these arguments we can see the enormous potential values of a book like Jones and Butman's. However, in an increasingly religiously diverse society it would seem an immense task to critique the increasingly diverse psychotherapy approaches from the perspective of the various spiritual orientations. Journals such as the *Scientific Study of Religion, Review of Religious Research*, the *Journal of Psychology and Christianity*, and the *Journal of Psychology and Theology* provide a forum for ongoing discussion of these issues. These are vital tasks. Additionally, books such as Koenig's (1998) *Handbook of Religion and Mental Health* and Richards and Bergin's (2000) *Handbook of Religious Diversity*, which discusses unique religious issues from a variety of religious perspectives is an important reference book for the modern day psychologist. Koenig includes chapters by authors from various traditions including Protestant, Catholic, Mormon, Buddhist, and others. It is important for therapists to be aware of these resources and the ongoing dialogues.

CONCLUSION

Religion and spirituality have become an integral part of the lives of many people. The rich resources inherent in religious/spiritual systems provide hope and comfort. However, they may also interfere with optimal functioning if being abused. Individuals who struggle with religious/spiritual issues need professional help in their coping. This presents a challenge to the mental health community that is generally not well equipped to handle religious/spiritual matters in therapy. Practitioners interested in treating religious/spiritual clients are encouraged to be familiarized with a variety of religious/spiritual topics and their implications that may emerge in counseling. Insight concerning discernment between religious experience and psychotic symptoms would help sharpen diagnostic skills. Clinicians need to be aware that their religiosity may affect their clinical approach. Ethical considerations must be given with respect to their professional presentation, their practice, and their limitations. A sensitive religio-therpeutic ecology would facilitate therapeutic relationships. Treatment may include a narrative approach that strengthens clients' observing ego, helping them seek meaning by deconstructing their background and reconstructing their self. Transference and countertransference issues may interfere with the therapeutic process and need to be addressed upon their emergence. Edification resources are recommended for further training. Practitioners may not be competent in treating clients with particular religious/spiritual concerns. Nonetheless, the combination of a solid clinical training and an empathetic, sensible, and respectable clinical demeanor would make it a good recipe for a sound practice, empowering clients to utilize the inherent healing power of their belief to progress through their predicaments.

REFERENCES

Abi-Hashem, N. (1999). Grief, loss, and bereavement: An overview. *Journal of Psychology and Christianity, 18,* 309-329.

Anderson, N. B. (Ed.). (2003). Spirituality, religion, and health. *American Psychologist,* 58.

Bergin A. E. (1980). Psychotherapy and religious values. *Journal of Consulting and Clinical Psychology, 48,* 95-105.

Bergin, A. E., & Jensen, J. P. (1990). Religiosity of psychotherapists: A national survey. *Psychotherapy, 27,* 3-7.

Bergin, A. E., Payne, I. R., & Richards, P. S. (1996). Values in psychotherapy. In E. P. Shafranske (Ed.), *Religion and the Clinical Practice of Psychology* (pp. 297-325). Washington, DC: American Psychological Association.

Bowen, E. S. (1998). Integrating religion into the education of mental health professionals. In H. G. Koenig (Ed.), *Handbook of Religion and Mental Health* (pp. 367-378). San Diego, CA: Academic Press.

Bowman, E. S. (1989). Understanding and responding to religious material in the therapy of multiple personality disorder. *Dissociation, 2,* 231-238.

Bullis, R. K. (1996). *Spirituality in social work practice.* Pristol. PA; Taylor & Francis.

Chamberlain, T. J., & Hall, C. A. (2000). *Realized religion: Research on the relationship between religion and health.* Philadelphia, PA: Templeton Foundation Press.

Cornett, C. (1998). *The soul of psychotherapy.* New York: Free Press.

Ellis, A. (1983). *The case against religion.* New York: Institute for Rational-Emotive Therapy.

Ellis, A. (1986). Do some religious beliefs help create emotional disturbance? *Psychotherapy in Private Practice, 4,* 101-106.

Frankl, V. E. (2000). *Man's search for ultimate meaning.* Cambridge, MA: Perseus Publishing.

Freud, S. (1960). Civilization and its discontents. In J. Strachey (Ed. & Trans.), *The Standard Edition of the Complete Psychological Works of Sigmund Freud* (vol. 21, pp. 64-145). London: Hogarth Press. (Original work published 1930).

Garfield, S. L. (1978). Research on client variables in psychotherapy. In S. L. Garfield and A. E. Bergin (Eds.), *Handbook of psychotherapy and behavior change* (2nd ed., pp. 191-232). New York: Wiley.

Gartner, J. (1986). Antireligious prejudice in admissions to doctoral programs in clinical psychology. *Professional Psychology: Research and Practice, 17,* 473-475.

Gartner, J. (1996). Religious commitment, mental health, and prosocial behavior: A review of the empirical literature. In E. P. Shafranske (Ed.), *Religion and the Clinical Practice of Psychology* (pp. 187-214). Washington, DC: American Psychological Association.

Gorsuch, R. L. (1984). Measurement: The boon and bane of investigating religiosity. *American Psychologist, 39,* 228-236.

Grame, C. J., Tortorici, J. S., Healey, B. J., Dillingham, J. H., & Winklebaur, P. (1999). Addressing spiritual and religious issues of clients with a history of psychological trauma. *Bulletin of the Menninger Clinic, 63,* 223-239.

Hall, T. W. & McMinn, M. R. (2000). Christian spirituality: Theoretical and empirical perspectives [Special issue]. Journal of Psychology and Theology, 28(4).

Hall, T. W. & McMinn, M. R. (2001). Christian spirituality: Theoretical and empirical perspectives - Part 2 [Special issue]. Journal of Psychology and Theology, 29(1).

Hawkins, I. L., & Bullock S. L. (1995). Informed consent and religious values: A neglected area of diversity. *Psychotherapy, 32,* 293-300.

Hill, P. C. & Pargament, K. I. (2003). Advances in the conceptualization and measurement of religion and spirituality: Implications for physical and mental health research. *American Psychologist, 58,* 64-74.

Hoge, D. R. (1996) Religion in America: The demographics of belief and affiliation. In E. P. Shafranske (Ed.), *Religion and the Clinical Practice of Psychology* (pp. 21-41). Washington, DC: American Psychological Association.

Humphries, R. H. (1982). Therapeutic neutrality reconsidered. *Journal of Religion and Health, 21,* 124-131.

Idler, E. L., & Kasl, S. V. (1997). Religion among disabled and nondisabled elderly persons, II: Attendance at religious services as a predictor of the course of disability. *Journal of Gerontology, 52B,* 306-316.

Jones, S. L. & Butman, R. E. (1991). *Modern psychotherapies: A comprehensive Christian appraisal.* Downers Grove, IL: InterVarsity Press.

Kelley, P. (1986). Narrative theory and social work treatment. In f. J. Turner (Ed.) *Social work treatment:Interlocking theoretical approaches.* (4th ed., pp. 461-479). New York: Free Press.

Koenig, H. G. (Ed.). (1998). *Handbook of religion and mental health.* San Diego, CA: Academic Press.

Koenig, H. G., Cohen, H. J., George, L. K., Hays, J. C., Larson, D. B., & Blazer, D. G. (1997). Attendance at religious services, interleukin-6, and other biological indicators of immune function in older adults. *International Journal of Psychiatry in Medicine, 27,* 233-250.

Koenig, H. G., McCullough, M. E., & Larson, D. B. (2001). *Handbook of religion and health.* New York: Oxford University Press.

Koltko, M. E. (1990). How religious beliefs affect psychotherapy: The example of Mormonism. *Psychotherapy, 27*, 132-144.

Kushner, H. S. (1981). *When bad things happen to good people.* New York: Schocken.

Kushner, H. S. (1996). *How good do we have to be?* Boston: Little, Brown.

Lannert, J. L.(1991). Resistance and countertransference issues with spiritual and religious clients. *Journal of Humanistic Psychology, 31, 68-76.*

Larson, D. B., Pattison, E. M., Blazer, D. G., Omran, A. R., & Kaplan, B. H. (1986). Systematic analysis of research on religious variables in four major psychiatric journals, 1978-1982. *American Journal of Psychiatry, 143, 329-334.*

McCullough, M. E., Pargament, K. I., & Thoresen, C. E. (2000). (Eds.) *Forgiveness: Theory, research, and practice.* New York: Guildford Press.

Meissner, W. W. (1996). The pathology of beliefs and the beliefs of pathology. In E. P. Shafranske (Ed.), *Religion and the Clinical Practice of Psychology* (pp. 241-267). Washington, DC: American Psychological Association.

Miller, W. R. & Thoresen, C. E. (2003). Spirituality, religion, and health. *American Psychologist, 58*, 24-35.

Moriarty, G. (2001). *The God image in individuals with depression: A clinical manual for understanding and treatment.* Unpublished doctoral dissertation, Forest Institute of Professional Psychology, Springfield, Missouri.

Northcut, T. B. (2000). Constructing a place for religion and spirituality in psychodynamic practice. *Clinical Social Work Journal, 28,* 155-169.

Nouwen, H. J. M. (1972). *The wounded healer.* New York: Image Books/Doubleday.

Oates, W. E. (1959). *The revelation of God in human suffering.* Philadelphia: Westminster Press.

Pargament, K. I. (1997). *The psychology of religion and coping: Theory, research, practice.* New York: Guilford Press.

Post, S. G. (1998). Ethics, religion, and mental health. In H. G. Koenig (Ed.), *Handbook of Religion and Mental Health* (pp. 21-29). San Diego, CA: Academic Press.

Powell, L. H., Shahabi, L., & Thoresen, C. E. (2003). Religion and spirituality: Linkages to physical health, *American Psychologist, 58,* 36-52.

Princeton Religion Research Center. (1996). *Religion in America.* Princeton, NJ: Author.

Richards, P. S. & Bergin, A. E. (2000). *Handbook of psychotherapy and religious diversity.* Washington, D. C.: American Psychological Association.

Rose, E. M., Westefeld, J. S., & Ansley, T. N. (2001). Spiritual issues in counseling: Clients' beliefs and preferences. *Journal of Counseling Psychology, 48*, 61-71.

Saari, C. (2000). Therapeutic dialogue as means of constructing identity complexity. *Smith College Studies in Social Work, 71,* 3-17.

Seeman, T. E., Dubin, L. F., & Seeman, M. (2003). Religiosity/spirituality and health: A Critical review of the evidence for biological pathways. *American Psychologist, 58,* 53-63.

Shafranske, E. P. (1996). Religious beliefs, affiliations, and practices of clinical psychologists. In E. P. Shafranske (Ed.), *Religion and the Clinical Practice of Psychology* (pp. 149-162). Washington, DC: American Psychological Association.

Shafranske, E. P. & Malony, H. N. (1991). Clinical psychologists' religious and spiritual orientations and their practice of psychotherapy. In H. N. Malony (Ed.). *Psychology of Religion: Personalities, Problems, Possibilities* (pp. 549-560). Grand Rapids, MI: Baker Book House.

Sittser, G. (1995). *A grace disguised.* Grand Rapids, MI: Zondervan.

Slater, W., Hall, T. W., & Edwards, K. J. (2001). Measuring religion and spirituality: Where are we and where are we going? *Journal of Psychology and Theology, 29,* 4-21.

Smedes, L. (1996). *Forgive and forget: Healing the hurts we don't deserve.* New York: HarperCollins.

Spilka, B. (1986). Spiritual issues: Do they belong in psychological practice? Yes-But! *Psychotherapy in Private Practice, 4,* 93-100

Strawbridge, W. J., Cohen, R. D., Shema, S. J., & Kaplan, G. A. (1997). Frequent attendance at religious services and mortality over 28 years. *American Journal of Public Health, 87,* 957-961.

Tan, S. Y. (1987). Cognitive-behavior therapy: A biblical approach and critique. *Journal of Psychology and Theology, 15,* 103-112.

Tan, S. Y. (1996). Religion in clinical practice: Implicit and explicit integration. In E. P. Shafranske (Ed.), *Religion and the Clinical Practice of Psychology* (pp. 365-387).Washington, DC: American Psychological Association.

Tortorici, J. (1993). *Abuse of the sacred and the need for spiritual healing in the treatment of MPD.* Paper presented at a Menninger conference on Dissociative States: Multiple Personality and other Trauma-related Disorders, Topeka, KS.

White, F. J. (1987). Spiritual and religious issues in therapy. In D. G. Benner (Ed.), *Psychotherapy in Christian perspective* (pp. 37-46). Grand Rapids, MI: Baker.

White, M. & Epston, D. (1990). *Narrative means to therapeutic ends.* New York: W. W. Norton.

Yalom, I. D. (1980). *Existential psychotherapy.* New York: Basic Books.

Yancey, P. (1990). *Where is God when it hurts?* Grand Rapids, MI: Zondervan.

16

SELECTED LITERATURE REVIEW ON SPIRITUALITY AND HEALTH/MENTAL HEALTH

Betty Ervin-Cox, Ph.D.
Dean of Students
Colorado School of Professional Psychology
Colorado Springs, CO

Louis Hoffman, Ph.D., M.A.T.
Vanguard University of Southern California
Costa Mesa, California

Christopher S. M. Grimes, Psy.D.
Forest Institute of Professional Psychology
Springfield, MO

Spirituality has come be viewed by many as unrelated to physical health and psychological well-being. However, this separation underestimates the power of spirituality while limiting our understanding of health and well-being. The purpose of this chapter is to review the current empirical literature regarding the relationship between spirituality and physical health and well-being. We will begin with the relationship between spirituality and health. Next, research on the relationship between spirituality and well-being will be reviewed. Finally, we will conclude with summary remarks and suggestion for future research.

DEFINITIONS

What do we mean by religion and/or spirituality? The various ways these terms have been defined are more diverse than time would allow us to review. This book alone lists several differing perspectives. The lack of consistent definitions of these concepts along with the intermingling of them can make it challenging to gain a coherent understanding of the literature on spirituality and religion. For the purpose of this paper, religion and spirituality will be defined as highly related, but conceptually distinct. Religion refers to the cognitive, behavioral, and systematic aspects of a person's belief system. The person's religious beliefs are based off what Frankl (2000) has termed "ultimate meaning." Spirituality refers to the transcendent and emotional qualities of life in relation to ultimate meaning (Frankl, 2000) or "whatever they may consider divine" (James, 1902/1958, p. 42). These conceptions of spirituality are similar to how Tillich (1957) defines "ultimate concern" in the context of faith. Unfortunately, the definitions used within the empirical research are not consistent between studies or with this definition. We will attempt to clarify the confusion due to altering definitions of religion and spirituality as they are encountered.

The confusion amongst definitions continues with the concepts of physical health and well-being. Fortunately, there is greater consistency with these terms in the literature. We will use the term health to refer to the various conceptions of physical health. The definitions within the mental health field are much more confusing. We have chosen to use the term well-being to refer to the various general conceptions of positive mental health. Well-being is best viewed as a multidimensional construct that includes positive affect, negative affect, and life satisfaction (Chamberlain & Zika, 1998). Within this conceptualization of well-being, the three factors are highly interrelated, yet they maintain distinctions. Psychological well-being is much more complex than simple lack of pathology. Again, the usage of various terms referring to what we conceptualize as well-being are not consistent within the literature. We will attempt to clarify the differing usage of terms.

SPIRITUALITY AND HEALTH: SETTNG THE CONTEXT

Healing is an integral part of health and has often been associated with various spiritual practices. The concept of healing permeates all cultures from the beginning of the human race and is practiced in different methods depending upon the culture being considered. The "healer" in some cultures is known as a "faith healer." If one studies the New Testament, Christ often ministered to the sick and the diseased and many may well have considered him a "faith healer." The disabled and sick sought out Christ for healing, therefore, we might say that religion was a place for the sick. Matthew, the disciple of Christ, wrote, "They that be whole need not a physician but they that are sick", (Matthew 9:12, King James Bible; KJV). What the KJV translates as "whole" has also been translated "healthy". Regardless, this reference of whole or healthy refers to a conceptualization of wholeness that includes mind, body, and spirit. This book is dedicated to the concept that spirituality is vital to the total health of every individual.

Spirituality within the definition of belief was paramount to the New Testament miracles and conversions. Belief is the communication that one has with the "higher being." The terms "religion" and "spirituality" must therefore be considered carefully in that religion may well be an institutionalized function while spirituality may be the relationship one has with that higher being regardless of the religion espoused. To this end, Easterbrook (1999) suggests that belief or spirituality rather than religious practice supports better health. However, we will see mixed support for this in the empirical research.

During the early twentieth century spiritually was a controversial issue for physicians, many of whom ignored spirituality all together. However, studies occurring in the last three decades have shown a marked interest in spirituality and health. Currently the medical profession is increasingly acknowledging that research confirms the connection between spirituality and health. "Beginning in the 1950's, several factors saw the pendulum start to swing back in favor of a wider consideration of environmental, social, psychological and behavioral determinants of health including religious identity and practice" (Chatters, Levin & Ellison, 1998, p.689).

Recently, during the final decades of the twentieth century and now into the beginning of the twenty-first century, more and more physicians are accepting the spiritual-health connection. Well-respected physicians have contributed significantly with their own research. Research conducted by medical schools and schools of public health gives reason to hold to the traditional view that belief, i.e., a close relationship to the higher power, promotes better individual health (Benson, 1996; Christy, 1998; Easterbrook, 1999; Ellison & Levin, 1998; Faneuli, 1997). There are numerous physicians who have joined the ranks of those willing to speak out publicly regarding the value of this relationship. Several insist that such a relationship is imperative.

Three recent books reflect the growing interest in spirituality in the medical and psychological fields. Chamberlain and Hall's (2000) book, *Realized Religion*, is an attempt to address the effects of being religious through a selected review of the literature. Plante and Sherman (2001) edited a collection of essays titled *Faith and Health* which examines psychological perspectives on the relationship of faith with physical health and psychological well being. Finally, *The Handbook of Religion and Health* by Koenig, McCullough, and Larson (2001) is the most extensive work on religion and health to date. The authors, who are three primary research contributors in the field, offer a comprehensive review of the literature and a discussion of the implications of their findings.

It is interesting that DSM-IV (American Psychiatric Association, 1994), the manual used for the diagnosing of mental disorders, includes a code for "Religious or Spiritual Problem" which is not classified as a disorder. This indicates that psychiatry and psychology are now considering the spiritual aspects of health to some degree. Research psychologists have recently demonstrated a renewed interest in understanding the relationship between spiritually and physical health (Larson & Larson, 2003; Powell, Shahabi, & Thoresen 2003;

Seeman, Dubin, & Seeman, 2003). Powell et al. utilized a levels-of-evidence approach in their review of literature regarding religion and spirituality's link to physical health. The levels-of-evidence approach, compared to meta-analysis, requires research to meet acceptable methodological standards in order to qualify for review. While overall the researchers judged past reviews to be overly optimistic regarding the positive relationship between religion or spirituality and physical health, they concluded that there is indeed a relationship between religion or spirituality and physical health, but that the relationship is more complex that suggested by some.

Various medical schools and graduate programs in psychology are adding courses on spirituality to their curricula and courses are required in many. These are positive signs that the professions of medicine and psychology are recognizing the growing body of research indicating that spirituality has a positive effect on health (Benson, 1996; Christy, 1998; Easterbrook, 1999; Ellison & Levin, 1998).

The general population may have been ahead of the scientific community all along. Gallup polls since 1948 show little change in the percentage of persons who pray. In 1948, ninety percent of Americans surveyed stated that they prayed, whereas in 1989, eighty-eight percent surveyed said they prayed (Poloma, 1993). Of those who do pray, fifty-seven percent say that they pray daily. Andrew Greely (as cited in Poloma, 1993), a sociologist and Roman Catholic priest, believes Americans are the most praying people of any modern nation.

PRAYER, RELAXATION, AND HEALTH

In a survey of Americans, Poloma and Gallup asked who prays, the forms of prayer used, and if prayer makes a difference in the health and well-being (Poloma, 1993). Four types of prayer were identified: colloquial, petitionary, meditative, and ritual. According to their findings, 60% of those surveyed used the meditative form of prayer when praying and perceived it as an intimacy or a close relationship with God. "Prayer for healing appears to contribute to greater life satisfaction and existential well-being for those who are in poorer health but not for those in good health" (Poloma, 1993, p.10).

Many of the persons questioned in the medical research on religion and health stated it was religion or prayer that gave them purpose and meaning to their life (Benson, 1996). They further stated that religion or prayer offered them peace and hope when faced with life threatening disease. Prayer, defined as communication with a higher power, was a source relied upon and provided strength to support them through their suffering. Without prayer, their predicaments would have presumably been despair. Instead, they were able to show a positive attitude that benefited their health.

Viktor Frankl (1959) revealed his depth of spiritual value in his lectures and book, *Man's Search for Meaning*. He emphasized that the desire of most people is to have a purpose and meaning to life. Frankl explains that in order to find the meaning of life, one must go outside of oneself and that there are three ways to do this: one may create or do a deed, one may love, or one may suffer. These are the methods by which one may fulfill the responsibility for finding the meaning in life. They are also searches for the higher spiritual purposes of life.

Clearly, religion or a belief system gives meaning to life for many individuals. Their belief system provides goals to achieve, values to satisfy, rituals to follow, a community that approves, purposes for daily living, and in summary, something *meaningful* to accomplish. Those who find purpose and meaning in life through religion seem to have a resource that they see as spiritual to draw upon as they go through life's experiences. Even those whose values and goals differ from our own have their own sense of accomplishment, although those accomplishments may be in opposition to ours.

The holistic concept of health includes the mind, body, and spirit. When faced with physical problems, people turn to the physician to take care of what is wrong with the body, usually without regard for the spiritual. The mind has been largely left to psychiatry and psychology with little attention paid to the spiritual. Spiritual health, for the most part, has been left to clergy. With some notable exceptions, spirituality has been left out of the equation for retaining or regaining health. The emerging trend in health care tends to consider the whole instead of the parts. This is clearly a healthier way of looking at the individual. What is amazing is that it has taken until the twenty-first century to begin accepting that the gestalt is more than the sum of the parts, and that the human person is certainly a gestalt. Medicine, psychology, and theology have tended to work in isolation preventing each other from fully benefiting from the others' contributions to the whole person.

Hawks (1994), in writing about spiritual health, recognizes this importance on the gestalt and places this in the context of holistic health. Spiritual health provides the individual with meaning, a value system, and self-esteem. Emotional health allows the person to express human emotions along with the ability to give and receive love within their relationships. Hawks proposes five dimensions of health: physical, intellectual, social, spiritual, and emotional. He juxtaposed his theoretical model of spirituality and holistic health with Maslow's hierarchy of needs: food and shelter, safety and security, love and acceptance, self-esteem, and self-actualization. Others have shown agreement with him, i.e., "meaning", Frankl; "value system", Allport, "self-esteem", Maslow.

Herbert Benson (1999), a Harvard University cardiologist, in his address at the American Psychological Association convention stated that persons with a spiritual or religious belief were more likely to be healed than individuals not professing to any spirituality. His experience and research suggests that prayer has favorably influenced the health outcome of persons who pray. Benson is one of the foremost physicians of the day in the discussion regarding spirituality and health. The American Psychological Association, not known for its emphasis on things spiritual, found Dr. Benson's session "standing room only," indicating another bellwether aspect in the consideration of spirituality and health among today's psychological community.

Benson (1996) states that individuals who continuously repeat a word and disregard intrusive thoughts experience physiological changes, such as decrease in respiration and pulse rate. These changes are the opposite of those brought on by stress. The repeating of a word is sometimes viewed as utilizing a "mantra." Many people, however, prefer to repeat a prayer, such as The Lord's Prayer, Psalm 23, or other specific prayers from their religious tradition. There is little doubt that this exercise has proven to be an effective therapy for the disease being treated. Benson calls this the "relaxation response" and emphasizes it has a calming effect on the body and mind. It appears that when belief is added to the relaxation response the body and mind are quieted significantly more than when the relaxation response is used alone. Benson's studies suggest the body's self-healing abilities are aided by a calm state of mind. Benson's five-year study found that patients who used meditation and felt a closeness to a higher power had more rapid recoveries and better health than those who did not make such claims. Psychologists and others trained in biofeedback and hypnosis use similar techniques to train patients to control their headaches and other stress-produced and stress-related body pains. Relaxation, meditation, Yoga, hypnosis, guided imagery, and prayer have much in common.

Prayer is usually seen as part of a relationship with God and also may be a form of meditation. Research studies indicate that persons who attend worship services at least once a week and pray have better health (Benson, 1996). These studies suggest that a calm mental state influences the healing of the body. Other studies suggest that individuals who pray have lower blood pressure than those in the control group (Christy, 1998; Easterbrook, 1999).

Chamberlain and Hall (2000) distinguish between petitionary prayer and intercessory prayer in their selective review of the research. Petitionary prayer is defined as making a specific request of God. The request can be for the self or others, i.e., healing physical or psychological illness. Intercessory prayer makes a request for the healing of another person. One of the more intriguing studies reviewed was conducted by R. C. Byrd (1988). This was a double blind study in which coronary patients were randomly assigned to one of two groups. The first group received intercessory prayer from a group of volunteers who had no contact with the patients. The second group was a control group. In his initial reporting of the results, Byrd indicated that the intercessory prayer had a positive effect on those being prayed for. Byrd, in a 1995 article, reported that the prayer group had better results in 21 of 26 health related categories. Despite the promising findings of this study, Chamberlain and Hall reported inconsistent findings in connecting intercessory prayer and petitionary prayer with better physical health.

Koenig et al. (2001) concur with the Chamberlain and Hall findings on intercessory prayer in their more extensive review of the literature. These authors reviewed 1997 research conducted by O'Laoire on intercessory prayer. O'Laoire looked at the effect intercessory prayer had on measures of mental health and physical health for both the person offering the prayer and the recipient of the prayer. While no significant findings were found for the recipients of the prayers, the results did suggest that the people offering the prayers did receive psychological benefits.

Prayer is not always associated with better health and well-being. Koenig et al. (2001) review several research articles suggesting a negative association between ritual prayer and aspects of mental health. The relationship between other types of prayer, including intercessory and petitionary prayer, generally have inconsistent associations with mental and physical health. Koenig et al. suggest one reason for the inconsistent findings between prayer and health is that people tend to increase prayer in times of trouble. Prior research on prayer, mental health, and physical health suggests the relationship between these factors can be very complex. Further research will need to take into account the effects of prayer over time (longitudinal studies) and must distinguish between various types of prayer.

Koenig, McCullough, and Larson's (2001) literature review suggests that people with an intrinsic faith may benefit more from their religiosity than those with extrinsic faith. Intrinsic faith, which will be discussed in more detail later, is more internalized, personal faith. Conversely, extrinsic faith is faith for the social and other personal benefits. When applying this finding to prayer, it seems logical that people with intrinsic religiosity may benefit more from the effects of prayer than those with extrinsic religiosity. Research that controls for this confounding factor may further illuminate the relationship between prayer, mental health, and physical health.

SPIRITUALITY AND HEALTH

The studies from medical schools indicate that individuals who practice in mainstream religions have fewer physical disorders than the overall population (Koenig, 1999). This finding is constant even when researchers control the variables such as the believers' health histories. Dr. Harold Koenig of Duke University even stated that religious belief may even extend the length of our lives. Many experts in the field assert that church attendance at least once per week benefits physical health. Koenig, in another study that controlled for physical functioning and chronic illness, found older persons who regularly attended worship services had lower blood levels of interleukin-6 than their cohorts playing golf on Sunday mornings (cited in Christy, 1998; Easterbrook, 1999). The psychoneuroimmunology of this finding is staggering!

Koenig (cited in Easterbrook, 1999) states the connection between religious participation and better health within Christianity and Judaism. In a study by Strawbridge (1982), women who attended a worship service at least once a week lived longer but this finding did not necessarily extend to men. Non-mainstream denominations indicate a different picture than individuals in the mainstream denominations. It may well be that the utilization of health services is significantly different for these two groups. Religious communities have differing beliefs and practices when accessing health service. For instance, some religious bodies oppose practices such as blood transfusions, organ transplants, or even basic medical care.

Given the connection between spirituality and health shown here, patients should be advised of this by physicians just as they are advised of other health supporting practices. Just as patients are asked about other habits and practices of their daily living, they should also be queried by their physicians about their spiritual practices and beliefs. This suggestion may seem unnecessary for the medical profession. If so, it will certainly appear intrusive to psychotherapists who many times consider asking about one's religion to be "off limits."

A Dartmouth-Hitchcock Medical Center study of 232 patients who had heart surgery found that drawing strength from religious faith was the best predictor of patient survival in the six months after their surgery (cited in Christy, 1998). For those patients without religious faith, the death rate was three times greater than the rate of those who did have a belief system.

Much correlational research has been conducted on the relationship between religious involvement and mortality. McCullough, Hoyt, Larson, Koenig, and Thoresen (2000) conducted a meta-analysis of data from 42 independent sample studies exploring this relationship. They found religious involvement to be significantly associated with lower mortality, meaning that individuals who scored high in religious involvement were more often alive at follow-up that those with less religious involvement. The authors reason part of the religious involvement-mortality association can be explained by the health-promotive behaviors of religious individuals.

There are several factors that may improve the health and well-being of individuals who regularly attend worship services. George, Ellison, and Larson (2002) suggest four psychosocial mechanisms are presented in the literature as possible explanations of the health-promoting effects of religious involvement. These include health practices, social support, psychosocial resources (i.e. self-esteem and self-efficacy), and providing a sense of coherence and meaning. Some religions explicitly prescribe good health habits while strictly prohibiting behavior linked to poorer health, such as use of tobacco, alcohol, or caffeine, and promiscuous sexual practices. Individuals who regularly attend worship services are within a group of concerned individuals who support others when there is a need. One's local place of worship is the base for social contacts and becomes a primary support system because it not only cares for spiritual needs, but helps those who are ill or in distress. At their best, these institutions extend themselves among their members and those in the community as well. This combination may actually extend the life span for the believer. The caring relationship also acts as therapy for the individual. A church, synagogue, or mosque provides a systematized faith and a value system that gives meaning and sense to life for the individual. Such a place of worship provides the symbols, rituals, creeds, liturgies, and formal structure in which to place the otherwise ambiguous elements of individual belief systems. Individuals benefit in their emotional, mental, physical health as they experience acceptance, love, hope, and contentment. Regular participation in communal worship may regulate mental and physical health behavior in a way that the risk of disease is lessened (George et. al., 2002; Ellison & Levin, 1998; Hawks, 1994; Larson & Larson, 1991; McGuire, 1993).

SPIRITUALITY AND HEALTH IN ADOLESCENTS

Minimal research has considered the relationship between religion and adolescent health. Wallace and Forman (1998) conducted a study of high school seniors using the relationship between religion and behavioral predictors of morbidity and mortality among adolescents. Religious youth were more likely to behave in healthy ways because they were less likely to use alcohol, to take illegal drugs, to carry weapons, and to engage in fights than were their non-religious peers. Historically, disease was the leading cause of death among adolescents. Today, adolescent death is largely due to environmental, social, and behavioral causes. The leading cause of adolescent death is injury, followed closely by homicide and suicide. For adolescents, motor vehicle-related injuries are the most common. Adolescents are more apt to drive while under the influence of alcohol or other drugs or ride with a driver who has been drinking, and less apt to use a seat belt. Firearms account for most of the homicides and suicides of adolescents. Spiritual values and practices undoubtedly influence the etiology of many of the leading causes of death in adolescents. For instance, accidents are frequently secondary to alcoholism, suicide is often a result of damaged interpersonal relationships and despair, homicides are frequently the result of unresolved anger, and disease (certainly sexually transmitted diseases) raise serious questions about morals, ethics, and values.

The behavior and the health care of adolescents during this period of life are key predictors of health in adulthood. Adolescents who engage in smoking, drug use, excessive or unsafe sexual activity, or poor dietary and physical activity often continue these high-risk behaviors later as adults. Adolescents who start smoking before they are eighteen and continue into adulthood are prone to suffer from the three leading causes of death in adults: heart disease, strokes, and cancer. Alcohol and illicit drug utilization are health behaviors that cause illness and death among both adolescents and adults. Adolescents who are sexually active increase their risk for pregnancy and sexually transmitted diseases. The ramifications of unwanted pregnancies, the choices regarding abortion, and the multitudinous decisions that revolve around sexually transmitted diseases are a few of the connections between physical health and spiritual values.

American youth report high levels of religious belief and that religion is important to them (Wallace & Forman, 1998). The importance of worship attendance and spirituality for adolescent health, behavior, and health needs to be stressed among this population. Although this encouragement is typically directed toward religiosity, greater attention might well be given to worship attendance as a preventive behavior for future health problems. This assumes that one's place of worship serves as a support group for the adolescent, encourages a life-style that aids better health, and reduces delinquent behavior patterns.

Frankel and Hewitt (1994) examined the relationship between religion and health among Canadian university students. They found that students who belonged to Christian groups on campus were healthier, more satisfied with life, and handled stress better than the students who did not have the support of such affiliation. The students affiliated with the Christian groups used the university health services less often than non-affiliated peers.

More research must occur with this age group to add to the body of knowledge and to specific areas of spirituality, physical health, and social aspects of the adolescent. The research showing a positive influence for mental and physical health needs to be shared with young people to encourage them to live a better life-style. This research needs to find its way into the literature of adolescents, their parents, their religious leaders, and not kept within the walls of the research laboratory. Programs connecting mosques, synagogues, temples, and churches with medical and educational communities will help adolescents understand the positive rewards for being involved in the church and a spiritual life style.

SPIRITUALITY AND HEALTH IN THE ELDERLY

Interest in the relationship between religion and aging emerged during the 1950s. Since then, however, the amount of research has declined. This is likely due to the assumption that religion in the elderly person does not contribute to the understanding of the aging process. During the last decade, there has been a renewed interest in spirituality and health resulting in renewed interest in the spirituality of the older adult. Gerontology journals have published articles describing the religious behavior and attitudes of the elderly. There is a need to be more specific in the study of religion and how it impacts the lives of the elderly, i.e., the relationship to reading scriptural texts, prayer, worship attendance, and the loss of ritual, communal singing, and other specifically religious practices that frequently occurs with aging.

Levin, Taylor, and Chatters (1994) considered race and gender in their research. Their findings indicated that on the whole, women were more religious than men. Women were more likely to be church members, take part in church activities, and to pray. Older persons of both African American and Caucasian ethnicity had high levels of religiosity. However, the level among African Americans was higher than among Caucasians. Religion was an important part of their life as well as church attendance and prayer. Older African American men reported more religious participation than did older white women.

Oman and Reed (1998) found that, after five years, older persons who attended church services had lower mortality rates than those who did not attend at all. One limit to this study was its sample. The sample did not include persons of color. In a study of an ethnically diverse older group, Idler and Kasl (1997a) found that church attendance was not a significant predictor of health after controlling for demographics and health status.

Idler and Kasl (1997a) also considered the relationship between religion and functional disability. Their findings suggest attendance at worship services was more important than religious involvement. They suggest that research in the experiences that individuals had, such as the music, rituals, and symbols in the services, and confession and forgiveness may be important for bodily health. Attendance may reflect the ability to participate with the group in the service rather than doing it alone at home. For the disabled, church attendance made a positive difference in terms of well-being and social activity. This study confirms research conducted with religious and non-religious elderly persons showing that religion does add to their quality of life. In a second publication, Idler and Kasl (1997b) stated that the worship experience may aid the elderly person to transcend to a state where

293

body affliction is not as important. There are indications that ability to participate in religious groups may help the elderly who have new disabilities in their recovery.

In an earlier study, Idler & Kasl (1992) addressed the relationships between religion, depression, disability, and the timing of death. The results were consistent with their later research findings in that religion was a source of comfort for those with disability. Additionally, religion provided protective measures against disability and depression. Public religiosity had a stronger inverse relationship with depression and disability than did private religiosity. An interesting aspect of this study was the inclusion of the timing of death as a variable. Their results found that both Christians and Jews had fewer deaths in the month prior to religious holidays in comparison to the month following. This suggests that meaningful religious events provide a protective measure for those who are religious.

Idler looked specifically at the spiritual aspects of religiosity in a 1995 article on nonphysical senses of self (spirituality). She reviewed three models that attempted to explain the relationship between religion and health. The first model was based of the work of Durkheim and suggested that religion, or religious activity, provided a protective cushion against health problems. The second model predicted an inverse relationship between religion and health due to people turning to religion in times of poor health. The final model predicted a complex relationship between religion and health. The results supported the third model. Idler found that disabled people were more likely to turn to religion in times of trouble but that several aspects of this religiosity were beneficial for health. Particularly, the results suggested a positive relationship between non-physical sense of self (spirituality) and better subjective ratings of health. She explained these results suggest that when physical health is deteriorating individuals may benefit from focusing on the non-physical aspects of the self that are not affected by the deteriorating physical body.

Koenig (as cited in Marwick, 1995) suggested many of the surveys of the older population indicate that they are more religious than the younger generation. Fifty percent of the elderly attend church at least once a week. Koenig studied older people with disabling disorders such as diabetes and heart disease and construct of religious coping. The study suggested that people who scored high in religious coping were less likely to become depressed. He defined religious coping as the use of prayer, Bible reading, and faith in God. Participants in the study were able to use this ability to deal with their stress.

SPIRITUALITY AND HEALING

Reference was made earlier in the chapter that various cultures have had many kinds of spiritual healers through the ages. In today's world, faith healing is common to many cultures and studies are being conducted with healers from other cultures. Targ carried out one study at California Pacific Medical Center in San Francisco (as cited in Wallis & McDowell, 1996). The study consisted of randomly selected AIDS patients. Half of them were prayed for and half were not. None knew which group they were in. Twenty faith healers were asked to participate in the study. One of the healers, Estonian-born and living in

Santa Fe, New Mexico, was not acquainted with the persons she prayed for during the study. She received a photograph of the patients and their first name and was asked to pray for them at least one hour a day or a ten-week period. The healer prayed for permission to heal the person she would picture in her mind. Her process was to look at the organs of the body and those organs that appeared dark she would "wash it." Targ was encouraged by the results of even a small study and stated it warrants conducting a larger study.

Krippner and Villoldo (1987), in the *Realms of Healing*, describe some of the healers and their performances when they observed when they visited healers in other countries. The healers they interviewed were from the Philippines and Brazil, as well as some from United States. After observing the healers and their paranormal skills, Krippner and Villoldo noted:

> It is my suspicion that much of the "healing" that occurs is "self-healing," inspired by the "healer's" pyrotechnical displays and "I guessed that even fraudulent "healers" could bring about "healing" in much the same way that a physician administers a sugar pill when the patient's complaint appears to be psychosomatic. In other words, the "placebo effect," which accounts for a sizeable proportion of "cures" in Western medicine, may also apply to both psychic and pseudopsychic "healing." (p.232)

When talking with the authors, some of the healers stated their healing was not "psychic" but "spiritual." The authors suggested that scientific research needed to be done with appropriate experimental design and safeguards to test the truth of the "healing." These authors are in agreement with others who believe that research regarding religion and health should be carried out using stronger scientific guidelines utilizing specific aspects of religious life such as prayer, faith, Bible reading, and church attendance.

Krause, Ellison, and Wulff (1998) reported an interaction between church-based emotional support and psychological well-being. The sample was comprised of clergy, elders, and lay-members of the Presbyterian Church in the United States. This is one of the few studies in the field of religion that considered the health or well-being of clergy, elders, and church leaders. The findings suggest that Presbyterian Church members believe that their participation in the church activities has some effect on their well-being. The clergy reported fewer benefits than did the church members. This may be due to the fact that they do not receive the same emotional support as the members. These results suggest the church needs to find a better method of emotional support for the professional staff. Although this study was limited to the Presbyterian Church, it is likely representative of many other denominations. Since it seems the clergy provide acceptable emotional support to the church members, denominational leaders might find ways to offer that same support to the clergy.

Support systems for the clergy need to be explored. Lee and Balswick (1989), in their book *Life in a Glass House: The Minister's Family in Its Unique Social Context*, review the many additional stressors that clergy must deal with in congregational life. It appears that most clergy do not look at their own local church for social and emotional support. It may be that clergy will need to organize themselves to meet such needs. If spirituality has a positive relationship to health, the benefits accrued by members are not being supplied to those who supply it to others.

Health and healing is an important theme among church and religious groups in America. Many persons hold holiness, spiritual growth, salvation, emotional and physical health, and well-being as interwoven concepts. The words "healing," "holiness," "wholeness," and "health" are all derivatives of the same Greek word, from which we get the concept of "holistic." Several religious groups promoting the "spiritual healing movement" are eclectic in practice. They have borrowed healing practices and rituals from other cultures as well as various Western traditions. Some of these groups view medicine as inadequate and consider other parts of the life as causes of illness, such as social roles. The "macho" male, the "women's place," and "successful doctor" are illustrations of social roles that may produce illness.

Many mainline church denominations practice healing using anointing with oil, the laying on of hands, prayer meetings, and other rituals specifically designed for healing services. Radio and television media are replete with clergy who consider themselves anointed with healing power and have amassed large followings of believers. Some extend their abilities to a handkerchief or a hand placed on the radio or television set. The impact of this phenomenon cannot be ignored when looking at the role of religious life, belief, spirituality, religious symbols, and rituals in healing.

SPIRITUALITY AND WELL-BEING

The concept of psychological well-being, as previously discussed, is one for which there is not much consensus in the mental health field. Throughout the history of mental health, there has been a much greater focus on pathology than on well-being. Often well-being has been assumed to be simply the lack of pathology. The authors have already addressed issues pertaining to the multidimensional conception of well-being that includes positive affect, negative affect, and life satisfaction.

Pargament (2002), whose research on faith and coping is reviewed below, suggested five conclusions regarding the relationship between religion and well-being based upon his review of current empirical literature. First, Pargament notes some forms of religion is more helpful that others. Research is relatively consistent in support of a positive relationship between well-being and internalized, intrinsically motivated religion based on a secure relationship with God. However, religion that is imposed, unexamined, and reflective of a tenuous relationship with God, is consistently negatively related to well-being. Second, Pargament presents evidence of advantages and disadvantages to even controversial forms of religion. Specifically, fundamentalism is linked to increased prejudice, but also linked to increased well-being. Pargament's third conclusion regarding the relationship between religion and well-being suggest that religion is most helpful to socially marginalized groups. This finding is likely related to the social support that comes from belonging to religious congregations and the positive benefits of participating in religious services mentioned earlier in this chapter. Forth, religious beliefs appear to be particularly helpful in stressful situations. Finally, Pargament notes that the efficacy of religion, in regard to well-being, is tied to the degree to which it is integrated into an individual's life. Individuals who have more well integrated religious beliefs are more likely to have greater well-being.

Koenig et al. (2001) found 100 articles that addressed the relationship of religion and well-being. Seventy-nine of the 100 articles found a positive association between religion and well-being, 13 found no relationship, 7 found a complex relationship, and only 1 found a negative relationship. Koenig and colleagues pointed out that much of the research that did not find a positive relationship demonstrated poor research designs and contained small samples. This is an improvement from an earlier meta-analysis conducted by Bergin. Bergin (1983) found that 47% of the studies reviewed discovered a positive relationship between religion and mental health, 30% found no relationship, and 23% found a negative relationship. The changes in these relationships may be accounted for by improvement in research methods, improved measures, and studies conducted with larger sample sizes. Additionally, Bergin's concept of mental health was broader than the conceptualization of well-being suggested by Koenig and colleagues.

Ellison (1991) looked at the relationship between religious involvement and well-being. The results indicated a positive relationship between religiosity and well-being. Several aspects of this research make it particularly interesting. The significant relationship between religion and well-being remained after controlling for a broad range of mediating variables. Ellison suggests this indicates a directional relationship between religious belief and well-being that cannot be accounted for by the protective behavioral aspects of being religious (promoting healthy behaviors, social support, etc,). Ellison also found that spirituality may act as a buffer to stress or trauma. A final interesting aspect of this study was that as religiosity increased with age so did life satisfaction increase, but not happiness.

In a particularly well-designed study, Levin and Chatters (1998) looked at three different ways of measuring religion and its connection to health and well-being. While controlling for several potential confounding variables, they developed a structural equation model that predicted subjective religiosity, non-organized or private religiosity, and organized religiosity would have a positive effect on health and well-being. They found a small, but consistent positive relationship between religion and health and well-being. The relationship was stronger with organized religion than with subjective or private religiosity.

Spirituality is a primary source from which people derive meaning for their lives. In a relatively recent study, Compton (2000) found that meaning was one of the strongest predictors of various measures of well-being when compared to self-esteem, locus of control, optimism, and social support. Chamberlain and Zika (1988) found meaning to be a primary moderator in the relationship between religion and well-being for women. They used three different measures of meaning, three measures of well-being, and a single measure of religiosity. They found that religion had a small, significant relationship with well-being. However, after controlling for meaning, the relationship became insignificant for two of the three measures of meaning. This suggests that meaning may be the primary means through which religion impacts well-being.

The indication the meaning is an important component of relationship between spirituality and well-being is quite significant. This would suggest that for religion to be beneficial to the individual, it must be able to provide some meaning for them. A research study by Hoffman and Whitmire (2002) which examined people's response to the terrorist attacks on September 11, 2001, supports the hypothesis that meaning is an important mediator. They found that people who were able to find "meaning that went beyond the individual" showed the highest levels of stress-related growth. The research further suggested that stress-related growth was primarily associated with relationships with God and other people.

Koenig, Kvale, and Ferrel (1988) included a measure of intrinsic religiosity when looking at the relationship between religion and well-being. This research suggested that intrinsic religiosity and organized religion have a positive relationship with well-being. Non-organized religion was not as closely related to well-being. Intrinsic religiosity can be defined "as a meaning-endowing framework in terms of which all of life is understood" (Donahue, 1985, p.400). Extrinsic religiosity, on the other hand, can be defined as "the religion of comfort and social convention, a self-serving, instrumental approach shaped to suit oneself" (Donahue, 1985, p.400). Again, it can be noted the differences of intrinsic and extrinsic religiosity in terms of the meaning dimension. Intrinsic religiosity can be seen as religion providing a meaning inherent in itself. While extrinsic religiosity may afford meaning, but it does through associated aspects of religion instead of religion itself.

Glik (1990) looked at three different religious groups (Christian charismatic, "New Age" groups, and other religious groups) and well-being. She found a positive relationship between religiosity and well-being. She predicted an inverse relationship between religiosity and well-being due to people turning to religion and times of high distress. The results partially confirmed this hypothesis. Whereas there was a positive relationship between religion and well-being in general, there was a negative relationship certain aspects of religiosity:

> Ideational Beliefs, Mysticism, and Salience of Religion represent certain features of religiosity, lined to psychological states of healing adherents. Use of these measures provided evidence that extreme or intense religiosity may correlate negatively with some mental health indicators, thus demonstrating the differential effects that religious beliefs can have on mental well-being within different religious contexts. (Glik, 1990, p. 173)

These results allude to the importance of not consolidating all types of spirituality together into a single construct.

SPIRITUALITY AND SPECIFIC ASPECTS OF WELL-BEING

Surprisingly, the concept of happiness has received little attention in the research literature until quite recently. As discussed earlier, happiness, or positive affect, can be seen as one part well-being. Francis, Jones, and Wilcox (2000) looked at the relationship between happiness and religion during adolescence, young adulthood, and later life. Happiness was measured by the Oxford Happiness Scale in this study. They found that happiness had a positive association with religion in all three age groups.

It is interesting to pay attention to distinctions in the various relationships between constructs within the multidimensional model of well-being. For example, Koenig, McCullough, and Larson's (2001) review of the literature shows that the connection between depression and spirituality is much less consistent than the relationship just discussed between spirituality and well-being. There may be a variety of explanations for this distinction. First, it is possible that the relationship between spirituality and depression is more complex than the relationship between spirituality and the more general construct of well-being. Second, because depression is a more precise construct than well-being, it is possible that the research has thus far been unsuccessful in teasing out the specifics of the relationship. Third, it is possible that spirituality and religion play as stronger role in promoting well-being than in protecting from pathology.

A fourth approach may suggest that religion and psychology frequently focus on different ideologies of mental health. While psychology has often focused on the lack of symptoms and the presence of happiness, religion and spirituality stress the existential nature of all emotions. The shift to well-being (positive affect, negative affect, and life satisfaction) as the indicator of mental health represents a different paradigm than what is frequently used in psychology today. This approach implicitly states that both positive and negative emotions are part of our existential nature, which is at its core spiritual, and thus both need to be embraced. This shift in how mental health is operationally defined has important implications for future research.

Gartner (1996) reviewed the literature on religion's association to several aspects of mental and physical health. He reports that several factors tend to be positively associated with being religious including physical health, mortality, suicide, drug use, alcohol abuse, delinquency, divorce, marital satisfaction, well-being, and depression. Several factors tend to have ambiguous or complex associations with religion including health, anxiety, psychosis, self-esteem, sexual disorders, intelligence, and prejudice. Finally, he reports authoritarianism, dogmatism, suggestibility, dependency, self-actualization, and temporal lobe epilepsy are aspects of pathology that tend to be associated with religion.

Koenig et al. (2001) found that two religious groups are more susceptible to depression. First, those who describe themselves as non-religious are at greater risk for depression. The second and more controversial group is those affiliated with the Jewish religion. There have been many attempts to explain why this population may be more prone to depression that include social, historical, and cultural explanations. Further research needs to better address these differences. However, given that much of this research has evolved over a time period in which the people of Jewish faith and cultural background have been grossly misunderstood and mistreated, it is very important to be cautious about any interpretations of this faith tradition as being unhealthy. It doesn't take too long of a look at the history of psychology to find many previous such interpretations which have been used in the service of further discriminating against a group of people.

Religious orientation appears to play a primary role in the relationship between religion and depression (Park & Murgatroyd, 1998; Koenig et al, 2001). Koenig and colleagues have reported two connected trends in the literature regarding these construct. Extrinsic religiosity appears to have an inverse relationship with depression. This suggests that people who tend to use religion for their own self-interest or personal gain tend to have a higher likelihood of depression. Conversely, those with intrinsic religious faith are less likely to be depressed.

In one particularly well designed study, Parks and Murgatroyd (1998) studied the relationship between spiritual orientation and depression in a sample of Korean Americans. Consistent with the trend previously noted, they found that extrinsically religious Korean Americans were more likely to be depressed. Additionally, they found that divorce, lower levels of education, and unemployment were strong predictors of depression for this population. They further discovered a strong relationship between extrinsic religiosity and depression that remained significant even after controlling for divorce, education level, and employment status. This study is particularly important because it extends findings to different cultures. Most current literature has examined samples that have been primarily Caucasian or African American.

Several studies have suggest spirituality can be a protective factor against depression during times of increased stress (Fehring, Brennan, & Keller, 1987; Young, Cashwell, & Shcherbakova, 2000) and may even help some people grow through stressful times (Hoffman & Whitmire, 2002). Young and colleagues found that negative life experiences were associated with increases in depression and trait-anxiety. Spirituality was a significant moderator between negative life events and depression, but not for anxiety. Thus, spirituality may help people better cope with some aspects of stressful events. Fehring and colleagues (1987) looked at depression and spiritual well-being during the transition to college. They found that the increase in depression during the transition to college was tempered by spiritual well-being. Fehring et al. used the Spiritual Well-Being Scale which defines spiritual well-being as the cumulative scores of the existential well-being and religious well-being subscales. When taking the subscales into account, the relationship between religious well-being was no longer significant while existential well-being remained significant. This suggests certain aspects of spirituality provide the protective effects.

Several studies have also looked at religion, loneliness, and well-being (Frankel & Hewitt, 1994; Schwab & Petersen, 1990; Stokes, 1985). Benson and Spilka (1973) found that individuals who perceive God as "angry and punishing" have negative feelings toward God and are more likely to feel lonely and suffer with lower self-esteem. The individuals who

300

have a positive attitude regarding God and see God as "loving and caring" are likely to have a better overall well-being and report higher self-esteem. These findings were consistent between the college population and an older adult population.

FAITH AND COPING

The concept of faith and coping has gained increased attention over the past ten years. A discussion of faith and coping adds an important, new level to the discussion thus far through its connection to both physical and mental health. Kenneth Pargament is one of the premiere leaders in research in the area of faith and coping and has strongly argued for a multidimensional approach to religious coping (Pargament, 1997; Pargament & Ishler, 1994; Pargament & Olsen, 1992; Pargament, Kennell, Hathaway, Grevengoed, Newman, & Jones, 1988; Pargament, Smith, Koenig, & Perez, 1998). Pargament et al (1998) report a general trend suggesting religious coping has beneficial functioning for mental and physical health. However, this relationship has often been found to be small and has been inconsistent in the research. Pargament and his colleagues argue that this is due, in part, to attempts to measure multidimensional, complex constructs in as a global, unitary construct. Research in the faith and coping arena has done much to begin to change this and move toward research that respects the complexity of these constructs. Furthermore, Pargament's arguments provide a good model to apply to other religious and mental health constructs which are not valued in their complexity.

Koenig, George, and Siegler (1988) looked at the use of coping strategies in an older adult population. They found religious coping skills to be the most frequently used of all coping skills followed by focusing attention elsewhere, "just accepting" the problem, and seeking support from family or friends. Pargament and Ishler (1994) further put the frequency of religious coping to the test. Most of the previous studies looking at the frequency of religious coping were retrospective appraisals of the frequency of religious coping skills. Pargament and Ishler looked at coping skills used during the 1990-1991 Gulf War. They found that religious coping skills were frequently used during the time of crises. Later research by Pargament et al (1998) found that religious coping was also employed during the Oklahoma City bombings, by college students having experience a traumatic experience, and by hospital patients suffering from physical illness.

Religious and non-religious coping skills do not appear to be completely independent from each other. Pargament and Ishler (1994) found that there was a small, consistent relationship between religious and non-religious forms of coping. This suggests that while religious and non-religious coping skills may frequently be used in conjunction with one another, they both contribute independently to aspects of dealing with the distress.

Research has provided conflicting results on the consistency of the usage and effectiveness of coping skills across different times and situations (Maynard, Gorsuch, & Bjork, 2001; Pargament & Olsen, 1992; Schaefer & Gorsuch, 1991, 1993). Pargament et al (1998) found that religious and non-religious coping were both related to poorer levels of health. The authors interpreted this stating that it is likely that people with poorer health are more likely to use coping skills in general, and religious coping skills in particular. The results do not necessarily indicate that religious coping negatively influences health. It does provide some initial evidence for the bi-directionality of the relationship between religion and health that will be discussed more later in the chapter.

Personality variables also appear to play a role in religious coping. Different religious orientations (or motivations for religion) and different beliefs about God influence preference for religious coping styles (Pargament & Olsen, 1992; Schaefer & Gorsuch, 1991, 1993). Pargament and Olsen (1992) looked at religious coping variables associated with intrinsic, extrinsic, and quest religious orientations. Intrinsic religiousness with a spiritual end or purpose is primarily associated with seeking God. People with this religious orientation tend to perceive negative life events as a spiritual threat, but they also see the event as an opportunity for growth. Intrinsic religiosity has been found to generally be associated with a collaborative or deferring coping style (Pargament et al, 1988; Schaefer & Gorsuch, 1991). A collaborative coping style is one in which the people see themselves as working with God. People who use a deferring coping style tend to rely on God primarily to resolve or deal with the situation.

Extrinsic religious orientation is generally associated with a self-directed coping style in which the people rely solely upon themselves in the absence of God to deal with stressful situations (Pargament et al, 1988; Schaefer & Gorsuch, 1991). Pargament and Olsen (1992) additionally found that people with this religious orientation tended to seek self-development as the end purpose of dealing with a negative life event. However, they did not see the negative life event as an opportunity to grow as did those with an intrinsic religious orientation. Extrinsic religiosity was associated with higher levels of distress. Individuals with high extrinsic religiosity were more likely to see negative life events as out of their control. Their religious coping often focused on religious action such as participating in good deeds or pleading to God for help.

The quest religious orientation was associated with viewing negative life events as having a spiritual purpose. However, this purpose was primarily searching for meaning (Pargament & Olsen, 1992). This is contrasted with intrinsically religious people who also view these events as having a spiritual focus, but they focus on searching for God. People with the quest orientation's response of perceiving the event as a spiritual threat and an opportunity to grow through it was similar to those with intrinsic religious faith. The quest orientation's religious coping was directed toward doing good deeds and voicing discontent with God.

Religious orientation has important implications for spiritual coping, well-being, and physical health as demonstrated by this review of the research and reviews conducted by others (Pargament, 2002) However, it is not the only dimensional aspect of religiosity that has implications for health and well-being. Schaefer and Gorsuch (1991) examined the influence of specific beliefs about God and their association to psychological adjustment. They found that while seeing God as loving and benevolent was associated with lower levels of trait anxiety, views of God as being impersonal and unpredictable were associated with higher levels of anxiety. Interestingly, views of God as wrathful were not significantly associated with anxiety. These results are consistent with the findings of Maynard et al (2001) who looked at religious coping style, God-concept (cognitive view of God), and personal religious variables. Their finding suggested that a person's view of God influences their religious coping style. Thus, religious orientation's association with well-being may be dependant upon which beliefs are intrinsically incorporated (Hathaway & Pargament, 1990). Religious orientation has earned a position of respect in the psychology of religion. However, it must not be the only multidimensional variable considered in understanding the complexity of religion and spirituality.

Hathaway and Pargament (1990) examined the relationship between intrinsic religious faith, religious coping, and psychosocial competency while controlling for potential response bias. Critics have argued that religious people may tend to answer in accordance with what is deemed socially appropriate (social desirability) and may endorse religious items in a positive manner regardless of the validity of this response (indiscriminate proreligiousness). The results discovered by Hathaway and Pargament suggest that social desirability and indiscriminate proreligiousness do not contribute significant response bias to religious research. Additionally, they found the relationship between intrinsic religiosity and competency to be partially mediated by a person's religious coping style. This supports the hypotheses that the relationships between intrinsic religion, well-being, and health are partially mediated by the type of intrinsic faith.

Larson and Larson's (2003) review of the literature on spiritual/religious coping led them to conclude that there is the potential for both positive and negative effects of spiritual/religious coping. They note that studies which have investigated spiritual/religious coping and well being suggest a large proportion of mental health clients turn to their religious/spiritual community and to their relationship with God or a Higher Power to help them cope with their illness. Often individuals report relying on their spiritual or religious beliefs provided a sense of comfort, hope, belonging, and feeling of being loved. However, Larson and Larson note that sometimes a individual's spiritual/religious beliefs led to a sense of guilt, condemnation, or abandonment. Other times the individual may misuse their spiritually/religion for avoidance.

MODELS OF THE RELATIONSHIP BETWEEN SPIRITUALITY, HEALTH, AND WELL-BEING

A review of the literature of spirituality, health, and well-being reveals at least four implicit models to explain their relationship. The first suggests that spirituality and religion have a positive impact on physical health as mediated by well-being. In other words, it is proposed that religion has a direct impact on improving well-being, but not on physical health. Well-being and various aspects of mental health have gained a great deal of acceptance as having a positive influence on physical health. Through improving mental health, religion may have an indirect role in improving physical health. Within this model there are two variations. The first variation of this model, represented in Figure 1, purports that spirituality's effects on well-being are moderated by certain aspects of organized religious activity (ORA) and/or non-organized religious activity (NRA) in addition to other religious variables. It denies spirituality having any direct effects on well-being. The categories (ORA, NRA, and other religious variables) are presented at basic classifications of the various moderating aspects of religion identified by different theorists. The second variation of the first model, represented in Figure 2, maintains that spirituality has direct, positive effects upon well-being in addition to the moderating effects of the other spirituality variables. However, this model seems unlikely in light of the research in this area. Comprehensive reviews of the literature reveal that the relationship between religion and health tends to be consistent even when the relationship between religion and well-being is not (Bergin, 1983; Koenig et al, 2001; McFadden, 1995).

Figure 1.

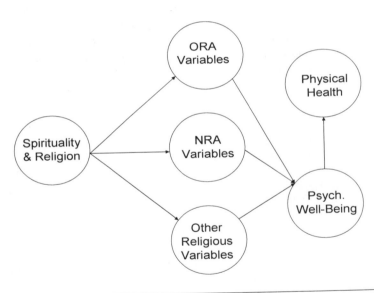

Figure 1. This figure represents Model 1a. ORA represents Organized Religious Activities and NRA represents Non-organized Religious Activity. The arrows indicate the direction of the suggested relationship between constructs.

The second model suggests that religion and religious behavior have a direct relationship with physical health, but not with well-being. Health, in turn, influences well-being. Thus, this model, represented in Figure 3, suggests religion has a positive influence on health and an indirect relationship with well-being as mediated by physical health. Spirituality's effects on health has been proposed as being direct or moderated through other spirituality variables as was previously illustrated in the first model. Levin and Chatters's (1998) structural model provides an example of this model. A third model better represents the relationship. This model proposes a complex relationship between religion, health, and well-being. In this model religion has direct and indirect effects on both health and religion as well as indirect effects that may be moderated by the other construct. This model is illustrated in Figure 4.

Figure 2.

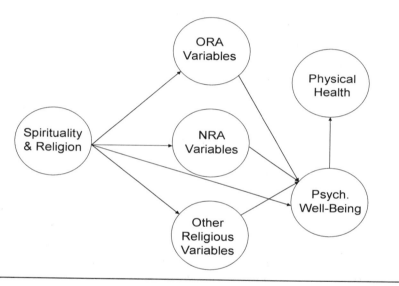

Figure 2. This figure represents Model 1b. The only difference from Model 1a is the addition of a predicted direct effect of spirituality/religiosity on well-being. ORA represents Organized Religious Activities and NRA represents Non-organized Religious Activity. The arrows indicate the direction of the suggested relationship between constructs.

We propose a fourth, more complex model. In this model, spirituality has both direct and indirect effects upon both health and well-being. Additionally, health and well-being may directly and indirectly impact spirituality. The relationship between physical health and well-being can better be seen in a web model in which all constructs influence other constructs while at the same time being influenced by them. It would also be assumed that these relationships can be both positive and negative, at times. This fourth model is still severely limited by the usage of a unidimensional representation of the constructs of spirituality, health, and well-being. This web model would be better represented by replacing the unidimensional constructs with the more specific, discrete aspects of these constructs. However, for simplicity's sake, we will leave the model as represented in Figure 5.

Figure 3.

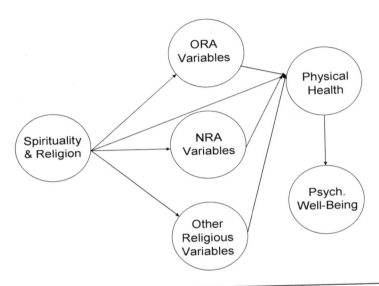

Figure 3. This figure represents Model 2. As with the first model, some theorists would omit the line representing the direct effect of spirituality on health. ORA represents Organized Religious Activities and NRA represents Non-organized Religious Activity. The arrows indicate the direction of the suggested relationship between constructs.

Many theorists and researchers have implied at certain aspects represented as unique in the fourth model, however, few have made these assumptions implicitly known. It is important that these assumptions be made implicit in order to develop quality theory. This theory then serves as the basis of future research models that can be tested. Koenig et al. (2001) have discussed the importance of clarifying distortions regarding the literature in this area of research. Implicitly identifying these assumptions are important in preventing and clarifying such assumptions. For example, while the bi-directional relationship between spirituality and mental health may be assumed in some research, these assumptions are made implicit. This can lead to interpretations of the literature as supporting a unidirectional relationship.

Figure 4.

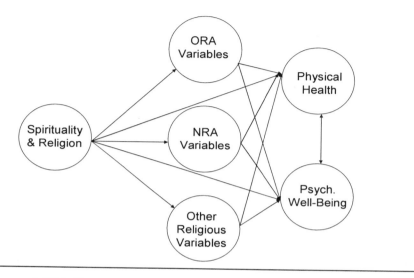

Figure 4. This figure represents Model 3. ORA represents Organized Religious Activities and NRA represents Non-organized Religious Activity. The arrows indicate the direction of the suggested relationship between constructs.

FUTURE DIRECTIONS FOR RESEARCH
IN SPIRITUALITY AND PHYSICAL/MENTAL HEALTH

The current research has only begun to understand the complex relationships between spirituality, health, and well-being. Given this, the most important direction for future research is developing a more comprehensive understanding of the multidimensional aspects of spirituality, health, and well-being. The complex relationships between these constructs may, at times, appear to be inconsistent or insignificant. At other times, it may appear so complex that any attempts at finding kernels of truth through research appear vain. However, we remain optimistic that though research will never be able to explain spirituality, we may be able to better utilize it as one of many approaches of seeking truth. More complex and rigorous research designs will be necessary to clarify the intricacies of these relationships and these constructs if we are to hope to accomplish this ambitious goal.

Figure 5.

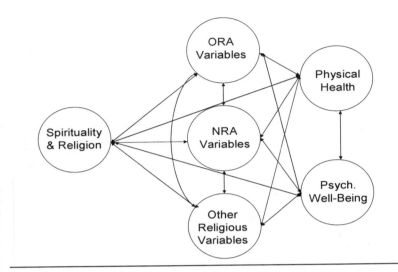

Figure 5. This figure represents Model 4. The relationship is assumed to be bi-directional in this model compared to the unidirectional predictions in previous models. ORA represents Organized Religious Activities and NRA represents Non-organized Religious Activity. The arrows indicate the direction of the suggested relationship between constructs.

Religious orientation has received the brunt share of the research attention. Several important articles have reviewed research findings on religious orientation and provided a critical analysis of the construct (Donahue, 1985; Hunt & King, 1971; Kirkpatrick & Hood, 1990). Additional research studies have associated intrinsic religiosity with better health and well-being outcomes than extrinsic religiosity. These demonstrate the importance of the multidimensional approach to religion. Religious orientation should maintain an essential place in the psychology of religion, but the manner in which it is used may need to evolve. When religious orientation is combined with measures of belief, the power of the construct may become more significant. For example, having a view of God as loving and forgiving may lack any power for a person's life if they are extrinsically religious. However, this same view of God will be of greater importance for a person with intrinsic faith. Religious orientation helps to clarify the understanding of how a person's belief is used in their life.

Koenig et al (2001) discuss several areas of religiousness that continue to need to be addressed. These include religious orthodoxy, certainty of belief, religious affiliation and Christian denomination, levels of involvement in organized religion, aspects of private religiosity, subjective religiosity, religious commitment, spiritual well-being, religious and faith maturity, religious orientation, and religious coping. Several of these have been discussed in this article. The recent publication by Peter Hill and Ralph Hood (1999), *Measures of Religiosity*, should facilitate accessibility to strong research tools.

More attention needs to be placed on translating theory and research into strategies for practice so that more people can reap the blessing from what we learn. Frequently, the only translation that occurs is through the popular media which, as Koenig et al. (2001) points out, is not always accurate. Malony (1995) provides one of the better examples of this translation in his book entitled The Psychology of Religion for Ministry. This book attempts to translate a professional level of psychology in to terms usable by church and lay professionals.

CONCLUSION

The literature reviewed in this chapter has demonstrated that spirituality and religion play important role in health and well-being. In general, the majority of the research purports that spirituality and religion have a positive impact on health, though this is not always the case. Others who have conducted similar reviews of the literature support this conclusion. Larson and Larson (2003) note that spiritual and religious coping often provide strength to persevere and a greater sense of well-being, but at other times spiritual distress can hamper one's health. The current state of the field is prepared to take great strides into new research domains.

This chapter reflects a snapshot of research to date. More research into the relationships here discussed will be conducted in the future. The National Institute of Healthcare Research (NIHR) has shown greater interest in this topic. In the past, much of this interest has focused on the elderly. Now, as popular culture, in addition to professional practitioners, shows greater concern for the role that religion plays in the holistic health of individuals of all age groups, the research agenda will change. So will its presentation. Medical doctors, psychologists, clergy, and others will need to review the research without fear of reprisal or of being considered less than scientific. Studies will become more specific and provide direction to individuals desiring to receive the best benefits. Professionals in the health care field may begin questioning patients regarding their relationship with a higher power and may even suggest that there is a connection between spirituality and better health. Currently, studies suggest that most professionals are less religious than are their patients. This may need to change. Physicians need to consider all aspects of life, including the benefits of spirituality, when telling a patient that they have a permanent physical disability. Patients such as Joni Anderson and Christopher Reeve are more than adequate illustrations of persons who lead the way for utilizing spirituality to overcome the daunting odds of physical disability. Whether health care providers will freely enter this area of prescription is questionable. Hopefully, research and writings such as in this chapter will assist in making such opportunities more acceptable.

It is the position of the authors that physicians should inform their patients of research indicating that worship attendance, prayer, and other spiritual activities will make a difference in their health. Further, proper patient education should include studies showing that the lack of religious involvement may be a risk factor for poor health. Physicians, psychologists, ministers, priests, and rabbis should be personally involved with the individuals whom they see. These professionals should be able to refer patients to spiritual programs currently in place. These professionals should also engage in developing new programs that respond to the evidence presented in the literature. These programs should be open to the community and supported by hospitals, schools, and churches, to ensure that a cross-section of ages receive the preventive information they need for better holistic health. Larimore, Parker, and Crowther (2002) offer evidence that patients wish to be offered basic spiritual care, and that many clinicians believe spiritual intervention can be helpful but lack the training to provide such interventions. The authors are optimistic, with the mounting empirical evidence of a positive relationship between spiritually and health and well-being, that professional organizations, medical training programs, and graduate psychology programs will begin to offer increased training in religious and spiritual issues.

The National Institute for Healthcare Research funds medical research that examines spirituality and health. David Larson, M.D., president of NIHR, states that medical students, i.e., the next generation of doctors, are interested in this type of research. Recent publications of the American Psychological Association and other professional journals indicate that many professions, as well as medicine, are joining in the research on spirituality and health. This increased interest, teamed with a funded organization interested in supporting it, should proceed in an educated manner to ensure that research not only contributes to the existing body of knowledge, but also makes appropriate contributions for professional practice.

REFERENCES

American Psychiatric Association. (1984). *Diagnostic and statistical manual of mental Disorders* (4th ed.). Washington, DC: Author.

Benson, H. (1996). *Timeless healing: The power and biology of belief.* New York: Simon & Schuster.

Benson, H. (1999, August). Paper presented at the 1999 Annual Convention of the American Psychological Association, Boston, MA.

Benson, P. & Spilka, B. (1973). God image as a function of self-esteem and locus of control. *Journal for the Scientific Study of Religion, 12,* 297-310.

Bergin, A. E. (1983). Religiosity and mental health: A critical reevaluation and meta-analysis. *Professional Psychology: Research and Practice, 14,* 170-184.

Byrd, R. C. (1988). Positive therapeutic effects of intercessory prayer in a coronary care unit population. *Southern Medical Journal, 81,* 826-829.

Chamberlain, K. & Zika, S. (1988). Religiosity, life meaning and wellbeing: Some relationships in a sample of women. *Journal for the Scientific Study of Religion, 27,* 411-420.

Chamberlain, T. J. & Hall, C. A. (2000). *Realized religion.* Philadelphia, PA: Templeton Foundation Press.

Chatters, L. M., Levin, J. S., & Ellison, C. G. (1998). Public health and health education in faith communities. *Health Education and Behavior, 25,* 689-699.

Christy, J. H. (1998). Prayer as medicine. *Forbes, 161(6),* 136-137.

Compton, W. C. (2000). Meaningfulness as a mediator of subjective well-being. *Psychological Reports, 87,* 156-160.

Craigie, F. C., Jr. (1999). The spirit and work: observations about spirituality and organizational life. *Journal of Psychology and Christianity, 18,* 43-53.

Donahue, M. J. (1985). Intrinsic and extrinsic religiousness: Review and meta-analysis. *Journal of Personality and Social Psychology, 48,* 400-419.

Easterbrook, G. (1999). Faith healers. *New Republic, 221,* 20-23.

Ellison, C. G. (1991). Religious involvement and subjective well-being. *Journal of Health and Social Behavior, 32,* 80-99.

Ellison, C. G. (1998). Introduction to symposium: Religion, health, and well-being. *Journal for the Scientific Study of Religion, 37,* 692-694.

Ellison, C. G., & Levin, J. S. (1998). The religion-health connection: Evidence, theory and future directions. *Health Education & Behavior, 25,* 700-720.

Faneuli, N. (1997). The spirituality of wellness. *American Fitness, 15,* 42-46.

Fehring, R. J., Brennan, P. F., & Keller, M. L. (1987). Psychological and spiritual well-being in college students. *Research in Nursing and Health, 10,* 391-398.

Ferraro, K. F., & Koch, J. R. (1994). Religion and health among black and white adults: Examining social support and consolation. *Journal for the Scientific Study of Religion, 33,* 362-375.

Francis, L. J., Jones, S. H., and Wilcox, C. (2000). Religiosity and happiness: During adolescence, young adulthood, and later life. *Journal of Psychology and Christianity, 19,* 245-257.

Frankl, V. E. (1959). *Man's search for meaning.* New York: Washington Square Press.

Frankl, V. E. (2000). *Man's search for ultimate meaning.* Cambridge, MA: Perseus Publishing.

Frankel, B. G. & Hewitt, W. E. (1994). Religion and well-being among Canadian university students: The role of faith groups on campus. *Journal for the Scientific Study of Religion, 33,* 62-73.

Gartner, J. (1996). Religious commitment, mental health, and prosocial behavior: A review of the empirical literature. In E. P. Shafranske (Ed.), *Religion and the Clinical Practice of Psychology* (pp. 187-214). Washington, D.C.: American Psychological Association.

George, L. K., Ellison, C. G., & Larson, D. B. (2002). Explaining the relationships between religious involvement and health. *Psychological Inquiry, 13,* 190-200.

Glik, D. C. (1990). Participation in spiritual healing, religiosity, and mental health. *Sociological Inquiry, 60,* 158-176.

Hathaway, W. L. & Pargament, K. I. (1990). Intrinsic religiousness, religious coping, and psychosocial competence: A covariance structure analysis. *Journal for the Scientific Study of Religion, 29,* 423-441.

Hawks, S. (1994). Spiritual health: Definition and theory. *Wellness Perspectives, 10,* 3-13.

Hill, P. & Hood, R. W., Jr. (Eds.). (1999). *Measures of religiosity.* Birmingham, AL: Religious Education Press.

Hoffman, L. & Whitmire, A. J. (2002, June). *The relationship between approach to coping and stress related growth in response to the events of September 11, 2001.* Poster session presented at the annual convention of the American Psychological Society, New Orleans, LA.

Hunt, R. A. & King, M. B. (1971). The intrinsic-extrinsic concept: A review and evaluation. *Journal for the Scientific Study of Religion, 10,* 339-356.

Idler, E. L. (1995). Religion, health, and nonphysical senses of self. *Social Forces, 74,* 683-704.

Idler, E. L. & Kasl, S. V. (1992). Religion, disability, depression, and the timing of death. *American Journal of Sociology, 97,* 1052-1079.

Idler, E. L. & Kasl, S. V. (1997a). Religion among disabled and nondisabled persons I: Cross sectional patterns in health practices, social activities, and well-being. *Journal of Gerontology: Social Sciences, 52B,* S294-S305.

Idler, E. L. & Kasl, S. V. (1997b). Religion among disabled and nondisabled persons II: Attendance at religious services as a predictor of the course of disability. *Journal of Gerontology: Social Sciences, 52B,* S306-S316.

James, W. (1902/1958). *The varieties of religious experience.* New York: The New American Library.

Kirkpatrick, L. A. & Hood, R. W., Jr. (1990). Intrinsic-extrinsic religious orientation: The boon or bane of contemporary psychology of religion. *Journal for the Scientific Study of Religion, 29,* 442-462.

Koenig, H. G. (1999). *The healing power of faith.* New York: Simon & Schuster.

Koenig, H. G., George, L. K., & Siegler, I. C. (1988). The use of religion and other emotion regulating coping strategies among older adults. *The Gerontologist, 28,* 303-310.

Koenig, H. G., Kvale, J. N., & Ferrel, C. (1988). Religion and well-being in later life. *The Gerontologist, 28,* 18-28.

Koenig, H. G., McCullough, M. E., & Larson, D. B. (2001). *Handbook of religion and health.* New York: Oxford University Press.

Krause, N., Ellison, C. G., & Wulff, K. M. (1998). Church-based emotional support, negative interaction, and psychological well-being: Findings from a national sample of Presbyterians. *Journal for the Scientific Study of Religion, 37,* 725-741.

Krippner, S. & Villoldo, A. (1987). *The realms of healing* (3rd ed). Berkeley, CA: Celestial Arts.

Larimore, W. L., Parker, M., & Crowther, M (2002). Should clinicians incorporate positive spirituality into their practices? What does the evidence say? *Annals of Behavioral Medicine, 24,* 69-63.

Larson, D. & Larson, S. (1991). Religious commitment and health: Valuing the relationship. *Second Opinion, 17,* 27-40.

Larson, D. & Larson, S. (2003). Spirituality's potential relevance to physical and emotional health: A brief review of quantitative research. *Journal of Psychology and Theology, 31,* 37-51.

Lee, C. & Balswick, J. (1989). *Life in a glass house: The minister's family in its unique social context.* Grand Rapids, MI: Zondervan.

Levin, J. S. & Chatters, L. M., (1998). Religion, health, and psychological well-being in older adults: Findings from three national surveys. *Journal of Aging & Health, 10,* 504-531.

Levin, J. S., Taylor, R. J., & Chatters, L. M. (1994). Race and gender differences in religiosity among older adults: Findings from four national surveys. *Journal of Gerontology: Social Sciences, 49,* S137-S145.

Malony, H. N. (1995) *The psychology of religion for ministry.* New York: Paulist Press.

Maynard, E. A., Gorsuch, R. L., & Bjork, J. P. (2001). Religious coping style, concept of God, and personal religious variables in threat, loss, and challenge situations. *Journal for the Scientific Study of Religion, 40,* 65-74.

Marwick, C. (1995). Should physicians prescribe prayer for health? Spiritual aspects of well being considered. *JAMA: Journal of the American Medical Association, 273,* 1561-1562.

McCullough, M. E., Hoyt, W. T., Larson, D. B., Koenig, H. G., & Thoresen, C. (2000). Religious involvement and mortality: A meta-analytic review. *Health Psychology, 19,* 211-222.

McFadden, S. H. (1995). Religion and well-being in aging persons in an aging population. *Journal of Social Issues, 51,* 161-175.

Moberg, D. O. (1968). Religiosity in old age. In B. L. Neugarten (Ed.), *Middle Age and Aging* (pp. 497-508). Chicago, IL: The University of Chicago Press.

McGuire, M. B. (1993). Health and spirituality as contemporary concerns. *Annals of the American Academy of Political & Social Science, 527,* 144-154.

Oman, D. & Reed, D. (1998). Religion and mortality among the community-dwelling elderly. *American Journal of Public Health, 88,* 1469-1475.

Pargament, K. I. (1996). Religious methods of coping: Resources for the conversation and transformation of significance. In E. P. Shafranske (Ed.), *Religion and the Clinical*

Practice of Psychology (pp. 215-239). Washington, D.C.: American Psychological Association.

Pargament, K. I. (1997). *The psychology of religion and coping: Theory, research, practice.* New York: Guildford Press.

Pargament, K. (2002). The bitter and the sweet: An evaluation of the costs and benefits of religiousness. *Psychological Inquiry, 13,* 168-181.

Pargament, K. I. & Ishler, K. (1994). Methods of religious coping with the gulf war: cross sectional and longitudinal analyses. *Journal for the Scientific Study of Religion, 33,* 347-361.

Pargament, K. I. & Olsen, H. (1992). God help me (II): The relationship of religious coping orientations to religious coping with negative life events. *Journal for the Scientific Study of Religion, 31,* 504-513.

Pargament, K. I., Kennell, J., Hathaway, W., Grevengoed, N., Newman, J., & Jones, W. (1988). Religion and the problem solving process: Three styles of coping. *Journal for the Scientific Study of Religion, 27,* 90-104.

Pargament, K. I., Smith, B. W., Koenig, H. G., & Perez, L. (1998). Patterns of positive and negative religious coping with major life stressors. *Journal for the Scientific Study of Religion, 37,* 710-724.

Parks, H. S. & Murgatroyd, W. (1998). Relationship between intrinsic-extrinsic religious orientation and depressive symptoms in Korean Americans. *Counseling Psychology Quarterly, 11,* 315-324.

Payne, B. P. (1990). Research and theoretical approaches to spirituality and aging. *Generations, 14,* 11-14.

Parachin, V. M. (1994). Facts of life. *American Fitness, 12,* 42-43.

Plante, T. G. & Sherman, A. C. (Eds.). (2001). *Faith and health: Psychological perspectives.* New York: The Guilford Press.

Poloma, M. M. (1993). The effects of prayer on mental well-being. *Second Opinion, 18,* 37-51.

Powell, L. H., Shahabi, L., & Thoresen, C. E. (2003) Religion and spirituality: Linkages to physical health. *American Psychologist, 58,* 36-52.

Schaefer, C. A. & Gorsuch, R. L. (1991). Psychological adjustment and religiousness: The multivariate belief-motivation theory of religiousness. *Journal for the Scientific Study of Religion, 30,* 448-461.

Schaefer, C. A. & Gorsuch, R. L. (1993). Situational and personal variations in religious coping. *Journal for the Scientific Study of Religion, 32,* 136-147.

Schwab, R. & Petersen, K. U. (1990). Religiousness: Its relation to loneliness, neuroticism, and subjective well-being. *Journal for the Scientific Study of Religion, 29,* 335-345.

Seeman, T. E., Dublin, L. F., & Seeman, M. (2003) Religiosity/spirituality and health: A critical review of the evidence for biological pathways. *American Psychologist, 58,* 53-63.

Stokes, J. P. (1985). The relation of social network and individual difference variables to loneliness. *Journal of Personality and Social Psychology, 48,* 981-990.

Strawbridge, S. (1982). Althusser's theory of ideology and Durkheim's account of religion: An examination of some striking parallels. *Sociological Review, 30,* 125-140.

Tacey, D. J. (1997). *Remaking men: Jung, spirituality and social change.* New York: Routledge.

Tacey, D. J. (2004). *The spiritual revolution: The emergence of contemporary spirituality.* New York: Brunner-Routledge.

Tillich, P. (1957). *The dynamics of faith.* New York: Harper & Row.

Wallis, C. & McDowell, J. (1996). Faith & healing. *Time, 147(26),* 58-63.

Wallace, J. M., Jr., & Forman, T. A. (1998). Religion's role in promoting health and reducing risk among American youth. *Health Education & Behavior, 25,* 721-741.

Whitaker, J. (1994). Religion may be good for your health. *Human Events, 50,* 8.

Young, J. S., Cashwell, C. S., & Shcherbakova, J. (2000). The moderating relationship of spirituality on   negative life events and psychological adjustment. *Counseling and Values, 45,* 49-57.

EPILOGUE[1]

Enchanted Agnosticism

Kirk Schneider, Ph.D.
Saybrook Graduate School
San Francisco, CA

Let's face it: with regard to faith and ethics today, we're between a rock and a hard place. The rock is extremist-fundamentalist religion and the hard place is postmodern free-market anarchy.

Fortunately, there is an alternative to these debilitating excesses which have the world in a vise-grip; I call it "enchanted agnosticism." Agnosticism has a long and many-layered history. In recent times it has come to be associated with scientific doubt (or the unverifiable); but there is another kind of agnosticism that takes doubt, and particularly the mystery of being, a step further. I call this alternative enchanted agnosticism.

By enchanted agnosticism, I mean bedazzled uncertainty, exhilarated discernment, and enraptured curiosity; I mean the openness and skepticism of science wedded to the zeal and exaltation of religion; I mean the veneration of mystery wedded to the solemnity of responsibility. To put all this in philosophic terms, I mean our existential faith in the inscrutable.

Enchanted agnostics believe that behind every institutionalized religion is a transcendent question, "But what is beyond that?" Our answer is that behind every bounded faith resides an evolving, indefinite faith. Beyond every bounded god resides an expanding, indecipherable god. Captivating as they may be, gods and goddesses, idols and icons, obsessions and fixations are but pale stand-ins for the inscrutable. Even concepts like the Absolute or Atman or the Void--to the degree they are decipherable--are but veneers of this mysterious power. As Paul Tillich (1952) put it in *The Courage to Be*, veneers (or pieces) of the holy must not be identified with the holy itself, which is a "God beyond God."

---

[1] An earlier version of this chapter was originally published in *Tikkun magazine*. I would like to thank *Tikkun* for allowing this paper to be reprinted in the current volume.

316

This radically new view of God, being, or creation is a view that trumps nihilism as it does dogma; purposelessness as it does certitude. It is a view that basks not in particular things, but in the amazement, astonishment, and bewilderment c/things. Whereas definable gods (such as those in the Old and New Testaments, ancient myth, and popular culture) tend to polarize us, either by containing and belittling us on the one hand, or inflating and exaggerating us on the other, the inscrutable fosters wholeness--not puritan or absolute wholeness, but dynamic, paradoxical wholeness. The inscrutable evokes our humility and our possibility at the same time, but instead of dictating these conditions from on high, it inspires us to negotiate them, to find our way within them. The result of this understanding is that devotees of the inscrutable are more inclined to see through their investments and be less driven by them. They are less entrapped--either by false hope or false despair--and they are enlivened by a poignancy to life, an overview, that heightens each attendant moment. Enchanted agnostics are the leaders-to-be of a new spiritual consciousness.

THREE PRINCIPLES

Faith in the inscrutable combines three intertwining perspectives: the magnificence of creation, the mystery of creation, and our responsibility to creation.

Magnificence

We don't need a directive or a definable god to feel the presence of divinity. The magnificence of creation demands it. That creation exists at all is magnificent, amazing, incomprehensible. So too, all that partakes in creation must be seen as equally amazing, equally magnificent--death as well as life. This magnificence measures the span of humanity's hope, and demands the tolerance that comes from being open to awe.

As Whitman reminds us:

Grand is the seen, the light, to me--grand are the stars,
Grand is the earth, and grand are lasting time and space,
And grand are their laws, so multiform, puzzling, evolutionary,
But grander far the unseen soul of me, comprehending, endowing all those...
(*Leaves of Grass*, n.d.)

Mystery

The flip side of magnificence is mystery One of the greatest dangers of our age is jadedness. The more jaded we become, the less we acknowledge Mystery; the less we acknowledge Mystery, the more we lose touch with its current and with the inscrutable itself. Magnificence and Mystery are a pair. We cannot have magnificence without uncertainty, and we cannot have mystery without hope. This paradox is often overlooked in mystical circles, which sometimes emphasize magnificence to the detriment of mystery, but was familiar to

Tillich (2001), who points out in *The Dynamics of Faith* that mysticism neglects "the separation of man from the ultimate. There is no faith without separation" (p. 100).

With separation comes anxiety; faith must live with this sense of unease. Uncertainty reminds us of our fragility, but it also reminds us of our possibility Again, Tillich (2001):

> [F]or man is finite, and he can never unite all elements of truth in complete balance. On the other band, he cannot rest on the awareness of his finitude, because faith is concerned with the ultimate and its adequate expression. Man's faith is inadequate if his whole existence is determined by something that is less than ultimate. Therefore, he must always try to break through the limits of his finitude and reach what never can be reached, the ultimate itself. (p. 57)

Responsibility

Creation's magnificence leads us to such foundational religious concepts as respecting the stranger, venerating God, and so on. Mystery however, leads us to responsibility, the challenge to respond. The call of magnificence can be answered by reflexive, even passive, approaches to worship. Mystery however, calls us to what Ernest Becker (see Keen, 1974) describes as reflective, even dialectical worship. Once we understand the mystery of the inscrutable, we understand that each of us, as individuals, must bear the brunt of decision-making.

We enchanted agnostics cannot passively defer to authority because there is no certain authority to accept our surrender. There is no marked path, no "highway to heaven," no inviolable canon. It is we who must sanctify the scripts, we who must find the path. But we are not rudderless when it comes to this process either; faith in the inscrutable does provide landmarks. The first, following Magnificence, is an appreciation for all being; the second, following Mystery, is an openness to what evolves; and the third, following Responsibility is a challenge to respond to or discern what evolves. That which Tillich (1967) calls "listening love" (which is akin to depth therapy as well as Buber's philosophy dialogue) is a concrete realization of the aforementioned principles. "Listening love," elaborates Tillich in *My Search for Absolutes*, is a whole-bodied immersion in a dilemma or concern. "It is a listening to and looking at the concrete situation in all its concreteness, which includes the deepest motives of the other person..." Tillich concludes, "The more seriously one has considered all the factors in a moral decision, the more one can be certain that there is a power of acceptance in the depth of life" (p. 111) --and in our own lives, I might add, for the decision we risk.

The responsibility to respond compels a mutable respect, a respect that leans on humanity Just as one can't apply a "fits all" product to a diverse and opinionated populace, one can't force a "fits all" ethic to a complex and changing existence. Instead, the principle of responsibility that is at the heart of enchanted agnosticism calls upon the deepest energies of democracy the fullest engagements of dialogue, and the keenest perceptions of context.

Nor is the principle of responsibility a kind of "situational" ethics, as that approach is conventionally understood. Enchanted agnosticism advocates an "awe-based" situational ethics, an ethics infused by the thrill and anxiety of living and the reverence, humility, and wonder of living. While other situational ethics tend to resort to intellectual or consensus-based criteria, an awe-based ethics is ever attuned to the whole, the embodied, and the relational in its deliberations (as in listening love, or person-to-person encounter).

THE WAY TO THE INSCRUTABLE

Enchanted agnosticism is thus very different from the reflexive faith of disciples, or the expedient faith of marketers, or the obsessive faith of fanatics (or even G.W. Bush's faith-based education!). Faith in the inscrutable is wrought from our encounter with these and other, singular faiths. It is a faith wrought from the encounter with the myopic, the fleeting, and the one-dimensional--a faith wrought from pain but not confined by pain. It is a faith born of deep self-inquiry deep presence to the results of that inquiry and deep trust in the unfolding of the results. It is a faith born of confidence that one can survive one s own intense grappling, BUT it is not just a faith in survival; it is a faith in that which permits survival to occur.

Awe-based faith entails a "giving up when there's nothing left," as Ernest Becker put it in 1974, a placing of ones trust in the "tremendous creative energies of the universe" to work through and with us when we are spent.

The key here is that such faith often requires that we struggle until we are spent. Struggle jolts the system, dents the armor, and jars the rails. But struggle is only the beginning. The shock and the awakening we experience are only preparatory. The next crucial question is how we pursue, engage with, and emerge from this struggle. We must learn to acknowledge, identify with, and yet somehow be more than that with which we contend.

Expediency, the catch-word of our time, is not a route to the inscrutable. It is a route to the definable, the consolable, and the delimiting. One cannot partake of the fruits of vibrancy, of the profound and the emancipating, through gimmickry There are no tricks to cultivating awe. The danger today is that we delude ourselves into believing in such tricks; that we mistake Isaiah Berlin's jigsaw puzzle universe for the brute and throbbing one into which we are thrust. Almost every cutting-edge technology poses this danger-virtually every designer drug, genetic manipulation, and robotic innovation holds the potential for abominable self-delusion. While we can be aided and, indeed, miraculously transformed by these developments, we must not lose touch with their partiality and their envelopment by the inscrutable.

VISION

If enchanted agnosticism were to become the norm, then, how would the world look? I envision a time when enchanted agnosticism is echoed in schools and in temples, in boardrooms and in embassies, in bedrooms and in alleyways--in every human sphere. This would be a time when churches throw open their doors to mosques, and mosques to synagogues; when Buddhist priests can perform sacred chanting rites before Hindu congregants; and when Jewish temples sanction Protestant services. It would be a time, perhaps, when every major denomination would regularly and on a rotating basis host every other major denomination and yet maintain their respective identities; when families of all faiths and backgrounds would pray together, break bread together, and partake in each others' heritage.

This would also be a time when enchanted agnosticism--awe-based living-is practiced in business and diplomatic circles; when politicians and mediators and entrepreneurs model the actions they expect of others; when they partake in interfaith ceremonies, avail themselves to intimate interchange, and open to diverse folk traditions. Then, and only then, will the spirals of hate, of tit-for-tat, and of intercultural estrangement be stanched. Then and only then will conciliation have a chance.

Further, this would be a time when diplomatic and trade meetings are attended not only by policymakers, but also by ethical philosophers, spiritual leaders, and organizational psychologists; when, for example, attendees participate in professionally facilitated process groups and promote frank exchanges of feeling; and when the input from scientists and philosophers matches that from legislators and generals. It would be a time when representatives can broach each others' personal fears as well as state or corporate agendas; when international relations can be spoken about in terms of interpersonal relations; and when hopes and trepidations can be coupled with predictions and averages.

Finally, this would be a time when people everywhere approach each other and our world from a stance of curiosity, wonderment, and potentially even attraction, for commensurate with the rise in enchanted agnosticism would be the corresponding rise in intra- and intercultural reassessment, trust, and cooperation, and with these developments, entire worlds will unfurl. Religious and scientific types, for example, would begin to perceive not only their respective divergences, but also their respective convergences, utility, and virtues. While adherents of doctrinal faith would reassess the value of openness and skepticism, devotees of calculation would reevaluate the legitimacy of veneration and faith; while spiritualists would rethink material realities, materialists would revisit the ethereal, poetic, and felt. Although hesitant at first, each of the respective parties would become increasingly appreciative of the others' legitimacy, lucidity, and sublimity.

Sound remote? Out-of-reach? Not necessarily. Social theorists from Carl Rogers to Michael Lerner have been promoting such interchanges for years and many have partaken of their fruit. As more partake in The Great Conversation, fewer will pine for The Great Detonation, or The Holy Vindication; and as some invite deepening and widening, others will permit risking, opening. In short, enchanted agnosticism--the embrace of mystery--has tremendous potential to address the confusion and spiritual hunger of our lives.

In her illuminating study of religion, *The History of God*, Karen Armstrong (1993) concludes that we in the West have reached a developmental milestone. We have witnessed the disasters of fundamentalist tyrannies and, equally, of post-Enlightenment oligarchies, and we are in need of something different. This alternative, Armstrong suggests, just might be what she calls "mystical agnosticism," which is very akin to my "enchanted agnosticism." The problem, Armstrong cautions, is that in order for such an alternative to be viable it must be "felt upon the pulse," or as Buber (Buber & Jaffee, 1988) put it, "hallowed in the everyday." That is precisely the challenge that I pose to readers today: to feel enchanted agnosticism upon the pulse.

REFERENCES

Armstrong, K. (1993). *A history of God*. New York: Ballantine.
Buber, M. & Jaffee, M. S. (1988). *Hasidism and modern man*. Atlantic Highlands, NJ: Humanities Press, International.
Keen, S. (1974, April). *A conversation with Ernest Becker*, 71-80.
Tillich, P. (1952). *The courage to be*. New Haven: Yale University Press.
Tillich, P. (1967). *My search for absolutes*. New York: Simon & Schuster.
Tillich, P. (2001). *The dynamics of faith*. New York: Perennial.